D1286606

IMMORTAL DIAMOND:

Studies in
Gerard Manley Hopkins

Gerard Manley Hopkins, S. J.

IMMORTAL DIAMOND:

Studies in
Gerard Manley Hopkins

Edited by
NORMAN WEYAND, S.J.

With the assistance of
RAYMOND V. SCHODER, S.J.

INTRODUCTION BY JOHN PICK

LONDON
SHEED & WARD
1949

FIRST PUBLISHED 1949
BY SHEED AND WARD, LTD.
110/111 FLEET STREET
LONDON, E. C. 4

821.89
H 794 w
78707

PRINTED IN GREAT BRITAIN BY
BRADFORD AND DICKENS, LONDON, W. C. 1

6-15-317 Aubrey Nouse, Phil. 1 #7.00

GERARDO

FRATRI EXIMIO

APVD REGEM TRIVMPHANTI

SOCII

DONVM HOC ET DEBITVM

SVB EODEM CHRISTI IESV VEXILLO

ADHVC IN TERRIS MILITANTES

ADMIRATI DEDICAMVS

In a flash, at a trumpet crash,
I am all at once what Christ is, | since he was what I am, and
This Jack, joke, poor potsherd, | patch, matchwood, immortal
      diamond,
            Is immortal diamond.

—That Nature is a Heraclitean
Fire and of the comfort of the Resurrection

PREFACE

Immortal Diamond: Studies in Gerard Manley Hopkins was conceived as an anniversary tribute to commemorate the one hundredth anniversary of the poet's birth on July 28, 1944.[1] The papers were, in fact, practically all completed in their present form during the year 1944.[2] War-time conditions, however, were the cause of many delays which made the appearance of the book during the anniversary year impossible.

Existing conditions account in part, too, for the fact that the work of other competent Jesuit scholars is not here included. Pressure of work prohibited the writing of some expected studies and prevented the editor from securing the cooperation of other desirable contributors. War-time academic demands in Jesuit

---

[1] The date June 11, 1844, has been erroneously given for Hopkins' birth. This date appears in Father Lahey's *Gerard Manley Hopkins,* published in 1930, and may well have for either its remote or its immediate source the Balliol College Register referred to below. When the *Times Literary Supplement* used this date for Hopkins' birth in its issue of June 10, 1944, Gerard Hopkins wrote as follows:

Sir,—It is unfortunate that an error about the date of Gerard Manley Hopkins's birth should have become current in his centenary year. It was first printed in the Balliol College Register, which gives June as the month of his birth. I have been at some pains to inquire into this matter, and wrote for information to the poet's younger brother Lionel, who has just celebrated his ninetieth birthday. He replied to my letter that the family list of births, marriages and deaths contains the following entry:—

Gerard Manley, son of the above; born at Stratford Grove, Essex, at 4.15 A.M., 28th July, 1844. Baptized at St. John's Church, August 24th, 1844.

There can, I think, be no doubt that July and not June was the month of his birth.

Yours faithfully,
GERARD HOPKINS

Oxford University Press.

[2] As a result, two important volumes on Hopkins, W. H. Gardner's *Gerard Manley Hopkins: A Study of Poetic Idiosyncrasy in Relation to Poetic Tradition* and Eleanor Ruggles' *Gerard Manley Hopkins: A Life,* as well as a number of recent periodical articles of significance could not be used by some of the contributors to this volume.

ix

colleges and universities throughout the United States overbur-
dened most teachers; chaplain's work in the armed forces of
the United States and added ministerial activities made scholarly work unthinkable for many. Chaplain John Louis Bonn,
U.S.N.R., was actually forced to complete his study, "Greco-
Roman Verse Theory and Gerard Manley Hopkins," while on
active duty. Yet the cooperation of all concerned, including a
number whose names do not appear, is a token of the esteem
for Gerard Manley Hopkins and of the great interest in his writing found among his fellow Jesuits in the United States.

The history of Hopkins' poems and the popularity which they
now command constitute a literary phenomenon. The long Holy
Saturday which the poems underwent after their creator's death,
coupled with the rapid spread of knowledge concerning them
after their resurrection in 1918, has few parallels in English literary history. The result is that the widespread interest in this
small body of poetry on the part of almost every type of reader
today [3] calls for studies in Hopkins by men who share the special
background and training which was his. There are aspects of
Hopkins which a Jesuit, naturally enough, is in the best position
to understand. The essays in this volume will, it is hoped, provide
a key to many of the beauties enclosed in the poetry yet locked
to numerous readers.

Some of the studies present, although in a rather indirect way,
a general introduction to Hopkins' poetic aims and techniques —
e.g. those of Fathers McNamee, MacGillivray, and Noon. Others,
such as the analyses of *The Windhover, The Wreck of the
Deutschland,* and *The Loss of the Eurydice,* despite the fact that
they are actually explications of the text and as such primarily
interesting to readers well acquainted with these poems, should
be valuable even to those unacquainted or but slightly acquainted

---

[3] The comprehensive bibliography herein given includes articles on Hopkins from a number of college periodicals, devotional magazines, and even a
few high school publications. These items when joined with those appearing
in scholarly and literary periodicals there listed indicate the variety of readers
to whom the poet appeals.

with Hopkins' poetry. The two metrical studies included will appeal to a more limited circle of readers.

The weakness of much work on Hopkins in recent years arises in part from one fact: the tendency of writers to snatch from Hopkins' letters and notebooks a phrase or sentence here, another there (some even apparently contradictory) without considering them in relation to the poet's views as a whole. It has been the aim of the writers in this volume to correlate in as careful a manner as possible all the available writings of Hopkins in relation to the topics they develop, and to view these against a background of Jesuit life and activities with which they themselves are familiar through long personal experience.

The importance of this background should be evident to anyone who has studied Gerard Manley Hopkins' poems and has even cursorily read his letters or notebooks. It is equally evident from a perusal of John Pick's valuable work *Gerard Manley Hopkins: Priest and Poet* or of Eleanor Ruggles' *Gerard Manley Hopkins: A Life*. Although the latter work will necessarily prove unsatisfactory in many points to an educated Catholic reader, it manifests the careful endeavor of a non-Catholic writer to present the background of religious life and aims indispensable to an understanding of either the poet or his verse.

Miss Ruggles' book is but one instance of the increasingly sympathetic attitude towards Hopkins the *Jesuit* which is gratifying to members of the Society of Jesus. A comparison of the 1944 anniversary tributes (such as those which appeared in the June 10th issue of the *Times Literary Supplement*) with many writings on Hopkins of a decade or more ago provides another. Then, to discover a non-Catholic instructor in a non-Catholic university writing a doctoral dissertation on the religious ideas in Hopkins' poems from a sympathetic viewpoint; to discover further, as this editor has recently done, that the teacher referred to chose this research topic because of disgust at the unintelligent prejudiced criticism of Hopkins as insincere or frustrated, is significant in two respects. It proves that the apprecia-

tion of the poet as a Jesuit whose religious life and beliefs are
the very stuff of his verse has progressed far in the past fifteen
years; it proves, too, that the impact of the poems carries with
it a strong communication of these religious truths and life to the
intelligent, open-minded reader, even though he may not share
the poet's religious heritage.

The contemporary interest in Hopkins' life and ideas, in addition to the perhaps more widespread academic interest in his
poetic technique, is also a consoling sign that a sense of spiritual
values, in fact a sense of the true hierarchy of values, persists in
many devotees of literature. Above the humanistic values which
W. C. Brownell, Irving Babbitt, and Paul Elmer More strove to
propagate in this country, and which Norman Foerster, Mortimer
Adler, Robert M. Hutchins, and Stringfellow Barr, among others,
are yet striving to promote, is the world of supernatural values
which Gerard Manley Hopkins incarnates in his verse. The discovery of these in the poet's verse has left a profound impress
upon the lives of many of his readers. It has, in fact (so far as
human judgment in these matters can determine), led a man
who on the basis of his published writings should be ranked as
the outstanding critic and interpreter of Gerard Manley Hopkins
in England today to embrace the faith which the poet himself
professed.

But regardless of specific religious influence, discerning students
of contemporary art and letters have no difficulty in recognizing
one fact: in an era marked by abstract, surrealist, materialistic,
and much intellectually and spiritually bankrupt indiscriminate
art, the influence of Hopkins is a salutary one in English letters.
The present volume will, it is hoped, bring readers to a clearer
understanding of the verse he wrote and of the character of the
man. He possessed the ideal, *Ad Majorem Dei Gloriam,* be-
queathed to him by the founder of his religious order, St. Ignatius
Loyola. He was motivated by the realization that this ideal could
only be achieved—as Father Burns has pointed out in his essay—
by denying himself, by sacrificing even the desire to write poetry

in carrying out the *agere contra* spirit of Ignatius Loyola and every true Jesuit.

It is quite fitting that John Pick, author of *Gerard Manley Hopkins: Priest and Poet*, should introduce these studies written by Hopkins' fellow Jesuits of a later generation.

NORMAN WEYAND, S.J.

Loyola University
Chicago, Illinois

ACKNOWLEDGMENTS

The editor wishes to express his sincere gratitude to the following, and to the many others, whose generous assistance made this volume possible:

The Reverend John Wellmuth, S.J., my former colleague at Loyola University, now Chairman of the Department of Philosophy of Xavier University, for invaluable aid and inestimable hours of service in critical reading and editing of the manuscript, as well as in proofreading and in constant encouragement.

Dr. Samuel M. Steward, formerly of the Department of English of Loyola University, for a careful reading of the manuscript and critical advice.

The Reverend William R. Hennes, S.J., of Xavier University, for reading a number of the studies contained in this volume and critical advice.

The Reverend Walter J. Ong, S.J., who, in addition to contributing the longest study in this volume, assisted in the editing of several of the other studies and in proofreading.

The Reverend D. A. Bischoff, S.J., who, after the volume was in the galley stage, read the sections pertaining to Hopkins' life in the light of his own recent discoveries in England. The essay "Gerard Manley Hopkins and the Society of Jesus," by Father Carroll, indicates our indebtedness to Father Bischoff for factual information which is to appear in the complete authorized later life of Hopkins which Father Bischoff is now preparing. It should be noted that the contributions of Father Bischoff were made possible largely through the kindness of the Very Reverend Martin C. D'Arcy, S.J., Provincial of the English Jesuits, who placed at Father Bischoff's disposal a considerable amount of unpublished manuscript material of Father Hopkins which is preserved in the archives of the English Province of the Society of Jesus.

Sister Mary Roberta, S.S.N.D., of Malden, Massachusetts, who, in addition to the bibliographical help indicated in the introduction to our "Chronological Bibliography," provided the portrait of the poet which serves as a frontispiece.

Mr. F. J. Sheed and Miss Patricia MacGill of Sheed and Ward for their sympathetic cooperation and patience in seeing the volume through publication.

Miss Annette Dawson, for invaluable services in the preparation of the index.

Miss Elizabeth Ann Kelly, Miss Catherine Kelly, Miss Mary R. Manzke, Miss Mary Ann Kay, and Miss Irene Wisz for gratuitous secretarial help in connection with the unexpectedly voluminous correspondence which the preparation of the book entailed.

The Very Reverend Leo Sullivan, S.J., Provincial of the Chicago Province of the Society of Jesus, my religious superior, for continued approval and material help necessary in the preparation of the book.

Acknowledgments for aid in the compilation of the "Chronological Bibliography of Gerard Manley Hopkins" are made in the introduction to that section of the book.

Furthermore, the editor wishes to express his gratitude to the following for permission to quote from publications:

The poet's family and the Oxford University Press, London and New York—*Poems of Gerard Manley Hopkins*.

Professor C. C. Abbott and the Oxford University Press, London and New York—*Letters of Gerard Manley Hopkins to Robert Bridges, Correspondence of Gerard Manley Hopkins and Richard Watson Dixon*, and *Further Letters of Gerard Manley Hopkins*.

Professor Humphry House and the Oxford University Press, London and New York—*Notebook and Papers of Gerard Manley Hopkins*.

Dr. John Pick and the Oxford University Press, London and New York—*Gerard Manley Hopkins, Priest and Poet*.

The Reverend Gerald F. Lahey, S.J., and the Oxford University Press, London and New York—*Gerard Manley Hopkins*.

Herbert Read, the Clarendon Press, Oxford, and the Oxford University Press, New York—*Essays and Studies, The English Association,* Volume 21.

Jacob Schipper, the Clarendon Press, Oxford, and the Oxford University Press, New York—*The History of English Versification.*

Henry Frowde, Oxford, and the Oxford University Press, New York—*Classical Metres in English Verse,* by Robert Bridges.

The Oxford University Press, London and New York—*Three Friends,* by Robert Bridges.

The Catholic Poetry Society of America—quotations from *Spirit: A Magazine of Poetry.*

Katharine Garrison Chapin and Harper & Brothers, New York—*Plain Chant in America.*

The Reverend James J. Daly, S.J., and the Bruce Publishing Company, Milwaukee—*Boscobel and Other Rimes.*

H. D. and the Liveright Publishing Corp., New York—*Pear Tree.*

Mr. T. S. Eliot and Faber & Faber, Ltd., London—*After Strange Gods* and *Murder in the Cathedral.*

Herbert Marshall McLuhan and New Directions, Norwalk, Conn.—"The Analogical Mirrors" in *Gerard Manley Hopkins, by the Kenyon Critics.*

Ezra Pound and Faber and Faber Ltd., London—"Dance Figure" in *Selected Poems,* ed. by T. S. Eliot.

Ezra Pound and New Directions, Norwalk, Conn.—"Dance Figure" in *Personae: The Collected Poems of Ezra Pound.*

Elizabeth Madox Roberts and the Viking Press, New York—"I, Adam" in *Song in the Meadow.*

Clive Sansom and the Favil Press, London—"Seagulls" in *The Unfailing Spring.*

ABBREVIATIONS

B   signifies   *The Letters of Gerard Manley Hopkins to Robert Bridges*

D   "   *The Correspondence of Gerard Manley Hopkins and Richard Watson Dixon*

F   "   *Further Letters of Gerard Manley Hopkins*

N   "   *The Note-Books and Papers of Gerard Manley Hopkins*

Jnl   "   "Journal" of Gerard Manley Hopkins, included in N, pp. 103–217

L   "   "Life," i.e. *Gerard Manley Hopkins,* by G. F. Lahey, S.J.

P   "   Poems of Gerard Manley Hopkins edited by Robert Bridges, 2nd. edition, 1930

BIOGRAPHICAL OUTLINE

1844.	July 28, born at Stratford, Essex.
1852.	Removal to Oak Hill, Hampstead.
1854.	Attended Highgate School.
1855.	Met Marcus Clarke at the Isle of Wight.
1857.	Tour through the Rhineland.
1859.	Prize-poem "The Escorial."
1860.	Tour through Southern Germany.
1862.	Received gold medal for Prize-poem "A Vision of Mermaids."
1863.	Won an Exhibition for Balliol College.
1866.	August, wrote to Cardinal Newman concerning his conversion.
	October, received into the Catholic Church.
1867.	Spring, took a double-first in "Greats."
	Autumn, taught at the Oratory School, Birmingham.
1868.	Tour through Switzerland.
	May, decided to enter the Jesuit Order.
	September 7, entered the Jesuit Novitiate, Roehampton.
1870.	Philosophical studies at St. Mary's Hall, Stonyhurst.
1873.	Taught Classics at Manresa House, Roehampton.
1874.	Theological studies at St. Beuno's College, North Wales.
1877.	Ordination to the Priesthood.
	Preacher at Farm Street Church, London.
	Sub-minister at Mount St. Mary's College, Chesterfield.
1878.	Preacher at St. Aloysius Church, Oxford.
	Renewed acquaintance with Canon Dixon.
1879.	Preacher at St. Francis Xavier's Church, Liverpool.
1881.	Third Year Novitiate, Roehampton.
1882–84.	Taught Classics at Stonyhurst.
	Met Coventry Patmore while at Stonyhurst.
1883.	Trip to Holland.
1884.	Chair of Greek at the Royal University, Dublin.
1889.	June 8, died.

CONTENTS

N.B. The "Interpretive Glossary of Difficult Words" has been placed in the centre of the book for the convenience of readers who may wish to keep this section open while reading Hopkins' poems.

INTRODUCTION

John Pick

A century has elapsed since the birth of Gerard Manley Hopkins, and over twenty-five years have passed since the posthumous publication of his poems in 1918. Yet it has been only in the last fifteen years that his place in the stream of English poetry has been analyzed and assessed. Enthusiasm for his work has grown, but it has been refined and tempered, and the influence of his poetry has become ever deeper and more subtly pervasive.

The main outlines of the history of his life are now the common property of a large body of readers and admirers. They know that this sensitive and artistic young man, precocious with so many gifts and so much promise, was born into Victorian England amid the warring schools of the aesthetic movement and of religious turmoil; that at Oxford he turned his back on his family and his friends and, following Newman's lead, became a convert to Rome. They know, too, that he entered the Jesuit novitiate and spent his short life, so full of joy and so desolate with pain, as a Jesuit fulfilling carefully and scrupulously the duties of his high office until he met his death unacclaimed and unsung, yet believing always that "Immortal beauty is death with duty."

And they have grown also to realize that his real life was an inner life, was "in hiding," but that in his poetry particularly is revealed the exaltation as well as the struggle which really was his life:

> But be the war within, the brand we wield
> Unseen, the heroic breast not outward-steeled,
> Earth hears no hurtle then from fiercest fray.

The story, too, that as a young man he was a conventional poetaster but that as a Jesuit he renounced poetry as a profession and henceforth considered it as secondary to that spirituality which ever after was his main concern, but that from time to time he wrote but never published those great poems which are now known as among the most intensely elaborate and yet most austerely stringent in the language—all these facts are also a part of the legend that has grown up around him.

The keeping of his poems he confided to his life-long friend Robert Bridges, who in 1918, almost thirty years after Hopkins' death, gave to the public that thin volume which has since won so many lovers. It has become a fashion among some unfairly to decry Bridges' delay, but the Poet Laureate had long paved the way by gradually introducing his friend's poems into various anthologies until he felt, towards the close of the first World War, that an era of poetry was under way that would be receptive to the poems of Hopkins. Nor was he wrong in his judgment.

Yet the appearance of Bridges' edition of the poems in 1918 inaugurated a number of fundamental misunderstandings which only now are being dispersed. For Bridges was unsympathetic both to Hopkins' religion and to his poetry. The latter, as is evident from his notes and comments, offended his sense of poetical decorum and his critical orthodoxy. And it was impossible for the Poet Laureate to conceive that the poet was sincere in his religious tenets and aspirations. Various aspects of these two problems have been the predominant ones for some twenty years.

On the one hand, Hopkins was adopted as almost an esoteric cult by a new generation of poets and versifiers, and his style was copied and heard in derivative volumes of verse. Yet it was with little real understanding of his sprung rhythms or of his syntactical audacities that others wore his garments.

And on the other hand, the religious aspect of his life and of his poetry was twisted and distorted by an unsympathetic audience intent on reading into his experiences and writings Freudian "complexes" and "repressions." Some were shocked, in an almost mock-puritanical manner, that here was a devotional poet so full of delight in the created world. Yet in Hopkins they failed to perceive how this was unified with his supersensuous vision. Others pointed their fingers at his famous "terrible sonnets" and said, "There is the suffering and the cry of impotence that must come from one who devotes himself to religious ideals."

And it has taken a long time for people to see that for Hopkins his religious vocation was an intensification and not a denial of life, and that his poetry was always an attempt to "Give beauty back . . . back to God, beauty's self and beauty's giver."

To this truer and more critical understanding great contributions were made by the publication of his letters and correspondence, his diaries, notebooks, and sermons. On the foundation of these, and of the pervasive influence of the *Spiritual Exercises* of St. Ignatius upon which his whole view of this world and the next world was based, and as a result of the efforts of numerous authors of articles, critiques, essays, and studies—from these has emerged a very different man and poet from the one that confronted the startled public of the 1920's.

Now it is no longer possible to think of his prosody, his colloquial vigorousness, his rugged subtleties, his highly patterned verbal orchestration as elements unintegrated with his most basic conceptions of poetry and art. No longer can one speak of him as a chaotic eccentric. Rather, critics see how highly disciplined was his attempt to make poetry once more a living and vital expression of the genius of the English language.

And critics can no longer speak of a conflict between his priesthood and his poetry. The Hopkins we now know is an integrated character whose verse is a counterpart to his integrated vision. And he shines forth as one of the great religious poets of all time. Indeed, he can teach the world what is meant by the very term *religious poet,* for he is one of those few exceptional spirits who combine the characteristics demanded by that concept. In Hopkins will be found the unity of the poet and the seer, a unity which in the history of poetry is always needed and is always rare.

And the distinction of the present volume is that it emphasizes and extends the twofold and yet single truth: Hopkins was a poet and at the same time a priest. The following essays are contributed by men whose lives are lived within the traditional framework of Hopkins' own religious ideals and who, therefore, have a sympathy and an insight with which the world of modern criticism is all too unfamiliar; they are written at the same time by men who know that his poetry is "the achieve of, the mastery of the thing." Our understanding and appreciation and love of Hopkins and of his poetry should emerge with greater stature and with greater vitality. With a new meaningfulness we can reassert the lines that Bridges wrote in a dedicatory Sonnet to the 1918 edition:

> Go forth: amidst our chaffinch flock display
> Thy plumage of far wonder and heavenward flight!

IMMORTAL DIAMOND:

Studies in
Gerard Manley Hopkins

GERARD MANLEY HOPKINS AND THE SOCIETY OF JESUS

MARTIN C. CARROLL, S.J.

Thee, God, I come from, to thee go

Gerard Manley Hopkins died in Dublin on June 8, 1889, just fifty days before his forty-fifth birthday. The last twenty-one years of his life were spent as a member of the Society of Jesus. Of these years it has, sadly enough, been said (F 249):

> Humanly speaking he made a grievous mistake in joining the Jesuits for on further acquaintance his whole soul must have revolted against a system which has killed many and many a noble soul; . . . To get on with the Jesuits you must become on many grave points a machine, without will, without conscience, and that to his nature was an impossibility. To his lasting honour be it said he was too good for them. . . .

To the minds of many Hopkins "chose, though he could not have preferred, the lonely and unresponsive corridors of a Jesuit house";[1] and "the rigid and pitiless Society of Jesus"[2] "exhausted, discouraged, and perhaps destroyed him."[3] Finally, the "pathos and the waste of such a situation" have so affected the well-meaning world of literary criticism that the twenty-one years which Hopkins spent as a member of the Society of Jesus are generally considered to have left him "a frustrated voluptuary, a genius blasted by asceticism, a soured and disappointed man."[4]

[1] Plures, "Father Gerard Hopkins," *Dublin Review*, 334 (July-Sept., 1920), p. 56.
[2] *Ibid.*, p. 49.
[3] Theodore Morrison, "The Man of the Month, Gerard Manley Hopkins," *The Atlantic Monthly*, Sept., 1935.
[4] "Editorial Comments," *The Month*, 166 (Dec., 1936), p. 487. Though this summary is of *The Month*, the sentiments, of course, are not. From the first it has pioneered in censuring such easy dramatics.

Now such an attitude on the part of critics is regrettable, for it is unjust to Hopkins and to the Society of Jesus. It leads to the type of criticism which makes something all right or all wrong, all black or all white; or to borrow, not unkindly, from Hopkins himself (B 275. May 25, 1888) :

. . . a criticism that they sling about between the bursting Yes and blustering No, for want of more things to say . . . it reminds me of my aunt's questions when she went shopping with her mother as a child, 'Is goose a poultry?'—not an unreasonable question in itself and even philosophical, for strictly speaking everything either is or is not poultry, but for the purposes of criticism not enough. . . .

Hopkins once expressed to Bridges his passion for explanation which, unless it be "personal, is always pure good," and without which "people go on misunderstanding" (*Ibid.*). One is tempted to believe that thus far there has not been enough explanation of the kind of life which Hopkins led once he became a Jesuit. For it is evident that much of the criticism levelled at the Society of Jesus and its role in Hopkins' life has arisen simply from misunderstanding and not from ill will or prejudice. All pay deference to the heroism and sanctity which Hopkins achieved as a Jesuit, and in an indirect and involuntary way, therefore, to the Society which the poet loved. But still there has been too much misunderstanding because there has been too little explanation. Until this misunderstanding is removed by proper explanation there will always be at least a hint of truculence in the approach made to Hopkins by those not of his faith.

How then explain, without becoming personal or without drawing yet another caricature of the real Hopkins and his real life? The problem can be solved by the correct use of two ready instruments. The first of these is the poetry of Hopkins. F. R. Leavis tells us that: "He is a poet because his interest in his experiences is not separable from his interest in words," [5] and we know from

[5] F. R. Leavis, *New Bearings in English Poetry* (Chatto and Windus, 1932), p. 13.

other sources that many of the poems which Hopkins wrote were autobiographical. Consequently it is possible to learn much of Hopkins and the Society of Jesus by a close examination of his poetry, and this has already been done. Not without danger, however, for it is easy to slip into the error of many critics by whom "the poet's inner life has been reached *through* the poems and the ideas found there applied *to* the poems." [6] A corrective to this circular procedure is necessary, and happily it is found in a second instrument, the letters which Hopkins wrote to his friends and the notebooks and journals which he kept throughout his life. Not all of these have survived. It is now known, for example, that Hopkins' spiritual diary was mistakenly returned to his family after his death. Acting on instructions written on the fly-leaf, his two sisters burnt the diary without reading it. Furthermore, many of his letters, especially those which he must have written to his immediate family, are not available. The handicap of working without these aids is often felt. This, however, is as Hopkins desired it, as it should be; and it is good to know that the advent of a poet's fame does not strip a man of all right to privacy or to the secret possessions of his own soul. With what we have we can be content. It will not, perhaps, give us a full and complete picture of what Hopkins called (N 309–310):

. . . my selfbeing, my consciousness and feeling of myself, that taste of myself, of *I* and *me* above and in all things which is more distinctive than the taste of ale or alum, more distinctive than the smell of walnut leaf or camphor, and is incommunicable by any means to another man . . . except so far as this, that other men to themselves have the same feeling.

Yet though the picture may not be full it will be true, for it is the picture drawn by Hopkins of himself as a Jesuit,

> . . . while there went
> Those years and years by of world without event.[7]

---

[6] Harris Downey, "A Pioneer of Poetry," *The Commonweal,* Apr. 13, 1934.
[7] *St. Alphonsus Rodriguez.*

It is the picture of his odyssey from God—through the years of his conversion to the Catholic religion and his vocation to the Society of Jesus, through the years of his quiet study and acceptance of the ideals of the Society as a novice, through the years of his preparation for the priesthood as a philosopher, teacher and theologian, through the years of his poetry and his priesthood—to God.

1. CONVERSION AND VOCATION (1866–1868)

It is the summer of 1866, and a young man of twenty-two, who has just finished his third year at Balliol College, Oxford, is writing to Newman (F 11. Aug. 28, 1866):

• I am anxious to become a Catholic, and I thought you might possibly be able to see me for a short time. . . . I do not want to be helped to any conclusions of belief, for I am thankful to say my mind is made up. . . .

To understand this decision of Hopkins it is necessary to go back a number of years to his student days at Highgate. What manner of boy he was is revealed by one of his fellow students (F 248–249). Hopkins, we are told, had by far a higher standard than that of his fellows, as, for example, when he persevered in reading regularly a part of the New Testament despite some minor flurries of ridicule from his roommates. He was loved and respected for his goodness and consistency, but these qualities did not detract from his popularity. In the face of personal injustice he was aroused mightily, and it seems that it was his misfortune frequently to run afoul of the authorities. On one occasion he had the entire school talking about him as the result of a bet he made after a conversation on seamen's sufferings and human powers of endurance. He felt that abstaining from all drink for three weeks was "the most trifling ludicrous little thing" (F 2. May 7, 1862), but his masters did not agree with him; and from

this point on, it seems, the atmosphere was so charged with misunderstanding that Hopkins could later say: "The truth is I had
no love for my schooldays and wished to banish the remembrance
of them . . ." (D 12. Oct. 5, 1878).

There can be little doubt that during his Highgate and Oxford
days religion was a compelling force in his life. Abstaining from
water could be a trifle, but only because it was his custom to fast
frequently, so much so that his mother found it necessary to forbid
continuance of the practice (F 60. March, 1864). He obeyed
her, but during Lent it was by adept compromise of cutting out
desserts and sugar and rationing himself to meat once a day (Jnl
53). During a stretch of minor illness he read *Romola* and made
himself wretched over the fall of Savonarola, "the only person
in history (except perhaps Origen) about whom I have a real
feeling, and I feel such an enthusiasm . . . that I can conceive
what it must have been to have been of his followers" (F 7. Jan. 6,
1865). His religion was more than enthusiasm about externals
and he was deeply attracted to union with God through the life
of the sacraments. In the summer of 1864 he tells his friend
A. W. M. Baillie that he has written some religious poems "of a
very Catholic character" which deal with the sacrament of the
Eucharist (F 66. July 20, 1864). Towards the end of the same
year he is confessing to Canon Liddon; in his journal (Jnl 41)
he refers to March 12, 1865, as "A day of the great mercy of
God" and thereafter mention of similar confessions occurs from
time to time (*Ibid.* 42, 53). As early as the autumn of 1865 he
is considering the possibility of leaving the Church of England:
"Note that if ever I should leave the English Church the fact
of Provost Fortescue is to be got over" (*Ibid.* 52). Finally, his
conversion to the Catholic religion, when it came, "was all in a
minute" (F 17, Oct. 4, 1866). The decision was actually made
on July 17, 1866:

It was this night I believe but possibly the next that I saw clearly
the impossibility of staying in the Church of England, but resolved

to say nothing to anyone till three months are over, that is the end of the Long, and then of course to take no step till after my Degree.[8]

The secret did not keep for long; a week later Hopkins reveals it to W.A.C. Macfarlane, who jots it down in his diary for July 24, 1866: "Walked out with Hopkins and he confided to me his fixed intention of going over to Rome. I did not attempt to argue with him as his grounds did not admit of argument" (F 250).

What were these grounds of Hopkins which did not admit of argument? Some very capable attempts have been made to isolate the motives for such a drastic step. The Oxford Movement of Newman, whose books Hopkins was reading, Tractarianism and Ritualism had all Oxford in a ferment, and it was inevitable that the student should consider his position as a member of the Established Church. It has been shown how "the young Oxonian, under the impetus of religious asceticism, chose the way of renunciation." [9] Attention has been drawn to the fuller vision of the sacramental life which opened before him,[10] and was then dimmed and clouded as a result of a conversation with Canon Raynal of the Benedictine monastery at Belmont, who impugned the validity of participation in the Anglican Communion (L 21–22). Hopkins began to feel within himself an urgent desire for a visible, manifest church and creed, and finally, "trusting his belief that Christ had founded a church . . . and drawn ever mystically toward God, even through Nature," [11] he became a Catholic.

The reasons for Hopkins' conversion to the Catholic Church

[8] Unpublished Journals recently discovered in London by Anthony Bischoff, S. J. Hereinafter referred to in text as (UJnl).

[9] John Pick, "The Growth of a Poet, Gerard Manley Hopkins, S.J.," *The Month*, 175 (Jan., 1940), p. 41. See also John Pick, *Gerard Manley Hopkins, Priest and Poet* (Oxford University Press, 1942), pp. 9–15.

[10] Egerton Clarke, "Gerard Hopkins, Jesuit," *Dublin Review*, 396 (Jan.-March, 1936), p. 129.

[11] Daniel Sargent, *Four Independents* (Sheed and Ward, 1935), p. 127.

were the customary ones; some were apologetic, others more deeply personal. The former are seen for the most part in the exchange of letters between himself and Canon Liddon which his imminent reception into the Church occasioned. From the beginning Hopkins seems to have been certain as to the authority of Rome (F 11. Aug. 28, 1866). He was more concerned with the manifest notes of the Church than with the need of historical and other investigations (F 256. Oct. 20, 1866). That the Church which Christ founded was one, holy, catholic and apostolic he did not doubt, and gradually it became clear to him that the Catholic Church alone, in its visible existence, possessed these notes. His assimilation of this truth is evident in a number of letters written at this time to E. W. Urquhart, who was considering a similar step Romewards. He felt that such apologetic arguments were unassailable, but, even more than these, deeply personal motives influenced his decision. The young student's apologetic reasoning had made the assent of faith intellectually possible; it remained for prayer and meditation and the grace of God to elevate this possibility into moral and psychological necessity. The wellsprings of this necessity were varied. For one thing, he found the grace of the sacraments indispensable for spiritual growth. As early as January, 1865, he comments bitingly on the lack of honest and manly opposition displayed by those who oppose the growth of sacramentarian and sacerdotal elements within the Anglican church (F 8. Jan. 6, 1865). It was in the following summer, after his conversation at Belmont, that he first began to realize that he had mistaken the shadow for the substance, and after his conversion he wrote to Urquhart (F 34. Dec. 31, 1867):

I am glad you go to confession although there is nothing of a Sacrament in the ordinance as you use it, but still it has its value *ex opere operantis* and in some cases the shadow of Peter may cure where the touch of Peter is not to be had. But this kind of reasoning is dangerous and likely to mislead.

Hopkins himself had found the substance by following the
shadow and by humble meditation on his own unworthiness, as
is revealed by a fragment found in his journal (Jnl 51. Sept. 28,
1865):

> Trees by their yield
> Are known; but I—
> My sap is sealed,
> My root is dry.
> If life within
> I none can shew
> (Except for sin),
> Nor fruit above,—
> It must be so—
> I do not love.

The consciousness of his own barrenness led him to describe himself as "by the mercy of God . . . a penitent waiting for admission to the Catholic Church" (F 13. Sept. 20, 1866). But
his approach is not negative: ". . . one is sure in these cases
that one is not alone but then if ever the saints and one's guardian
angel are praying for one" (F 16. Sept. 24, 1866). This help
from on high manifested itself in a clarity of vision transcending
the triviality and sordidness of life as men must lead it. The
triviality, he felt, was corrected and avenged by the doctrine of
eternal punishment and by a belief in the future life as taught by
theology, but more especially by the incredible condescension of
the Incarnation in which Our Lord submitted not only to the
pains of this life and the Passion but also to the mean and trivial
accidents of humanity (F 8. Jan. 22, 1866). As for the sordidness
of things, which one is compelled perpetually to feel, he believed
that it was (F 79. Sept. 10, 1865):

the most unmixedly painful thing one knows of: and this is (objec-
tively) intensified and (subjectively) destroyed by Catholicism. If
people cd. all know this, to take no higher ground, no other induce-

ment wd. to very many minds be needed to lead them to Catholicism
and no opposite inducement cd. dissuade them fr. it.

These and similar considerations prepared his soul for the touch
of the finger of God which, when it came, had the inevitable
force of a summons from heaven. He realized the silence and
severity of God in a moment of prayer that answered the searching questions of his heart (F 37. June 13, 1868):

Will it comfort you at death not to have despaired of the English
Church if by not despairing of it you are out of the Catholic Church?
—a contingency which by the fact of doubt you contemplate. Will
God thank you for yr. allegiance and will He excuse you for it? He
asks obedience before everything else. Make half an hour's meditation on death and suppose you have received what you call the last
sacrament: it will then occur—*perhaps* this is not a sacrament and if
not it is a mockery to me and God; secondly, if it is, *perhaps* it is
received in schism and I have wounded my soul with the 'instrument of salvation': this *perhaps* which gives little trouble on an
ordinary Sunday will be very terrible then . . . above all things
say *Domine quid vis ut faciam?* Say it and force yourself to mean it.
Until you prefer God to the world and yourself you have not made
the first step.

Hopkins' answer to the question *Domine quid vis ut faciam* was
his reception into the Catholic Church on October 21, 1866.
Henceforth he could with confidence sing (Jnl 26):

> He hath put a new song in my mouth,
> The words are old, the purport new,
> And taught my lips to quote this word
> That I shall live, I shall not die,
> But I shall when the shocks are stored
> See the salvation of the Lord.

The motives which impelled Hopkins to enter the Catholic
Church have been considered in some detail. They form a neces-

sary introduction to his life as a Jesuit, since his conversion and
his subsequent vocation, though separated by two years, seem,
nevertheless, to have been the result, under God's grace, of the
same intellectual and volitional drive. Less than two months after
becoming a Catholic Hopkins was advised by Newman: ". . . it
seems to me a better thing not to hurry decision on your vocation.
Suffer yourself to be led on by the Grace of God step by step"
(F 258. Dec. 6, 1866). This he did quietly and prayerfully,
meanwhile occupied with the trying tasks of reconciling his family
to his conversion and of preparing for Greats which he took most
successfully. In the autumn of 1867 he assumed for a time a
Master's position at Newman's Oratory school, but at the end
of the year another letter from Newman indicates a desire on Hopkins' part to reach a final decision by going into retreat at Easter
(F 260. Dec. 30, 1867). Actually the retreat but reinforced a decision which had been previously made. As early as January he tells
Bridges that he expects to go into retreat to decide whether he has
a vocation to the priesthood (B 22. Jan. 9, 1868), while on
February 12th he announces to his friend Baillie (F 84. 1868):

I am expecting to take orders and soon, but I wish it to be secret
till it comes about. Besides that it is the happiest and best way it
practically is the only one. . . . I want to write still and as a priest
I very likely can do that too, not so freely as I shd. have liked,
e.g. nothing or little in the verse way, but no doubt what wd. best
serve the cause of my religion.

It would be interesting to know the full inner story of the
reasons why this young convert decided to apply for admittance
to the Society of Jesus. As it is, only recently have the fragments
of past events shattered by the impact of time been painstakingly
reassembled by Anthony Bischoff, S.J. For Hopkins the way to
Damascus did not lead swiftly along one single path, was not
illumined by a sudden blinding light. Here failed him his in-
tuition, which in other races could rush to the heart of a poetic
truth. As he considered his vocation he had three questions to

answer slowly and thoughtfully: Shall I be a priest? Shall I be a religious? To what religious order or congregation shall I apply?

The answers to the first two questions were not long in coming after his conversion, though their final ratification did not occur until his retreat in 1868. It was the answer to the third question which gave him pause. His first inclination favored the congregation of Newman whose guidance he had sought upon his conversion and at whose school he was teaching. A fragment of an undated letter written from the Oratory in early 1868 to his aunt, Laura Smith, indicates this: "I do not expect to be long here: if I get a vocation to the priesthood, I should go away (I should [wish] to be an Orato[rian]. . . ." Another possibility which appealed strongly to him was that of the Benedictines, whose Canon Raynal of the monastery at Belmont had at a critical time directed his steps towards the true Church. Finally, there were the Jesuits. It was to their house at Roehampton that he retired on April 27, 1868, to make a retreat in which he hoped to find the definite answers to all three questions. On May 2nd, he notes: "This day I think, I resolved" (UJnl). On May 7th, he states after the retreat: "Home, after having decided to be a priest and religious but still doubtful between St. Benedict and St. Ignatius" (UJnl). The doubt was not for long. There is a letter of Newman, dated May 14th, expressing both his surprise and pleasure at Hopkins' information that he had decided to apply for admission to the Society of Jesus (F 261). The application was made on May 19th in an interview with Father Alfred Weld, S.J., provincial, at 111 Mount Street; it received prompt attention so that by May 30th he could record that he had "Fr. Weld's acceptance" (UJnl).

So much for the train of events, the outer story behind the weeks and months of weighing possibilities and of coming to a decision. The reasons for this decision can be conjectured, the possible motives can be weighed, but the real secret of his vocation seems likely to remain unknown. Only that he familiarized himself thoroughly with the ideals and practices of the Jesuits before making his decision is evident from his letters. He tells his friends that after his entrance he will not be able to write frequently to them (B 23. June 27, 1868), and that, moreover, the letters he receives from them will be first read by his Superiors (B 24. Aug. 7, 1868). Knowing that he will not have any books of his own, he copies out many of the poems of Richard W. Dixon which he admires so enthusiastically (D 1. June 4, 1878). In informing Newman of his decision he apparently calls the Jesuit discipline hard, and Newman gives the perfect answer: ". . . it will bring you to heaven" (F 261. May 14, 1868). A month later Hopkins echoes his appreciation of this answer (F 37. June 13, 1868):

It is enough to say that the sanctity has not departed fr. the order to have a reason for joining it. Since I made up my mind to this I have enjoyed the first complete peace of mind I have ever had. I am quite surprised—at the kind and contented way my parents have come to take the prospect.

2. NOVICE AND PHILOSOPHER (1868–1873)

Hopkins left home for the Jesuit Novitiate at Roehampton in the evening of September 7, 1868, a "dim, fine and very hot" day (Jnl 119). The anniversary of this departure he could never forget, for even twenty years later he reminds Bridges: ". . . my eyes are very, very sore. Also there goes ten. Goodnight. Sept. 8 (it is now 20 years to a day since I began my noviceship)" (B 283). On that day Hopkins entered into a new and different kind of life. His immediate reaction to this newness and this difference are not recorded. Only the testimony of his regular weather-journal bridges tenuously the gap from day to day until the beginning of the Long Retreat. Were we to judge solely from this it would seem that he left home with almost undisturbed nonchalance. "In the evening when I had said good-bye at home I found my train did not go for three quarters of an hour, so I walked to Victoria Road in the meantime" (Jnl 120).

During the week that followed, his entries of "fine, but dim," "dull, thick and with an east wind" continue uninterruptedly. On September 16th the Long Retreat began and on the 18th his entries appropriately cease with the exception of one made on the first day of repose, when the retreat routine of silence and prayer is somewhat modified: "Henceforth I keep no regular weather-journal but only notes."

It is not our intention here to discuss the effect which the Spiritual Exercises of St. Ignatius had upon the young novice. This has already been done by others, and its importance deserves even fuller study. For the present, however, a faithful description of the normal life which Hopkins led as a Jesuit is desired. It is hoped that such a description will serve to remove some of the unfortunate impressions that have resulted from uninformed and piecemeal perusal of his notes and letters. Throughout his entire noviceship Hopkins was laying the foundations, broad, wide and deep, of his spiritual life. Some scattered hints of this will appear from time to time in his journal, but for the rest it can only be said that the motives which inspired his conversion and vocation were now heightened and deepened. He advanced in wisdom, age and grace, not through pitiless violence and discipline, which is foreign to the Society of Jesus, but through prayerful understanding of the vocation which he had been called to follow.

In this understanding and growth Hopkins was not unique among Jesuits. Their most important work before God is the cultivation of their own souls, and it may be said that upon the success or failure of this interior work depends proportionately the true success or failure of that external apostolate which almost immediately comes to mind when one thinks of the Society of Jesus. The Long Retreat, or thirty days of Spiritual Exercises, which the novice enters upon shortly after his admittance, is only the beginning of this spiritual growth. Into these thirty days is packed in miniature the spiritual life which the Jesuit must live if he is to survive in his vocation. Once the Long Retreat has been concluded and the novice has dedicated himself anew to the service of Christ, the real work of living a Christlike life begins. It is a work which can be sustained, not by militant dramatics or dead obedience, but only by individual responsibility and individual initiative. The Society of Jesus does not aim to produce impersonal automatons stamped with a patented stamp and moulded to a rigid mould. It places before its young men the only ideal it has always cherished — Christ the God-Man who in obedience to the will of his eternal Father came upon earth that all men might be saved. To know Christ, to love him, to imitate him, this is the labor of a Jesuit's lifetime. The Society of Jesus therefore has made special provisions to facilitate this work for all its members, but particularly for its novices who are taking their first faltering steps along a new road.

Hopkins' early notes and letters make but passing reference to these fundamental ideals and practices of Jesuit life, and precisely because of this our picture of him as a novice is apt to be thrown out of focus. Certain aspects of the noviceship which are only secondary in importance catch the attention of the unwary observer who is liable to emphasize them out of all correct proportion. Actually the major preoccupation of the novice after the Long Retreat is Christ, and all his energies are primarily directed towards learning more about Christ, towards loving Christ, towards imitating Christ. Such knowledge and imitation cannot be achieved and assimilated in a vacuum, and consequently the novice's life is carefully planned to give the utmost opportunity for the spontaneous exercise of all the virtues. There are household tasks to be performed, work in the fields or on the grounds, catechism to be taught to neighboring children, classes to attend as well as group and private conferences given by the Master of novices for the purpose of guiding his charges or explaining to them certain norms and directives of Jesuit life.

All of these somewhat social activities of the noviceship are important for testing a man's fitness for his vocation, but by far the greatest emphasis is placed upon the time which the novice

spends in private prayer and study of the spiritual life. Each
morning shortly after arising he devotes an hour to personalized
prayerful meditation on the life and teaching of Christ. Immediately after this he assists at the holy sacrifice of the Mass.
Throughout the rest of the day periods of time are regularly set
aside for the continuance of this spiritual work. After breakfast
there is a private review of the hour previously spent in prayer.
Following close upon this comes spiritual reading either of the
rules of the Society or of some book on the fundamentals of the
religious life. As one duty yields to another during the day the
novice pauses for a moment of thanksgiving for the work he has
just accomplished and of petition for God's blessing on that he
is about to begin. Before the noonday meal he spends fifteen
minutes examining his conscience to discover wherein during the
past hours his conduct could have been made more fully Christlike in fact and motivation. After the period of recreation which
follows the noonday meal he joins with the other novices in a
half hour of vocal prayer. Late in the afternoon he devotes additional time to private prayer and meditation similar to that in
which he was engaged in the early morning. Finally, before his
day is completed there is further spiritual reading either of the
life of Christ or of some saint, another examination of conscience
and time set aside for preparing the subject matter on which he
will meditate the following morning.

It was these and other spiritual activities which loomed most
significantly on the horizon of Hopkins' days as a novice. Whatever else he did was only secondary. The practice of obedience,
of common life, of mortification is necessary in a religious house,
but only as means to the practical sanctification of one's soul and
the more expeditious despatch of the external work to which the
community is dedicated or for which it is preparing. Hopkins and
his fellow novices accepted and used these means. However, their
acceptance and use was not made in a burst of wild abandon or
with a deadly blindness which blotted out their own personalities.
It is precisely to prevent this kind of dedication that the Society

of Jesus during the noviceship offers its younger men two years
of prayer, of looking upon Christ, of understanding how the
rules and spirit of this new way of life attempt perfectly to imitate
the rules and spirit of Christ himself. All this Hopkins saw and
understood; his soul began to grow to spiritual manhood.

Nothing better reflects this prayerful growth than the record
of the quiet, even tenor of his early life as a Jesuit. These young
years, it is true, were not without their trials, disappointments and
hardships, but:

It is the blight man was born for . . .[12]

Hopkins could no more escape such moments than any other
man. They came to him in the Society as they had come to him
before his entrance. Now, however, his religion and his vocation
enabled him to bear them with fortitude.

As a new Jesuit novice Hopkins is serious about the business
of learning to know, love and imitate Our Lord. That he may be
better recollected during his first year, he deliberately prevents
himself from seeing much of the world of nature around him for
six months (Jnl 121). Despite this penance he records some of
the delicate observations which his moments of leisure as a Jesuit
student are to make possible through all his years of study. With
the other novices he works in the nearby fields under the direction
of the brother who has charge of the grounds. He marks down in
his journal peculiar words, the use of which always fascinates
him, and for some time he studies closely the variations in the
Latin pronunciations of the Fathers in the community. But one
letter survives from his first year as a novice. It is a letter of
condolence to Bridges on the death of his sister and in it Hopkins'
ready sympathy and spiritual growth are unmistakable: "What
suffering she had! . . . it appeared in her face. But sufferings
falling on such a person as your sister was are to be looked on
as the marks of God's particular love and this is truer the more
exceptional they are" (B 25. Apr. 29, 1869).

[12] *Spring and Fall.*

At the end of his first year at Roehampton the master of novices was changed. "Fr. Fitzsimon," Hopkins notes almost with surprise, "left us suddenly and without a Goodbye and Fr. Gallwey took his place" (Jnl 123). It was Father Gallwey who in later years as Provincial of the English Jesuits was to treat Hopkins with the understanding kindness characteristic of the Society towards those who are ill. Now, however, he undertook the guidance of the young novice during the second year of his spiritual training. How well he did his work will be seen when some phases of Hopkins' spiritual life are discussed.

It seems unlikely that Hopkins was visited during the noviceship either by his parents or by other members of his immediate family. Such visits were rare at Roehampton; the *Minister's Journal* and Novice *Porter's Log,* Manresa, make mention of them but fail to record any made by Hopkins' relatives. Instead it was two of his friends whom he entertained, Bridges in October, 1869,[13] and in May, 1870, Baillie,[14] for whom Hopkins cherished a particular affection. Shortly after the visit of Bridges, the novice was assigned to preach the annual panegyric which is given in honor of St. Stanislaus, the patron of Jesuit novices. His heart must have warmed to his subject, for he delivered a sermon "which for its brilliancy and beauty was remembered long afterwards by those who heard it" (L 128). A month later, on December 12th (Jnl 126, 129) he became porter, and in this office, until February 19th, he was occupied with the task of ringing the many bells that punctuate the life of a novice, of accommodating the few visitors to the novitiate and of despatching the flow of mail. A day or so after he was made porter, he had a most unusual experience which he attempted not quite successfully to analyse in his journal. The first year novices were making the long retreat, and during the third week in which the Passion of Our Lord is the main subject of prayer and consideration (Jnl 128):

[13] B 26–27 (April 2, 1871).
[14] F 86–87 (May 11, 1870).

they were reading in the refectory Sister Emmerich's account of the Agony in the Garden and I suddenly began to cry and sob and could not stop. I put it down for this reason, that if I had been asked a minute beforehand I should have said that nothing of the sort was going to happen and even when it did I stood in a manner wondering at myself not seeing in my reason the traces of an adequate cause for such strong emotion—the traces of it I say because of course the cause in itself is adequate for the sorrow of a lifetime. I remember much the same thing on Maundy Thursday when the presanctified Host was carried to the sacristy.

The winter of 1870 was quite severe and the novice had an opportunity to study in detail the inscapes of snow and clouds of snow-dust, "which caught the sun as they rose and delightfully took the eyes" (Jnl 129), and at another time he turned physicist when "In taking off my jersey of knitted wool in the dark with an accidental stroke of my fingers down the stuff I drew a flash of electric light. This explains the crackling I had often heard" (Jnl 130). He was making spiritual discoveries, too, for in May he jotted down a little reminder: "Devotion to Our Lady not only in particular but under particular attributes —There is this in Spain to Our Lady of Mt. Carmel" (Jnl 133). During the same month he knew the beauty of Our Lord through the beauty of the bluebell whose inscape is mixed of strength and grace (Jnl 133–134).

On September 8th, 1870, his noviceship ended, and he took his three perpetual vows of poverty, chastity and obedience, praying humbly (as the words of the Vows put it) that God in his immense goodness and mercy might accept this holocaust in an odor of sweetness. His friend and former adviser Newman congratulated him on an event "so solemn and joyful" and promised to say Mass "for your intention upon it" (F 261. Sept. 26, 1870). We can imagine what his intention was when, eleven years later, he could say (D 75. Oct. 12, 1881):

As for myself, I have not only made my vows publicly some two and twenty times but I make them to myself every day, so that I should be black with perjury if I drew back now. And beyond that I can say with St. Peter: To whom shall I go? *Tu verba vitae aeternae habes.*

With the completion of his noviceship, Hopkins entered upon an entirely new phase of Jesuit life. The foundations of his spiritual life had been laid carefully and well, the blueprint was before him, and his further spiritual growth was insured by the many helps which the Society of Jesus provides. These helps he would never neglect; their influence in ways seen and unseen would pervade his entire life. But henceforth primary and manifest emphasis was to be placed upon his studies and upon preparation for the priesthood. Some of these studies had already been completed at Balliol, and because of this, the customary two years which the young Jesuit devotes to the classics and to the mastery of poetry and rhetoric were omitted. On September 9th he left Roehampton to begin his course in philosophy at St. Mary's Hall, the Jesuit seminary adjoining Stonyhurst.

There is nothing spectacular about the years which a young Jesuit spends in study. In Hopkins' case but one activity distinguishes him from the many who have lived through these quiet years of training. His journal is filled with page after page of observations which he made on natural phenomena and then recorded in an orderly fashion. Some things were always to appeal to him—sunsets, sunrises, clouds, flowers, trees, skies, flow of water; but for the rest he seems to have concentrated throughout the seasons on one or two special manifestations of the physical world until he exhausted their possibilities. In the winter of his first year as a philosopher he "made many observations on freezing" (Jnl 136); in the spring, on clouds "and evaporation, for instance over our Lenten chocolate" (Jnl 139). From the end of March to the beginning of April—"This is the time to study inscape in the spraying of trees, for the swelling buds carry them to a pitch which the eye could not else gather" (Jnl 141). As the nature-lover passed from observation to observation he must at times have been a strange sight to his fellow students. There is an interesting story told of the effect which Hopkins' studies had upon the gardener at Stonyhurst:

When an aged Father of the community drew his attention to Hopkins and said: "That young man is a very clever student," the gardener replied: "You don't say so! I watched him the other day while he kept staring at a piece of glass in the pathway and walking around it and examining it from all angles. I thought that he was a simple sort of fellow." [15]

We can feel sure that few of his brother Jesuits were as naive as the gardener, but still it is a fact that even to his friends outside the Society Hopkins was frequently an enigma. In later life Bridges took him to task for this, and the Jesuit could only reply (B 126. Apr. 27, 1881):

You give me a long jobation about eccentricities. Alas, I have heard so much about and suffered so much for and in fact been so completely ruined for life by my alleged singularities that they are a sore subject.

In addition to his nature and weather notes Hopkins copies from Whitaker's Almanack a series of important news events that occurred during his last year as a novice. He feels the need of bringing himself up to date on what is happening to the world and also to his friends, for in April he asks Bridges "Please tell me all about yourself" (B 26. Apr. 2, 1871). At the end of the same month he informs his fifteen year old sister Kate: "I want to know two things by the next person who writes" (F 42. Apr. 25, 1871). It is characteristic of Hopkins that the two things were particulars about an American yacht whose successes he has marked down in his journal, and whether or not the cuckoo had come unusually early that year.

The letter to Kate is a delight to read. Hopkins speaks of being vaccinated and the passage is full of tumbling good humor even

[15] André Bremond, *Etudes*, Oct. 5, 1934.

though, as he admits, the vaccination and medicine thereafter taken make him feel miserable. He tells her of the bounding and spinning lambs, an observation taken from his journal: "They toss and toss; it is as if it were the earth that flung them, not themselves" (Jnl 143). At the end we see his quick sensitivity to the pain of others (F 42. Apr. 25, 1871):

One thing made me very sad. . . . As I came down one of the galleries from the room [infirmary] I saw one of our young men standing there looking at a picture. I wondered why he stayed by himself and did not join the rest and then afterwards I remembered that he had had the smallpox and was deeply marked with it and all his good looks gone which he would have had and he did not want to face the others at that time when they were having their fun taking safe precautions against catching what it was too late for him to take any precautions against.

Other homely details of his life these days are caught in his journal. He mesmerizes a duck by the well known method of drawing chalk lines from her beak, painted upon the surface of a black table (Jnl 144). He studies the peacock with its spread train and once more is baffled by the inscape of bluebells as he draws his fingers through them (Jnl 144–146). Finally, towards the end of the scholastic year, on Whit Monday he goes to nearby Preston to see the procession, and "Though not very splendid, it moved me" (Jnl 148).

An excellent appraisal is given of his first year of philosophy in a letter addressed to Baillie during the Easter holidays. Strangely enough for one of his ability, he finds the study of logic difficult: "I am going through a hard course of scholastic logic . . . which takes all the fair part of the day and leaves one fagged at the end for what remains. This makes the life painful to nature. I find now too late *how* to read" (F 87. Apr. 10, 1871). He gives a compelling description of the vicinity and a comment on fishing that is almost epigrammatic: "There is good fishing for those who do not see that after bad fishing the next worse thing is good fishing." Hopkins concludes: ". . . this life here though it is hard is God's will for me as I most intimately know, which is more than violets knee deep."

His Easter mood, born of a time when all Jesuit students in houses of study begin to feel themselves harried somewhat by the prospect of difficult final examinations, was not to last. During the summer the philosophers went to Inellan on the coast of the Frith of Clyde for their vacation. From this point, in short expeditionary trips Hopkins visited Aman, Edinburgh and Glasgow. On August 30th he was back at Stonyhurst for the annual retreat of eight days. During this time, devoted exclusively to prayer and other spiritual activities, he re-lived the Spiritual Exercises which he had first made during the Long Retreat of the noviceship. These days offered him an opportunity to review the past year, to rest spiritually from the routine and cares of a student's life, to renew the spirit of his first dedication and to strengthen himself interiorly for the year ahead. This was an opportunity which Hopkins appreciated and he noted in his journal that it pleased him very much (Jnl 153). At the conclusion of the retreat his brother Cyril paid him a three day visit and then accompanied Gerard part of the way to Hampstead where the Jesuit found his father and eldest sister. He remained here, seeing relatives and friends for two days, and then proceeded to Hampshire where his mother and the rest of the family were waiting to welcome him. The remainder of the week he spent happily reunited with his family until September 18th, when he returned to Stonyhurst for the resumption of his philosophical studies.

During his second year of philosophy, cosmology and psychology occupied most of the curriculum. His mastery of these subjects is on many later occasions noticeable, and it developed in him a habit of careful, correct thinking that was to flourish all his days. In criticising a paper of Patmore's which appeared in the St. James on the text of Newman: "Man is not a reasoning animal; he is a seeing, feeling, contemplating, acting animal," he shows his uncanny ability to strike at the heart of a paradox.

Patmore must have frowned ever so slightly when he read (F 240. May 6, 1888):

the matter is philosophical, the title is so, the reference is to a philosophical work, and therefore philosophical precision would be in place and I in reading crave for it . . . after all there is nothing like the plain truth: paradox persisted in is not the plain truth and ought not to satisfy a reader.

Intellectual precision is the result of years of study, and for Hopkins the days spent in such study passed by with but few noteworthy interruptions. He rescues a kitten from its precarious perch because (Jnl 156):

I heard her mew a piteous long time till I could bear it no longer; but I make note of it because of her gratitude after I had taken her down, which made her follow me about and at each turn of the stairs . . . try to get up to lick me through the bannisters from the flight above.

In December there was frost and some skating and during the Christmas holidays there were plays and concerts presented by the boys at the College. It is a happy time, as is evidenced from some typical Hopkins humor directed at his friend Baillie (F 90. Jan. 4, 1872):

I ask for your professional opinion which I should receive with deep respect just as I should expect you to respect what I might hold *de gratiis gratis datis, de motibus primoprimis,* or *de satisfactione et satispassione* (you would be juiced green if you did, for I have not read a work of theology yet . . .)

Early in March, however, the Jesuit's tranquillity was broken. Henry William Challis, a friend and like Hopkins a convert, wrote saying that he had left the Church. The news was deeply disturbing, and for a week Hopkins was troubled as he reviewed his own position. The climax came on March 13th (Jnl 158):

After a time of trial and especially a morning in which I did not know which way to turn, as the account of De Rancé's final conversion was being read at dinner the verse *Qui confidunt in Domino sicut mons Sion* which satisfied him and resolved him to enter his abbey of La Trappe by the mercy of God came strongly home to me too, so that I was choked for a little while and could not keep in my tears.

The time of trial passed, however, and the year drew to a close with his sense of sympathy for the hardships and losses of others so deepened that it betrays itself even when he steps into a great shadowy barn and "looking at the great rudely arched timber-frames . . . I thought how sadly beauty of inscape was unknown and buried away from simple people and yet how near at hand it was if they had eyes to see it and it could be called out everywhere again" (Jnl 161). Just before the annual vacation which was spent at Douglas in the Isle of Man, Hopkins began to read the Commentary of Scotus on the Sentences of Peter Lombard. As a result he "was flush with a new stroke of enthusiasm," which "may come to nothing or it may be a mercy from God." It was a mercy from God; and the influence of Scotus can be seen frequently in Hopkins' poetry and more especially in almost every line of his Notes on the Spiritual Exercises of St. Ignatius. That summer he thought of Scotus during his vacation when he took in any inscape of sea or sky. There were many opportunities for this as he spent his time walking, swimming, boating and fishing. These days he enjoyed and further he found the Manx people the most good-natured he had ever met (F 93. Dec. 3, 1872).

When the philosophers returned to Stonyhurst on August 20th, 1872, Hopkins narrates how with a gesture characteristic of the devotion of the Society of Jesus to its younger men, "Fr. Rector came over to wait on us at supper, which touched me" (Jnl 167). Further manifestations of this devotion were soon to appear, for about this time there occurs the first break in his health. There is mention of it on October 27th, about two weeks after the marriage of his brother Cyril, to whom Gerard sent as a wedding present the orange and yellow feathers which a vagrant golden-crested wren had scattered about his room. It was evening and

Father Gallwey, now the provincial, who was then visiting
Stonyhurst, before night litanies "came to my room as I lay on
my bed making my examen, for I had some fever, and sitting
by the bedside took my hand within his and said some affectionate
and most encouraging words" (Jnl 170). Encouragement was
needed, not so much because of the seriousness of his illness but
rather because of its weakening and disagreeable nature. Apparently Hopkins had been subject from time to time to weakness
brought about by what he calls "my old complaint." He suffered
such a severe hemorrhoidal attack in the beginning of November
that it was decided an operation was necessary.

Meanwhile, however, he manages to overlook his illness. He is
teaching himself how to play the piano and when Dr. Vaughan,
the new Bishop of Salford, visits the community, he sheds twenty-
four Greek iambics with much ado at an academy in honor of the
event (F 91-92. Dec. 3, 1872). In studies "they are having at me
with ethics and mechanics" (F 91) and apparently the latter subject is occasioning him some initial difficulty. It is about this time,
too, that he must have begun his course in natural theology, a
subject which appealed to him greatly, as his first meditation in
his Notes on the Spiritual Exercises of St. Ignatius shows. Here
he develops with skilful subtlety his own variations on the cosmo-
logical argument for the existence of God. In his hands the scholastic dilemma—"Am I due (1) to chance? (2) to myself, as
selfexistent? (3) to some extrinsic power?"—assumes new vitality
(N 310-317).

Studies were broken off for the Christmas holidays. Hopkins'
superiors had decided that the necessary operation should be delayed no longer. The sweet was mingled with the bitter, however,
for their decision enabled him to return home to Hampstead and
spend the holidays with his parents. On Christmas there was a
reunion of the Hopkins family, and on December 30th the operation was performed by two of the family physicians (Jnl 172).
The Jesuit remained at Hampstead, happily visited by a number
of his closest Oxford friends, and after three weeks departed for

Roehampton on the 21st. One is tempted to believe that Father Gallwey had a hand in these arrangements, for Hopkins rested at Roehampton for two more weeks, returning to Stonyhurst a few days before the semi-annual triduum preceding the renovation of vows.

The remainder of the school year was a busy time, for the philosopher now had to prepare for the hour's oral examination *de universa philosophia* in which he was responsible for the matter of the past three years. Between long periods of work over his books he continued to find relaxation in his study of nature. The aesthetic experience had become such a reality to him that when one of the ash trees in the corner of the garden was felled, "I heard the sound and looking out and seeing it maimed there came at that moment a great pang and I wished to die and not to see the inscapes of the world destroyed any more" (Jnl 174). During the spring and early summer he is especially interested in the flight and actions of birds — how the corncrakes cry at night, how the "swifts round and scurl under the clouds in the sky," how the "turkey and hens will let a little chick mount their backs and sit between the wings," how the pigeons in the kitchen yard "look like little gay juds by shape when they walk, strutting and jod-jodding with their heads," and how "sometimes," he says, "I hear the cuckoo with wonderful clear and plump and fluty notes" (Jnl 175–176).

His final examination was on June 23rd, and a week later he is given his first taste of active work when for a few days he takes over some of the classes at the College. On August 1st vacation begins, once more at Douglas Castle on the Isle of Man. A letter is written during his stay there while "people all about are reading extracts of the *Manx Sun* and *Mrs. Brown* and repeating a constructive pun I found my way into at supper and so on" (F 43. Aug. 4, 1873). He is reading Arnold's poems "with more interest than rapture," and he has been delving into Newman's *Grammar of Assent*. In between times he goes on long hikes with his fellow Jesuits. Despite his operation he suffers during these

days from recurrent attacks of weakness, some of them undoubtedly occasioned by his own carelessness. On one expedition
he stops in the rain to sketch a stream, and then, not content
with this foolhardiness, jumps into the water, which was almost
up to his waist, to get a better view of his subject (Jnl 180).
Upon return to the College at the end of vacation, "being unwell
I was quite downcast: nature in all her parcels and faculties
gaped and fell apart, *fatiscebat*, like a clod cleaving and holding
only by strings of root. But this must often be" (Jnl 182).

There was nothing to do now but wait until he should receive
his appointment for the coming year. This arrived on August
27th; he was assigned to teach rhetoric at Roehampton, his students being some of the younger Jesuits who had but a year before
taken their vows. Before he took up his new duties, an entry in
the journal brings to a close this period of Hopkins' Jesuit life:
"At Manresa I caught the Provincial who spoke most kindly and
encouragingly" (Jnl 182). It is appropriate that these first five
years of his Jesuit life should end on such a note.

3. TEACHER AND THEOLOGIAN (1873-1877)

The year which Hopkins spent as professor of rhetoric at
Roehampton was to have a forceful influence upon his metrical
development. As Humphrey House points out: "It is important
to realize that the stimulus to formulate his thoughts about metre
came directly from the teaching he was officially given to do"
(N xxviii). Some idea of the subjects he taught and the manner
in which he taught them can be gleaned from his lecture notes
on rhetoric (N 221-251). His classes could not have been large,
for there were only twenty students at Roehampton during this
year, and it is doubtful if all of these attended his lectures. The
work should not have been difficult, though Hopkins would seem
to have made it so. Looking back over the year, he felt that he
had taught painfully and badly (B 30. Feb. 20, 1875). Certainly
his notes were painstakingly compiled; the finished product is

a masterpiece of detail and subtlety. It seems to lack clearness, however, and that simplified ordering of knowledge which is essential if it is to be communicated, especially to young men such as Hopkins had under him. We do not know what his students thought of his classes, and we can only hope that they gained as much by the hours spent with their teacher as Hopkins himself did by the metrical advances of his later work.

Beyond these few details little can be learned about his teaching days at Roehampton either from his letters or his journal. An interesting analysis occurs of a nightmare which he experienced shortly after his arrival. The immediate and remote reactions are characteristic of the man: "I cried on the holy name and by degrees recovered myself as I thought to do. It made me think that this was how the souls in hell would be imprisoned in their bodies as in prisons" (Jnl 185). His nature notes are briefer now, interspersed for the first time in his Jesuit days by studies of various paintings which his visits to nearby galleries made possible. The Christmas holidays were again spent at Hampstead with his family, though now they are pleasantly free from the shadow of illness. Upon his return, the regular routine of teaching is broken by visits from some of his friends, one of whom he exhorts to "Be pregnant, bring thoughts, news, strokes, touches, Moncure Conway, friends (not in the body), butts, bulls, blunders" (F 45. Apr. 19, 1874).

The school year ended on July 31st, and Hopkins thus summarized his year of teaching (Jnl 199):

I was very tired and seemed deeply cast down till I had some kind words from the Provincial. Altogether perhaps my heart has never been so burdened and cast down as this year. The tax on my strength has been greater than I have felt before: at least now . . . I feel myself weak and can do little.

The truth of the matter seems to be that Hopkins had not learned and probably never would learn the limit of his own physical and intellectual endurance. He was always reaching out above

and beyond the capacity of his naturally weak body. There are
evidences of this even in his nature studies which he considered a
relaxation. On one occasion during the year he visited the
Academy and inspected paintings until "my eye was fagged with
looking at pictures" (Jnl 197). In his spiritual life it was the
same. On a visit to the Jesuit house at Beaumont he felt that he
had talked too freely and unkindly at dinner; in reparation for
this fault, on the way back he kept his eyes downcast so that he
did not see the loveliness of the day (Jnl 199). He could never
be satisfied with mediocrity, imperfection or superficiality, and in
all things was too severe a judge of himself. Nothing better illustrates this horror of things half done than a criticism he passed
upon himself after he had spent some hours first in Westminster
Abbey and then in the National Gallery: "As I hurried from picture to picture at first these words came to my mind—'Studious
to eat but not to taste'" (Jnl 209). Although the cup of weariness and discouragement was often to be of his own brewing he
was determined to taste its depths.

On August 26th, 1873, after a vacation spent at Teignmouth,
Hopkins heard definitely that he was to go to St. Beuno's College
in North Wales to begin his theological studies. It was news heard
under a good star, for a week before "the stars came out thick:
I leant back to look at them and my heart opening more than
usual praised Our Lord to and in whom all that beauty comes
home" (Jnl 205). The next three years of his life were probably
the happiest he spent as a Jesuit, for each day brought him consciously nearer to the priesthood in an atmosphere and a country
that was instressed with charm. It was at St. Beuno's that Hopkins could write:

> I remember a house where all were good
>   To me, God knows, deserving no such thing:
>   Comforting smell breathed at very entering
> Fetched fresh, as I suppose, off some sweet wood.[16]

[16] *In the Valley of the Elwy.* The house referred to was that of a London
family, the Watsons of Shooter's Hill.

Upon his arrival two of the scholastics "met me at St. Asaph, Mr. Bacon put scarlet geraniums in my room, and everyone was very kind and hospitable" (Jnl 209). Shortly after this, however, he experienced for a time the difficulties to which all young Jesuits— and some old—are subject when they come to a new house. Kindness and hospitality can never completely counterbalance the inevitable trials of unpacking and settling down in different surroundings and among different companions. Perhaps, too, the thought of the difficult course of studies to be completed before ordination dismayed and even discouraged him. During the retreat he says: ". . . I was very bitterly feeling the weariness of life and shed many tears, perhaps not wholly into the breast of God but with some unmanliness in them too, and sighed and panted to Him" (Jnl 210). But this period passed; at the end of the retreat he received minor orders and on the next day was present at his first Jesuit Ordination. "At the singing of the *Veni Creator* and giving of the Orders I was by God's mercy deeply touched" (Jnl 213) by the thought and prospect, no doubt, of his own ordination which the reception of minor orders had brought so much closer.

There are only a few pages in his journal devoted to these first weeks at St. Beuno's, and they are all filled with good cheer. With his fellow theologians he took many long walks, "and returned very joyously" (Jnl 214). The views are fresh, noble and delightful. The days are fine and clear; the flowers are splendid. There are lovely sunsets "of rosy juices and creams and combs" (Jnl 213), and the white and grey smoke of Denbigh "creeping upon the hill, what with sun and wind give fairy effects which are always changing" (Jnl 216). It is as if Hopkins and his companions are like a multitude of starlings he saw one day, and of whom he wrote: "I thought they must be full of enthusiasm and delight hearing their cries and stirring and cheering one another" (Jnl 215).

The journal comes to an end in early February, and thereafter we must depend on correspondence for details of the remaining time he passed at St. Beuno's. Once again he finds his classwork difficult (B 31. Feb. 20, 1875):

The close pressure of my theological studies leaves me time for hardly anything: the course is very hard, it must be said. Nevertheless I have tried to learn a little Welsh, in reality one of the hardest of languages.

More important than Welsh is an unrecorded but larger "Nevertheless" which forty-five years later was to be placed by Bridges as a great dragon guarding the gate of Hopkins' poetry. In the winter of his first year as a theologian, following a wishful hint expressed by his superior, Hopkins' poetic pen, practically unused for ten years, began to write:

> On Saturday sailed from Bremen,
>   American-outward-bound,
> Take settler and seamen, tell men with women,
>   Two hundred souls in the round—[17]

The Wreck of the Deutschland interests us at this point not only because it marks the definite resumption of poetic production for Hopkins, but mainly because he said of it to Bridges (B 47. Aug. 21, 1877):

I may add for your greater interest and edification that what refers to myself in the poem is all strictly and literally true and did all occur; nothing is added for poetical padding.

We have studied the story of Hopkins' odyssey from God back to God in the unpretentious pages of his letters and journal; but here in *The Wreck of the Deutschland* is the fullest story of his dedication to Christ. Here is the song he sings:

of the hours of prayer that resulted in his conversion (ll. 19-21):

> . . . where was a, where was a place?
>   I whirled out wings that spell
> And fled with a fling of the heart to the heart of the Host.

[17] *The Wreck of the Deutschland,* ll. 89-92, B 44 (Aug. 21, 1877).

of his vocation (ll. 29, 31–32):

> I steady as a water in a well, to a poise, to a pane,
> . . . a vein
> Of the gospel proffer, a pressure, a principle, Christ's gift.

of his days spent in loving observation of nature as a young Jesuit (ll. 38–40):

> . . . tho' he is under the world's splendor and wonder,
> His mystery must be instressed, stressed;
> For I greet him the days I meet him, and bless when I understand.

of his hours of trial when he discovered (ll. 69–70):

> Beyond saying sweet, past telling of tongue,
> Thou art lightning and love, I found it, a winter and warm;

of his prayer for himself and all men (ll. 73–76):

> With an anvil-ding
> And with fire in him forge thy will
> Or rather, rather then, stealing as Spring
> Through him, melt him but master him still:

After the composition of *The Wreck of the Deutschland* silence closes about the activities of Hopkins for two years. Of these he might say only:

> Away in the loveable west,
> On a pastoral forehead of Wales,
> I was under a roof here, I was at rest . . .[18]

His studies continued apace and he began now to take a more active interest in poetic production. In January, 1877, eight months before his ordination, we hear of him again. He is preparing for his final examination in moral theology, and many in a similar position will agree with his sweeping description of the subject: "You see, moral theology covers the whole of life and to know it it is best to begin by knowing everything, as medicine, law, history, banking" (F 95. Jan. 6, 1877). Hopkins could not

[18] *The Wreck of the Deutschland*, ll. 185–187.

begin by knowing everything, but he did end by knowing moral theology. His analyses of the nature and essential elements of sin, of free will and grace which occur in his Notes on the Spiritual Exercises of St. Ignatius make this abundantly clear, as does a short explanation of the sin of presumption which he gives to Patmore.[19]

Preparation for the examination in this subject is always exhausting, and Hopkins found it unusually so, for afterwards he admitted that he was "very very tired, yes 'a thousand times and yet a thousand times' and 'scarce can go or creep' " (B 33. Apr. 3, 1877). His weariness, however, did not prevent him from writing to Bridges a long and detailed criticism of the latter's poems. Bridges had objected to Hopkins' superiors reading his letters. The Jesuit had attempted to explain this practice common to religious orders, and when Bridges apparently said that he didn't like Jesuits anyway, Hopkins' answer was simple and experimental: "Did you ever see one?" (B 40. Apr. 3, 1877). One is tempted to feel that neither then nor at any other time did Bridges really see a Jesuit, for despite the intimacy of their association he never really understood his friend. His unfortunate blindness is frequently manifested in Hopkins' letters and is shared by all too many of those who have professed admiration for Hopkins' poems and have pioneered in publicizing them.

The study of theology came to an end on September 27th when Hopkins was ordained to the priesthood. This most important event in his life must pass by without comment, for comment there is none save for two letters of congratulations he subsequently received.[20] But no matter, since Hopkins and his brother Jesuits ordained with him:

Christ minds: Christ's interest, what to avow or amend . . .
Their ransom, their rescue, and first, fast, last friend.[21]

[19] F 174 (Oct. 25, 1883). See also on sin N 317–321; on free will and grace N 322–328; on infused virtue of faith N 336; on Incarnation N 346–351.
[20] F 262 (Nov. 13, 1877) and F 267 (Oct. 23, 1877).
[21] The Lantern out of Doors.

4. PRIEST AND TERTIAN (1877–1882)

After his ordination at St. Beuno's Hopkins leaves the retire-
ment of a life of study and becomes engaged in active priestly
work. Events crowd upon us and it becomes impossible here to
follow his activities in detail. For the purpose of our subject the
remaining twelve years of his life fall into three inevitable periods.
The first spans the years which he spent principally at Mt. St.
Mary's College, Chesterfield; at St. Aloysius', Oxford; and at St.
Francis Xavier's, Liverpool. During this time he has his first contact with the work for which he had been prepared. At the conclusion of these four years Hopkins is given an opportunity during
the tertianship to evaluate the past and to adjust himself, his
plans and his spiritual life to the active ministry as he has found it.
Finally in the last six years of his life he returns once more to the
active ministry at Stonyhurst and later at University College,
Dublin.

During this first period it was evidently the intention of superiors
to test the aptitude of the new priest in various positions. At Mt.
St. Mary's, where he remained for only seven months, his work
was mostly administrative; at Oxford and Liverpool he was engaged in the duties of a parish priest, hearing confessions, preaching and visiting his flock. In none of these positions did he distinguish himself, but it is not therefore to be imagined that he was a
dismal failure. Rare indeed is the preacher who achieves immediate success. Hopkins, a novice in this type of work, could only
hope to emulate such men as his Liverpool superior, Father James
Clare, S.J., who had long been acknowledged as a master of sacred
eloquence. Even before Hopkins had become a convert, Father
Clare's reputation and ability as a preacher had drawn large
crowds to the Jesuit church at Farm Street. Beside the accomplish-
ments of such a man, the efforts of any newly ordained priest
would seem unsuccessful. Certainly Hopkins' efforts seemed unsuccessful to himself, but it can be seriously doubted whether his
audiences took such a harsh view of the matter. Because of the

unfortunate reception which greeted one of his sermons given at
St. Beuno's it has been concluded that "the immediate effect
even of his serious preaching was likely to be comic or disastrous"
(N xxxi). Reading his sermons it is hard to credit such a conclusion. The 'Dominical' episode during which some of his fellow
Jesuits "laughed . . . prodigiously" has no significance — as any
Jesuit who has given a practice sermon and seen what manner of
reception it received, will agree. In Jesuit houses of study such
sermons occur at community meals sometimes as frequently as
four times a week during the regular school year. They are given
in the presence of men who are primarily assembled for the purpose of eating. Throughout the entire sermon there are distractions: mumbled requests for service, waiters walking back and
forth, attending to the needs of their tables or stacking plates on
serving carts, dishes rattling and even on rare occasions tumbling
with a crash to the floor. The sermon itself is addressed, not to
the community but to some imaginary group, and many a would-
be Bourdaloue finds this a serious handicap. He cannot hope to
overcome the distractions of his position by moving his audience
directly, for at most they only overhear remarks supposedly directed at others. In such surroundings even the most eloquent may
arouse prodigious laughter. It is interesting to note that when
Hopkins as a novice addressed the community directly in his
panegyric on St. Stanislaus, he made a deep impression on his
audience. At Liverpool difficulties were to be expected when he
preached to congregations which Father Clare and others more
experienced than Hopkins had addressed. These difficulties were
mostly infelicities of phrase, expression or comparison. Hopkins,
conscientious, severe in his judgment of himself, may have magni-
fied the importance of his faults, but his superiors only suggested
one or two corrections and then "poohpoohed the matter and
would not look at it" (N 433).

Intimates of Father Hopkins in these years were impressed
mostly by his priestly spirit. As a young priest he could say sin-
cerely (B 64. Jan. 29, 1879):

And I take leave to repeat and you cannot but see, that it is a noble thing and not a miserable something or other to give alms and help the needy and stint ourselves for the sake of the unhappy and deserving.

During these years the priest gave abundant alms of himself in the performance of his sacred duties. The influence of his zeal embraced both his flock and his friends, though with the latter he had little success. He was repeatedly rebuffed despite the frequent efforts he made to arouse in Bridges an awareness of the supernatural. It was to be a source of sadness to him throughout his entire life. He could say: "As I am criticising you, so does Christ, only more correctly and affectionately, both as a poet and as a man" (B 73. Feb. 23, 1879). He could urge Bridges to approach God with "the humblest and most earnest prayers" (B 118. Jan. 26, 1881). At one time he could enter most gracefully the door to Bridges' heart, telling him (B 263. Nov. 2, 1887):

I do not know whether I told you . . . but for fear it should never have been said, I may write now that . . . I had the impression I had never in my life met a sweeter lady than Mrs. Bridges. You may wear a diamond on your finger and yet never have seen it in a side light, so I tell you.

At another time he could try to have Bridges enter the door of his own heart by explaining to him the Catholic religion and his own vocation (B 186. Oct. 24, 1883). But to the end his friend was a disappointment to him, as for example, when he expressed satisfaction over the defection from the Church and the priesthood of one of Hopkins' closest boyhood friends (B 298. Oct. 20, 1888):

It is as you say about Addis. But why should you be glad? Why at any rate should you burst upon me that you are glad, when you know that I cannot be glad? It seems there is something in you interposed between . . . the Christian and the man of the world which hurts, which is to me like biting on a cinder in bread. Take the simplest view of the matter: he has made shipwreck . . . I feel the same deep affection for him as ever, but the respect is gone.

Such is the relationship between them that we can expect to find but few references in Hopkins' letters to the priestly work he is doing. He refers to visiting the sick and administering the last sacraments (B 123. Jan. 26, 1881), he interrupts a letter to visit the workhouse (B 95. Oct. 22, 1879), he tells Bridges of a boy, about whom he had written one of his poems: "The little hero of *The Handsome Heart* has gone to school at Boulogne to be bred for a priest and he is bent on being a Jesuit" (B 92. Oct. 8, 1879). We learn of his revulsion over the sad lot of the city poor huddled in their own dirt and grime, spawning immorality and crimes. He who was so sensitive not only to sin but even to imperfection that he would penance himself for an unkind word, who sang of:

> Head, heart, hand, heel and shoulder
> That beat and breathe in power—[22]

wept bitterly over the multitude that would not hear him. Fagged, harried, gallied up and down, he was at times so dismayed that he could exclaim: "And the drunkards go on drinking, the filthy, as the scripture says, are filthy still: human nature is so inveterate. Would that I had seen the last of it" (B 110. Oct. 26, 1880). It is the cry of the priest who knows that his best efforts will go unheeded and that his success must be patterned after the apparent failure of Christ.

The time had come for building up his reserves of spiritual strength, and on October 10th, 1881, Hopkins began his year's tertianship at Manresa, Roehampton. Here he found rest and contentment while newspapers and world events, poetry and literary criticism were for a time left behind. Shortly after his arrival he tells Canon Dixon, with whom he had resumed acquaintance during the first year of his priesthood (D 75. Oct. 12, 1881):

[22] *Morning, Midday and Evening Sacrifice.*

. . . in the midst of outward occupations not only the mind is drawn
away from God, which may be at the call of duty and be God's will,
but unhappily the will too is entangled, worldly interests freshen, and
worldly ambitions revive. The man who in the world is as dead to the
world as if he were buried in the cloister is already a saint. But this is
our ideal.

How close Hopkins came to fulfilling that ideal is seen in his
evaluation of the importance of poetry in his priestly life.

As a young convert about to enter the Society of Jesus Hopkins
had decided that the writing of poetry would interfere with his
vocation and hence "resolved to write no more, as not belonging
to my profession" (D 14. Oct. 5, 1878). One is tempted to doubt
the wisdom of this decision and to hope that it was not made independently of the prudent advice of his confessor. Perhaps what
C. C. Abbott says may be true, that at this time "there was danger
to his soul in the exercise of his gift as a poet. He feared the
temptation as one of the secret solicitations of the world"
(B xxxvi). Or perhaps he felt that it was unworthy of him:

> Having the infinitely great
> Therewith to hanker for the small! [23]

This resolution Hopkins kept until his rector at St. Beuno's expressed the hope that someone would write a poem on the wreck
of the *Deutschland,* a hope which Hopkins readily fulfilled. He
made one attempt to have this poem and another subsequent work
published. Although these attempts failed, he continued to write
from time to time as inspiration and occasion offered. This was
not often, as he tells Bridges: "I shall never have leisure or desire
to write much" (B 54. May 30, 1878), and "I cannot in conscience spend time on poetry, neither have I the inducements and
inspirations that make others compose. . . . Then again I have
of myself made verse so laborious" (B 66. Feb. 15, 1879). The
wellsprings of his poetry were either professional experiences or
deeply personal emotions which Hopkins could not refrain from

[23] *A Voice from the World,* N 20.

expressing in verse. While some of this work was sent to Bridges and Dixon for them to admire and criticise, he was convinced that "The only just judge, the only just literary critic, is Christ, who prizes, is proud of, and admires, more than any man, more than the receiver himself can, the gifts of his own making" (D 8, June 13, 1878).

Of the fame which publication of his poems might bring him he was wary (D 6.):

it is a great danger in itself, as dangerous as wealth every bit, I should think, and as hard to enter the kingdom of heaven with. And even if it does not lead men to break the divine law, yet it gives them "itching ears" and makes them live on public breath.

Hence he could say that he will make no attempts to publish his works and could feel that if they were published even by his superiors he would not be altogether glad.[24]

When at the importunate promptings of Dixon he did submit to Hall Caine some sonnets which were refused, he subsequently poked fun at Caine whose "manner was that I was 'a young aspirant' and he a judge by whose nod I stood or fell—a thing not to be thought" (B 129. May 14, 1881). Dixon felt bad about this refusal of Caine, but Hopkins had candidly warned him: "The life I lead is liable to many mortifications but the want of fame as a poet is the least of them" (D 28. May 12, 1879).

At Roehampton Hopkins once more, and now for the last time, reconsiders his evaluation of the importance of poetry in his life. The long retreat began during the second week of November, and after some days spent in silence and prayer the first day of repose or break-day, as it is sometimes called, occurred. At this point the usual retreat order was suspended to some extent, silence was lifted and the retreatants were encouraged to rest and refresh themselves in preparation for the next week of the retreat. On this day Hopkins received a letter from Dixon who placed the

---

[24] B 66 (Feb. 15, 1879). See B 196 (Aug. 12, 1884) for a list of the few persons to whom Hopkins showed his poetry during his lifetime.

problem of poetry squarely before him. His heart bleeds, he says, for the choice that his Jesuit friend has made, and while he recognizes the high spiritual motives which prompt Hopkins he clings "to the hope that you will find it consistent with all you have undertaken to pursue poetry still, as occasion may serve. . . . Surely one vocation cannot destroy another" (D 90. Nov. 4, 1881). If the Jesuit had been inclined to defer reviewing his position towards poetry he could no longer do so. During the second week of the retreat while he was following Our Lord in His Public Life and rededicating himself to the standard of the King of kings, he considers the decision which he made as a novice. On the second break-day he begins to write his answer to Dixon; but time does not permit its conclusion and once more he returns to prayer, this time sorrowing as his Leader during the Passion deliberately chooses humiliation, suffering and death that He might, as He says, give us an example. The third break-day arrives and Hopkins finishes what he has to say to his friend. His decision has been made and he will not, after viewing Christ's sacrifice, fail in his generosity or willingness to imitate his Master. Still the letter is not sent to Dixon until the end of the retreat after Hopkins has meditated on the glory of the risen Christ and sealed his dedication with an act of purest love. In this dedication there was no haste, no compulsion, no heroic immaturity, but only the considered judgment of a man who had walked for a month by the side of Christ and there found how best to serve Him. Before such a determination our murmurs of disappointment must be reverently stilled. Hopkins, whose vision was clearer than our own, knew that Christ Our Lord: "if he choose to avail himself of what I leave at his disposal he can do so with a felicity and with a success which I could never command" (D 93. Dec. 1, 1881).

After the long retreat Hopkins spent much of his time preparing sermons for the tour of work which was later assigned him during Lent. He was also occupied with gathering materials on the subject of sacrifice and beginning his projected commentary on the Spiritual Exercises. Just before the end of the tertianship Bridges visited his friend and was present at the Corpus Christi procession, which all agreed was not brisk and joyous, but heavy and dead (B 148. June 10, 1882). Perhaps Bridges agreed too vehemently, for Hopkins found it necessary to remind him that while such things has no significance for his friend (*Ibid.*),

what is strange and unpleasant is that you sometimes speak as if they had in reality none for me and you were only waiting with a certain disgust till I too should be disgusted with myself enough to throw off the mask . . . Yet I can hardly think you do not think I am in earnest. And let me say, to take no higher ground, that without earnestness there is nothing sound or beautiful in character . . .

These words should be noted by students of Hopkins who are inclined to feel that the priest was forever looking back with longing upon the sacrifice of the muse he had intelligently and heroically made. To read into Hopkins' occasional complaints about the lack of poetic inspiration an importance they did not assume, is, as Hopkins himself said, "unreasonable and is to make difficulties" (B 163. Mar. 26, 1882). We should remember what Bridges failed ever to realize: that Hopkins was deeply in earnest about this, and "a man who is deeply in earnest is not very eager to assert his earnestness, as they say when a man is really certain he no longer disputes but is indifferent" (B 163).

5. JESUIT AND POET (1882–1889)

In the beginning of September, 1882, Hopkins became a member of the Stonyhurst faculty. From that time until his death in 1889 he was engaged in teaching, correcting papers or examinations, and collecting materials for a number of projects which he hoped would eventually find their way into print. Both at Stonyhurst and later at Dublin, where he went in 1884, he labored to achieve (B 173. Feb. 3, 1883)

that chastity of mind which seems to lie at the very heart and be the parent of all other good, the seeing at once what is best, the holding to that, and the not allowing anything else whatever to be even heard pleading to the contrary.

During his long retreat in the tertianship he had seen what was best for him, and now he held on to it with vigor, not allowing anything else to be heard pleading to the contrary. If at that time the mind rather than the heart embraced renunciation of poetry for a higher good, his choice was then made "with the elective will, not the affective essentially; but the affective will will follow" (N 416). It did follow, for two years before his death he wrote calmly to Dixon: "What becomes of my verses I care little, but about . . . what I write or could write on philosophical matters, I do" (D 150. Jan. 27, 1887). Like Patmore he did not think he was (F 214. Apr. 7, 1885)

uselessly employed. Dont you think that a soul wh. has filled itself very full of a great unspoken and unspeakable thought may, if it attain its last end, teach the world by uttering it into the hearts of men in some far more powerful way than words?

Hopkins could never join with those who would make poetry and art an absolute good. For him it was a luxury to be placed in his determined scale of values after the priesthood, after teaching, after his professional writing, after his study of literature and music. To those who would exalt it above all these things, but especially above his vocation given to him by God, to those who, misunderstanding the Jesuit, attempt to understand the poet by slighting the priest, Hopkins might well say, firmly but kindly (D 146. Oct. 23, 1886):

For myself literally words would fail me to express the loathing and horror with which I think of it and of man setting up the work of his own hands, of that hand within the mind, the imagination, for God Almighty who made heaven and earth.

The Jesuit poet's last years at Dublin were filled with many trials and sufferings. He had said that want of fame as a poet was the least of the mortifications in the life he led; but there were others which could not be so easily borne. The first of these, and the one which cannot be overstressed, was ill health. When a young teacher at the Oratory in 1868 he had complained of this (F 84. Feb. 12, 1868), and as we have seen, he was subject to intermittent attacks during his first years as a Jesuit. The operation which he underwent while a philosopher seemed to bring only temporary relief. We know that he was ill just before his ordination (F 267. Oct. 23, 1877) and during the year which followed his departure from St. Beuno's. Weariness from overworking himself, from diarrhoea and vomiting, often sapped his strength and caused, naturally enough, fits of deep depression in which he cried out "in that coffin of weakness and dejection in which I live" (B 214. Apr. 1, 1885). His satisfaction on hearing of the Dublin appointment was subdued, particularly because he felt that he was not at all strong and did not see how he was to become so (B 190. Mar. 25, 1884). As one year at Dublin yielded to another he began to be more subject to murderous colds and rheumatism, to nervous prostration approaching madness, to blinding eye trouble of a particularly painful nature. These things he reveals mostly in his letters to Bridges, who was a doctor and whom he had consulted for professional advice.[25] Such, finally, is his decline in health that on the third anniversary of his arrival in Dublin he says sorrowfully: "I only need one thing—a working strength" (B 251. Feb. 17, 1887).

One might expect that such a man would take prudent care of himself, would use every legitimate opportunity for necessary change and rest. Hopkins did not do this; he was forever applying the spur to his weary body and mind, and only utter exhaustion could make him succumb. In the winter of 1885 he refuses to spend the Christmas vacation at Hampstead with his family, and by New Year's Day he is jaded (B 201. Jan. 1, 1885). During a short visit to Clongowes Wood College he spends his time reading and working over his criticism of one of Bridges' books. In March his health and appearance are so bad that one of his brother

[25] *Vid.* 61 B 84 (June 22, 1879) and 78 B 138 (Oct. 22, 1881).

Jesuits "will have it that I am dying—of anaemia" (B 208. Mar. 24, 1885), and Hopkins admits that he is "weak in body and harassed in mind." The Easter holidays find him in the same unsatisfactory condition, but he continues to work hard over some musical compositions. By the middle of May the burden of "work, worry, and languishment of body and mind" (B 216. May 17, 1885) is so great that he confesses to Bridges: "my fits of sadness, though they do not affect my judgment, resemble madness. Change is the only relief, and that I can seldom get." How closely ill health was companioned by desolation and the thought of despair will be seen from the important fact that during these months the Dublin sonnets, unbidden and against his will, were written, as he says (B 221. Sept. 1, 1885), literally in blood.

In addition to his health, which was ill enough to crush anyone, there were other trials. To the inevitable loneliness of the priest were added the loss of former friends and grief over the spiritual barriers which his conversion had raised between his family and himself. It is indeed true that "the kind and contented way" (F 37. June 13, 1868), in which his parents received the news of his conversion and of his vocation, had been a great comfort to him; throughout all his Jesuit life Hopkins' relations with his family remained familiar, loving, free of restraint. So, too, it was with the companions of his earlier years; his correspondence with them continued to be that easy, intimate exchange which exists only between close friends. However, despite such intimacies, between himself and all these others there was a difference too great to be ignored. He had so much he wished to share with them, so many gifts of peace and truth which he himself had found since his conversion to the Catholic Church. Yet he stood alone (No. 44):

> To seem the stranger lies my lot, my life
> Among strangers. Father and mother dear,
> Brothers and sisters are in Christ not near
> And he my peace my parting, sword and strife.

Nor was this enough. The Irish question troubled him excessively, and his love for England made it painful to contemplate any decadence in her government or peoples. Finally there was the bitter disappointment contained in his growing realization that he would never finish or print anything that he considered of importance. Though he had rejected any possibility of recognition or fame as a poet, he was convinced that his position as professor of classics and as fellow at the Royal University demanded scholarly research and composition. His spirit of indifference as far as his poetry was concerned, did not extend itself to these other fields. This was part of his work, the job he felt he had been given to do; and so he wanted to write, he longed to publish. His career as a Jesuit was strewn with the dying and dead hopes of books and papers he had planned on innumerable subjects—*The Spiritual Exercises,* Sacrifice, St. Patrick's Confession, Metrics, The Dorian Measure, Philosophy of Art, Aeschylus, Sophocles, The Greek Negatives, Statistics and Free Will, Light and the Ether, Welsh, and Music. He had spoken to his superiors about these subjects, had received their encouragement (B 150. Sept. 26, 1882), but it was to no avail. His health and consequently his spirits failed him and he could not go on in the face of uncertainties: ". . . but when shall I finish it? or if finished will it pass the censors? or if it does will the *Classical Review* or any magazine take it?" (B 270. Jan. 12, 1888).

Through these frequently dark days at Dublin the fortitude of the Jesuit poet shines clear. In a fragment of his spiritual notes he reminds himself: "—take it that weakness, ill health, every cross is a help. *Calix quem Pater meus dedit mihi non bibam illud?"* (N 416). As for the others, few could have guessed his real condition. When Bridges told him that Andrew Lang was deeply discouraged and compared Lang's condition to that of the Jesuit, Hopkins quietly replied: "I am sorry for poor Lang, if his dejection is so deep as you describe (only that, since you speak of me, I may say that I must conceal myself or it, which it seems he does neither of)" (B 247. Dec. 11, 1886). Now, of course, it is different. The emergence of Hopkins as a major Victorian poet has made public property of what was once known only to a few special friends, to some of his brother Jesuits and to his superiors. Like most public property the information has been frequently ill used. Sincere but inconsiderate and patchwork quoting from Hopkins' eminently quotable letters and notebooks has often produced sad results. Thus students of English literature have done Hopkins and themselves and their study a grave injustice. Perhaps this was an inevitable adjunct to the strictly literary approach which is interested in Hopkins primarily because he was a poet, and is prone to evaluate all other things in relation to his poetry. In Hopkins' case such an approach is not to be rejected utterly, but it must be bridled, it must be fitted to the facts which Hopkins himself has given and which have been seen in this narration of his daily life as a Jesuit.

Among all these facts two shine forth clearly and unmistakably. The first is negative—a negation of the importance of poetry in his life. One may not like this fact, may even conjecture such a negation to be unnecessary or imprudent, but one must accept it. Even as a young convert anticipating the possibility of a vocation to the priesthood, Hopkins had felt that poetry must play a minor part in his life. Throughout his early years as a Jesuit student this conviction persisted and in his tertianship it was sealed forever. Henceforth he might nod at the Muse but never seriously court her.

The second fact is positive—an affirmation of the supremacy of the supernatural in his life. Because he hoped for such a supremacy he became a Jesuit, and the Society of Jesus carefully nourished this hope until its object became a reality. Now such supremacy is not achieved overnight; the natural man cannot be slipped off like an old overcoat. And yet there are many who would tragically dramatize the fact that Hopkins, like his Hero and Leader Christ, often found in his work of saving souls, not peace but a sword. There seem to be many who mistakenly conceive dedication to Christ as a blissful state in which one enjoys ecstatic resignation to a *fait accompli,* made easy and secure by immunity to all the ills and weaknesses of poor human nature. The heart of the matter is that sanctity does not consist in freedom from trials. The true lover of Christ is anxious to suffer as Christ Himself did, is most perfectly fulfilling his dedication when despite his suffering he cleaves to Christ because he loves Him. This Hopkins did; the Jesuit in him had already grown to full stature long before his death.

But what of the poet? It is, of course, foolish to conjecture what kind of poet Hopkins would have been had he followed a different vocation. Though his early works show great promise, it is upon the poetry of his Jesuit years that his reputation rests. The contribution which the Society of Jesus made to this poetry is incalculable. It could not make Hopkins a poet in spite of himself, but in wisely guiding and tenderly caring for Hopkins the Jesuit and the priest, the Society of Jesus, more than can ever be known, formed Hopkins the poet. It fostered in the man those interests of mind and qualities of character that constitute the universality of his poetic appeal. His work as a teacher stimulated research in metrics and led directly to the development of his metrical innovations. His years as a student afforded him ample opportunity to indulge a spontaneous love of the natural world and of natural beauty, while his spiritual growth during those same years elevated that love of nature in all its moods and appearances, enabling him to experience supernaturally "the dearest freshness deep down things," [26] the stress of the Divine hand as it moves over mountains and streams, inscaping the world to its own likeness. Hopkins' intense spiritual life, born of the *Spiritual Exercises* of St. Ignatius, daily strengthened by meditation and vividly realized in every hour of joy or hardship, finds its full expression in the passionate and personal force of his verse. Hopkins' priesthood was the food of that rare insight, quick sympathy and love of humanity which made his poetic masterpieces. It is no accident that his poems awaken an immediate

[26] *God's Grandeur.*

response because of their vigorous, uncompromising honesty. For the Society of Jesus desires and exhorts all her sons to avoid self-deception, to strive for perfect humility which is nothing but genuine honesty, and to make such honesty the guiding rule of every thought, word and deed.

Had Hopkins never become a Jesuit he would, without doubt, still have achieved distinction as a poet. But it would have been a different Hopkins, and much that his poems now possess to perfect measure, would be strangely missing.

Towards the very end of his life Hopkins seems to have achieved a balance which time and experience might have made more permanent. His letters to Bridges indicate that his last year at Dublin found him happier at his work. Perhaps, had he lived, some of the peace and patience of his Jesuit student days might have arisen from all this suffering. The same fragment of his spiritual notes indicates such a prospect. After jotting down the fact that man was created to save his soul he continues: "Consider in this life the meaning of these words. Consider peace, contentment, a good conscience" (N 417). A good conscience, yes, but utter peace and contentment, it seems, were not for him in this life. His eyes were turned to the storm-driven hills and he knew "how the joy of seeing Christ Our Lord is from having lived for him." He prayed therefore earnestly to do this.

His prayer was answered in his life as a Jesuit and in the joy which we may hope came to him, seeing Christ Our Lord, on June 8, 1889, just fifty days before his forty-fifth birthday.

HOPKINS AND CREATIVE WRITING

Arthur MacGillivray, S.J.

I

Three Irish children, Maeve, Rory, and Eileen, were acting out passages from history. Maeve, describing the Irish Queen Maeve, read from the book:

"A tiara of solid gold encircled her head, and a torque of gold her white neck."

"What's a torque?" demanded Eileen.

"For the love of God," Maeve said passionately, "what should a torque be, by the very sense of the words I'm speaking, but a thing to go round the neck?"

Eileen drooped her head in contrition, while Rory turned and gave her his rare crooked smile, saying, "If we don't understand it, let's shut up. The thing is to feel it." [1]

Before bringing up the suggestion that Hopkins be used as a model for a creative writing group, a preliminary question might be asked: Can students be taught to write poetry? Theodore Maynard says that he has yet to hear of anybody who has been made a poet by instruction. Though he believes with the rest of us that creativeness cannot be created, he is willing to admit that the student can be taught or shown to look at the world through his own eyes, that he has a vision of the world that is unique. Similarly, Allen Tate, contending that instructors cannot teach students to write, is quick to append his belief that instructors can, by developing students as readers who see the creative problem in poetry, prepare them to teach themselves. They don't understand

[1] Howard Spring, *My Son, My Son!* (The Viking Press, 1938), pp. 153-154.

the magic key for composing; they can't find it, but they can be awakened to feel it.

What should be pointed out in addition is the fact that the creative writing group, under an instructor's direction, is *already* interested in the art of composition. We are not talking about a freshman college group that has yet to be converted to the *liking* of poetry, but rather of a group that has looked into its collective heart, asking itself the question, "Must I write?" and answering with a strong and simple "I must." This group, it will be admitted, *can* be taught, not how to find "inspiration" so called, but how to make the most of experience that lends itself to a poetic theme, how to profit by the successes and failures of real poets, how to acquire a technique arresting, individual, and by all means adaptable to what the poet must say.

Every poet who ever was a poet has been taught or influenced by another; he was present in a classroom, in the companionship of a study, walking the roads, or within the pages of a book. We are told that Hopkins himself was influenced by Dryden, Milton, Swinburne, Wordsworth, Christina Rossetti, Tennyson, Spenser, Shakespeare, Herbert, and who knows how many others? And did he not learn something from his conversations and correspondence with Bridges and Patmore?

In this sense poetry can be taught. It has been so taught in our day by Robert Frost (Dartmouth), David Morton (Amherst), Robert P. Tristram Coffin (Bowdoin), Theodore Morrison (Harvard), John Ciardi (Harvard), Paul Engle (Iowa), John Malcolm Brinnin (Vassar), John Holmes (Tufts), Rev. John Louis Bonn, S.J. (Boston College), Theodore Roethke (Michigan State), John Frederick Nims (Notre Dame), John Crowe Ransom (Kenyon), Yvor Winters (Stanford), Mark Schorer (California), Genevieve Taggard (Sarah Lawrence), Robert Penn Warren (Minnesota), and Morton Dauwen Zabel (Loyola)—to indicate partially what has been done.

Recalling the years when she taught creative writing to the

students of the University of Miami (Florida), Eunice Tietjens emphasizes her belief in the fact that poets are both born *and* made:

Unquestionably, a true poet must have somewhere under his brainpan, a subtle personal sense of organic rhythm and the individual fashion of looking at the world which gives his utterances their content. But he must have far more than this. He must have technical control; he must know how to use the tools of his trade, how to make his lines telling and how to avoid the numberless pitfalls which beset the tyro. It is this craft side of poetry which can be taught, and learned.[2]

Let those who are unconvinced be unconvinced. If Hopkins, after living a hundred years on this our earth, were interested in anything other than how to prepare himself for his departure, conceivably he might have something to say about the problems of a poet writing in the nineteen forties. He, as an adviser, as a teacher, might emphasize the importance of writing in ordinary modern speech heightened and excited, not necessarily in the obvious capitalization manner of Fearing, but as John Holmes has suggested, rediscovering our living speech and ceasing to compose, Chinese-fashion, in a literary language—writing more for the ear than for the eye. Hopkins might consider the possibilities of radio as a poetic medium which offers a living audience more numerous than the troubadours ever dreamed of, whereby poetry could come out of the boudoir and the study to match itself against the world.

What the future of poetry will be is anybody's guess. The poets of the thirties, David Daiches has reminded us, were confused about their audience; having been concerned with diagnosing the ills of their time, they tended to equate the diagnosis with cure. Using intricately rich techniques derived from Hopkins,

[2] Eunice Tietjens, "On Teaching the Writing of Poetry," *Poetry: A Magazine of Verse* 47 (Nov., 1935), pp. 92–93.

Donne, the French Symbolists, Eliot, Pound, and some personal choices, they tried to express in crowded verse their view of the nature of their discontents—producing some exciting poetry, it is true, but never ceasing to sound like experimentalists. Getting back to the golden aura of peace will involve much private warfare among the poets who, it can be prophesied, will *still* sound like experimentalists. And that is where Hopkins enters and offers a technical helping hand.

"Our century likes thorny, tangled poetry like that of Donne and Hopkins," says Elizabeth Atkins,[3] perhaps, we might say, because we live in a thorny, tangled century wherein our reading preferences reflect our private and public concern. And we have several poets who though not ostensibly imitating Hopkins, have caught his breath to express whatever wonder and awe they have found in the world about them. Katherine Garrison Chapin's "Look, more than beauty beckons, more than sheer, sharp height!"[4] contains the Hopkins magic, reminiscent of

> O the mind, mind has mountains; cliffs of fall
> Frightful, sheer . . .

while Elizabeth Madox Roberts in the remarkable *I, Adam,* almost echoes the compound active images which mirrored Hopkins' mind:

> I named the birds and all the cattle . . .
> Lump-backed, web-foot, keel-breast, fish and fowl.
> When God made the ox he brought it before me
> To see how I would him call.
>
> 'What is it?' God said, and he set a thing on a stone.
> Hooked-beak, have-take, swoop-snatch, and swift talk
> Of a short, crooked claw, and I said,
> 'It is the hawk.'

[3] Elizabeth Atkins, *Edna St. Vincent Millay and Her Times:* (Chicago University Press, 1936), p. 205.

[4] Katherine Garrison Chapin, *Plain-Chant for America* (Harper & Brothers, 1942), p. 74.

Or again: God put in the grass and the air . . .
'What is it?' (God's laughter) A bubble of dark
Re-winded water, wing beat up and over.
And I flung, 'Hark, hark, the lark . . .'[5]

Francis Maguire, evidently a scholar of Hopkins' "Glory be to God" school, voices his theme nicely in *These Things:*

Today the wind narrowed; the thunder-black clouds
Are chill-June, and good against the under-side-swept leaves.
And O, for this day and its like—for wind-heaves
That curdle cloy-air, for rain's crowds
In solitudes of sun, for hail, for a crow's call
For things that make dark the sun-white, tart the sweet—
A snorting stallion, cats jungle-neat—
Glory, glory to the Wonder Maker of them all—

For these are the things that keep the soul, that spill
Tempests of peace when bright rebellion singes
The lone, inflammable mind, when loud, proud,
The tongue would hail tongue; the will, will.
These soothe when the heart would pull earth from its hinges,
Life from the planets, death from its soft shroud.[6]

Perhaps Mr. Maguire's poem is too Hopkinslike, with its hyphenations, alliteration, monosyllabic colorful verbs, internal rhyme, ellipsis. Despite the tour de force, he has produced a poem.

Similarly Clive Sansom's *Seagulls* is patterned somewhat after Hopkins' famous *Windhover* "off, off forth on swing":

More than birds' music,
Than all their movement
Swift curve of swallow,
Kestrel's poising or plunge of falcon,
I admire the strong smooth flight of gulls.
They are so effortless in their planing,

[5] Elizabeth Madox Roberts, "I, Adam": *Poetry: A Magazine of Verse,* 54 (April, 1939), p. 24.
[6] Francis Maguire, "These Things": *Spirit* 4 (March, 1937), p. 17.

> Drifting so lightly over the water
> On wind-current and their strength
> Lifting to beat the wind—
> Parting its waves swiftly—
> Ploughing with steel wings
> Then, mastering in surrender—
> Anchoring for a moment in the wind,
> Returning on its full tide, wing-spread, at Schneider speed,
> Lovely—O, lovelier than all birds' movement,
> Than all their music! [7]

Where Hopkins actually makes his Windhover fly lone and beautiful without aid, Mr. Sansom seems to be directing his bird by radio beam, counselling it to return at *Schneider* speed! But withal, again, a poem.

Hopkins' delight in *The Starlight Night* where he makes us "Look at the stars! look, look . . ." suffuses W. R. Rodgers' *Stormy Day* with the expected air of surprise:

> O look how the loops and balloons of bloom
> Bobbing on long strings from the finger-ends
> And knuckles of the lurching cherry-tree
> Heap and hug, elbow and part, this wild day,
> Like a careless carillon cavorting;
> And the beaded whips of the beeches splay
> And dip like anchored weed round a drowned rock,
> And hovering effortlessly the rooks
> Hang on the wind's effrontery as if
> On hooks, then loose their hold and slide away
> Like sleet sidewards down the warm swimming sweep
> Of wind. O it is a lovely time when
> Out of the sunk and rigid sumps of thought
> Our hearts rise and race with new sounds and sights
> And signs, tingling delightedly at the sting
> And crunch of springless carts on gritty roads,
> The caught kite dangling in the skinny wires,

[7] Clive Sansom, *The Unfailing Spring*: London: The Favil Press, 1943), p. 6.

The swipe of a swallow across the eyes,
Striped awnings stretched on lawns. New things surprise
And stop us everywhere . . .[8]

This poem sounds so much like Hopkins, that if he himself had written it, we should justly accuse him of being what he would call "Parnassian," writing according to a mannerism without effort of inspiration. For Rodgers to have written it is merely another instance of how the Hopkins tradition has been perpetuated in our day.

2

Until now, we have walked around our subject; now we look in. Hopkins is a good choice for a student model, not because he is necessarily the best poet who can aid the creative writer (cases could be made out for Donne, Shakespeare, Milton, Browning, Thompson, Claudel, Auden, Eliot, Rukeyser, and many others), but because he exemplifies so surely what a novice-poet should first seek: insight, inscape, looking through an object to determine its poetic qualities, what reality it contains, is. We do not limit the model to Hopkins for fear of keeping the poet on the pedestal too long, tiring not himself but his onlookers. Younger, more contemporary poets like Karl Shapiro, John Frederick Nims, John Ciardi, Winfield Townley Scott (though it may be dangerous to canonize them poetically in their youth) have much to offer the student and can beneficially be used for their honesty of approach, frankness, and almost paradoxically, their understatement. But Hopkins, the grandfather of them all, is a root that has fed countless branches; it is not only a sense of piety but a mark of intelligence for the branch — once granted the rationality of trees! — to probe into the vitality of the root.

Direct imitation of a poet has its limitations and dangers, no matter who the model is, and for purposes of instruction should

[8] W. R. Rodgers, *Awake! and Other Wartime Poems* (London: Secker and Warburg, 1941), p. 43.

be discouraged. Hopkins himself, we learn, leaned toward Milton, Keats, the Bible, Whitman. He took what he wanted from them and wrote in his own style. Again and again the serious student in the creative writing group of which we have spoken should be counselled to read, read, and read the best poets, think through a great deal, and write much. After a while it may be that destructive criticism on the instructor's part, showing the student what literary sins he has committed, may be of more benefit to him than telling him what he ought to do. Meanwhile, he can learn a few lessons from Hopkins, by reading so much of him that he begins to see even Hopkins' Parnassian; by that time he will have seen the absurdity of affecting another's style. "The effect of studying masterpieces," wrote Hopkins, "is to make me admire and do otherwise. So it must be on every original artist to some degree, on me to a marked degree" (B 291. Sept. 25, 1888). Of course, our student is not an original artist; yet, even original artists must take time to study the best work of other artists and learn tricks.

Even though many—poets like William Butler Yeats, for example—have found difficulty in reading Hopkins, not being able to focus attention for more than a few minutes, still under direction the student can go through Hopkins' poems, select a dozen images or so, and with profit he might build a poem with the Hopkins bricks on any theme he chooses. The result will not be a poem, but at least he has begun to play with the Erector set. His own images may be used as well, provided they have fibre; after this experiment, the instructor will be satisfied with two "poems" like the following, which were written by students:

SAINT ISAAC JOGUES

For this wild whipping can I not complain,
O Lord, and just Thy judgment of my ways;
My broken bleeding back on cut Thy flays,
And mind not how feel I this precious pain.

Wild whip me, bruisen me again, again,
And set this willing blood of me ablaze,
A crucible afire no end of days;
Nor freshen, cool me—dyke Thy mercy-rain!
What wonder! dream! aside flung Thou the rod,
Bound me to Thy breast, a wounded thing,
And let me press and kiss the feet that trod
Me! touch the hand chastised me, glory sing!
There is no comfort like, my Lord, my God,
(I know, oh how I know) Thy rod, staff bring!

TO GERARD MANLEY HOPKINS

Why does a summer sky this snow-blown day
Brook deep a heart with summer-shout, now cold,
Now dumb, now everything but mild-May—
Wise, June-fresh? (It hath stern February mould!)
Under daylight darkness thickens here
Where once the dour-lid bold-eyed daisy made
Much of sun and rain. Have you an ear
Tried and tuned, whorled by the wind-in-glade,
Sea, mount, soft to Spring's fingers in hair,
Quick to Spring's touch? My ear is full of things,
Thrush-nests, willow at water's-end (who knows where?),
And red-flanked flowers flaring in rows where wren sings.

Whose beauty this, Whom praise, what winters flay us?
Hid Beauty flows out Him, Domine Deus.

Did we mention the dangers of direct imitation? These two students, discreetly warned after the writing of these experimental
verses, have since published commendable pieces in such magazines as *Poetry: A Magazine of Verse, America, Spirit, Saturday
Review of Literature, Voices,* to name but a few.

"Some poets," according to Marshall Schacht, "begin their art
by making a noise, then learning how to play the flute or trumpet. . . . Others . . . first carve the instrument, hoping to fill

it later with their breath." [9] Our students are the *others*, carving the instrument, reedlike as it may be in the above two examples. Such carving should exclude the writing of religious poetry which students undertake so readily and lamentably. T. S. Eliot's advice has either not been heard, or if heard, stupidly rejected:

> Why, I would ask, is most religious verse so bad; and why does so little religious verse reach the highest levels of poetry? Largely, I think, because of a pious insincerity. The capacity for writing poetry is rare; the capacity for religious emotion of the first intensity is rare; and it is to be expected that the existence of both capacities in the same individual should be rarer still. People who write devotional verse are usually writing as they want to feel, rather than as they do feel.[10]

Hopkins' religious poetry is always honest and unaffected; he was incapable of poetic padding to which the over-pious young "poet" easily resorts. (There are many Catholic minor magazines and major newspapers, whose names we shall charitably omit, which could positively aid the struggling Catholic Revival by not cultivating every pious little blossom that shoots up on the managing editor's desk.) Once poetic maturity has set in, the writer may try his talents on this difficult theme, but not before.

Observation is what the youthful writer should keep in mind. Keep the eyes and the mind open! As unlike a Dostoyevsky character as possible, he should not walk down the street seeing almost nothing of the external world. His eyes should be open always to the inner reality of all he sees, whether it be tree, trolley car, rock, or bum. Let him keep asking himself, "What does *this* resemble?" Hopkins saw a cuckoo, heard a cuckoo, and found that it varied much (B 145–146. June 5, 1882):

> In the first place cuckoos do not always sing at the same pitch or in the same key: there are, so to say, alto cuckoos and tenor cuckoos.

---

[9] Don Stanford, Review of *New England Earth*, *Poetry: A Magazine of Verse* 60 (May, 1942), p. 107.

[10] T. S. Eliot, *After Strange Gods* (Faber & Faber, Ltd., 1934) pp. 28-29.

In particular they sing lower in flying and the interval is then also least, it being an effort to them to strike the higher note, which is therefore more variable than the other. When they perch they sing wrong at first, I mean they correct their first try, raising the upper note.

In a delicate fragment Hopkins is entranced by the sound:

> Repeat that, repeat,
> Cuckoo, bird, and open ear wells, heart-springs,
>   delightfully sweet,
> With a ballad, with a ballad, a rebound
> Off trundled timber and scoops of the hillside ground,
>   hollow hollow hollow ground:
> The whole landscape flushes on a sudden at a sound.[11]

Or again, in the fragment called *The Woodlark,* he hears the sound:

> *Teevo cheevo cheevio chee:*
> O where, what can that be?
> *Weedio-weedio:* there again!
> So tiny a trickle of song-strain;
> And all round not to be found
> For brier, bough, furrow, or green ground
> Before or behind or far or at hand
> Either left either right
> Anywhere in the sunlight.
> Well, after all! Ah but hark—
> 'I am the little woodlark.' [12]

Easily would Hopkins have agreed with St. Thomas Aquinas, had he come across the passage, as he may have done:

The perfection of knowledge requires that a man should know distinctly all that is in a thing, such as its powers, parts, and properties. On the other hand, love is in the appetitive power which regards *a thing as it is in itself:* wherefore it suffices for the perfection of love that a thing be loved according as it is known in itself. Hence, it is,

[11] *Poems,* p. 85.
[12] *Poems,* p. 83.

therefore, that a thing is loved more than it is known; since it can be loved perfectly even without being perfectly known.[13]

A note-book in which to keep fragmentary impressions is helpful. As an example of one who had no outstanding reputation for his sensitivity to nature, John Barrymore might be cited, the Barrymore who on a sea voyage wrote in his log:

The sky was wonderful, bright-chocolate color and bright-silver, with a long low rainbow, distinct and beautiful, on one side; on the other, brilliant cerulean blue, with heavy spattered clouds, through which shone bright rays onto the horizon, like celestial searchlights.[14]

That passage might have come from Hopkins' *Notebooks and Papers*. In another section Barrymore writes: "Beautiful electric storm came up. Sky wonderful, looked like painting by Lucifer." [15]

Any student can be taught to catch what Henry James called "the tone of things." Just as Pare Lorentz gave us a rhythmical category of rivers, the neophyte poet can be taught to put his experience together as did Joseph Mitchell's gloomy, defeated, ex-Greenwich Village poet, called by his intimates *Eddie Guest,* who was fond of reciting the names of many of the walk-up hotels on the Bowery:

The Alabama Hotel, the Comet, and the Uncle Sam House, the Dandy, the Victoria House and the Grand Windsor Hotel, the Houston, the Mascot, the Palace, the Progress, the Palma House and the White House Hotel, the Newport, the Crystal, the Lion and the Marathon. All flophouses. All on the Bowery. Each and all my home, sweet home.[16]

3

Many young people, intent upon writing creatively, are handicapped for subject-matter by their lack of experience. The love-theme, the religious-theme, these are pitfalls for the poet. The

[13] *Summa Theologica*, I–II^{ae}, q. 27, art. 2, ad 2um.
[14] Gene Fowler, *Good Night, Sweet Prince* (The Viking Press, 1944), p. 248.
[15] *Ibid.*, p. 250.
[16] Joseph Mitchell, "Mazie," *The New Yorker*, December 21, 1940, p. 26.

nature-theme, always safe for beginners because it allows for unlimited subjective reactions to objects unceasingly variable, Hopkins used frequently. Look up his poems on a landscape, a lake, the grandeur of God in creation, dappled things, a starlight night, spring, May, air, evening, spring and fall, trees, the sea and the skylark, a bird in flight, a caged bird, harvest. See what he made of these themes, the insight he held firm, the excitement he conveyed.

Always Hopkins wrote of what he knew, the life about him. Being interested in the spiritual life, he wrote of a picture of a saint, a silver jubilee, the cloister, a nun's profession, the life of a lay-brother, sacrifice, the Virgin Mary, a soldier's first Communion, resurrection. Being interested in human beings, he wrote poems for a friend, on a dead musician, a ploughman, a dead blacksmith, a soldier, brothers, a wedding, the unemployed. Looking about him, he saw themes in the wreck of a ship, an inn, a house in a valley, a lantern in the night, a candle, Oxford, Beauty. And looking within, he examined the heart, peace, patience, despair, loneliness, disappointment, being in exile, the purpose of being. Is even one of his finished poems written on a bookish theme?

When studying any one of Hopkins' poems for creative writing work, the aim should be to try to find out not how Hopkins wrote his poems, but rather how a poem may be developed after the initial idea or emotion has, to use Sara Teasdale's term, been *irritated*. Take, for example, *Spring and Fall:*

> Márgarét, are you griéving
> Over Goldengrove unleaving?
> Leáves, líke the things of man, you
> With your fresh thoughts care for, can you?
> Áh! ás the heart grows older
> It will come to such sights colder
> By and by, nor spare a sigh
> Though worlds of wanwood leafmeal lie;
> And yet you wíll weep and know why.

> Now no matter, child, the name:
> Sórrow's spríngs áre the same.
> Nor mouth had, no nor mind, expressed
> What heart heard of, ghost guessed:
> It ís the blight man was born for,
> It is Margaret you mourn for.

We do not ask how the idea came to Hopkins, but how *could* the idea have come to him. Example: maybe he came upon an autumn forest and looked for a word to describe it: Goldengrove. What is happening in Goldengrove? The leaves are falling. Condense the expression: Goldengrove unleaving. Naturally, with this concept, we find beauty and sadness. Question: why is the scene sad? Because of our longing for beauty that lasts. Everything that is physical decays, all goes back to original sin. How make this unoriginal idea new and compelling? Introduce action. A young girl. Crying. *Grieving* comes easily as a rhyme for *unleaving*. What name shall we choose for the girl? A quiet, lingering name. Margaret. Explain to Margaret why she is grieving, but don't tell her too much because she is too young to understand. How explain to her without suggesting that she is listening to a sermon? Should she inject a question or two? It would be more subtle to suggest by an answer that she has already asked a question, viz. "What is the name of this thing?", "Why should it happen?" Should the answer be given directly, or at the close of the poem for suspense? Choose the latter and make it simple.

How long will the poem be? We don't know. We shall wait to see whether we have said everything we have to say, condensed as much as possible. What tricks of technique shall we use? Certainly alliteration and assonance. What metre shall we use? Let it follow from the first two lines, which we already have:

> Margaret, are you grieving
> Over Goldengrove unleaving?

Rhymes? Rather not think about them until we have made our thought follow along the pattern of what we must say.

Let us begin. We have the first two lines. Now what? The falling of leaves is a natural sign for all sorrow that comes to everyone. And if one sorrows at the falling of leaves, there is bound to be greater sorrow as one grows older. *Older . . . colder.* What gets colder? A concrete image is what we want. Margaret? No, but a more concrete image for Margaret—her heart. "Ah! as your heart grows older." No, better make it more universal, "as *the* heart grows older." And so on, and so on. The students should be allowed to finish the poem; most of them will not have seen it before, or if they have, they will have forgotten its pattern. Finally, the results can be compared with Hopkins' version, which undoubtedly will not suffer. Allow the students to criticize the model, introducing then the result of I. A. Richards' experiment with the same poem narrated in his book, *Practical Criticism* (pp. 81–90), and commenting on the criticisms. After the student has assimilated the Hopkins idea, he may try his hand at writing a poem in his own idiom, recalling the principles behind the Hopkins idea (freshness of image; hard, forceful verbs, etc.). Class discussion on the merits and demerits of each performance can be encouraged.

For the sake of variety, the Hopkins manner in prose may be examined, as for example in this quotation from Richard Eberhart:

. . . Lest we be engulfed, lest there be no further year, no further book, lest by any direction we find indirection out, put it out, pile it up, piece it together: have it at the hand.[17]

Or the following paragraph from Gilbert Frankau's *Mustard-Pot—Matchmaker* might be adapted to the Hopkins rhythm:

Ensued frantic seconds—seconds of slip and slide and scramble, of plunge and stumble and miraculous recovery—seconds when it

[17] Review of *New Directions 1941*, edited by James Laughlin, *Poetry: A Magazine of Verse* 60 (June, 1942), p. 165.

seemed to the horseman as though no power on earth could keep him from pitching yards over that enormous down-stretched yellow neck —seconds when the head, neck and shoulders reared up like a giraffe's before his eyes as Mustard-Pot glissaded fifty sheer yards on his tail—seconds when the loose iron-stone of the hillside rained like shrapnel from their hoof-strokes—seconds when the tree-roots tip-tilted them at every bound—seconds when it seemed as though they left solid and flew, flew for dear life down the whistling void.[18]

Every Hopkins student readily grants the presence of faults, glaring faults, in the Hopkins technique and manner. Robert Bridges without apology was the first to acknowledge them; they should be pointed out to the writing group as eccentricities to shun. First, there are his ellipses, liberties of grammar, in such lines as "guess the beauty (that has) been"—"comfort (that) serves in a whirlwind." We know Hopkins' purpose behind such obscurity, to cut out unimportant words, to make his images do all the poetic work. But when such omissions, though they speed up the performance, allow the intellect to slacken, poetic damage is done. Secondly, inversion as a poetic device to allow for end rhymes is not only old-fashioned but cumbersome. "Fair thy fling," "thy creature dear," "mighty a master," "aspens dear," "disappointment all I endeavour end," "your round me roaming end, and under be my boughs" are negligible compared with

> Leáves, líke the things of man, you
> With your fresh thoughts care for, can you?

These lines bring up the third defect to remember, forced rhymes. Though original for the most part, they are distracting for the reader: "communion—boon he on," "eternal—burn all," "England—mingle and," "portholes—mortals," "righteousness—no or yes," "Saviour—gave you a," "disregarded—jar did." Possibly the listener would not detect the abnormalities of "snowstorm—coast or (m)," "electric—wrecked her he (c)," "unvisited—busy to

---

[18] Gilbert Frankau, *Men, Maids and Mustard-Pot* (London: Hutchinson & Company, 1923), p. 250.

(d)," "Irish—sire he (sh)," but the reader, admiring their ingenuity, condemns their falsity.

Hopkins' virtues, having been pointed out many times by others,
need only to be mentioned here, where the student can ponder
over a masterful technique and learn by example. Apt use of
alliteration used for a purpose predominates: "Thou hast bound
bones and veins in me, fastened me flesh," "feel thy finger and
find thee," "heeds but hides, bodes but abides." The effect of all
alliteration, making a word out of a phrase, gives us the Hopkins
excitement, setting off an explosion all at once in the reader's
consciousness: "skies betweenpie mountains," "fallowbootfellow,"
"the O-seal-that-so feature," "drop-of-blood-and-foam-dapple,"
"that blue is all in a rush with richness," "the achieve of, the
mastery of the thing!" *Interior rhymes* are used with effect: "steep
or deep," "plod safe shod sound," "bones built in me, flesh filled,"
"heart wants, care haunts," "first, fast, last friend," "hell's spell."
Often we find the presence of *three verbs,* usually monosyllabic:
"do, deal, lord it," "fall, gall themselves, and gash," "reckon but,
reck but, mind but," "I walk, I lift up, I lift up," "caps, clears,
and clinches." *Hyphenated words* ("jay-blue heavens," "moth-
soft Milky Way") are obvious. Activity, aliveness, alertness are
achieved by the use of *imperatives*: "come, plant the staff,"
"come, swing the sculls," "look at the stars! look, look" (the
word occurs seven times in one poem), "come . . . let be; call
off . . . leave comfort," "fold home, fast fold thy child," "hush
there!", "resign them, sign them, seal them, send them, motion
them," "buy then! bid then!"

Hopkins' use of *repetition,* always a poetic device, usually adds
another idea: "bone-house, mean house," "sweet fowl, song-fowl,"
"own nest, wild nest," "for John, young John," "wants war,
wants wounds." *Statement,* used more frequently today than ever,
breathes honesty: "I'll not play hypocrite to own my heart," "I
muse at that and wonder why," "Nothing is so beautiful as
spring," "I kiss my hand to the stars," "With witness I speak this."
And then we come to the overflowing emotional verse that actu-

ally *stutters*: "I caught this morning morning's minion, kingdom of daylight's dauphin," "Have fair fallen, O fair, fair have fallen," "How to keép — is there ány any, is there none such, nowhere known some, bow or brooch or braid or brace, láce, latch or catch or key to keep . . ." Stuttering verse can become too much of an eccentricity and should not be used too often lest the poet be accused of forced emotion. Likewise, the use of direct emotion, whose effect is usually flat, should be discouraged: "I muse at that and wonder," "I admire thee, master of the tides." One modern poet (it would be unkind to mention his name), an admirer of Hopkins, surfeits his emotion so frequently that his forty-seven years belie his naïveté: "My heart is so elated," "the memory of you . . . makes the soul to start," "I . . . have felt a start," "I have loved thee for thy lowness," "the reverence loving-like I feel towards this saint of ours."

4

To return for a moment to what we have said before, that we are not teaching how to find inspiration, but rather how to induce a creative response on the part of the students, it is difficult to reduce the technique to any set formula. Charles Glicksberg, of Newark, New Jersey, speaks with the knowledge derived from classroom experience when he says:

It is not so much what the teacher says as how he says it; in other words, it is the general, intangible atmosphere of confidence, enjoyment, free discussion, and mutual trust which is of paramount importance. For the time being the pupils of the class are liberated from the compulsory and, from the creative point of view, inhibitory discipline of the traditional classroom where the emphasis is placed on learning, on information, on covering a given area of subject matter. What a relief to escape from that standardized, memory-straining situation! To experience the freedom of the individual self! Each one is literally exploring and prospecting on his own. It is difficult to make the pupils believe that these reminiscences and impressions, these shamefaced but persistent fears and anxieties—that these, if honestly presented, are precious and creatively revealing.[19]

It requires all the art, the practical art, that the teacher possesses to *awaken* the creative response. Once he has done that, he has performed a noble function. As Emerson has said:

Colleges . . . can only highly serve us when they aim not to drill but to create; when they gather from far every ray of various genius to their hospitable halls and by the concentrated fires, set the hearts of their youth on flame.[20]

We do not believe, as Emerson implies, that the highest aim of a college is to turn out creative writers, leaving the drilling, the formative and informative elements to those who seemingly possess no great ideals; but we do believe that awakening the creative response is a vocation noble in itself. The formula, yet to be discovered, centers about the teacher's ingenuity and enthusiasm.

"Too many young poets," according to A. M. Sullivan, "are willing to be thin echoes of yesterday," [21] when the need today, as always, is for passionate and concrete statement. Hopkins supplies the model for the teacher and the student, manifesting the urge to reveal the complexity of his experience and to accent its personal flavor. That is the onus of the lyric poet today, says Elizabeth Drew, "to reveal the whole content of the poet's mind, his whole response to living. The result is that words have had to work harder than they have ever worked before as an interpretative medium, and that there has been an absorption in the craft of conveying the utmost density of consciousness in the smallest possible compass of language." [22]

Evidently Hopkins is the master here "in communicating his

[19] Charles Glicksberg, "Creative Efforts and Achievements of a Low Senior Class," *The English Leaflet,* 39 (Dec., 1940), p. 133.

[20] Ralph Waldo Emerson, "The American Scholar," in *Nature Addresses and Lectures* (Houghton, Mifflin & Company, 1903), p. 93.

[21] A. M. Sullivan, "The Dull Poetic Void": *America* 67 (October 3, 1942), p. 718.

[22] Elizabeth Drew in collaboration with John L. Sweeney, *Directions in Modern Poetry:* (W. W. Norton & Company, 1940), p. 260.

closely woven texture of thought and feeling." [23] The poetic diction of Elizabeth Barrett Browning, William Morris, and James Russell Lowell died in our grandfather's day. In a letter to Canon Dixon (D 99. Dec. 1, 1881), Hopkins expresses this idea:

To waive every other objection, it [i.e. standardized diction] is essentially archaic, biblical a good deal, and so on: now that is a thing that can never last; a perfect style must be of its age.

Commenting on the Dixon letter, the critic T. C. Wilson says that the tradition of poetic diction which Hopkins himself did so much to reinvigorate is the one into which the significant verse of our own time fits. And its chief characteristics, he enumerates,[24] are precision of phrase, an extension of the functions and subject matter of verse to include images from contemporary life and the rhythms of everyday speech, as opposed to the vagueness and otherworldliness of the late-romantic diction and imagery. Not only Eliot, Pound, Williams, Marianne Moore, and Auden, but Hardy, Lawrence, Yeats, and Wilfred Owen belong to this living tradition.

Who better than Hopkins had at his command the emotional possibilities of image and sound, words most carefully chosen to express exact shades of meaning which he was always ready to explain by paraphrase? "He may try to say too many things at once," says Helen C. White, "he may demand a wider span of application than the usual reader is accustomed to give, but he has the gift of projecting his state of mind to the point where it stirs all the sensibilities of his reader." [25]

His application of the sprung-rhythm theory was based on the desire to approximate the rhythms of contemporary speech to poetic form, to heighten, as he said, current language. "It enables the poet," Yeats observed, "to employ words taken over from sci-

[23] *Ibid.*
[24] T. C. Wilson, "The Muse and Edmund Wilson": *Poetry: A Magazine of Verse*, 52 (June, 1938), p. 151.
[25] Helen C. White, *The Metaphysical Poets* (The Macmillan Company, 1936), p. 19.

ence or the newspaper without stressing the more unmusical syllables, or to suggest hurried conversation where only one or two
words in a sentence are important, to bring about a change in
poetical writing like that in the modern speech of the stage, where
only those words which affect the situation are important." [26]

And Hopkins, like Keats who was his first master in the use
of compounds, loved words, fresh flowers of speech with the dew
still clinging. He relished a term with a tang on it, with a savor
and flavor all its own, with sharpness of edge. Some of these
words he found in Welsh poetry, compound words of noun-noun,
noun-adjective, adjective-adjective; often he did not stop at compound words but used the epithet formed of the object and the
verb—"rollrock," "dare-gale," "lack-lustre," lacing the sense so
tightly that it can hardly breathe. He could ring adjectives like a
chime of bells:

> Tatter-tassel-tangled and dingle-a-dangled
> Dandy-hung dainty head.

Stringing his words together more by instinct than by intellect,
he found it "dreadful" to explain the meaning of a phrase in cold
blood. Yet in his explanation he shows how unerring are his sense
impressions, always searching for the apt comparison, the precise
word (B 164. Nov. 26, 1882):

The *skein* and *coil* are the lark's song, which from his height gives
the impression of something falling to the earth and not vertically
quite but trickingly or wavingly, something as a skein of silk ribbed
by having been tightly wound on a narrow card or a notched holder
or as twine or fishing-tackle unwinding from a *reel* or *winch* or as
pearls strung on a horse-hair.

His humor, rarely mentioned by the critics, further emphasizes
his fondness for words:

We were all vaccinated the other day. The next day a young
Portug(u)ese came up to me and said: 'Oh Misther 'Opkins, do you

[26] William Butler Yeats, Introd. to *Oxford Book of Modern Verse* (Oxford
University Press, 1936), pp. xxxix–lx.

feel the cows in yewer arms?' I told him I felt the horns coming through. I do I am sure. I cannot remember now whether one ought to say the calf of the arm or the calf of the leg. My shoulder is like a shoulder of beef. I dare not speak above a whisper for fear of bellowing—there now, I was going to say I am obliged to speak low for fear of lowing. I dream at night that I have only two of my legs in bed. I think there is a split coming in both my slippers. Yesterday I could not think why it was that I would wander about on a wet grass-plot: I see now. I chew my pen a great deal. The long and short of it is that my left forequarter is swollen and painful (I meant to have written arm, but I could not). Besides, the doctor has given us medicine so that I am in a miserable way just now.[27]

Will teaching the students to fall in love with words create a talent for writing poetry? No. Can the art of writing truly be taught? We think not. But it can be learned. And if we have said one good thing in this article that needs to be said, it is that Hopkins is a good master and influence for learning to write poetry. Once the young writer has exhausted what Rossetti calls "the soulless self-reflections of man's skill," once he has completed a laborious training in the perfection of a technical instrument, he might in some inexplicable way catch fire in the telling of what he must tell, and then he will have written a poem. Invariably he will return to Hopkins, as Charles Williams has prophesied, as to a source, not a channel, of poetry.

[27] F 41 (Letter written from Stonyhurst to his younger sister Kate, April 25, 1871).

GRECO-ROMAN VERSE THEORY AND GERARD MANLEY HOPKINS

John Louis Bonn, S.J.

In the history of the development of metrical art forms there are three things that are incontrovertible—first, that there may be a good deal of difference between the theory and the practice of a poet; second, that theories invented posteriorly to the writing of poems by an experimentalist may have little in common with the way in which, as a creative artist, he actually conceived his rhythmic pattern; and third, that a false theory may lead to excellent metrical and architectonic effects. To these general facts the work of Gerard Manley Hopkins was no exception. His theory and his practice are widely different; his researches into Greek metric and his serious studies in them followed rather than preceded his main experimental period. Where his theory was sound, his practice was not infrequently unsound; and where his practice was sound, his theory was often inadequate. While none of these things seems to have more than mere historic import in a study of Hopkins as a metrist or more particularly as a metrical innovator and artist, each is decidedly to the point in any study of Hopkins as a theorist in Greek and Latin metric.

It is first of all instructive to observe that while from the very beginning Hopkins realized his indebtedness to more primitive English sources, he also believed that there were strong similarities between his rhythms and the rhythms of the Greek choruses. In this he acted more upon a suspicion, a guess, than upon any studiously investigated certainty. The progress of his metrical knowledge is, in this regard, informative. In 1873 he had written *Rhythm and Other Structural Parts of Rhetoric-Verse*. In 1876 he wrote the *Deutschland*. In 1878 he writes of "new metrical

73

effects" which he has discovered and which, he says, are similar to those in Greek choruses. In 1879 he asserts that his metres are logaoedic. In 1882 he says that in employing his sprung rhythm he is writing in a manner similar to the Greek. But in 1883 we find him confessing that at that time he had read none of the German commentaries on Greek metric which were then current and that he intends to study them (cf. F 105). This was in January. By November of the same year we find that he is cognizant of the work of J. H. Heinrich Schmidt, sufficiently at least, to disagree with him, and that he is acquainted with the work of Hadley and agrees with him. Three years later he begins his researches on the theory of Dorian rhythm, and in the following year, 1887, he announces that he has discovered the scientific basis of metre and music!

It seems obvious then that while from the beginning he had a feeling that his work was somehow related to what he called Greek logaoedic he had given little more than a cursory glance toward the then modern researches into the nature of Greek metres. It seems that he made a guess from his reading of Greek choruses that this logaoedic method was one which was common in Greek usage. Whether these speculations preceded or followed his actual experimentation is impossible to know, for they may either have been explanations after the event or convictions which led to the development of his practice. If the latter be the case, then we have the same phenomenon as that which led to the invention of the English Pindaric—a wrong conception producing a new and satisfactory English verse-form. The settling of this problem does not, however, lie within the scope of this paper which is to discuss not Hopkins' experimentation (save in the relations of his own metric to Greek verse), but to investigate his statements regarding Hellenic metric and to point out a bit of his theory as it developed.

Hopkins' statements about Greek "logaoedic" are these: "Logaoedic, as when in classical and therefore strictly timed metres dactyls are mixed with trochees, which feet are of unequal length. . . . It is enough that we [in English] can interchange

two-syllabled with three-syllabled feet" (D 21. Feb. 27, 1879).
In the Preface of the *Poems* he writes, "The trochee and dactyl
may be mixed . . . and then what the Greeks called a logaoedic
rhythm arises." And again, "And hence sprung rhythm differs
from running rhythm in having or being only one nominal rhythm,
a mixed or 'logaoedic' one instead of three. . . . In Sprung
Rhythm as in logaoedic rhythm, generally, the feet are assumed
to be equally long or strong and their seeming inequality is made
up by pausing or stressing."

Now it just so happens that not very much of this statement is
true. The word "logaoedic" is not ancient but relatively modern;
it is not used by the Greek rhythmists, at least not in this sense,
and does not occur thus in Aristoxenos. True, it was used by
Aristides Quintillianus (Keil, *Metrici Graeci,* vol. ii) and in the
way in which Hopkins employs it, but Aristides was a late metrist
(third century A.D.), an eclectic who, though he had many
strangely penetrating things to say, was in the habit of giving
metrical descriptions of the Greek verses at least as often as he
gave rhythmical analyses of them.

To make this distinction quite clear, the metrists as a whole
were quite able to say that the Glyconic, for instance, could be
formed by a spondee, a dactyl, a trochee, and a single syllable.
Metrically, then, it was composed of four different feet, and in
this sense was, in Aristides' metrical terminology, logaoedic. As a
description of the syllabic occurrences in the phrase it is all very
well in its way, but it certainly is not a rhythmic analysis of the
true nature of the Glyconic. Indeed, if nothing else were false
about it—and as rhythmic analysis as distinguished from metrical
description nearly everything about it is false—no Greek rhythmist
would allow a single syllable to stand in place of a foot. This is
purely metrical speculation and not rhythmic analysis.

Yet Aristides' system of logaoedic description attained great
vogue. In the eighteenth and early nineteenth centuries nearly
every phrase of synthetic Greek metric was divided into logaoedic
parts, composed of every type of foot, strung together in some

arbitrary and uninvestigated fashion. The book which Hopkins
himself used in the classroom was a decadent adaptation of
Alvarez's grammar, "Englished" and formalized under the name
of Alvary by one Canon Geoghegan. The section on metric, now
something of a curiosity, shows no trace of anything except the
"logaoedic" theory. It is no wonder that Hopkins, unacquainted
with rhythmic theory, should think that the Greeks did, indeed,
string their unrelated feet together in this amazing hodge-podge.
What is remarkable is that with his keen sense of the difference
between accentual and timed verse he did not perceive that such
a thing would be impossible in a time-art even though it is
possible in a stress-art such as English.

I am not saying of course that Greek verse did not allow and
sometimes employ mixed metres, for nothing seems better established in the history of Greek metric than that such cola did occur;
I merely say that such mixed metres were not mixed as Hopkins
and the general run of his contemporaries thought they were. The
mixed metres were made from cola or phrases of divergent metrical feet—but individual cola were never formed except by legitimate and highly regulated substitution of feet of divergent time-
lengths. The Glyconic is of diplasion structure throughout and
allows an ison only as an exception, usually in the first position.
One of the so-called Archilochian groups, however, common in
Greek lyric, is composed of three repeated cola, the first composed
of four dactyls, the second of three trochees, the third of six
trochees of which the first is acephalous. It is, as always, the cola
which are mixed; but the feet within the cola are not mixed.
Consequently, when Hopkins says that his sprung rhythm is similar to Greek logaoedic metre because dactyls are mixed with
trochees, he is quite wrong. This was not Greek usage. Furthermore although it is highly probable that in Greek some form of
rhythmization increased the unity of the felt pattern, this rhythmization was not as Hopkins felt it was. It is not true, as Schmidt
and his host of American, some English, and no German metrists
believed, that these divergent feet "are assumed to be equally

long." This late and added speculation, appearing after Hopkins became acquainted with Schmidt's theory, led him into the same bypaths of error which thwarted true metrical advance throughout the latter quarter of the last century and still disturb students of even our most modern textbooks, which as every metrist knows are a good fifty years behind solid metrical knowledge.

Now in this general theory of logaoedic and mixed verse, Hopkins accepted the teaching of his time. In this he followed what he thought was a Greek system. Yet in his own work and in his own metrical speculations we find many departures from the "Greek" law, which probably explain why he says that his verse is *like* Greek choruses rather than identical with them even in theoretic construction. In Hopkins one syllable can make a foot. This he reiterated so constantly that there can be no doubt about his strong belief. Yet as we have mentioned, no Greek rhythmist holds this view. The whole principle of Greek versification was founded on a system of time-relationships, the relationship of 2:1 or 1:2 in the diplasion (iambo-trochaic) measures, and of 2:2 in the ison (dactylo-anapaestic) measures. No single syllable possesses such relationship. And the Greeks went on from this so that in the most common stichic verse, the iambic dipody trimeter, the unit of measurement is not the single foot, but the dipody, as the name implies. And in choric verse a further development made the syzygy, or unification of two feet by inversion, the unit; and beyond that, the synthesis or anaclasis of more than two feet formed the unit, and so on to the long periodic unities of the involved forms. Plainly the Greek tendency was to larger and larger relationships of parts and away from the impossible arrhythmy of the monosyllable. In Hopkins the relationship is of no importance. The single syllable may be the entire foot. The number of slack syllables, while held down from excess, is of no metrical importance. The thesis alone counts; the arsis may vary at will. And in this Hopkins was Anglo-Saxon in his concept, certainly not Greek.

Yet he felt oddly that his verse was more like Greek than like

Greene. In 1882 he writes, "No, but what it is like is the rhythm of Greek tragic choruses or of Pindar: which is pure sprung rhythm. And that has the same changes of cadence from point to point as this piece" (B 157. Oct. 18, 1882); or again: "Greek and Latin lyric verse, which is well known, and the old English verse seen in *Pierce Ploughman* are in sprung rhythm" (Preface). Both these statements go a great deal further than his more conservative early statement of 1878: "It contains metrical attempts other than any you have seen, something like Greek choruses, a peculiar eleven-footed line for instance" (B 54. May 30, 1878). And this advance of subjective certainty would seem to identify his own sprung rhythm with what he thought in his increasing study was the principle underlying Greek choruses.

Some things must be noted in these statements which he made. When he asserts boldly that the rhythm of Pindar and of the Greek tragic choruses is pure sprung rhythm, or even more that Greek and Latin lyric verse—now nearly all-inclusive—*and* the English verse of *Piers Ploughman* are all in sprung rhythm, it would appear that his theory was beginning to run so far beyond the facts that only enthusiasm could explain it. Actually, outside of a certain surface similarity there is very little in common between his sprung rhythm and Greek choral rhythm; his early conservative statement was true. His later studies led him astray.

One assertion however, must not go unnoted. The observation on the changes of cadence from point to point in Pindar and in his own work is significant and sound, as well as of great importance. His fine ear, rather than his metrical researches, dictated this accurate observation. And what Hopkins has contributed, primarily, to English metric is an ability to shift from one type of cadence to another much as Pindar and the dramatists did, though the means which an English poet used were as dissimilar as the genius of the Greek and English languages demanded.

The Greek shift or "metabole" from cadence to cadence is far more involved, far more intricate, than a mere shift from falling to rising rhythm. Greek counterpoint is a subtle thing, so dependent upon so many technical factors that I despair of describing it here, since a hasty sketch would be confusing and an adequate one of unwieldy length. Let us say then, only this—that Greek metabole shifted the cadence from one rhythmic mode to another kindred mode, thus shifting the emotional significance of the cadences by means of studiedly satisfactory "intermediate" phrases, by the use of pauses, by contraction and resolution impossible in English, by catalectic devices of rare subtlety, by prolongations of the phrase through hypercatalexis. It was never abrupt and always significant. Yet, however involved the Greek methods of metabole were, the fact which Hopkins perceived and utilized was that the Greeks *did* shift their cadential values with apparent ease and with great artistic advantage, and that a similar shifting process was necessary in English beyond the limited possibilities presented in regular or Running Rhythm. And again, Hopkins as a working poet was a sufficiently great artist to use the English means which were at his disposal and never, so far as I can see, to attempt to adapt Greek methods to English. In this he was far shrewder than many other experimenters; nor did he allow his false metrical guesses to interfere with his good poetic practice.

I have already suggested that Hopkins' own and uninfluenced speculations, the things which he learned from his own ear, were in general better than those which he borrowed from contemporary theory. Yet even this was not always true. Certain hints which he picked up after he had begun to study the prosodists of his time he found valuable, if not in creating his own metric, at least in explaining its apparent eccentricities, and these were, in the main, related to the musico-mathematical theories which had been formulated by Westphal and Rossbach. So we find his musical preoccupation appearing in a letter to Baillie, where he says, "There are, I believe, learned books lately written in Germany on the choric metres and music, which if I could see and read them would either serve me or quench me" (F 105. Jan. 14, 1883).

Yet, long before this, in a letter to Bridges (B 45–46. Aug. 21, 1877), there are strong hints of at least a surface acquaintance with some of the Greek theory then current. His description of his own "outrides," for instance, which, while not Greek at all (for his outrides occur within the verse-phrase) looks something like the adaptation of the common misapprehension of "anacrusis" which Blass had foisted on a gullible scholarly world. Again, his tendency to scan all verses with the thesis first, "for convenience" as he says, though his own ear told him that this was not a sound scheme and his constant practice is consciously opposed to it, is certainly derived from the corollaries to the then current theory of anacrusis.

The similarity of theories lies here—that the outrides were a recognized extra-metrical effect, "part of the metre in aesthetic effect and not part of the metre in counted or metrical effect," and this was true of the anacrusis, which was conceived to be somehow "extra metrum." Also, the outride belongs to counterpointed verse, supposing an unforgettable standard rhythm. So does the anacrusis belong, as far as it has any significance, to Greek synthetic verse, although it is not exclusively synthetic. The sole difference was that the anacrusis occurred only at the beginning of the phrase, the outride within the phrase. But the basic rhythmic principle is clearly the same—that certain syllables may occur which are not to be counted in the regular scansion (cf. B 45; D 15, 41).

Now while modern theory has rejected the anacrusis as a complete fabrication, it has not totally rejected the idea of syllables "extra metrum." And as far as counterpointing goes, supposing an unforgettable standard rhythm, that still remains as the basis of most modern speculation, as in Headlam, Thomson, Wilamowitz.

At this point a word of criticism of Hopkins' ear, his aesthetic sense, must be made. In this one place at least his theory was better than his practice, for it is not always true that in his verses the basic rhythm is set up strongly and unforgettably and that the superimposed rhythm can then be heard as counterpoint to it. His metrical first statements are not infrequently ambiguous — a mistake one finds in Shakespeare, never in Sophocles, seldom in Aeschylus, infrequently in Euripides.

Be it noted that Hopkins, in reading verse, was never led astray. In this his ear was true. His criticism of Milton for failing to let the auditor know what is the ground-rhythm of his counterpointed verse is correct.

The first line should announce the true rhythm so that the ear can catch the verse-tune clearly before the counterpointing begins. Yet in this Hopkins is a great offender. Of the many poems which begin with ambiguous lines these are but a few:

(7) The world is charged with the grandeur of God.
(13) Glory be to God for dappled things.
(16) I remember a house where all were good.
(31) Margaret are you grieving.
(34) As Kingfishers catch fire, dragonflies draw flame.

All these lines are first lines and all are ambiguous. The first three are intended to be pentameters. They might quite as well be tetrameters. The ear has no way of knowing. In the first, "grandeur" is probably a trisyllable. The second is an error which most schoolboys know how to avoid—the beheading of a pentameter for an acephalous iambic pentameter is an atrocity. By the third I am completely baffled, for it yields a tetrameter to me at every reading. The fourth line sounds to my American ear like a trimeter, and only a strong British stress on the last syllable of Margaret,[1] which pushes two strong syllables into unpleasant juxtaposition, can twist it into the tetrameter which it must be. The fifth line is a free pentameter, but only the later context, not yet established, makes me reform it from what my ear has told

[1] In the text, Hopkins does place a stress mark on the third syllable of the word (Márgarét). For further consideration of this point confer "Hopkins' Sprung Rhythm and the Life of English Poetry," p. 93 of this volume.— *Editor.*

me is a clear hexameter—whereupon my desire to balance strong stresses on *catch fire* and *draw flame* is frustrated.

When I mention that Shakespeare made the same mistake, I say it because I have the impression that it was for the same reason. This error, which appears notably in "When icicles hang by the wall"—in a first reading almost always read as a trimeter and then corrected to a tetrameter—is probably due, in one not otherwise noted for indelicacy of ear, to a strong first musical inspiration. The music of the song preexisted the words, and I think it highly probable that Hopkins, with his well-known pre-occupation with music, conceived of his poem first as musical tune. I do not mean by this that the tune was clear or even fixed, but rather that his first impulse—a common enough occurrence among practicing poets—was musical. With the tune established at least in cadential form, the words seemed to fit it so exactly that he could not conceive of any other possible reading. Hence his insistence on reading his verse aloud, from which, he claims, perfect ease in understanding will result, and this claim is largely substantiated. From this also came his almost belligerent insistence on the objective clarity and ease of his own really very difficult cadential values. Only if he *heard* them clearly himself could he make such claims; and he could only make such claim for himself and put such strictures upon others if he heard them *first*.

At the basis of his entire musical theory both in its early form and in its later and uninfluenced developments is, of course, his appreciation of the place of stress in English and of time-lengths in Greek. What he says, if a bit labored, is at least clear:

"The Greek accent was a *tonic accent,* was tone, pitch of note: it may have included a stress, but essentially it was pitch. In like manner the English accent is *emphatic accent,* is stress; it commonly includes clear pitch but essentially it is stress" (F 179. Nov. 7, 1883).

This distinction, which precedes a rather lengthy description of stress and the nature of stress which has no divergencies from the traditional and no very remarkable advances of presentation, is fundamental enough. It must be noted however that Hopkins here is discussing Greek accent and not that Greek time-length which he knows is the focal point of Greek metric. Later he describes this accent very well indeed. "The paragraph on tonic accent . . . The best thing I have read on Greek accent is an essay by the late American Professor Hadley (in his collected Essays). It seems to me that, looking at such facts as you here cite, we shall be justified in saying the acute tonic accent was the best marked pitch in each word; which pitch was commonly a rise (say of a fifth to the dominant—the most natural interval) from the keynote or readingnote; but sometimes a fall of, say a fourth, to the same dominant. I mean of course the octave of the other, below. In like manner the grave accent, which Hadley reasonably says means not a lower note, that is, one lower than the keynote or readingnote, but only one not so high as the acute above it, will commonly be a rise of, say a major third to the mediant, but sometimes a fall of, say, a minor third, to the submediant. The circumflex is no doubt a sort of turn or shake, two notes to a syllable instead of one or a rise and fall instead of a rise only. It is to be remarked that men seem to have found it hard to reach the simple notion of a note. In the passage you quote at p. 15 Cicero says there are only three sounds in music, the turn, the rise and the fall—for so I interpret him; and it is believed that our present musical notation arose from a complicated system of accents, rising, falling, and so on (a great variety of marks, now unnecessary, may be seen in books on the history of plain chant, e.g., Helmore's Primer in Novello's Music Primer series); as though men first were struck by the change or passage of sound and later seized the points of departure and arrival. It is true this does not agree with what I have said above about the grave accent, but modern critics, as Roby and Munro, strongly suspect Cicero, Quintilian and the Latin writers of bungling on the subject and misapplying Greek theory to Latin . . ." (F 181–182. Nov. 7, 1883).

"As then the English accent is stress and yet we can make the

stress on the unaccented syllables of an emphatic word more
marked than on the accented of an unemphatic one, the general
or rhetorical emphasis overriding the particular and syllabic, so
in Greek, no doubt, it was possible for the accent to be ordinarily
a high tone and yet for the lowest note of one word to be higher
than the highest of another or even for the note usually raised
on occasion to be lowered as markedly, the general and rhetorical
intonation here too controlling and modifying the syllabic and
particular. More shortly, emphasis does not destroy our accent of
stress nor need intonation have destroyed their accent of tone and
I should have liked something of the sort to be expressed here"
(*Ibid.*, p. 182).

All this is admissible as sound enough theory, to which disagree-
ments will also be theoretical. Only one thing is truly noteworthy,
and that is Hopkins' tendency to an over-exactness in determining
the precise degree of pitch-change. The idea of musical intervals is
probably quite erroneous since it is improbable from the evidence
which we possess that spoken words approached as nearly to song
as this conjecture implies. Certainly Aristoxenos, who mentions
all sorts of musical intervals both harmonic and unharmonic,
would not have allowed such a phenomenon to go unnoted; and by
parity with his theory of artistic prolongation, I fancy he thought
the voice's rise and fall to lie "somewhere between" settled intervals rather than a fifth above or a third below. There is in
Hopkins a strong tendency toward mathematical accuracy, which
shows not only a good deal about his general character but also
seems to indicate the nature of his rhythmic studies, which were
becoming, I fear, more and more musico-mathematical, more
and more Rossbachian. The precise pleased him. He was not only
tortured by decisions between fifths of a point in examination
marks but fascinated by the idea of mathematical precision.

The distinction between emphasis and tone is important and
true; the distinction between stress and length is of greater importance and of greater value to the rhythmist. These two things,
stress and length, only the veriest tyro would confuse, and I find

nothing very remarkable in Hopkins' treatment of the distinction, though I do find something rather remarkable in his insistence on so elementary a point. Moreover I find three very disturbing statements about accent, which he must have dashed off hurriedly, for they neither fit into the rest of his theory nor are they at all true in themselves. In fact, he knows better. Yet he says in his 1873 lecture notes on Rhythm (N 223), that musical pitch is not an element of verse; that (p. 226) the vowel, in Greek, is held before a diconsonant to make a long by position, and that the accent of words, the sense-words, goes for nothing.

What he means by the first misleading statement is that musical pitch is not a *primary* element of Greek and English verse. This is true. It is not, as he says elsewhere, to be considered as a metrical factor but only as an aesthetic factor. Yet this is so inadequate as to be confusing, since the rise and fall of the voice is most decidedly a rhythmic factor—as in the arrangement of the verse-cadence, which depends upon spoken variation of pitch and which he clearly recognizes. As a secondary element, then, pitch enters, and the universal denial is simply untrue.

The difficulty about the vowel before the diconsonant is more easily explained—a more common misapprehension. It is not true that the vowel is lengthened before a diconsonant and that the vowel then becomes long by position; much less, long by nature. The vowel does not change at all. In a time-art such as Greek the vowel retains its normal semeion value, but the time taken in pronouncing the double consonant, the time elapsing for changes in tongue and teeth, adds another semeion or part of a semeion to the syllable, so that the syllable, not the vowel, is long. It is wrong to say that the value of the vowel changes before the diconsonant.

To say that the accent of the words, the sense-words, goes for nothing, is again false. This accent is the main point of variation, as length in English is the main point of English variation. It must be remembered that three things enter into all language— stress, pitch, length. In English, where stress is the principle of unity, length fulfills a dual role—either replacing stress when and after the stress unity has been established, or serving as contrapuntal variation to the stress repetition. It is peculiarly important as a principle of variety where over-strong stress repetition would tend toward monotony; and it is bad art to have coincident stress and accent over a long period, though in English any really insufferable monotony is practically defeated by the nature of the language, which decreases length in ratio to strength of stress and weakens stress in ratio to length of prolongation.

In Greek, length is the principle of unity. A strongly tonic language and a weakly stressed one, the pitch becomes the first principle of variation, never, however, in classical times, replacing the primary element of length. The Greeks did not feel the need to avoid monotony by having the main time-length different from the accented syllable, for it is more often coincident than diverse; and this, probably, because the third element—that of stress—however weak, was present in the basic syllable, so that the contrapuntal effect, the variational effect, could be achieved when the pitch-emphasis and the length-emphasis agreed.

But the statement that none of these elements save length matters or is an element of verse is almost beyond belief. Fortunately we have so many statements of Hopkins which explain what he really meant that we can only consider these amazing slips as the nodding of Homer; and I point them out merely because somebody might pounce upon them and try to assert that Hopkins erred in his most fundamental ideas. But let them be considered according to the distinction which he makes in the letter to Dixon, Dec. 22, 1880 (D 39), as simply statements regarding the doing, not the well-doing of the prosody—"the writing it somehow and the writing it as it should be written; for written anyhow it is a shambling business and a corruption, not an improvement. In strictness then and simple εἶναι it is a matter of accent only, like common rhythm, and not of quantity at all." This is what he meant, then: that the subsidiary or contrapuntal features were not important to the doing, though they may have been very important to the well-doing; or as prosodists would have it, accent and stress are not part of the metric but of the rhythmic.

Two things, then, enter strongly into his later speculations and these two things, music and mathematics, are the bases of the Rossbach-Westphal theory, further mathematicized by J. H. Heinrich Schmidt, whose work Hopkins knew. The main thesis is that an original lost musical setting modifies the time-lengths of the syllables and, in Schmidt's theory at least, with an accuracy that is so exact as to be artistically and indeed practically impossible. It is a credence in this false view of metric which makes Hopkins regret his lack of mathematical knowledge in his researches in Pindar. "I cannot do what I would for want of mathematics," he says (F 128. Dec. 23, 1886), and his general belief in the musical and mathematical theory is clear enough in many places, noticeably in page 222 of the *Notebooks*, and frequently in the *Letters* (as B 230, F 244-245, etc.).

Yet somehow he felt that despite his mathematical lacks—his musical lacks he never admitted even when they were pointed out to him—he could write, "I believe that I can now set metre and music both of them on a scientific footing which will be final like the law of gravitation" (F 229. Jan. 20, 1887). This is a great subjective advance from a statement made a month previously "My book on the Dorian Measure is going on . . . in fact it needs mathematics, but how can I make them up?" (B 246-7. Dec. 11, 1886). What solution he had come to we shall probably never know, but the statement about the scientific footing is, in its way, somewhat pathetic, for it is a basic misapprehension too common in theories of art. The *apparentia rerum* which is art can never be confused with the exactness necessary in science, and a single hint from Aristoxenos would have spared him much labor and doubtless great disappointment. Yet in his futile work he had his moments of exuberance. In November, 1886, he had written, "I am hoping to write . . . a paper on the Dorian Measure, the true scansion of perhaps half or

more than half of the Greek and Latin lyric verses. I do believe
it is a great and it is an unexpected discovery" (F 226).

As to his theory and how it was progressing, we have ample
evidence. Brushing aside as inconsequential his statement that
the Dorian Measure is the key to half or more of Greek and
Latin lyric, which it certainly is not, the Aeolian, Ionian, Paeonic
being each, possibly, more common—let us look for a moment
at his explanation:

"I added two metrical schemes to my Greek verses for you.
They are inconsistent; that is to say, one is fuller than the other.
I have made what I think is a great discovery; it is of a fundamental point; and I hope to publish something on it. It is shortly
this. The Dorian rhythm, the most used of the lyric rhythms,
arises from the Dorian measure or bar. The Dorian bar is originally *a march step in three-time executed in four steps to the bar.*
Out of this simple combination of numbers, three and four, simple to state but a good deal more complicated than any rhythm
we have, arose the structure of most of Pindar's odes and most
of the choral odes in the drama. In strict rhythm every bar must
have four steps. Now since four were to be taken to three-time,
say three crotchets, (1) one crotchet had to be resolved, (2) only
one at a time, and that (3) never the last. Hence the two legitimate figures of the Dorian bar were these: ∪ ∪ — — (the rising
Ionic) and — ∪ ∪ — (the choriambus). But the following irreg-
ularities were allowed ∪ ∪ — ∪ (the third paeon), either by pro-
longing the third syllable (∪ ∪ —⌐ ∪) or by irrationally lengthening the last (∪ ∪ — ∪̆); — ∪ — — (the second epitrite), (which
is not as Schmidt thinks —⌐ ∪ — —, for that wd. destroy the
three-time, but ⌐∪ — —), by resolving the first long into three
instead of two, exactly as we employ triplets in music and write
3 over them; lastly the very irregular but important combination of these two licenses — ⌐∪ —⌐ ∪ or ⌐∪ — ∪̆ (the double
trochee). The beautiful figure ⌐∪ — — is the one most important characteristic of the rhythm: Hephaestion calls it the
Carian foot.

"When the measure is more loosely used two new licenses appear—syncopation, by which syllables are lengthened so that three fill a bar and so that the last of one bar becomes the first of the next; 'and triple resolution, so that a bar can have five syllables. By means of syncopation the measure can be made dactylic and practically brought into common time. The strict Dorian can only be found in odes meant to be marched to.

"I shd. say a word of the accentuation or stressing. Naturally the strongest place in the Dorian bar is the second crotchet, not the first, and I have so marked it in the schemes I sent, but perhaps it would be best to mark the first as strongest: it is made so, so to speak, by a correction, to redress the heaviness of the second crotchet. Pindar and all the poets continually pass from heavier feet, like ‾ʋ — — or ɯ — — , to lighter, — ʋ ʋ —, where by the stress falling sometimes on a long or crotchet, sometimes on a short or quaver, a beautiful variety is given and the variety is further enhanced by making an imperfect Ionic follow a choriambus, thus: — ʋ ʋ —/ ʋ ʋ —, by which a dactylic cadence is given but with the stress falling on different syllables of the dactyls. With all this the rhythm came to have an infinite flexibility, of which the Greeks seem never to have tired.

"Thus you are not to mark

ἔρως ἀνί|κατε μάχαν. || ἔρως ὃς ἐν | κτήμασι πίπτεις, as here, but as here:

ἔ|ρως ἀνίκα|τε μάχαν. || ἔ|ρως ὃς ἐν κτή|μασι πίπτεις.

However the musicians no doubt took their own way with these things" (B 233–234. Oct. 21, 1886).

Let us examine some of the statements made here:

First: The Dorian measure — ʋ ʋ — ʋ ʋ — — is not made up of "three crotchets," as there is no basis for assuming a musical triplet formation in Greek similar to that found in modern music. It is not true that the final long syllable of this measure is never resolved, for it can be found not too infrequently in the form:

— ∪ ∪ — ∪ ∪ — ∪ ∪. Nor is it true that only one long syllable at a time may be resolved, since the form may occur completely resolved into short syllables. Hopkins' data were insufficient for his generalization.

Second: The second epitrite — ∪ — — is a prolonged trochaic dipody and may be charted thus: — ∪ — > and is neither —⌐ ∪ — — as Schmidt has it nor ⌐∪ — — as Hopkins has it. Theoretically Schmidt's analysis is farther from the truth than Hopkins', since Schmidt's scansion makes the measure dactylic, which it certainly is not, and Hopkins' general analysis recognizes some relationship with a basic diplasion form.

Third: From the *loci classici* in Plato and Aristophanes we know that there is a measure in 3/4 time which is similar to (κατὰ) the 4/4 or dactylic march measure and that this 3/4 measure is the Dorian phrase. This makes it impossible for the true Dorian to be a march measure as Hopkins believes.

Fourth: Hopkins does not seem to be aware of the two types of Dorian phrases, the falling — ∪ ∪ — ∪ ∪ — — used with — ∪ — —; and the rising — — ∪ ∪ — ∪ ∪ — used with — — ∪ —. However, this omission may simply be an effort to condense and to avoid complication.

Fifth: The phrases mentioned in the above paragraph are the true characteristics of the Dorian Rhythm, not the first epitrite ∪ — — — as Hopkins believes.

Sixth: The rhythm is not syzygic—that is, composed of the equivalent of two basic feet — ∪ ∪ — and ∪ ∪ — —, but synthetic, composed of four basic iambo-trochaic feet — ∪ ∪ — ∪ ∪ — — in a combination of twelve times and used with a dipody synthetic and prolonged.

Seventh: The syzygy as such ∪ ∪ — — is peculiar to the Ionian, not to the Dorian mode; the syzygy — ∪ ∪ — to the Aeolian and not to the Dorian.

Eighth: There is no necessary prolongation of a syllable in the paeonic substitution and no necessary truncation of a syllable in the epitrite ⌐∪ — — or ⌐∪ — ∪. Substitutions are of their

nature different from that for which they substitute and their
normal time-lengths remain substantially unchanged, as in the
substitution of a spondee for an iambus in simple rhythmic
—— — for ᴜ —. The underlying aesthetic principle here is that
substitutions are of their nature artistic variations; *in Greek these
variations are divergencies in time-length from the regular pattern*. But if the times of the "irrational syllable" are made, in
speech or song, to conform by abbreviation of the long or prolongation of the short to that of the normal or regular short or
long, there is no variation from the regular time-pattern and the
reason for their introduction is destroyed.

Ninth: Syncopation does not mean the lengthening of syllables
so that they fill out a bar. There is no authority for this statement
in Greek metric and the passage sometimes quoted from Aristoxenos to prove it is a restoration so complete as to amount almost
to a forgery. Not more than twenty words are clearly visible on
the manuscript fragment; the rest are "conjectures" made to fit
a preconceived theory.

Tenth: The last of one bar does not become the first of the
next. Although overlapping rhythmical phrases occur within
longer cola, the individual phrases retain their own metrical
identity.

Eleventh: The phrase quoted from *Antigone* (781) is not
Dorian, as Hopkins should have known from similar prosodic
phrases in Aeschylus' *Prometheus*.

From these eleven strictures it should be clear enough that
Hopkins was following a most misleading trail in the Dorian
theory and that no solution could have been forthcoming. It is
unnecessary to say more.

Now, as I remarked in the beginning, nothing of this confusion
or theoretical error detracts from Hopkins' reputation as a great
metrist, innovator, and restorer in English; and, as I have attempted to show, the ideas which he received from his interest
in Greek metric were of some help to him in working out his own
system of English metric. As a metrical theorist in Greek lyric,

however, his contributions cannot be said to be great. Some few realizations were in advance of his time; some few were speculatively interesting to students of Greek metric.

Truly then, as a theorist in metric, particularly in Greek and Latin metric, Hopkins holds no great place. And yet this is a minor thing for one who as a practitioner has given so much, has broadened the scope of English rhythms, has left a fluid and flexible patternization which has proven of such vast value to all who follow. Hopkins' faults both as theorist and practitioner were the faults of the pioneer, as his virtues were also pioneering virtues—strength, daring, power. And that is enough.

HOPKINS' SPRUNG RHYTHM AND THE LIFE OF ENGLISH POETRY

WALTER J. ONG, S.J.

> Soun is noght but air y-broken,
> And every speche that is spoken,
> Loud or privee, foul or fair,
> In his substaunce is but air.
> —The egle to Chaucer in *The Hous of Fame*

"In the winter of '75 . . . I had long had haunting my ear," so Gerard Manley Hopkins writes to Richard Watson Dixon, "the echo of a new rhythm which now I realized on paper. To speak shortly, it consists in scanning by accents or stresses alone" (D 14. Oct. 6, 1878).

This was Hopkins' celebrated "sprung rhythm," christened by its author with a name which is at once vigorous as the rhythm itself, colorful but disenchanting, and, for the better or worse fortune of the rhythm it designates, not a little hoydenish.

In the case of Hopkins, it may be possible to convict Chaucer's eagle of understatement. For sprung rhythm, which characterizes most of Hopkins' poems, is so integral to the whole poetic texture where we find bedded his deep-rooted raciness that we may expect an investigation of it to prove altogether more fruitful than an ordinary pursuit of metrics. Investigation here should be capable of something more than physical measurements, than counting the pieces of broken air. This is plain not only from the rhythm itself as heard, but from the remarks about it winding through Hopkins' correspondence in a trail which, for all its apparent errancy, hints at a secret consistency on a level which explanation so far has not reached.

93

Investigation is needed. We can gather, for instance, with
W. H. Gardner in his article on *The Wreck of the Deutschland,* which touches on the movement of Hopkins' verse as closely
as any study so far, that sprung rhythm "is virtually a stress-
meter derived from two main sources—the 'irregular' choruses
of Milton's *Samson Agonistes* and the free rhythms of popular
jingles and nursery rhymes."[1] But why is it also, to cite Hopkins'
own statement, "the rhythm of common speech and of written
prose, when rhythm is perceived in them"? (Author's Preface,
Poems, p. 5.) Certainly this latter pedigree, which is often neglected, outranks the former, which is frequently enough cited;
furthermore, if the two pedigrees are connected, because the
rhythm of the Samson choruses, the rhythm of nursery rhymes,
and the rhythm of prose are the same, such a connection is not
by any means evident.

Hopkins' remarks on his new rhythm are often oblique, *obiter
dicta,* and since the appearance of the four volumes of his papers,
others' comment or study in the vicinity of his rhythm has simply
taken similar oblique paths with regard to the rhythm itself.
Moreover, an accumulation of prosodic detritus against which
I. A. Richards protested some years ago,[2] has further obscured
the view; and statements such as Dr. Richards' that Hopkins
"gave himself complete rhythmical freedom," while they brush
aside the detritus ("the absurdities of prosodists"), do not leave
fully lighted the vistas they have opened. What is Dr. Richards'
"complete rhythmical freedom"? To say what the movement of
Hopkins' poetry is not—it is not what prosodists ordinarily
try to count, it is free from this thing they would make rhythm
out to be, it has "complete rhythmical freedom"—this is to say
something, and in the present case something worthwhile. But it
is to open the proper question, not to close the discussion. Sure

---

[1] *"The Wreck of the Deutschland," Essays and Studies* (English Association), XXI, collected by Herbert Read (Oxford: Clarendon Press, 1936),
p. 127. A more recent study of Hopkins' rhythm is discussed in the note at
the end of Part II below, p. 145.

[2] "Gerard Hopkins," *Dial,* LXXXI (Sept., 1926), p. 203.

now of one thing it is not, we may still wish to know what the movement of Hopkins' verse is.

The present study attempts to account for Hopkins' sprung rhythm and at the same time to design a key to his vast number of scattered remarks about the rhythm by showing both his practice and his comment on his practice against a general pattern of development in English verse.

I

THE WAYS OF DISCOVERY

In opening a discussion of Hopkins' verse, first steps must be taken carefully so as to avoid false starts. Even yet there are plenty of such starts possible, and a preliminary excursion through Hopkins' papers will be necessary to recognize them for what they are and to find the proper point of departure.

The Question of Old English

At first sight, one of the most promising starts is the indisputable connection, often enough observed, between Hopkins' sprung rhythm and Old English verse. As we shall see, this connection leads us, in a way, toward explanation, but the way is so roundabout as to be misleading. It is easy to mention the connection without adverting to the fact that, instead of providing explanation, it really raises a sprawling genealogical problem. In Hopkins' day, knowledge of Old English was not easy to come by, and the nature of Old English poetry by no means entirely clear. It was not until 1885, ten years after the writing of the *Deutschland,* Hopkins' first sprung rhythm poem, that Eduard Sievers first published in *Paul und Braune's Beiträge* his "Zur Rhythmik des germanischen Alliterationsverses," the definitive work setting forth—and that in German, in which Hopkins shows little interest—the structural principles of Old English poetry.

Late in 1882 Hopkins admits that he does not know for certain whether his sprung rhythm occurred in Anglo-Saxon verse: it does, he says, "so far as I know—I am enquiring and presently I shall be able to speak more decidedly" (B 156. Oct. 18, 1882). A month later Hopkins writes that he is (only then) learning Anglo-Saxon (B 163. Nov. 26–27, 1882).

Hopkins' acquaintance with the work of William Barnes, "good soul, of Dorset-dialect poems," looks promising at first sight but goes little further in the way of explaining the connection of Hopkins' new rhythm with Old English. Barnes had indeed published in 1849 an Anglo-Saxon collection, but Hopkins nowhere mentions it. His acquaintance with Barnes seems to have been confined principally to the latter's own Dorsetshire dialect poetry: but even if this poetry were capable of suggesting sprung rhythm to Hopkins, his interest in it was too slight to matter. He writes in 1879, again after the completion of the *Deutschland* and other sprung rhythm pieces, that he had never read any of Barnes' poems since his own undergraduate days "except the one quoted in Gosse's paper" (B 87. Aug. 14, 1879). Everything else in Hopkins' acquaintance with Barnes is too late to help account for sprung rhythm. At the instigation of Patmore, Hopkins later went over more of Barnes' Dorsetshire poems, but this was in 1885, when sprung rhythm was ten years old.[3] His acquaintance with Barnes' *An Outline of English Speech-Craft* (B 162–163. Nov. 26, 1882), with its insistence on "pure" English and its abhorrence of Latinisms might possibly have accounted for some of Hopkins' idiom which seems the fiber of his verse movement, had Hopkins' acquaintance with the book been possible earlier. But the work did not appear until 1878; Hopkins' idiom was well matured in 1875.

There remains *Piers Plowman* as apparently Hopkins' only means of establishing contact with Old English poetry before his sprung rhythm was already formed. This late fourteenth-century poem preserves enough of the early Old English rhythmic

[3] F 218 (to Patmore, June 4, 1886); B 221, Sept. 1, 1885.

movement to make it a possible source, and Hopkins mentions it often. But even the part played by *Piers Plowman* in introducing the new rhythm to his ear, and still more in furnishing him a *detailed* theory, is highly questionable. It is true that in his lecture notes prepared in 1873–74 he quotes a few lines from the poem. In 1880, however, he writes Bridges that he had not studied it enough to know whether or not it employed triple time in its verse (B 107. Sept. 5, 1880); and it is not until two years later that he reports, "I am reading that famous poem and am coming to the conclusion that it is not worth reading" (B 156. Oct. 18, 1882).

With this last remark, we finally come upon Hopkins' first definitive statement, repeated when he wrote "in '83 or not much later" [4] the Preface now published with his *Poems,* that "the old English verse seen in Pierce Ploughman" is in sprung rhythm.[5] Clearly, this by no means explains the source of Hopkins' rhythm: it simply states a fact which Hopkins had discovered.

The Question of Later Authors

Similarly, with regard to specific authors after the Old and Middle English periods, Hopkins' treatment of their sporadic manifestations of sprung rhythm is on altogether too undecided a basis to indicate that they were really sources: often Hopkins cannot make up his mind whether they use sprung rhythm or not. He mentions Milton so often in his correspondence that it has been easy to suspect he derived his rhythm from Milton, especially from the *Samson Agonistes,* and the ease of making this conjecture has obscured the fact that Hopkins nowhere says that he learned sprung rhythm from Milton. Rather, he approaches Milton as one who judges, not as one who learns, and he can never quite make up his mind whether Milton's rhythms

---

[4] See Bridges' notes, *Poems,* p. 100.
[5] *Poems,* p. 6; B 156 (Oct. 18, 1882).

are sprung or not. The *Samson* choruses, which Hopkins first mentions in his now printed papers on April 3, 1877 (B 38), are, he writes to Bridges later the same year, "intermediate between counterpointed and sprung rhythm," but in the same breath he adds, "In reality they are sprung" (B 45. Aug. 21, 1877). Later, he calls Milton "the great standard in the use of counterpoint," but states definitively that Milton did not use sprung rhythm: "When . . . secondary or 'mounted rhythm,' which is necessarily a sprung rhythm, overpowers the original . . . you reach simple sprung rhythm. Milton must have known this but had reasons" for not going so far.[6]

It is well to remember that the interest Hopkins shows in Milton's rhythms is not all his own. A large part is the reflection of the interest of Bridges, his constant correspondent, who was on his way to writing *Milton's Prosody*.

Shakespeare is the one cited in Hopkins' letters at the first mention of anything promising to develop into sprung rhythm. This occurs in a postscript to Bridges just before Hopkins enters the novitiate:

I hope you will master the peculiar beat I have introduced into St. Dorothea. The development is mine but the beat is Shakspere—e.g.
Whý should thís desert be?—and
Thoú for whóm Jóve would swear—where the rest of the lines are eight-syllabled or seven-syllabled (B 24–25. Aug. 7, 1868).

As indicated by Hopkins in at least one of the versions of his poem, the beat is:

> I bear a basket lined with grass.
> I' am só light' and fair'
> Men are amazed to watch me pass
> With' the básket I beár.[7]

[6] D 15 (Oct. 6, 1878). For the nature of "counterpoint" or "mounted rhythm," see below, pp. 148 ff.
[7] *Poems*, p. 141.

This looks promising, but with this particular beat other authors besides Shakespeare are associated in Hopkins' lecture notes for rhetoric made in 1873–74 (N 221–248). In these notes, although he does not use the term "sprung," Hopkins describes a kind of verse which is unmistakably that destined to become in his hands the new rhythm. This is the "stress verse," verse which builds with stresses only, disregarding how many other syllables there may be. Hopkins contrasts it with quantitative verse, such as classical Greek and Latin, and with "counted" or "numbered" verse, which regards the total number of syllables, stressed and unstressed. He mentions that the rhythm of verse without count of syllable, that is, the pure stress rhythm like that he was later to make his own, is to be found in the ancient Saturnian Latin verse and in *Piers Plowman*. In *Piers,* he notes, each half-line gets two beats commonly, but sometimes three or four. He goes on to say that such stress or beat rhythm can be found occasionally in Shakespeare, Campbell, and Hamilton, quoting from them four, one, and four lines respectively. There are other unusually acute observations on this verse which regards only stress without taking into account the total number of syllables—we shall come to some of these remarks later—and finally Milton is mentioned as having "made experiments in accentual counterpoint," as (with Hopkins' own marks)—

Hóme tó his móther's hóuse prívate retúrned

This is the only line from Milton quoted in the lecture notes, although Hopkins tells Dixon that he had paid "a good deal of attention to Milton's versification" when the notes were being got up (D 13–14. Oct. 6, 1878).

Derivation and What It Means Here

When these lecture notes were being assembled in 1873–74, sprung rhythm was undoubtedly in the offing, and, indeed, the lectures may well have been occasion for Hopkins' giving full attention to the rhythm—it was only a year later that the *Deutschland* appeared, after Hopkins had had the echo of the new rhythm "long . . . haunting" his ear. Yet it is impossible to state that Hopkins "derived" his rhythm from any of the authors mentioned in these lecture notes, for the passages he quotes here give every evidence of being *loci* which Hopkins could cite as instances of his rhythm rather than "sources" for it. "Single lines and single instances of it [sprung rhythm] are not uncommon in English and I have pointed them out in lecturing," he writes Bridges (B 45. Aug. 21, 1877), quoting from these same authors and others. The Shakespeare passages early connected with *St. Dorothea,* which are really the most promising as genuine sources, are too meager to account for sprung rhythm as such. Hopkins appreciates this and in his lecture notes simply lists them, without special mention, with the other lines which serve merely as instances.

It seems true, then, to say that Hopkins' statement giving the most definite information about the source of the new verse is the one quoted earlier: "I had long had haunting my ear the echo of a new rhythm" (D 14. Oct. 6, 1878). Conclusions that Hopkins' meters derived, or that he even thought they derived, from their being used in this or that particular author are wide of the mark. Hopkins testifies only to the fact that the new rhythm was "haunting" his ear. It might be said that he noticed *what* it was when it was already in his own possession, after he had already picked it up. Whether Hopkins himself could have named all the really proximate sources, we simply do not know. This much is certain: the real sources of a rhythm which makes such a radical claim on a language as that of being the rhythm of the language's prose can hardly be narrowed to one or two authors or to nursery rhymes, though these may provide quite valid instances of the rhythm's appearance. Sources for a rhythm with such roots must be more widespread than that. If Hopkins' claims for his rhthym are acceptable, he must have been, consciously or unconsciously, hearing it everywhere.

Whether Hopkins' first susceptibility to the movements of the new rhythm was occasioned by his speculating on its possibility or directly by his hearing it, is not at all evident from his printed papers and perhaps will always remain an unsolved question. At any rate, once his enthusiasm for sprung rhythm had begun, about the time he set down the *Deutschland,* he began to find it in more and more places. This is hardly strange, for had the rhythm which Hopkins found been other than something basically widespread, it would very likely not have been the sort of thing that could have worked. For, practically speaking, there can be no question of a poet's introducing into a language the bases of a rhythm—various stresses, lengths of syllables, other hinges on which a language turns. He can utilize what is there, perhaps change it subtly. But the rhythms of a language are already rooted when the poet arrives, and the real question to be answered concerning Hopkins' sprung rhythm is, What was this thing he was discovering all around him? or What is the life of this rhythm in the language, what are its claims on our speech?

This is the sort of question Hopkins himself was gradually solving. Where the new rhythm came from and what its implications were Hopkins was at first not sure. The St. Dorothea piece he associated with Shakespeare in 1869 is an important but only equivocal hint and an entirely inadequate explanation of what was to come. But by 1873–74 Hopkins certainly had a skeleton theory erected for a verse which counted stresses only and disregarded the number of syllables in a line. A theory so stated was capable of differentiating the "new rhythm" from other rhythms which had been the ordinary concern of metrists. But that was all. What was the full economy of such a pure stress verse in English, Hopkins could not yet answer. His ear had caught a rhythm and he could describe it. But it would take time to know how it would work, what organization it demanded, just as it would take time to know the principal places where it might be found.

From here on, Hopkins begins listening for the rhythm and

listing instances of its occurrence, blocking in areas of theory as he proceeds. Leaving the theory for later discussion, we can remark that not only do *loci* of the rhythm increase in number as Hopkins becomes more familiar with the rhythm by using it himself, but *loci* which, such as that of ordinary rhythmical prose, would be most likely important sources (because they were most commonly in his ear or in anyone's ear) are mentioned latest in Hopkins' discussion of his discovery.

The crisis is reached in 1882–83. By 1882 Hopkins had come to the point where he was ready to give his sprung rhythm a brief and tentative history in a letter to Bridges: he suspects that it (B 156. Oct. 18, 1882)

existed in full force in Anglo saxon verse and in great beauty; in degraded and doggerel shape in *Piers Ploughman* . . . ; Greene was the last who employed it at all consciously and he never continuously; then it disappeared—for one cadence in it here and there is not sprung rhythm and one swallow does not make a spring. (I put aside Milton's case, for it is altogether singular.)

This is the skeleton of the view given in the Preface published with his *Poems,* but this Preface, written as we have seen within approximately the next year, lists as additional *loci* of the rhythm weather saws, nursery rhymes, and songs, and caps all with the astonishing and sweeping statement that sprung rhythm "is the rhythm of common speech and of written prose, when rhythm is perceived in them." [8]

Thus we come upon the inevitable question with which we began. If this sprung rhythm is, being the rhythm of prose, the commonest and most ordinary rhythm of the language, how did it happen that Hopkins did not from the first give it its fullest pedigree by stating such a fact? In 1877 he was still writing to Bridges that it is not the rhythm of prose but "the nearest to the rhythm of prose" (B 46. Aug. 21, 1877). The answer lies in Hopkins' only gradually opening awareness of the genealogy of

[8] *Poems,* p. 5.

his own new rhythm and of the rhythm's economy and connections.

Although in his 1883 Preface he says everything in summary when he says, "It is the rhythm of common speech and of written prose when rhythm is perceived in them"—although this indeed "caps, clears, and clinches all," this statement still needs its implications developed. With things at such a pitch, however, in the press of work which in his own case as in that of Brother Alphonsus,

> Could crown career with conquest while there went
> Those years and years by of world without event

Father Hopkins himself went quietly to God, "lover of souls, swaying considerate scales." This was in 1889. Had he lived longer, he might have explained more: "And there it is," he writes Bridges (B 275. May 25, 1888),

> I understand these things so much better than you: we should explain things, plainly state them, clear them up, explain them; explanation—except personal—is always pure good; without explanation people go on misunderstanding; being once explained they thenceforward understand things; therefore always explain: but I have the passion for explanation and you have not.

A frank avowal and the truth. For Hopkins was always trying desperately to explain his rhythmic practices.

But the mass of brief comment dispersed through his letters and his all-too-brief Preface leaves much explaining still to be done.

Hopkins' misunderstandings of Greek and Latin rhythmic usages, which derived from the mistakes of scholars of his age, led his speculation on classical meter over unsafe ground, as Father John L. Bonn explains elsewhere in the present volume. Since Father Bonn's work discusses separately what here might have proved a troublesome enough distraction, the matter of Greek and Latin meters need not enter the present study. Fortunately, Hopkins was not constructing a rhythm on Greek theory, however much Greek theory may have provided him false analogies in Greek for his rhythm. The validity of his work is independent of speculation on Greek metric: Hopkins knew sprung rhythm because he *heard* it in English.

We must keep in mind the cardinal problem, which, despite the direction taken by much thought on the matter, is not why Hopkins is different, but why he is not different. Hopkins' poetry, which is not separable from the vehicle of his rhythm, has a hold on the English language as unshakable and as permanent as that of St. Thomas More, Shakespeare, Donne, Dryden, or, indeed, quite absolutely, anyone else at all, though his grasp may not be so ample as the grasp of some of these. Now Hopkins' differences from his contemporaries are obvious. But simply to be different is no virtue. The virtue of Hopkins' difference and the thing which wants explaining lies in the fact that in an age when most of the major poets—major at least with regard to their contemporaries—were out of contact with a living language, Hopkins was able to reestablish contact with one.

Scott, Southey, Landor, Arnold, Rossetti, Swinburne, much of Tennyson—and Newman, to take a poet whose importance is lesser but whose basically religious views of reality were the same as Hopkins'—these have little life to supply the serious poet of the present century. A minor poet of the seventeenth century, such as King, is likely to be far more alive today. But upon the appearance of his poems in 1918, Hopkins' work was found to have carried forward a fecund vitality into a new age which its author had not lived to see.

Hopkins, rhythm and all, had taken up his position at a place over which the living current of the language was moving, when men whom his age thought great were, as it latterly appears, stogged to the right and to the left in drying sloughs. This is what needs explaining. The question is not the one often heard: How did Hopkins break with tradition? Hopkins is in a tradition or he could not have survived. Nor is it, What did Hopkins invent?

For, though many men have found a tradition, no one yet has invented one. Hopkins' entire discussion of his rhythm, as we have seen, evinces that he *found* something, his ears were opened, and once they were, he began to hear about him more and more evidence of the same thing.

Our question, then, can be put this way: What did Hopkins come upon?

II

ANOTHER ECONOMY IN ENGLISH VERSE

From speech, from music, or from the mere miscellany of activity about him, man's ear is being fed constantly with a complex wave of sound. Though sound is "noght but air y-broken," the texture of this wave, when its source is speech, can be exceedingly rich and variable, and in its manifold many patterns of diverse kinds and diverse degrees of fixity can be discovered—patterns noticed or made by adverting to pitch or to phrasing or to syllabic length or to the number of syllables or to the strange phenomena grouped together under the title of stress or accent, which is something easily recognized but, with its variable mixtures of pitch and force, not easily defined or even described. Sound pattern, and hence verse, can exist in terms of any of these things or of combinations of them, or in terms of other things as well.

The Alternating Stress

One pattern in English speech, at least in Modern English speech, is quite easy to identify. For English, as we pronounce it, demands, with a few exceptions to be noted later, a stress of some sort on every two or three syllables: that is, however few the stresses demanded by sense may be, other stresses are scattered through English speech so that generally no more than two syllables pass without one. If at least every third syllable takes a sense stress, this will serve: thus we would say *And nów let us gó* or *And nów let ús go,* as the sense might demand. But if the sense demands no particular stress on any special word or words in a group of monosyllables such as this, we ordinarily must put stresses on some of the words anyhow, making our own one or another of the possible alternating stress patterns: we would hardly say, as a Frenchman speaking English might say, *And now let us go,* with all the syllables equi-accented and only a slight tonic elevation on the last. Or again, no matter what the sense of a phrase in which the word occurs, we pronounce poly-syllables with alternating stresses, the longer the word, the greater the number of stresses. Thus we say *in″com-mu″ni-ca-bil′i-ty,* or perhaps *in″com-mu″ni-ca-bil′i-ty″.* This rule is general enough to set up throughout our speech the feeling for alternating or pulsing between syllables which are stressed and syllables which are not. We may call the stress this feeling demands, the alter-nating stress.

In non-versified speech the pattern of this alternating stress and its correlative slack is irregular. Thus we might scan (since the alternating stress asserts itself with some flexibility, other scansions would be equally admissible in places):

Foūrscŏre ănd sēvĕn yēars ăgō oŭr fāthĕrs broŭght fŏrth ŏn thĭs cōntinēnt ă nēw nātion, cŏnceĭvĕd ĭn lībĕrty, ănd dĕdĭcātĕd tō thĕ prŏpŏsĭtiŏn thăt āll mĕn āre crēatĕd eqŭăl.

Now, one way of writing English verse is to create a regular rhythm by so arranging words that the alternating stress sets up a quite regular beat of stress-slack, or stress-slack-slack, and so on. Thus in Gray's *Elegy Written in a Country Church-Yard:*

> The Curfew tolls the knell of parting day;
> 　The lowing herd winds slowly o'er the lea;
> The plowman homeward plods his weary way,
> 　And leaves the world to darkness and to me.[9]

[9] *The Poetical Works of Gray and Collins,* ed. by Austin Lane Poole (London: Oxford University Press, 1917), p. 90.

Or in Spenser's "Mutabilitie" cantos:

> When I bethinke me on that speech whyleare
> Of Mutabilitie, and well it way.[10]

Here the alternating stress sets up a simple one-two beat like that of very elementary, unsophisticated, measured music—how far actual time is an element of the beat need not concern us here; we need only note that the beat pattern is somehow an element—and once the beat is set up, it may be varied by reversing or making undecided occasional slack-stress "feet" so long as the variations are not great enough to destroy the measured rhythm. Thus Shakespeare in *Sonnet XXXIII* (reversed foot):

> *Stealing* unseen to west with this disgrace; [11]

or in *Sonnet XXX* (undecided feet):

> And with *old woes new wail* my dear time's waste.[12]

Sometimes this beat of the alternating stress is so marked in its timing that it admits either one or two slacks indiscriminately, the two when they occur receiving each approximately half the time of one. For instance, Coleridge's *Christabel*:

> The lovely lady, Christabel,
> Whom her father loves so well,
>
> . . . . . .
>
> She had dreams all yesternight
> Of her own betrothed knight;
> And she in the midnight wood will pray
> For the weal of her lover that's far away.[13]

[10] *The Fairie Queene*, Bk. VII, Canto viii, in *The Complete Poetical Works of Edmund Spenser* (Boston: Houghton Mifflin Co., 1908), p. 676.

[11] *The Complete Works of William Shakespeare*, ed. by Sidney Lee *et al.*, after the Cambridge Edition of William Aldis Wright ("Renaissance Edition"; Cambridge, Mass.: The University Press, 1907), XXXIII, 33. Italics mine.

[12] *Ibid.*, p. 30. Italics mine.

[13] *The Poetical Works of Samuel Taylor Coleridge*, ed. by James Dykes Campbell (London: Macmillan and Co., 1914), p. 116.

With proper allowance for this latter kind of verse, it is plain
that the verse made from the alternating stress—we call such
verse, with Hopkins, "common" or "running" rhythm [14]—deter-
mines the number of syllables in a line in determining the number of alternating stresses.

The Breakdown of Alternating Stress

With regard to this kind of rhythm, Hopkins' "new rhythm"
is evidently "sprung." This running rhythm limps badly in a
passage like this from stanza 8 of the *Deutschland*:

> Is out with it! Oh,
> We lash with the best or worst
> Word last! How a lush-kept plush-capped sloe
> Will, mouthed to flesh-burst,
> Gush!—flush the man, the being with it, sour or sweet,
> Brim, in a flash, full!

Or again in stanza 13:

> And the sea flint-flake, black-backed in the regular blow.

The reason for the breakdown here of running rhythm, the
rhythm of the alternating stress, derives from the fact that the
general rule that English speech proceed by stresses alternating
with one or two slacks between them cannot always be observed
in English. The place where it most commonly cannot be observed is where the sense demands that two stresses be juxtaposed: *lush-kept,* or *plush-capped,* or *flint-flake.* From the particular effect which arises here in contrast to the demands of
running rhythm, Hopkins designates this other rhythm as
"sprung" (D 23. Feb. 27, 1879).

Often, indeed, even this juxtaposition of stresses yields to the
general tendency of English to proceed by alternating stresses

[14] Author's Preface, *Poems,* p. 1.

and slacks. In the first place, occasionally the juxtaposition of two stresses will be taken care of by a complete break in the rhythmic structure. When there is opportunity for such a break, as, for instance at the end of a phrase or clause or sentence in prose, the juxtaposition of two stresses means nothing: one rhythm is stopped and another started again. Moreover, when there is not an occasion for this kind of pause, we can adjust two juxtaposed stresses to the feeling for alternation of stress and slack in either of two ways: (1) we may add equivalently a slack after the first syllable by pausing slightly between the two syllables or by drawing out the first; or (2) we may, in a certain context, make one accent actually predominate.

An example might be that used by lexicographers: *The room is airtight*. *Airtight* is one of the not uncommon English words which varies its accent precisely for purposes of rhythmic adjustment, "according to the rhythm of the syllables in the context." [15] Careful advertence will show that the feeling for alternating stress easily intrudes in the example just cited, so that either (1) between the beginning of the syllable *air-* and the beginning of the syllable *-tight* there is a prolongation of time which produces at least a felt pause (so that saying *The room is airytight* would not change the timing), or else (2) the word tends to become *airtight'* or *air'tight*.

The meter generally heightens one or the other stress in this second way (*airtight'* or *air'tight*) when running rhythm uses equi-accented words; if such words must really remain equi-accented, running rhythm usually will not use them at all. Hopkins was aware of this and bridled at it, setting down as a virtue of his sprung rhythm its ability to assimilate juxtaposed stresses. In some running rhythm measures, indeed, the two stresses are given full value, as in the third line at the opening of Coleridge's *Christabel* (this third line, like all the other lines, has a total of four stresses):

[15] "A Guide to Pronunciation," *Webster's Collegiate Dictionary* (5th ed.; Springfield, Mass.: G. and C. Merriam Co., 1938), p. ix.

> 'Tis the middle of night by the castle clock
> And the owls have awakened the crowing cock.
> Tu—whit!——tu—whoo!
> And hark, again, the crowing cock,
> How drowsily it crew.[16]

But this is somewhat unusual. Running rhythm, for the most part, is averse to two or more consecutive stresses, and hence Hopkins seizes on the more general affinity of his sprung rhythm for such stresses as a characteristic feature roughly differentiating it from most alternating stress measures. Differences between it and the *Christabel* rhythm have to be worked out in more detailed formulae. But there are differences: Hopkins says only that the *Christabel* meter "might be developed into" sprung rhythm (D 21. Feb. 27, 1879).

Hopkins' juxtaposed sprung rhythm stresses are to be found, for example, in the last two words in this line from stanza 20 of the *Deutschland*:

> Christ's lily and beast of the waste wood,

or in the last three in this line from stanza 11:

> The sour scythe cringe, and the blear share come.

Almost all the instances of his new rhythm that Hopkins first rehearses are cases of these juxtaposed stresses marked by him as such (N 235–236; cf. B 24–25. Aug. 7, 1868):

> Shakespeare—
>   Toád that únder cóld stóne
>   and—
> Sleép thou fírst i' th' chármed pót
>   and—
>   Why should thís désert bé
>   and—

[16] *Loc. cit.* The passage from Coleridge's note to *Christabel* is quoted in D 173. Cf. Hopkins' comment on the poem in D 21. Feb. 27, 1879.

Thoú for whóm Jóve would swéar—;
Campbell—
Ás ye swéep thróugh the déep.

Without arguing over the validity of these instances, we can see plainly here what Hopkins was taking note of. His "new rhythm" he describes later as being based on the principle that only stresses, and not stresses and slacks, are counted. Hence these juxtaposed stresses are not its only manifestations: it may manifest itself as well by merely unequal numbers of slacks between stresses. But the juxtaposed stresses are symptomatic. Ordinarily they are not found in running rhythm as such. From their characteristic abrupt effect—by no means the only effect of sprung rhythm—Hopkins takes the name for his new verse (D 23. Feb. 27, 1879).

Sense Stress

The working of these consecutive sense stresses shows the effect of sense interpretation in overruling on occasion the tendency in English toward an alternating stress. The sense stress is important on an even larger scale in determining another group of sound units in English apart from those made by the alternating stress. Syllables which carry a sense emphasis, particularly if this is very marked, tend to pull surrounding syllables to themselves, forming units with the sense stress as a core; or a sense stress by itself may even constitute a unit of this sort. One resolution into such units—other resolutions are possible, for units will vary somewhat with varying interpretations—might be indicated thus, the virgules marking off the unit formed around each stress:

Foúrscore and seven|yéars ago|our fáthers|brought fórth|on this cóntinent|a néw nation,|concéived in liberty,|and dédicated|to the propositíon|that áll men|are creáted|équal.

Or, in a highly dramatic style (with rather marked pauses at the virgules):

Fóurscore| and séven| yéars| agó| óur| fáthers| bróught| fórth| on thís| cóntinent| a néw| nátion,| concéived| in líberty,| and dédicated to the proposition| that áll| mén| are créated| équal.

This patterning is not entirely independent of the pulsing or alternating stress, for many stresses here would be picked up by the alternating stress, which, as we have seen, utilizes sense stress without being restricted to it. Yet it is apparent that this kind of rhythm is not that of the alternating stress as such: this rhythm does not merely utilize sense stresses; it grows out of them, is constituted by them alone. It arises when the sense is being wrung out of the words. If this rhythm were somehow built up into verse, the basic rhythmic movement of such verse would not be constituted by (at least implied) stresses placed evenly along a line which thereby flows steadily in one direction and is thus styled iambic, or trochaic, and so on. Rather, it would be assembled from units which are heavy stresses alone or heavy stresses with slacks on either or both sides: reversed or "antispastic" effects are *of* this rhythm, not variations on it.

Now, from units of this sort Old English verse is made. And, although we have seen that the fact does not argue Old English as a source, from the same kind of units is built the sprung rhythm of Gerard Manley Hopkins. The following analysis is based on this hypothesis.

The Affinities of Old English and Hopkins

The comparative study of two independent bodies of verse separated by such wide intervals as Old English verse and Hopkins' can be productive of more valuable results than might otherwise be hoped for. It will be seen again and again in the following analysis how apparently accidental features arising spontaneously in both Old English verse and in Hopkins' sprung rhythm appear by this very fact for what they really are—not accidental at all, but integrated parts of an economy which must be seen as a whole before we can know what sort of thing Hopkins discovered.

Affinities Rooted in Interpretive Speech

The resemblance of the two bodies of verse is deepest in the relation of each to dramatic delivery, to the spoken language. The case for Old English has been made by Professor Kemp Malone:

The rhythm of Old English verse grew naturally out of the prose rhythm, by a process of heightening and lowering. . . . The lifts [*hebungen,* stresses] in a line of verse regularly coincided with syllables which would (or might) take stress if the line were read as prose; in like manner, the drops [*senkungen,* slacks] coincided with syllables which would (or might) be without prose stress.[17]

Hopkins' final conclusion that his sprung rhythm was "the rhythm of common speech and of written prose, when rhythm is perceived in them"[18] comes to the same thing. He remarks earlier that his verse "is oratorical, that is the rhythm is so" (B 46. Aug. 21, 1877).

The great regularity of alternating stress which makes running rhythm is not a virtue in prose. The existence of a very marked pattern relatively independent of sense is out of keeping with prose psychology. But prose can operate effectively with pure sense-stress units. These are intimately connected with interpretation: increase in feeling tends to heighten and draw out the stress and countenances hurrying over unimportant syllables so that otherwise disparate units come to be equivalent to one another. In this fashion, if the equivalence of the units is made only a little more marked than it might be in prose, the passage from the *Gettysburg Address* already quoted could slip into a

[17] Kemp Malone, "Life-Patterns in Old English Verse," *English Literary History,* VIII (1941), p. 74.
[18] Author's Preface, *Poems,* p. 5.

kind of Old English verse rhythm. Thus it might be arranged with four stresses to a line:

> fóurscore|and séven|　　yéars|agó|
> óur|fáthers|　　bróught|fórth|
> on thís|cóntinent|　　a néw|nátion|

As verse this is weak-kneed and perhaps somewhat footless, but it makes evident the tendency prose enjoys. The difference between rhythmically patterned prose and verse, as Hopkins observes (N 221), can be only one of degree. This is true to some extent even in the case of running rhythm, when freed from the label of rhyme: there are the passages in Shakespeare which may be intended either for verse or for prose. But in sense-stress patterning the difference between prose and verse is less marked because sense-stress rhythm differs from running rhythm in this important psychological feature: whereas emotion does not naturally re-assort words so that the alternating stress is placed evenly to produce running rhythm, emotion does naturally heighten the irregular sense stresses and in doing so can assert its tendency to rhythm by balancing the weight of the segments of speech of which these sense stresses form nuclei. This is what happens in the passage just cited when read as scanned. The connections here indicated bring out the all-important fact about this rhythm, the fact which fixes its psychological bearings and stabilizes it as emotional currency: heavy stressing, dramatic interpretation, high feeling are the life of the rhythm itself, so much so that the more dramatic the rendition of a passage becomes, the more marked the rhythmic movement is. The converse of this statement is equally true and perhaps more important: the more the heavy stress which constitutes this rhythm is brought out, the more the sense clears and the feeling rises.

Specious Differences and Real

This is a point of great difference between the rhythm of these sense-stress units and running rhythm. In the latter, sense stress often reverses and plays *against* the (running rhythm) pattern, and bringing out the sense makes this rhythm *less* marked, as in the line Hopkins quotes from Milton:

Home tō hǐs móthĕr's house private rĕtúrned.[19]

Even where the sense does not thus reverse the rhythm, bringing out each metric stress heavily does not help the sense but rather makes the rhythm monotonous and distasteful. The reason is plain. These stresses are not all really closely connected with sense or feeling. Thus in Gray's *Elegy,* if the running-rhythm pattern is read like a sense-stress pattern so as to be very marked, it becomes intolerable and makes the sense difficult to follow:

> The Cúrfew tólls the knéll of párting dáy;
> The lówing hérd winds slówly ó'er the leá;

Since their units have one stress each but a varying number of syllables, the lines of Old English verse or of Hopkins' sprung-rhythm verse can be distinguished from those of running rhythm by the fact that they count only stresses, whereas running rhythm, the rhythm of the alternating stress, counts the total number of syllables per line. Hopkins, as has been seen, occasionally points out his sprung rhythm by means of this difference, and it is common to differentiate Old English verse from later English verse on the same basis. But this guide can prove to be vicious as well as serviceable, for it diverts attention from the deep-seated psychological disparities between the two rhythms. Difficulty arises if the supposition is encouraged that the stress which Old English or Hopkins' sprung rhythm counts and the stress which running rhythm counts are the same thing, for they are not. That they are in part alike adds confusion, for the psycho-

---

[19] N 241. I use the marks — and ᵕ to mark the stresses and slacks respectively of the fixed running rhythm pattern (to which the real stresses and slacks do not always correspond) ; the marks ' and ˣ to mark stresses and slacks, respectively, considered as incorporated in sense stress rhythm, including Hopkins' sprung rhythm. Stress marks on Hopkins' verse are his own unless it is otherwise indicated.

logical values of the two patterns are at opposite poles. Moreover, unless the divergent polarity of the two systems is pointed out, many phenomena of the Old English-Hopkins rhythm appear as mere adventitious accretions instead of what they are, parts of an ordered verse management.

The case for Old English is clear. The stress of its verse is always the sense, or interpretive, stress. Thus Jacob Schipper says in *A History of English Versification:*

Each hemistich must have two syllables which predominate over the rest in virtue of their logical and syntactical importance and have on this account a stronger stress.[20]

And Dr. George T. Flom in his *Introductory Old English Grammar and Reader:*

Here in every case [of the examples cited] the accent in the successive measures coincides absolutely with the natural accent. . . . Thus it is seen that the metrical stress always rested upon the important word and the naturally accented syllable. Weak words . . . could not have the rhythmic emphasis.[21]

Hopkins' *obiter dicta* regarding the stress in sprung rhythm show an early awareness that this stress was not that of running rhythm. Not only does he insist that in sprung rhythm stress alone, not stress as alternating, is essential to a foot (D 39. January 14, 1881), but he also notes that the sprung rhythm is "more *of* a stress" than that of running rhythm, "in which less stress is laid" (D 39. Jan. 14, 1881; italics Hopkins' own). But to establish further the identity of Hopkins' sprung rhythm stress with the sense stress here described will require close collation of his many and scattered remarks, with one another and with the operation of stress in his verse and in other verse of a similar nature. To this collation we now turn.

[20] (Oxford: The Clarendon Press, 1910), p. 30.
[21] 2d ed. (Boston: D. C. Heath and Co., 1930), pp. 152–153.

Hopkins' persistent plea for oral, interpretive reading of his poems shows that this "more *of* a stress" was, just as the stress in Old English, the dramatic or interpretive stress. He tells Bridges (B 51–52. May 21, 1878):

You must not slovenly read it [*The Loss of the Eurydice*] with the eyes but with your ears, as if the paper were declaiming it at you. For instance the line "she had come from a cruise training seamen" read without stress and declaim is mere Lloyd's Shipping Intelligence; properly read it is quite a different thing. Stress is the life of it.

We know from a letter to Dixon that Hopkins wanted the line here mentioned to be read, "She had cóme from a crúise tráining séamen" (D 40. Jan. 14, 1881). This is plainly the way the sense of the verse would demand. The other rhythm which Hopkins evidently wanted to avoid is suggested not by the sense but by an alternating stress pattern induced by the first half of the line (ᴗᴗ — ᴗᴗ —),which would make the whole line read, "shĕ hăd cōme frŏm ă crūise trăining sēamĕn." Only the sense stress pattern fits into Hopkins' stanza, which requires a four-stress line where this one occurs.

Hopkins, indeed, wanted more than "rhetorical" reading for the higher tension of poetical rendition. The sense emphasis is a more intense thing here than in oratory, for the pitch of feeling to which his poetry rises makes its performance demand "not reading with the eye but loud, leisurely, poetical (not rhetorical) recitation, with long rests, long dwells on the rhyme and other marked syllables, and so on. This sonnet [presumably *Spelt from Sibyl's Leaves*] shd. be almost sung: it is most carefully timed in *tempo rubato*" (B 246. Dec. 11, 1886).

An interesting gloss on these quotations which, by linking his verse with oral delivery, confirm the primacy in it of sense emphasis, is Hopkins' own half-shamefaced admission to Patmore that he made his verse orally and only wrote it down "with repugnance" (F 231. May 12, 1887).

There is evident throughout Hopkins' writings a marked sensitivity to the difference between kinds of stress which indicates his ability to feel sense stress as different from other kinds and thus as a stress which can be used apart from others to construct a rhythmic pattern. The "lightsome French or Chaucerian rhythm," he writes, is used by Dixon; but, he adds thoughtfully, "Chaucer properly read is heavier stressed than we think" (D 78. Oct. 23, 1881). His description of "To What Serves Mortal Beauty" as "common rhythm highly stressed" [22] points both to the same sensitivity to differences in kinds of stresses and to a realization that common rhythm ordinarily is not stressed highly. Moreover, keeping in mind his earlier remark that sprung rhythm uses "more *of* a stress," we read with interest his statements to Bridges that sprung rhythm "lends itself to expressing passion" (B 92. Oct. 8, 1879) and that in the *St. Winefred's Well* fragments, "as the feeling rises the rhythm becomes freer and more sprung" (B 212. April 1, 1885). Set against the earlier remark, this means that as the dramatic emphases assert themselves under the influence of feeling, the rhythm becomes more of a sprung rhythm. The dramatic stress makes the sprung rhythm pattern.

There is, moreover, no difficulty in seeing how a sensitivity to the value of the heavy or dramatic stress is at one with Hopkins' whole attitude toward poetry. For him a poem was not to be grafted on language, but grown from it. Rhythm, if it is a mode of conveying feeling, gains by being drawn out of the interpretive stress, for this stress naturally mounts with the feeling. This line of thought accords with Hopkins' remark to Bridges (B 89. Aug. 14, 1879) that

the poetical language of an age shd. be the current language heightened, to any degree heightened and unlike itself, but not (I mean normally: passing freaks and graces are another thing) an obsolete one. This is Shakespeare's and Milton's practice and the want of

[22] Notes in *Poems*, p. 113.

it will be fatal to Tennyson's idylls and plays, and to Swinburne, and perhaps to Morris.

Hopkins tells Bridges in the same place that he avoids inversions

because they weaken and because they destroy the earnestness or in-earnestness of the utterance. Nevertheless in prose I use them more than other people, because there they have great advantages of another sort. Now these advantages they should have in verse too, but they must not seem to be due to the verse: that is what is so enfeebling (for instance the finest of your sonnets to my mind has a line enfeebled by inversion plainly due to the verse, as I said once before ' 'Tis joy the falling of her fold to view'— . . .). . . . So also I cut myself off from the use of *ere, o'er, wellnigh, what time, say not* (for *do not say*), because, though dignified, they neither belong to nor ever cd. arise from, or be the elevation of, ordinary modern speech.

It might be noted that Hopkins' "what while we, while we slumbered" in *The Leaden Echo and the Golden Echo* arises not from any Spenserian archaizing but from dramatic disturbance.

With an extraordinary consistency, Hopkins' musical sensibilities reflect the same bent as his poetic. He is an admirer of the Church's plain chant, which is eminently the elevation of speech (B 214. Apr. 1, 1885). (It is, indeed, interesting to speculate what the effect would have been on him had the Solesmes Benedictines' work of restoring the original chant been completed before his death so that the real rhythm of the chant would have been available to him in its fullness.)

It does not come as a surprise that the mind in evidence here would hit upon a rhythm built from the interpretive, sense stresses which are a normal mode of conveying feeling in English and which tend themselves to become more prominent as the feeling rises. "Why do I employ sprung rhythm at all?" Hopkins asks (B 46. Aug. 21, 1877), apparently echoing a query of Bridges'.

Because it is the nearest to the rhythm of prose, that is the native and natural rhythm of speech, the least forced, the most rhetorical and emphatic of all possible rhythms, combining, as it seems to me, opposite and, one wd. have thought, incompatible excellences, markedness of rhythm—that is rhythm's self—and naturalness of expression—for why, if it is forcible in prose to say 'lashed:rod', am I obliged to weaken this in verse, which ought to be stronger, not weaker, into 'láshed birch-ród' or something?

My verse is less to be read than heard, as I have told you before; it is oratorical, that is the rhythm is so. I think if you will study what I have here said you will be much more pleased with it and may I say? converted to it.

Similarly, he writes to Dixon later that he believed his rhythm was based on "a better and more natural principle than the ordinary system, much more flexible, and capable of much greater effects" (D 14–15. Oct. 6, 1878). His claim that his poetry had a popular style, which claim amused Patmore (F 207. Patmore to Hopkins, Apr. 5, 1884), derived largely from this same conviction that its rhythms grew naturally out of normal emotional language.

In the light of these texts, it is unmistakable that Hopkins consistently views his rhythm as a rhythm derived not from any stresses, but from high stresses important to sense, from the strong stresses which arise in the normal rhythms of emotional prose. This picture coincides with the picture we have of the rhythm of Old English poetry. Further examination of the practice of Hopkins and the Old English poets confirms this conclusion, showing, as we shall see, that the rhythms are identified with one another in a surprisingly intimate fashion.

Juncture of Sense-Stress Units

Whether we take a prose passage such as that from the *Gettysburg Address* already used, or a passage of Old English poetry, or one of Hopkins' sprung rhythm poems, it is noteworthy that there is a great variation in the ways in which the sense units of the sort indicated articulate with one another. Although sense-stress verse seems to demand that the time intervals between stresses, generally speaking, be felt as being somewhat equal, the spacing of the slacks within these time intervals between the stresses will follow various arrangements, depending on the varying amount of time required for the pronunciation of different syllables, natural pauses or rests in or between certain words or syllables, various ways of counterbalancing minor accents, and so on. Thus all sorts of rhythmic complications and syncopations can arise, like those of a very complicated and varied dance figure.

For instance, longer units are enunciated relatively faster, and monosyllabic units are drawn out and perhaps receive compensating emphases, as in the arrangement of the *Gettysburg Address* passage, which may stand as a prose counterpart of Hopkins' poetry —

> Fóurscore| and séven| yéars| agó|
> óur|fáthers| bróught|fórth|

— or as in Hopkins' *Spelt from Sibyl's Leaves* (with scansion developed from Hopkins' own incomplete marks):

> With:| Óur| évening|is óver ús;|óur níght| whélms,|whélms,|ánd|will énd ŭs.
> . . . . Héart,| yŏu róund mĕ| ríght

(I indicate here one possible resolution into sense-stress units, although, in view of the close interlocking of the units in actual rendition, the virgules dividing them off from one another are elsewhere in this paper usually omitted.) Moreover, the various internal movements of these sense units—rising, falling, rocking —are not leveled off into a simple one-two or one-two-three pattern, but all the natural variety of spoken utterance as such is incorporated into the verse movement.

The intricate ballet is perhaps the best analogy. We could take as representing the sense-stress units small groups of individual steps ranging, let us say, from one to four (or more) steps each. The individual steps (in verse the stress and slacks) in these groups would be some longer, some shorter, and would represent in timing quarter, eighth, and sixteenth notes, for example; these would be arranged in various groupings, perhaps with some pauses included, and with a kind of ictus or principal step (corresponding to the stress) placed within each group, but not necessarily always in the same position with regard to the other steps (slacks) in the group. These groups of steps, then, to form a complete ballet, would be woven together so as to engage with a rhythmic background. The principle would be, in general, to keep the ictuses (stresses) at rather equal distances, except when some special syncopation is desired, and to work the slacks in as they naturally fit best by making minute adjustments. Similarly, in verse the sense-stress units would be woven together across a rhythmic background, which would vary from poem to poem, being perhaps now a kind of 4/4 time, now 6/8, or again something like the free rhythm of plain chant (as, for instance, the opening line of *The Leaden Echo and the Golden Echo*).

Normal pronunciation, which does not permit the complete equalization suggested by regular stress and slack alternation, does allow minor adjustments in accentuation and timing depending on the rhythmic context of the sense-stress units. This is plain in prose, where at one time a phrase will be pronounced one way and at another time another, the timing within a phrase being always somewhat *ad libitum*. When sense-stress units are woven into a rhythmic setting, these minor adjustments will be made according to the rhythmic background, but because they are adjustments of the usual sort, they will not destroy naturalness of utterance.

Here, of course, a given number of slacks between two stresses will not necessarily demand always the same pattern. Everything will depend on the timing which pronunciation demands. There will be hovering on some syllables and complete rests here and there, such as normal enunciation sprinkles with great freedom all about our speech, as well as special adjustments in timing and accentuation which high feeling may demand. Some slacks will themselves receive various minor accents. (Professor Malone has commented on varying weights of stresses in Old English verse.[23])

Thus, for instance, in the *Spelt from Sibyl's Leaves* passage just scanned, the second syllable of *evening* would be a kind of grace note, as also might be the *is,* which yields to its common tendency to suppress its vowel. But the other slacks have more time and weight. Poems like *The Windhover* and the *Deutschland* are full of examples of elaborate rhythmic variations of the sort described: the syllables might be represented variously as something like quarter notes, eighth notes, sixteenths, grace notes, and there will be a variety of rests to correspond.

All this makes the organization of a line in this kind of rhythm a matter for delicate workmanship, as Hopkins was well aware. There must be accommodation to a marked rhythm without loss of the natural timing and stressing which words can demand. Indeed, the natural movements must be built up instead of de-emphasized. Speaking of the sprung rhythm pattern superimposed on certain other verse patterns, Hopkins observes that the beats of the sprung rhythm are "so subtly hung and distributed and balanced that scarcely any two are alike." [24] This is indicative of his recognition of the rhythmic complication of which we have been speaking, as is also his remark, already cited, that a sonnet, *Spelt from Sibyl's Leaves* most probably, "is most carefully timed in *tempo rubato*" (B 246. Dec. 11, 1886). "Robbed time," with its reference to the lengthening of some notes at the expense of others, is an excellent label for the variegated and often syncopated effects resulting from the combination of pro-

[23] Malone, *op. cit.*, pp. 74–80.
[24] N 236. For the superimposing of one rhythm on another, see the discussion of counterpoint below, pp. 148 ff.

tracted sounds with shorter ones in the unlike groupings of sense-stress units.

Of course, this kind of rhythmic complication, which can arise by virtue of the variable sense-stress units we have been considering, is foreign to the simple throbbing of pure running rhythm. It demands sensitivities other than those demanded by running rhythm, a sense of complex timing. This, too, Hopkins was aware of. Because of Bridges' lack of this sense, Hopkins complains to him (B 81–82. May 26, 1879): "Since the syllables in sprung rhythm are not counted, time or equality in strength is of more importance than in common counted rhythm, and your times or strengths do not seem to me equal enough."

In a letter to Dixon, Hopkins shows his feeling for his sprung verse as a product assembled out of units consisting of stresses with their adhering slacks. In this letter (D 22. Feb. 27, 1879), he speaks of "an easily felt principle of *equal strengths,*" which

supposes not only that, speaking in the abstract, any accent is equal to any other (by accent I mean *the* accent of a word) but further that each accent may be considered to be accompanied by an equal quantity of slack or unaccented utterance, one, two, or more such unaccented syllables; so that wherever there is an accent or stress, there there is also so much unaccentuation, so to speak, or slack, and this will give a foot or rhythmic unit, viz. a stress with its belonging slack. But now if this is so, since there are plenty of accented monosyllables, and those too immediately preceded and followed by the accents of other words, it will come about that a foot may consist of one syllable only and that one syllable has not only the stress of its accent but also the slack which another wd. throw on one or more additional syllables, though here that may perhaps be latent, as though the slack syllables had been absorbed. What I mean is clearest in an antithesis or parallelism, for there the contrast gives the counterparts equal stress; e.g. 'sanguinary consequences, terrible butchery, frightful slaughter, fell swoop': if these are taken as alternative expressions, then the total strength of *sanguinary* is no more than that of *terrible* or of *frightful* or of *fell* and so on of the substantives too.

In stating here, "by accent I mean *the* accent of a word," Hopkins shows clearly that he is not concerned with the alternating stress, which may in some words occur three or four times.

His marking of strong stresses, pauses, quivers or circumflexions (one syllable read as two), syllables to be huddled together, and so on,[25] are all attempts on Hopkins' part to indicate by a notation not a strange manner of reading, but how the rhythmic adjustment actually works out in a heightened, feeling enunciation. The presence of such marks provides further evidence of the workings of the sense-stress economy we have been describing.

A similar organization seems to be quite evident throughout Old English measures, where the articulation of units in which the stress always followed the sense resulted in a verse which Professor Malone calls "an instrument subtle and sophisticated enough," by reason of the fact that "systematic alternation of lift and drop was avoided, presumably because of the mechanical, monotonous rhythm which such an alternation all too often produces." [26]

The question of the juncture of the sense-stress units with one another to form a complex whole goes to the very heart of sense-stress rhythm. We are here in the realm of rhythmic complication such as the simple throb of running rhythm does not know. But the detailed theorems according to which the articulation of the sense units with one another is carried out, although of capital importance for the complete understanding of sprung rhythm, would be too intricate to be worked out in the broad outline being sketched in this present study. It has seemed worth while to sketch the broad outline first, confining attention to the presence of the sense units themselves rather than looking to the more minute details of their organization. (But see the note on pp. 145–47 below.)

[25] See, for example, the facsimile of the *Harry Ploughman* autograph, B opposite p. 262; cf. Bridges' remarks in *Poems*, p. 95.
[26] Malone, *op. cit.*, p. 80.

Hovering Accents

However, within the sense-stress units themselves, a special manifestation of rhythmic complication in Hopkins merits some special attention. This is the effect achieved—again the closest analogy is perhaps dance movement—when two successive stresses are used almost as one prolonged stress. Often managed with the aid of a simple device, repetition of the vowel sound of the first stressed syllable in the second so as to minimize the syllabic break (*beak-leaved* or *tool-smooth* below), this quasi-prolongation is rather distinctive of sprung rhythm, which here proceeds with successive stresses, not after the manner of running rhythm by reducing one equivalently to a slack, liquidating it within the fixed pattern, but by balancing the two against one another so as to make of them a kind of one. The verse can often be read with two juxtaposed accents almost equal so as to constitute a single hovering stress. Thus *beak-leaved* or *tool-smooth* or *bleak light* in *Spelt from Sibyl's Leaves* (the stress marks are mine):

Ónly the béak-lèaved bóughs drágonish⏋   dámask the
     tóol-smòoth bléak lìght; bláck,
Ever so black on it.

The reader of Hopkins will recognize this effect as very common. It is also perhaps a feature of Old English, as in the examples scanned by Schipper as *Béowùlf* or *hríng-nèt*.[27] So in *The Seafarer:*

síþas sécgan   hú ic geswíncdàgum.[28]

The use of such a hovering accent by Walt Whitman has been noted by Dr. Sculley Bradley.[29] It is significant that Hopkins con-

[27] Schipper, *op. cit.,* p. 28.

[28] 2, in *The Exeter Book,* ed. by George Philip Krapp and Elliot van Kirk Dobbie ("Anglo-Saxon Poetic Records," III; New York: Columbia University Press, 1936), p. 143.

[29] "The Fundamental Metrical Principle in Whitman's Poetry," *American Literature,* X (1938–1939), pp. 437–439.

sidered Whitman's verse "an irregular rhythmic prose" at times quite near highly wrought sprung rhythm (B 155, 157. Oct. 18, 1882).

Reversal of Movement

It is in keeping with the principle of equal strengths that the units in a line of sense-stress verse need not all proceed in the same direction. Some may have the stress at their beginning, some at their end, some toward their center—all this without constituting exceptions to the movement, since this incorporates the units not as moving in any particular direction with alternation of stress and slack, but simply as more or less equal weights, each with a stress as the core. The operation of this law has been seen in the scanned *Gettysburg Address* passage. The operation of the same law in Old English leads Schipper to classify Old English half-lines into ascending, descending, and ascending-descending,[30] and leads Professor Malone to note how the drops (*senkungen,* slacks) serve both to lead up to and to lead away from the lifts (*hebungen,* stresses).[31] The same law is seen in operation in the passage just scanned from *Spelt from Sibyl's Leaves,* and can be observed throughout Hopkins' sprung rhythm verse. And Hopkins' own explicit statement of the law's exerting its force in his sprung rhythm presents the clearest possible evidence that he conceived this rhythm in terms of what we have described as sense-stress verse. Hopkins' practice of scanning with the stress always first in the "foot" was a mere convenience, and Hopkins recognized it as such,[32] as he had also recognized his earlier practice of scanning with the stress last to be a mere convenience (D 40. Jan. 14, 1881):

though it is the virtue of sprung rhythm that it allows of "dochmiac" or "antispastic" effects or cadences, when the verse suddenly changes from a rising to a falling movement, and this too is strongly felt by

[30] Schipper, *op. cit.,* p. 35.
[31] Malone, *op. cit.,* p. 80.
[32] Author's Preface, *Poems,* pp. 1–2, 3–4.

the ear, yet no account of it is taken in scanning and no irregularity caused, but the scansion always treated, conventionally and for simplicity, as rising. . . . Bridges in the preface to his last issue says something to the effect that all sorts of feet may follow one another, an anapaest a dactyl for instance . . . : so they may, if we look at the real nature of the verse; but for simplicity it is much better to recognize, in scanning this new rhythm, only one movement, either the rising (which I choose as being commonest in English verse) or the falling (which is perhaps better in itself), and always keep to that.

Of course, the sense stress need not be always irregularly placed among the syllables. It may for special effects alternate with slacks quite regularly, as in the line from *Spring and Fall* which scans (my marks):

By ănd bý, nŏr spáre ă sígh.

Predilection for Antithesis

From the complexity of rhythmic structure within each unit, it might be expected that the organization of sense-stress verse on the stanzaic level would remain relatively simple. In Old English it does. The patterns used here were regularly confined to antithetical or antiphonal arrangements of half-lines with two stresses in each, occasionally shrunk to one or extended to more than two stresses (Professor Malone notes many lines with three, five, six, or even seven). And among the many points of agreement of Hopkins' verse with Old English, none is more remarkable than the uncanny tendency to fall into similar half-line patterns.

Developing an intricacy of organization set deep within the economy of the language—the kind of "intricacy" found in villanelles and rondels only disgusted him, and "I wish we were rid of them," he writes Bridges (B 277. May 25, 1888)—Hopkins' sprung rhythm veers decidedly toward the Old English antiphonal movement. His discussion of parallelisms already noted [33] has an obvious relation to this movement. Moreover, he deliberately favors alexandrines in sonnets,[34] and his treatment of them there is telling. *To what serves Mortal Beauty* has the half-line breaks *marked* with a virgule. This shows Hopkins' tendency to use alexandrines for the precise reason that they break in the middle, and not in such a way as to conceal their tendency to do so, a tendency which indeed has bothered most poets. Similarly, the *Moonrise* fragment (No. 65) has its lines divided, as does *That Nature Is a Heraclitean Fire. Spelt from Sibyl's Leaves,* too, is divided into four-stress half-lines, which Hopkins would consider as alexandrines, since he held that in these latter "each half line is by nature a dimeter; two bars or four feet, of which commonly one foot is silent or lost at the pause" (B 212. Apr. 1, 1885). Indeed, Hopkins' feeling for dimeters in alexandrines makes his alexandrine verse movement correspond more closely than ever to Old English, for it introduces an antiphonal movement into each half-line and eliminates from his alexandrines the three-beat unit which would be unusual in Old English as a fixed pattern.

In accord with the general principle that the complexity of rhythmic structure within each unit of sense-stress verse calls for simplicity of stanzaic structure, we should expect something to happen if a complicated stanza form were attempted. So it does. Hopkins' most ambitious stanza form is the sonnet, and here it is that the dissolution into simpler half-line antithesis takes place.

Hopkins himself supplies the obvious explanation of the impulse of sense-stress rhythm to develop antithetical movement when he explains to Dixon in the passage already cited above that the correspondence of units in this rhythm "is clearest in an antithesis or parallelism." [35] (His remarks on the four-beat line in common use in English, despite the promise of the sub-

[33] See p. 124 above.
[34] B pp. 157 (Oct. 18, 1882); 203 (Jan. 1, 1885); cf. 212 (Apr. 1, 1885); 80 (Apr. 22, 1879); 92 (Oct. 8, 1879).
[35] D 22 (Feb. 27, 1879); see p. 124 above.

ject itself, yield little or nothing of value here—B 119-20. Jan. 26, 1881.)

Operation of the grammatical parallelisms to which Hopkins here refers is evident throughout Old English poetry. It can be seen for instance, in the last verses of *The Wanderer,* in the *Riddles* (for example, "The Nightingale"), or at the opening of *The Seafarer:*

earfoðhwile	oft þrowade
bitre breostceare	gebiden hæbbe,
gecunnad in ceole	cearselda fela,
. . . . . .	. . . . . .
dyde ic me to gomene,	ganetes hleoþor
ond huilpan sweg	fore hleator wera,
mæw singende	fore medodrince.[36]

Stretched Lines

Even the rhythmical variations which Hopkins calls "hangers" or "outrides" establish another *rapport* with Old English verse. Just as Old English admitted occasional "long lines"—lines with more than four stresses—so Hopkins occasionally stretches his lines with his "hangers" or "outrides," which he describes as "one, two, or three slack syllables added to a foot and not counting in the nominal scanning," so called "because they seem to hang below the line or ride forward or backward from it in another dimension than the line itself." [37] At first Hopkins thought these could be used only in counterpointed rhythm (a mixture of common rhythm and sprung—B 45. Aug. 21, 1877), but he soon describes them as "natural to Sprung Rhythm." [38] The correspondence of hangers or outrides and the Old English long lines can, I think, be pushed closely only at the cost of great subtleties, but it is plain that both Hopkins and the Old English

[36] 3-5, 20-22, *The Exeter Book,* pp. 143-144.
[37] Author's Preface, *Poems,* pp. 4-5; cf. p. 107. For explanation of counterpoint, see below, pp. 148-150.
[38] Author's Preface [written 1883], *Poems,* p. 4.

poets had here in common at least the practice of varying rhythm by lengthening verses.

Hopkins' lengthening also includes what he calls "burden lines." Thus in *Harry Ploughman:*

> . . . . Back, elbow, and liquid waist
> In him, all quail to the wallowing o' the plough;
> 's cheek crimsons; curls
> Wag or crossbridle, in a wind lifted, windlaced—
> See his wind— lilylocks —laced;

The last line here is a "burden line," and indeed it appears from his marks in the manuscript reproduced in facsimile in the volume of letters to Bridges (B opposite p. 262), that Hopkins perhaps even intended it as an outride, in which case outrides and burden lines would come to merge into one another, as they do at least in part in being both expansions or extensions for rhythmic effect.

The extreme of psychological effectiveness in the use of line lengthening is found in *The Leaden Echo and the Golden Echo,* where the nervous protraction of the opening line dramatizes the drive of high emotion which will not be brooked:

> How to kéep—is there ány any, is there none such, nowhere
> known some, bow or brooch or braid or brace, láce,
> latch or catch or key to keep
> Back beauty, keep it, beauty, beauty, beauty, . . . from vanishing
> away?

Hopkins nowhere does intelligible and intense feeling a greater service than when he defends here the choice and position of "Back" (*Poems,* p. 113).

Thunder, Echoes, and Chimes

The economy of the rhythm we have been describing is hardly reducible to rules of thumb. However, since the reason for this is not that the rhythm is amorphous, but that it is alive and flexible with the life of high perception and feeling—"stress is the life of it," and this stress is the stress of dramatic interpretation—we can at least observe that the economy of the rhythm demands the heightening of stress. Regarded in perspective with this fact, the alliteration and assonance, the partial rhymes and other echoes, the consonantal clangor—all the heavy arms with which Old English verse equipped itself and which are likewise present up and down Hopkins—these become understandable. The recurrence of these devices with the revival of Old English rhythms by Hopkins hints that the devices are not adventitious ornament in sense-stress verse. As a matter of fact, they are invaluable helps to the poet in bringing out what dramatic interpretation he wants (for dramatic interpretation, on which stress depends, is always somewhat *ad libitum*), and in enabling him to build up the intensity of the stresses so that the pattern may be evident despite the variable and often large number of slacks between stresses.

The working of these sounding devices is observable in any Old English poetry. *The Seafarer* opens:

> Mæg ic be me sylfum soðgied wrecan,
> siþas secgan, hu ic geswincdagum
> earfoðhwile oft þrowade
> bitre breostceare gebiden hæbbe,
> gecunnad in ceole cearselda fela,
> atol yþa gewealc. . . . .[39]

In the second half of the second line here, alliteration both cues in and builds up the stress on -*swinc*-. The heavy consonantal load -*ft þr*- in the short half-line "oft þrowade" works to the same end: the echoes of the sounds amplify one another in the hearer's ear. In brief, the more we allow the necessary mechanics of the language to operate here, the more the sense is clarified, the more the feeling mounts, the more marked the rhythmic movement becomes. Rhythm and interpretation interlock, and

[39] 1–6, *The Exeter Book*, p. 143.

monotony is no danger because of the free-jointed movement of
the verse loosed from syllabic count.

Similar analyses can be repeated throughout Hopkins. We
find in *Harry Ploughman:*

> Breathed round; the rack of ribs; the scooped flank; lank
> Rope-over thigh . . . .

This can be compared with a line such as this from the Old
English *Genesis,*

> Abrægd ða mid ðy bille,   brynegield obhread,[40]

and there is found similar alliteration, assonance, internal rhyme,
all working to the same end of leading in with great force the
sense-stressed syllables.

This force, in Hopkins as in Old English, is cumulative. By
the use of alliteration, partial rhyme, assonance, and consonantal
bunching not only on the syllables with the sense emphasis but
throughout the verse as well, the emphases of the sense stresses
require a proportionately greater heightening so that often very
heavy verse emerges, as in *Harry Ploughman:*

> In him, all quail to the wallowing o' the plough;
> 's cheek crimsons; curls
> Wag or crossbridle . . . .

The heavy consonantal load *'s ch—*, made heavier than usual
by the elision, in combination with the long *ee* of *cheek* forces
a very heavy stress onto the first syllable of *crimsons* because the
sense demands that this latter word receive more emphasis than
cheek.[41] So, for example, in the Old English *Phoenix:*

Swa se gesælige [42]

---

[40] *Genesis* 2932, in *The Junius Manuscript,* ed. by George Philip Krapp
("Anglo-Saxon Poetic Records," I; New York: Columbia University Press,
1931), p. 86.

[41] See facsimile of autograph, B opposite p. 262.

[42] *Phoenix,* 350a, in *The Old English Elene, Phoenix, and Physiologus,* ed.
by Albert Stanburrough Cook (New Haven: Yale University Press, 1919),
p. 62.

the *se* receives some additional prominence because of an alliteration with the preceding *swa,* but the second and third syllables of *gesælige* must override the effect of this alliteration and hence demand relatively stronger stresses.

Hopkins has drawn a red herring across his own trail—not without effect—in his remark to Dixon that the *Deutschland* uses "certain chimes suggested by the Welsh poetry" he had been reading (D 15. Oct. 6, 1878). If this is taken to mean that the rich texture of sound in Hopkins is a conscious importation which is not a growth integral to the management of the English verse he is writing, it is entirely misleading. For it is within his verse itself that the elaborate network of Hopkins' sound effects gathers its strength and has its meaning. Hopkins himself writes to Bridges that he got the chimes only "in part from the Welsh" (B 38. Apr. 3, 1877), and his mention of them to Dixon occurs while he is explaining how *natural* his new system is. The Welsh influence undoubtedly helps account for the relatively richer chiming of Hopkins' verse as against Old English, but beyond this it does not go.

The integrating value of assonance, alliteration, and the other sound equivalences comes home when one reads *London Snow* or the other poems done by Bridges in Hopkins' "new rhythm" as Bridges conceived it. Examination of these poems shows how much the neglect of Hopkins' rich overlaying of echo on echo results in the loss not of a grace but of the rhythm's self.[43]

A more surprising, because an apparently less essential yet exact point of resemblance to Old English, is to be found in Hopkins' theory that all vowels alliterate with one another. The agreement with Old English here is underlined by Hopkins' firmness in holding to his theory—he argued it out with Patmore—and his explicit statement concerning its origin (F 183–184. Nov. 7, 1883):

---

[43] See Hopkins' criticism of Bridges' sprung rhythm, B 71 (Feb. 22, 1879); 81–82 (May 26, 1879); 111 (Oct. 26, 1880); 122–123 (Feb. 5, 1881); F 187, to Patmore (Nov. 14, 1883).

I should like you to reconsider the matter of alliteration in vowels. To my ear no alliteration is more marked or more beautiful, and I used to take it for granted as an obvious fact that every initial vowel lettered to every other before ever I knew that anything of the sort was practiced in Anglo Saxon verse. I cannot agree that this alliteration is destroyed by using the same vowel. . . . How this alliteration arises is, I know, very hard to say, but to my ear there is no doubt about the fact.

Schipper follows Sievers in explaining the alliteration of unlike vowels in Old English by supposing a glottal catch missing in Modern English, in which language, we are told "the harmony or consonance of the unlike vowels is hardly perceptible . . . and does not count as alliteration." [44] This theory rests on the supposition that perception of "harmony or consonance of unlike vowels" is carried on independently of any particular artistic economy. But we are used to alliteration in a standard type of context where it is a grace. Do we know how to look for alliteration which is more integral to verse? What would it sound like if we heard it? In Hopkins' case an ear attuned to modern verse *organized like Old English* is taken by the same resemblance in the current language which caught the ear of the Old English poet.

Development, But No Shift in Direction

Correspondences between Hopkins' rhythms and Old English are remarkable enough so far, but they do not stop with the pointing of similarities, however remarkable these may be, for even the characteristic features of Hopkins' verse which are not found in Old English are, for the most part, explainable on the same grounds as the similarities themselves and operate in accord with them. This is to say, the same principle which we have been invoking to explain the characteristics of Old English and of Hopkins' rhythms—the fact that both develop from interpre-

[44] Schipper, *op. cit.*, p. 14.

tive or sense stresses in the language—serves also to explain a great many of Hopkins' individual "peculiarities."

Hopkins' Rhymes

With the odd petulancy which always pinches the genuine appreciation he has for Hopkins, Bridges objects to the latter's rhymes. Now rhymes Old English verse had not used to any extent. Rhyme came into English when the Old English sense-stress verse was being displaced by running rhythm. Hence Hopkins, in introducing rhyme into sense-stress verse, was transplanting it from the special culture in which it had grown to a new. The notion that this fact might to some extent change the appearance and function of rhyme Bridges seems never to have entertained. He might have been helped to the notion by Hopkins' desire that his sprung rhythm poems be in most cases not broken at the end of lines, where the formal rhyming occurs, to the extent usual with poems in running rhythm,[45] as well as by the whole movement of Hopkins' sprung rhythm verse. But Bridges—though we must not forget to remember him gratefully for his gift of Hopkins' poems nor fail to appreciate his genuine affection for their author—seems indeed never to have known Hopkins' verse in full movement. His persistent stumbling over "exaggerated Marianism" or over "some perversion of human feeling, as, for instance the nostril's relish of incense 'along the sanctuary side'" (Bridges had his mind made up that emotion was forced if it ran in "theological or sectarian channels"), or his frequent detours around "unpoetic lines" and excursions after peccadillos for argument[46]—all this must have so mingled with annoyance his progress through any one of Hopkins' poems that his powers of perception were seriously dissipated.

Had Bridges' perception been freer to operate, he might have observed that what happens in the rhyming of words at the end

[45] See B 86 (Aug. 14, 1879); cf. D 40 (Jan. 14, 1881), and Author's Preface, *Poems*, p. 4.
[46] See Bridges' notes in *Poems*, pp. 96–100.

of lines in Hopkins' verse is, on the whole, not particularly remarkable within the great skeleton of internal rhyme, assonance,
alliteration, and other sound echoings bracing the entire verse
structure. Thus in a typical passage from *Spelt from Sibyl's
Leaves,* the end rhymes are only fuller developments continuous
with effects built everywhere into the verse:

Only the beak-leaved boughs dragonish| damask the tool-smooth
  bleak light; black,
Ever so black on it. Óur tale, O óur oracle!| Lét life, wáned,
  ah lét life wind
Off hér once skéined stained véined varíety| upon, áll on twó
  spools; párt, pen, páck
Now her áll in twó flocks, twó folds—black, white;| right, wrong:
  reckon but, reck but, mind
But thése two; wáre of a wórld where bút these| twó tell, each
  off the óther; of a rack
Where, selfwrung, selfstrung, sheathe– and shelterless,| thóughts
  agaínst thoughts ín groans grínd.

Moreover, sprung rhythm lines vary so much in syllabic length
that it is most often impossible to anticipate the exact place of a
rhyme's occurrence: the rhyme loses inevitability, as, for instance,
in the first four lines of *The Windhover:*

> I caught this morning morning's minion, king-
>   dom of daylight's dauphin, dapple-dawn-drawn Fal-
>   con, in his riding
>   Of the rolling level underneath him steady air, and
>   striding
> High there, how he rung upon the rein of a wimpling wing.

This all means that the perfect chiming of endings is not so
much demanded, for endings are not felt as belonging so closely
to one another.

In the light of this principle the consistency becomes apparent
in Hopkins' frequent demand that sprung rhythm poems be
read through with less break at the line endings than is the case

with running rhythm poems: "the scanning runs on without break from the beginning, say, of a stanza to the end and all the stanza is one long strain, though written in lines asunder." [47] The same principle explains the fact that (*ibid.*)

it is natural in Sprung Rhythm for the lines to be *rove over,* that is for the scanning of each line immediately to take up that of the one before, so that if the first has one or more syllables at its end the other must have so many the less at its beginning.

This means that Hopkins' nominal scansion with stress first is preserved by considering slacks at the beginning of a line as going with the last stress of the preceding line and not being extra-metrical.

The special applications of this principle to certain relatively swift four-beat measures (such as *Spring and Fall*) are too detailed for attention here. [48]

The nature of the sprung rhythm stress, which is "more *of* a stress," and the whole economy of a verse which it dominates again provide the explanation and justification for rhymes such as *eternal* and *burn all,* or *and some* and *handsome* which nettle Bridges. [49] The same is true of rhymes which break words, such as *king-* (*king-dom*) and *wing* in the opening lines just quoted from *The Windhover,* and *overbend us* and *an end, as-* (*an end, as-tray*) in *Spelt from Sibyl's Leaves:*

> Her fond yellow hornlight wound to the west,⎪ her wild
> 　　hollow hoarlight hung to the height
> Waste; her earliest stars, earl-stars,⎪ stárs principal over-
> 　bend us,
> Fíre-féaturing heaven.　For earth⎪ her being has unbound,
> 　　her dapple is at an end, as-
> tray or aswarm, all throughther, in throngs;⎪ self ín
> 　　self steepèd and páshed—quíte
> Disremembering, dísmémbering⎪ áll now.　.　.　.　.　.　.

---

[47] *Poems*, p. 4.
[48] B 120 (Jan. 26, 1881); see note at end of Part II (p. 145).
[49] *Poems*, p. 99.

Hopkins' practices here are understandable when viewed in their relationship to all the parts of the closely geared machinery: line endings are less marked, exact rhyming has therefore less purpose, and the force of the stresses in a context already ringing with verbal echoes brings out resemblances which would be lost elsewhere. It is worth noting in this connection that Dr. Henry Lanz's recent studies have shown how imperfect forms of rhyme work better where accent is heavy.[50] Russian, for instance, which shows on Dr. Lanz's oscillograph records as a language of relatively intense explosive sounds, uses assonance where other languages use rhyme. Plainly, there is a parallel here with the English verse which takes a markedly heavy stress. In keeping with such a fact, we find Hopkins, who despised eye-rhymes but not imperfect rhyme and assonance (N 244–248), insisting on the interpretive reading of his verse as the test for his rhyming. The kind of reading which sprung rhythm demands makes his rhymes work. "My rhymes," he writes to Bridges, "are rigidly good—to the ear" (B 44. Aug. 21, 1877). And, discussing the matter later, he adds (B 180. May 11, 1883):

Some others again there are which *malignity may munch at* but the Muses love. To this class belongs what you quote. You will grant that there are things in verse which may be read right or wrong, which depend for their effect upon pronunciation.

How badly Bridges failed to follow Hopkins in the latter's discerning sensitivity to sound is apparent when one compares Bridges' remarks on Hopkins' rhymes [51] with the discussion of rhyme in Hopkins' lecture notes on rhetoric (N 244–248).

Omission of the Relative

The place accorded dramatic stress in sprung rhythm likewise helps explain even such "peculiarities" as the omission of the

[50] *The Physical Basis of Rhyme* (Stanford University, California: Stanford University Press, 1931), pp. 94–100.
[51] *Poems*, pp. 98–99.

relative pronoun at which Bridges munches again, though this omission in Hopkins is rare enough to deserve little comment. Omission of the object relative pronoun is a common English practice: *the man I saw, the room he lived in.* But the omissions in question are of subject relatives: "O Hero [that] savest," or "Squander the hell-rook ranks [that] sally to molest him." [52] Now, the speaking of the phrase "O Hero that savest" with heavy stresses on the *He-* and *sa-* will show the tendency of the relative to disappear: it can, in feeling delivery, easily become "O Hero 't savest," and in the breaking of deep emotion drop altogether. Similarly with the other line Bridges quotes.

Bridges' explanation does Hopkins justice in stating that these omissions were not "carelessness in Gerard Hopkins," but that Hopkins

banished these purely constructional syllables from his verse because they took up room which he thought he could not afford them: he needed in his scheme all his space for his poetical words, and he wished those to crowd out every merely grammatical colourless or toneless element. [53]

Bridges' use of the expression "poetical words" shows a mind veering far off the line of thought which holds that "the poetical language of an age shd. be the current language heightened." We wonder how Bridges' distinction between constructional and poetical would explain the stresses Hopkins often marks on prepositions. The distinction is, at best, pointless. Hopkins omitted relatives at times, not because they are not "poetical," but because in language highly stressed and emotional they may really tend to be crowded out. This is "the current language heightened." Hopkins' building with dramatic stress (both lines quoted by Bridges are from sprung rhythm poems) explains his practice: he was carrying forward—how advisedly need not be argued here—a tendency which that stress creates.

[52] *Poems*, pp. 97–98.
[53] *Poems*, p. 97.

Unusual Sense Stresses

The same emphasis on dramatic interpretation explains a practice of Hopkins to which little attention has been paid but to which attention will at some time surely be diverted. This is his marking of stresses in places unusual for sense stresses. It is true that most of the instances of stress marks inserted by Hopkins in his poems are self-explanatory: the rhythm of sense-stress verse is not always unambiguous, and in places Hopkins wishes to indicate his preference for one interpretation over others which would be easily suggested and which would scan, too. Thus, in general, he marks the metrical stress, as he indicates at the foot of the *Harry Ploughman* manuscript, "in doubtful cases only" (B opposite p. 262). Often the mark indicates an interpretation dictated by unusual emotional pitch, as the stress on *and* in *Spelt from Sibyl's Leaves*:

. . . . Heart, you round me right
With: Óur évening is over us; óur night   whélms, whélms,
        ánd will end us.

But an instance like this in the first line of *Spring and Fall* brings at first sight more difficulty:

Márgarét, are you gríeving
Over Goldengrove unleaving?

If this is sprung rhythm, how justify the stress on the last syllable of *Margaret*? Does not theory here dissolve into a fiction? Sprung rhythm uses sense stresses, and is not the sense stress here on the first syllable of the name? Is it not true that the ordinary way of emphasizing a polysyllable is to stress the member with the principal accent? The ordinary way, yes; but not the only way. The answer here lies, I think, in the thoughtful deliberation which marks the emotion of this poem and which brings to the interpretation an unusual second heavy accent as the speaker begins slowly and pensively. This second accent need not have the exact physical volume of the first, although it should be heightened psychologically at least. There is no need to explain this kind of enunciation in any other way than by noting its natural place in emotional speech. The touch here is exquisite. Other examples of a second metrical stress added by the feeling to a polysyllable may be found in Hopkins, for instance, in *Spelt from Sibyl's Leaves* on *dismémbering* (and *disremémbering* as well, though Hopkins has not made this explicit with stress marks, probably because the stresses are not juxtaposed):

```
. . . . . . . For earth|        her being has unbound, her
     dapple is at an end, as-
tray or aswarm, all throughther, in throngs;|      self ín
     self steepèd and páshed—quíte
Disremembering, dísmémbering|       áll now. Heart, you
     round me right
With: Óur évening is over us; óur night|      whélms, whélms,
     ánd will end us.
```

This is again "the current language heightened," and other cases of unusual accent in Hopkins are explainable as being the same sort of thing.

It is plain, then, that sense-stress rhythm, when it utilizes stresses which would ordinarily be only alternating stresses, does not do so without making them in context equivalently sense stresses. Thus in a line such as

Over Goldengrove unleaving,

where the stress of the sprung rhythm coincides exactly with the regular alternating stress and hence with a running rhythm, the line is read not as such lines are read in running rhythm, with the regular beat in the background, to be got away from as much as possible, but it is read with the stress heavy and prominent. The regularity of beat, which is not intrinsic to the rhythm, is simply explainable as arising from other sources, in the present case perhaps the suggestion of the senseless back-and-forth motions of a numbing grief and the measured sobs of the little Margaret. This regularity, which would become monotonous and shortly destroy altogether the feeling of a real sense stress, is lifted in the next line of the poem.

Rhythm Which Is Feeling's Self

Finally, what has been said of the parts of Hopkins' rhythm may be said of the whole, of the sweep and the ring which is its very self,

. . . . the strong
Spur, live and lancing like the blowpipe flame,[54]

which gives it life. For in the last analysis, the power driving this "line of masculine expression" is nothing other than the interpretive stress of the language assimilated in its full force, allowed its full play. The secret of this verse is that its rhythm thus bears up under the most emotional declamation. Hopkins' intensity, his dramatic suppression of words, his telescoping of grammatical structure, are possible and are demanded because with them and in them the interpretive stress mounts in value, and thus the rhythm grows. In brief, Hopkins' language and structure are what they are because his rhythm can support the kind of feeling for which such language is a normal vehicle. He is "strange" only to those not used to this pitch of emotion in verse. His language and structure are genuine, are commonly found in extra-poetical emotional contexts, and are foreign only to a "continuous literary decorum."[55] They are "the current language heightened." If they are more than some verse will stand, because this idiom reaches heights in its stresses and lows in its slacks which would entirely dismember the poetry of an Edmund Spenser, they are the concomitants of feeling which provide the

[54] "To R. B.," *Poems*, p. 69.
[55] Bridges' Notes in *Poems*, p. 96.

movement on which Hopkins' rhythm thrives. Thus in the *Deutschland* (st. 7 & 8):

> The dense and the driven Passion, and frightful sweat;
> Thence the discharge of it, there its swelling to be,
> Though felt before, though in high flood yet—
> What none would have known of it, only the heart, being hard at bay,
>
> Is out with it! Oh,
> We lash with the best or worst
> Word last! How a lush-kept plush-capped sloe
> Will, mouthed to flesh-burst,
> Gush!—flush the man, the being with it, sour or sweet,
> Brim, in a flash, full! . . . .

If the poem calls for shouting, the shouting need not be kept imaginary for fear the beat of the rhythm will go. Shout, declaim, and you will only have thrust this rhythm home. So, too, if the shout should need to die to a whisper, as in Poem No. 71:

> Strike, churl; hurl, cheerless wind, then; heltering hail
> May's beauty massacre and wispèd wild clouds grow
> Out on the giant air; tell Summer No,
> Bid joy back, have at the harvest, keep Hope pale.

Or there may be neither whisper nor declaim, but only a light passage in *The Woodlark*, with its bright rhythmic movements integral to entirely other feelings and tones:

> 'The blue wheat-acre is underneath
> And the braided ear breaks out of the sheath,
> The ear in milk, lush the sash,
> And crush-silk poppies aflash,
> The blood-gush blade-gash
> Flame-rash rudred
> Bud shelling or broad-shed
> Tatter-tassel-tangled and dingle-a-dangled
> Dandy-hung dainty head.

. . . .

And down . . . the furrow dry
Sunspurge and oxeye
And lace-leaved lovely
Foam-tuft fumitory

.   .   .   .

Through the velvety wind V-winged
To the nest's nook I balance and buoy
With a sweet joy of a sweet joy,
Sweet, of a sweet, of a sweet joy
Of a sweet—a sweet—sweet—joy.'

All this is the language of high feeling, and the rhythm. As Professor Malone has remarked of Old English, this is "an instrument subtle and sophisticated enough." And "stress is the life of it." Hopkins, who had a knack for happy expressions, never hit upon a happier. "In sprung rhythm the stress is more *of* a stress." The key to the understanding of the movement of Hopkins' sprung rhythm verse is the recognition that this stress, unlike that of "common rhythm," is not the stress which the mechanics of English make us want to put on every second or third syllable—though it may often coincide with this—but the stress of declaim, the stress of interpretation, the stress which grows from sense and feeling. On this stress the verse lives.

Note.—Since the present study was written, the *Kenyon Review* for the summer of 1944 has appeared with four Hopkins anniversary essays, one of them an interesting study entitled "Sprung Rhythm," by Harold Whitehall. Deriving from the theory which Professor William Ellery Leonard advanced some years ago for Old English and drawing on the work done in ballad measures by George R. Stewart, Jr. (I believe, although the reference, as it is given, is to a "G. B. Stewart"), the article advances the thesis that sprung rhythm is really a system of dipodies, feet conceived of as equivalents of musical 4/4 time.

In Parts II and III of the present study, I have attempted only
to put sprung rhythm in a general rhythmic setting without
going into details either in stress scansion or time equivalents. Dr.
Whitehall is undoubtedly correct when he says that in treating
stress independently of time, English metrics has abstracted too
far. Whether Hopkins' time equivalences which I have considered from the point of view of dramatic emphases, can be
reduced in whole or in part to "dipodies" is worth consideration.
There is evidence for it in Hopkins' discussion of four-beat
measures (B 119–120. Jan. 27, 1881) as well as in the apparent
movement of many of his poems, and in his tendencies to binary
development to which I have drawn attention.

But there is much evidence against it. It is hard to believe
with Dr. Whitehall that sonnets like *Carrion Comfort* are really
to be read in lines of four units and that the five-stress reading
which Hopkins commonly intended for sonnets not in halved
six-stress or eight-stress lines is therefore spurious. Other places,
for example, in *St. Winefred's Well* and *The Leaden Echo and
the Golden Echo* seem to resist fiercely any Procrustean tailoring.
And how are we to get stanzas 29 and 31 and 35 of the *Deutschland* to lie down in the same dipodic bed?

Moreover, if Hopkins' sprung rhythm is always dipodic, the
counterpoint in running rhythm must be dipodic, too, for by
sprung rhythm Hopkins meant the kind of rhythm found in this
counterpoint (D 15. Oct. 6, 1878; *Poems*, p. 5). Can we hear
dipodic rhythms over Milton's pentameters listed by Hopkins?
Again, how is it that the rhythm of ordinary speech must be
dipodic? For it, too, is a sprung rhythm (*Poems*, p. 5). The very
fact that Hopkins found sprung rhythm in Old English is at best
an equivocal argument for the dipodic theory since it is exceedingly doubtful that Hopkins read Old English poetry in a rhythm
not formally proposed for it until well within the twentieth
century.

Hopkins' description of the way he wants his verse read
(B 246. Dec. 11, 1886) confirms his awareness of the value of

time in rhythm, but does not help in the reduction of all sprung rhythm time to dipodies.

The difficulty, which we must honestly face, is that in the manifold of sound which is speech, there are many patterns. Sometimes a simple one is obviously emphasized. But at other times more subtle patterns exist. Such patterns may tend to dissolve into simple patterns even when this dissolution is not desired or desirable. Piano players know how triplets intended to equal together the time of a quarter note will, if one is not careful, dissolve into an eighth and two sixteenth notes. The Kyrie of the ordinary Gregorian Requiem Mass all too easily slips into the 6/8 time to which a poor performance distorts it. If we hold a frame of fours in our mind, a set of "dipodies," we can find ourselves slipping all sorts of movements into it.

There remains, however, the possibility of some kind of correlation between a dipodic movement, a hypothetical basic time pattern against which normal irregular English speech rhythms have their being, the counterpoint on ordinary English running rhythm, and the peculiar effects of Hopkins' sprung rhythm, including the relation of his stresses to sense and his picturing of reversed feet as part of the real movement of verse (*Poems*, p. 1). Is what I have called sense-stressing a syncopation of, a kind of compromise with, a basic rhythm represented in another way by alternating stress? These questions, involving the greatest psychological subtleties, are not easy to answer. Further study is still needed.

III

NOT BIRTH, BUT RESURRECTION

With the knowledge, then, that Hopkins' sprung rhythm is a rhythm built out of the dramatic or interpretive or sense stresses of the language, a rhythm the units of which are sense stresses

each with its belonging slacks, and with the understanding that
the "peculiarities" of Hopkins—his lines weighted with alliteration, assonance and other *retentissement,* his tendencies toward
antithetical verse movement, his use of rhyme, the very sweep
and lancing of his verse, "the roll, the rise, the carol, the creation," even to his variations of meter by "outrides" or "hangers"
or by burden lines—with the understanding that all this is not
mere ornament here but the stuff which "gathers to a greatness"
to form the substance, the organism, the essential machinery and
the accomplishment of a delicately adjusted rhythmic mechan-
ism, just as phenomena of the same order had gathered to form
the early sense-stress verse of Old English—with this understanding we return to the earlier question, What did Hopkins find?
It is not enough to say that he found the kind of basis for rhythm
that Old English had used, for this does not give all the credentials of his rhythm. To be understood, Hopkins' discovery must
be seen in its relation to conditions in his own time, which themselves are only understandable as the live ends, the wave front,
of a long past.

As a matter of fact, the rhythm which Hopkins found has a
history in verse which is not restricted to Old English. (Since it
is plainly always bound close to English prose, from its history
in this medium we prescind.)

Two Rhythms at Once: Counterpoint

Since running rhythm and sprung rhythm are concerned with
different elements in the language, there is the interesting chance
that they may coexist in one piece of verse. Verse with both
rhythms would be such that we could attend now to one rhythm,
now to another. Early in his discussions of sprung rhythm Hopkins pointed out instances of the coexistence of the two movements, calling the verse which employs both at once by the fortunate name of "counterpoint" verse. Counterpoint, he says
arises in running rhythm with the reversal of "two feet running,

especially so as to include the sensitive second foot." [56] Thus it arises in a line such as

Home|to his mother's|house|private|returned,

cited by Hopkins from Milton.[57]

Here the variations which the running rhythm allows can be taken as setting up a pattern of their own. Moreover, they are rooted in the sense stress. If such patterns based on this irregularly placed stress existed by themselves, that is, if only the kind of rhythm which is here called the reversed rhythm were heard, we should have sprung rhythm.

In a passage redolent of Hopkins down to details of diction, Bridges notes in *Milton's Prosody* the confusion possible when the two kinds of verse concur. The system of counting only stresses to the neglect of syllabic enumeration

is a perfectly different system from that which counts the syllables. It seems also the most natural to our language; and I think that the cause of this distinction not being recognized is the fact that stress cannot be excluded from consideration even in verse that depends primarily on the number of syllables. The two systems are mixed in our tradition . . . But if once the notion be got rid of that you must have so many syllables in a line to make a verse, or must account for the supernumerary ones in some such manner as the Greeks or Latins would have done, then the stress will declare its supremacy; which, as may be seen in Shakespeare and Milton, it is burning to do.[58]

[56] Author's Preface, *Poems*, p. 3; cf. D 15 (Oct. 6, 1878).

[57] N 241; D 15 (Oct. 6, 1878), where a note gives the reference *Paradise Regained*, iv, 639. The scansion marks here are mine, but are based on Hopkins'.

[58] (Oxford: Henry Frowde, 1901: in the same volume with *Classical Meters in English Verse* by William Johnson Stone), pp. 72–73. Hopkins' diction is repeated by Bridges, perhaps unconsciously: Hopkins had written to Bridges that if earlier poets had known of sprung rhythm, "they would have used it. Many people, as we say, *have been 'burning,'* but they all missed it."— B 156 (Oct. 18, 1882); italics mine.

Bridges does not discuss his pure-stress verse here precisely in terms of sense stress. If he had, it would be plain that the persistent absorption of sense stress by the alternating stress of English explains the confusion which he decries: sense-stress verse and alternating-stress verse are always alike and never quite the same.

Hopkins calls attention to the fact that a second or counterpointed rhythm can arise in running rhythm but not in sprung.[59] The reason is plain. The sprung-rhythm pattern is based on the sense stress. But the real or basic running-rhythm pattern, while not based on the sense stress, always includes it, never runs counter to it. Hence, reversals of stresses and slacks which make a counterpointed rhythm can arise only when a regularly alternating basic pattern is imported to a given line from the other lines of the poem. The sprung-rhythm pattern is never fixed enough for this, and such importation can therefore only be accomplished in a poem the basic rhythm of which is the running rhythm.

Now all this could be mere drumming at the higher poetical mathematics were not the roots of Hopkins' rhythm struck so deep into the language. As it is, the principle of counterpoint opens English poetry along its center and from end to end.

Hopkins had no idea how far this was true. By academic profession a Greek scholar who disclaimed wide reading in English literature (D 87. Oct. 29, 1881), he knew English poetry only as confined pretty closely to the recognized authors, who, for reasons to be noted later, were precisely the ones least likely to exhibit strong counterpoint.

Middle-English Survivals of Sense Stress

Sense-stress rhythm did not disappear from English with the advent of the Normans. This is a well known fact. The first volume of Saintsbury's *History of English Prosody* turns on a dis-

[59] B 45 (Aug. 21, 1877); Author's Preface, *Poems,* p. 4.

cussion of the persistence of the Old English rhythm within the later running rhythm which spread through English from Medieval Latin, French, and, later, Italian grafts. This persistence is not merely a matter of isolated poems such as *Sir Gawain and the Green Knight,* here and there reverting consciously to the old forms. It enters far deeper into rhythmic perception than that. Hopkins' guess that Chaucer "properly read is heavier stressed than we think" (D 78. Oct. 23–25, 1881) has been substantiated by the conclusions of the late Professor Manly and Miss Rickert, which help relate the movement of Chaucer's verse to the "rough," heavy sense-stress rhythms of Old English. "It is still uncertain," they conclude in the eight-volume collation of the *Canterbury Tales* manuscripts,

whether Chaucer's versification should always have the regularity assumed for it by the scholars of the late 19 C. . . . Current theories of Chaucer's versification are based, not upon the text as found in the MSS, or as established by critical processes, but upon an artificial text made regular by all the devices at the disposal of the scholar.[60]

The line, for instance, which is usually given as

Hath in the Ram his halve cours yronne

should be deprived of the smoothing final *e* so as to read,

Hath in the Ram his half cours yronne,[61]

in which one observes a movement remarkably like an Old English line:

$$Háth | \acute{i}n\ th\breve{e}\ R\acute{a}m | \qquad his\ h\acute{a}lf\ c\grave{o}urs | \acute{y}r\acute{o}nn\breve{e}. |$$

The alliteration in evidence in this line is too common in Chaucer and, as we shall see, in later poets to be dismissed as coincidence.

[60] John M. Manly and Edith Rickert, *The Text of the Canterbury Tales* (Chicago: The University of Chicago Press, 1940), II, 40–41.
[61] *Ibid.,* III, 3; the line is from the Prologue.

Renaissance Survivals

To omit the century following Chaucer's death, when the force of Old English rhythms is heard on every side, in the early sixteenth century Bishop Gavin Douglas' translation of the *Aeneid* overlays the decasyllabic running rhythm, which it seems to follow, with an unmistakable heavy sense-stress pattern, complete with the alliteration, consonantal weighting, and complex echoings of sound which help constitute sense-stress rhythm. If one halves its lines, the verse becomes practically indistinguishable from Old English in rhythm:

And áll|in váne| thŭs quhíle Enéăs|cárpit,|
Ane blústĕrănd|búb,| óut fră thĕ nórtht|bráying|
Gáne|óur thĕ foírschìp| ín thĕ bák sàil|dýng.|

. . . .

Héich ăs ăne híll   thĕ lăw ŏf wáttĕr brák,
And ín ăne héip   cŏme ón thăme wĭth ăne swák.
Sŏme hésĭt hóvĕrănd   ŏn thĕ wállĭs hýcht,
And súm thĕ sŏwnchănd sée sŏ láw gărt lýcht,
Thăme sémĭt thĕ ĕrd óppĭnĭt   ămýd thĕ flúde;
Thĕ stówr ŭp búllĕrĭt   sánd ăs ĭt were wúid.[62]

In this same period, Skelton's typical short lines, his "ragged rhymes," are largely sense-stress, often again developing the usual alliteration:

Ĭt wăs sŏ préttý|ă fóle|
Ĭt wŏuld sýt|ŏn ă stóle|
And lérned|ăftĕr mў schóle|
Fŏr tŏ képe|hĭs cút,|
Wíth, Phýllĭp,| kĕep yŏur cút!|[63]

[62] *The First Buik Eneados*, 6–18, in *The Poetical Works of Gavin Douglas, Bishop of Dunkeld*, ed. by John Small (Edinburgh: William Paterson, 1874), II, 28.

[63] *The Poetical Works of John Skelton*, ed. by Alexander Dyce (London: Thomas Rodd, 1843), I, 54. Italics mine.

It will be seen that these skeltonics, from *Phyllyp Sparrowe*, include a rhythm like the Old English antithesis, each line here being equivalent to an Old English half-line. Skelton's *Speke Parrot* is even more markedly counterpointed with sense stress. The declaim is evident in this heated diatribe against Wolsey, and the sense-stress pattern has the common tendency to move in fours. Breaking the lines like Old English, we get:

So myche raggyd ryghte	of a rammes horne;
So rygorous revelyng	in a prelate specially
So bold and so braggyng,	and was so basely born;
So lordlye of his lokes	and so dysdayneslye;
So fatte a magott,	bred of a flesshe flye;
Was nevyr suche a ffylty gorgon,	nor such an epycure,
Syns Dewcalyons flodde,	I make thé faste and sure.[64]

The alliteration cannot be missed.

Analysis of the verse of the period of Wyatt and Surrey shows how firmly the Old English half-line held the language even when a conscious attempt was made to establish the syllabic count imported from Latin sources. Thus in a sonnet attributed to Surrey or Vaux, a marked sense-stress pattern, alliteration and all, overlays the running rhythm; and the lines can easily be broken to bare the sense-stress movement:

Bríttlĕ|bĕautiĕ,|	thăt nátŭre|măde so fráil,
Whĕreŏf thĕ gíft|iš smáll,|	ănd shórt|thĕ séasŏn,|
Flowring today,	to morowe apt to faile,
Tickell treasure,	abhorred of reason,
Daungerous to dele with,	vaine, of none auail,
Costly in keping,	past not worthe two peason,
Slipper in sliding	as is an eles taile,
Harde to attaine,	once gotten not geason,
Iewel of ieopardy	that perill dothe assaile,
False and vntrue,	enticed oft to treason,
Enmy to youth:	that most may I bewaile.

[64] *Ibid.*, II, 24.

Ah bitter swete   infecting as the poyson,
Thou *f*arest as *f*ruit   that with the *f*rost is taken:
To day *r*edy *r*ipe,   to morow all to shaken.[65]

There is not this much alliteration in most of Wyatt and Surre*y*, but there is enough, and enough out-and-out antithetical movement to point to part of the answer to the question which has persistently troubled metrists: What were Wyatt and Surrey trying to do?

Elizabethan Drama, the Great Reservoir

It is not strange that the movement of a rhythm based on the declamatory stress should be most effectively preserved on the Elizabethan stage. For, to say the truth, it is practically impossible for running rhythm to be recognized if blank verse is declaimed as the sense demands. Whatever Elizabethan and Jacobean convention may have been, when the sense is given full play in Shakespeare's blank verse, the rhythm becomes indistinguishable in kind from the rhythm of Shakespeare's high stage prose. The same is true of Fletcher, Webster, and the rest. Hopkins, indeed, mentions a playwright, Gree*n*e, as the last to use sprung rhythm consistently, but the other playwrights, with the exception of Shakespeare, he gives little evidence of having read: concerning Marlowe's works, he writes Bridges, "I could flog myself for being so ignorant" (B 227. Oct. 2, 1886).

To confine illustration, for brevity, to one dramatist, Shakespeare is full to bursting with sense-stress movements, often cued

[65] "The Frailtie and Hurtfulnes of Beauty," *Songes and Sonnettes (Tottel's Miscellany)*, ed. by Edward Arber (London: 1870), p. 10. Italics mine. It has been the fashion to dismiss such verse as this as being merely crude and stumbling, on the assumption that Wyatt, Surrey, and others must have been trying to write syllabic-count verse. Since the original draft of this present study, D. W. Harding has ably contested this assumption in "The Rhythmical Intention in Wyatt's Poetry," *Scrutiny*, XIV (1946), 90–102. He finds that often Wyatt "positively chose the pausing line composed of dissimilar rhythmical units" and believes it an untenable theory which would hold that Wyatt's was only a stumbling performance (p. 99).

in with alliteration and other sound echoes, even in his early plays. *The Comedy of Errors* yields many passages such as this; which can be arranged like Old English by halving the lines:

> And *p*iteous *p*lainings   of the *p*retty babes,
> That mourn'd for *f*ashion,   ignorant what to *f*ear,
> *F*orced me to seek delays   *f*or them and me.
> And this it was,   *f*or other means was none:
> The *s*ailors *s*ought   *f*or *s*afety by our boat.[66]

But the later plays are even richer in examples; such as:

> Lów-crookĕd|cúrt'sĭes| ănd báse|spániĕl-făwning,[67]

or

> Thĕ *w*éariĕst|ănd *m*ost *l*óathĕd| wórldlў|*l*ífe|
> Thăt *á*ge,|áche| *p*enúrў,|ănd imprísŏnmĕnt|
> Căn láy|ŏn nátŭre| . . . .[68]

In many passages, the running decasyllabic rhythm is almost completely concealed under the sense-stress movement, which is loaded with echoes:

> . . . . Gone already!
> Ínch-thĭck, knée-dèep   ŏ'er hĕad ănd éars ă fórk'd òne!
> Gŏ, *p*láy, bŏy, *p*láy: thў móthĕr *p*lăys, ănd Í
> Pláy tóo;   bŭt sŏ disgráced ă părt, whŏse íssŭe
> Wĭll híss mĕ tŏ mў gráve:.   cŏntémpt ănd clámŏur
> Wĭll bĕ mў knéll.   Gŏ, *p*láy, bŏy, *p*láy . . . . .[69]

Prosodists have frequently called attention to the tendency of modern English decasyllabics to use lines with three or four real stresses.[70] Indeed, it seems altogether likely that its ability to take

---

[66] I, i, 73–77, *Works*, I, 6. Italics mine.
[67] *Julius Caesar*, III, i, 43, *ibid.*, XXIX, 58.
[68] *Measure for Measure*, III, i, 130–132, *ibid.*, XII, 63. Italics mine.
[69] *The Winter's Tale*, I, ii, 185–190, *ibid.*, XV, 15. Italics mine.
[70] See, for instance, Paull F. Baum, "The Character of Anglo-Saxon Verse," *Modern Philology*, XXVIII (1930–31), 155; or Geoffrey Tillotson, *On the Poetry of Pope* (Oxford: The Clarendon Press, 1938), p. 125.

on the sense stress movements inherent in the language since Old English is one of the principal reasons for the success of heroic blank verse. Passages such as these last need not be here multiplied from Shakespeare or the other dramatists, for, especially in the most feeling passages, they are easy enough to find.

In the Dramatic Tradition: Wit Poetry

Now the strange fertility of Elizabethan drama seems largely attributable to the fact that keeping contact with it meant keeping contact with heavily counterpointed verse. The debt which the metaphysical poets, particularly, owe the drama is definitely connected with the survival of sense stress rhythms. Terence Heywood has observed that

masculinity and ruggedness were, as we know, a special cult of the metaphysicals. It is probable that Hopkins would not have considered Dryden "the most masculine of our poets" had he known Donne. . . . To me it seems certain, though I know that some still doubt it, that Donne and many of his followers were striving for a natural speech-rhythm in English poetry.[71]

It would perhaps be helpful to emphasize that Donne and his followers, as well as Jonson and his—and from these two fountainheads the stream of wit flows—*had not lost contact* with a natural speech rhythm, that their verse perpetuated the sense-stress design which, without perhaps being fully conscious of the fact, they had inherited from the first poets of the language.

It is certainly more than a coincidence that almost universally the lyrics of the metaphysicals, or, more inclusively, the wit poets, do not meditate but talk. They fall naturally into the tones familiar on the stage, where one character is addressing another.

---

[71] "Gerard Manley Hopkins: His Literary Ancestry," *English*, III (Spring, 1940), p. 20. Cf. R. W. Short, "The Metrical Theory and Practice of Thomas Campion," *PMLA*, LIX (1944), 1003–1018. This article discusses the great irregularity in the number and position of accents together with the connections of Campion's rhythm with music.

This inspiration is observable in the titles typical of Jonson's lyric pieces: *To Dr. Donne* or *To My Mere English Censurer* or *To My Booke-seller,* which last, for example, begins with the characteristic conversational tone:

> Thou that mak'st gaine thy end, and wisely well
> Call'st a booke good, or bad, as it doth sell,
> Use mine so, too: I give thee leave. . . . .[72]

Sometimes the dialogue is with the audience, as in *Her Triumph* from *A Celebration of Charis in Ten Lyrick Pieces,* which opens, "See the chariot at hand here of Love." [73] Even Jonson's epitaphs, like his famous songs such as *To Celia,* preserve stage presence and address.

This same attitude carries over into the poetry of the Sons of Ben. Thus Herrick's *Corinna's Going a-Maying* is spoken directly to Corinna and echoes Jonson's brusque vigor:

> There's not a budding Boy, or Girle, this day,
> But is got up, and gone to bring in May.
> A deale of Youth, ere this, is come
> Báck, ănd with *White-thòrn* láděn hóme.[74]

It is evident from the way he turns into his last stanza that Carew's elegy, *Maria Wentworth,* is conceived in his mind as a direct address; the last line slips pretty much from the running rhythm pattern and at the same time turns to echoing:

> Learn from hence, Reader, what small trust
> We owe this world, where virtue must,
> Fráil ăs oŭr flésh, crúmblĕ tŏ dúst.[75]

---

[72] *The Poems of Ben Jonson,* ed. by Bernard H. Newdigate (Oxford: The Shakespeare Head Press, 1936), p. 3.

[73] *Ibid.,* p. 91.

[74] *The Poetical Works of Robert Herrick,* ed. by F. W. Moorman (Oxford: The Clarendon Press, 1915), p. 69.

[75] *Poems of Thomas Carew,* ed. by Arthur Vincent (London: George Routledge and Sons [no date]), p. 79. Italics mine.

So, too, George Herbert writes with a sense of declaim and a quite loose alternating-stress movement even in such a poem as *The Collar,* where meditation sends him not into a reverie but into the heart of a dispute:

> I struck the board and cry'd, "No more!
> I will abroad."
> What, shall I ever sigh and pine?
> My lines and life are free; free as the road
> Loose as the winde, as large as store.
> Shall I be still in suit? [76]

And Donne, though neither a dramatist nor a Son of Ben, is almost invariably in his lyric pieces talking to someone, while counterpoint grows unmistakably. *The Computation* ends (I halve the lines):

> Yĕt căll nŏt thís lóng lìfe;   Bŭt thínke thăt Í
> Ăm, bў bĕing déad, Ímmórtăll;   Căn ghósts díe? [77]

And in *Love's Alchemy*:

> Sŏme thăt hăve déepĕr dígg'd   lóves Mỳne thĕn Í
> . . . .
> Bŭt shŏuld Ĭ lŏve, gĕt, téll,   tíll Ĭ wĕre óld. [78]

The poetry of wit, with its tone of direct address, is the principal non-dramatic vehicle in which the sense stress rhythms of the language are carried on. The habit of direct address moves forward to Pope, whom Frank R. Leavis has discerningly identified as the last of the line maintaining connections with Jonson or Donne.[79] Pope does not uniformly use the tone—for instance, in the romantic pieces such as *Eloisa to Abelard* it is

---

[76] *The Complete Works of George Herbert,* ed. by Alexander B. Grosart ("The Fuller Worthies' Library"; London: private printing, 1874), I, 175.

[77] *The Poems of John Donne,* ed. by Herbert J. C. Grierson (Oxford: The Clarendon Press, 1912-1915), I, 69.

[78] *Ibid.,* p. 39.

[79] *Revaluation* (London: Chatto and Windus, 1936), pp. 71, 91.

missing—but in his better pieces he does: the *Epistle to Dr.*
Arbuthnot opens with

> Shut, shut, the door, good John! fatigued I said:
> Tíc úp thĕ knóckĕr; săy Ĭ'm síck, Ĭ'm déad.[80]

Pope is still able to utilize the variegated speech rhythms of the
language for poetical purposes, but in this he stands apart from
nearly all his contemporaries.

Spenserian: The Other Tradition

For another line of poets had learned other manners. Within a
rhythmic tradition such as that which was carried from Old
English into Elizabethan times, it was natural for his contemporaries to single out Spenser as "the new poet." For into the tradition Edmund Spenser hardly fits. Something might be done to
introduce him in part into the tradition on the score of "Febru-
arie" and "Maye" in *The Shepheardes Calender,* although this
is uncertain, but all the important rhythmic achievements of this
poet tend to divert English verse into pure running-rhythm channels with no sense-stress tributaries.

We are so close to the Spenserian tradition even yet that it is
difficult to realize the extent of the revolution Spenser effected.
His full influence in establishing the eighteenth- and nineteenth-
century feeling for a "continuous literary decorum," which so
easily associated itself with the quiet throbbing of the smooth
alternating-stress verse he perfected, is only beginning to be
recognized as comparable to that of his greater disciple Milton,
for whom he had everywhere paved the way. Saintsbury was not
only making a supposition common in his day, but he was calling
attention to a fact when he said that Spenser was the Joshua who
brought English prosody into its promised measure and rhyme.[81]

[80] *The Works of Alexander Pope,* ed. by Whitwell Elwin and William
John Courthope (London: John Murray, 1871–1889), III [241].

[81] George Saintsbury, *A History of English Prosody* (London: Macmillan
and Co., 1906–1910), I, 351.

Saintsbury's supposition would find little support now: that Spenser's achievement was inevitably progress is at best a gratuitous assumption. But the importance Saintsbury assigns to Spenser is not exaggerated. To appreciate the revolutionary effect of Spenser's verse, we need only look to the diffidence of Elizabethan prosodists toward the "feet" which become the stock in trade of prosody in the late Spenserian tradition we have known. And to see the extent of his influence long after his death, we can recall that all the poets disapproved of by the eighteenth century, and by the nineteenth following its lead, have uniformly been those who are outside the Spenserian tradition. Generally speaking, to the eighteenth and nineteenth centuries rhythmic crudity was equivalent to non-Spenserian verse movement. It is significant that eighteenth-century prosody outlaws alliteration.[82]

It is a simple fact that the smooth Spenserian rhythms cannot stand much sense interpretation or declaim. But no need for declaim was felt by the Augustans. The demand was for a standard currency, a guaranteed emotional tender insured against inflation. Since it provided this, the Spenserian tradition cannot be said to have achieved nothing: it does one of the things which poetry can do. And yet the reduction of all poetry to this sort of thing was bound to be disastrous. This reduction forms one facet of the "dissociation of sensibility" which T. S. Eliot has described [83] and which took place when Spenser's influence was in the ascendency. Here, indeed, the language was developed (along a simple enough line), but the feeling became more and more vulgarized as it became more and more standard, less responsive to its object, for no matter what their object, all vehicles had to follow the same road, not because it reached the destination, but because it was smooth. Of course, this road runs out in album verse and poetry as a "polite accomplishment." More-

[82] *Ibid.*, III, 541.
[83] "The Metaphysical P~ets," *Selected Essays, 1917–1932* (New York: Harcourt, Brace and Co., 1932), p. 247.

over, this is the road which leads verse off the English stage: as verse in general loses ability to declaim, the age of prose drama is ushered in.

It is difficult not to believe that the taste for smoothness which remained an accepted touchstone of good English poetry from Dryden's day, when Mr. Waller had only lately improved our numbers, till some time around the turn of the present century, is intimately associated with the whole intellectual milieu of this period. In this bright and shining world of a successful Newtonian physics, a Cartesian mathematical solvent for all reality, and a naive materialism, there is something which inevitably gave body to a "continuous literary decorum." Like the decimal measurement systems, Spenserian smoothness represented great achievement to the enlightened mind.

The effects of Spenser's canonization persist on all sides in Hopkins' age. They appear in the fact, already mentioned above, that Hopkins, reading the English poetry ordinarily read in his day, never came across the greater bulk of the poetry which would have interested him most, as the natural antecedent of his own. They are manifest in Saintsbury, who, proclaiming in his *History of English Prosody,* "It is the 'Progress of Prosody' which the present writer, not being able to 'sing,' is ambitious to 'say,' " [84] considers it a foregone conclusion that in the march of progress, Spenser is the Joshua. The same tradition accounts for the judgments of a Sir Sidney Lee in the *Dictionary of National Biography.* Without a glance aside at Gavin Douglas or Skelton, Sir Sidney hits with predictable accuracy on Sackville's *Induction* as the greatest poem between Chaucer and Spenser. It "has no rival." [85] The reason is not hard to find: it is almost the only thing like Spenser until Spenser himself.

Other evidence is available in the development of the lyric. In the Spenserian tradition, the lyric of Jonson and Donne, which

[84] II, 26.
[85] *Dictionary of National Biography,* ed. by Leslie Stephen and Sidney Lee, XVIII (London: Oxford University Press, 1921-22), 586.

had built on the strength of declamatory stress a strong idiom of counterpoint now regarded as making the verse too rough, had been discarded in favor of the staid and sober ruminations of Akenside and the Wartons. The tone of direct dialogue is replaced at best by bursts of apostrophe before an audience either unconscious or absent. It is here rather than in the twentieth century that poetry begins talking to itself. And this tradition was in possession when Hopkins put in his appearance. How thoroughly it had proscribed an oratorical delivery by its exclusive exploitation of running rhythm is evident in any representative poem, such as Shenstone's *The School-Mistress*:

> Ah me! full sorely is my heart forlorn,
> To think how modest worth neglected lies;
> While partial fame doth with her blasts adorn
> Such deeds alone, as pride and pomp disguise;
> Deeds of ill sort, and mischievous emprise!
> Lend me thy clarion, goddess! let me try
> To sound the praise of merit, ere it dies;
> Such as I oft have chaunced to espy,
> Lost in the dreary shades of dull obscurity.[86]

Any tendency to develop a pattern built on sense-stress here is entirely masked by the steady drone of the Spenserian meditative machinery. Indeed, the only sense or feeling which can exist here is that capable of moving with the special motion of this verse. Earlier verse had not all known such a restriction: this movement was only a phase in the varied rhythms found in the dramatists, even in their lyrics. But in the eighteenth and nineteenth centuries it pretty well held the field all the way from light lyric pieces to Thomson's staid heroics. It is little wonder that the mind which restricted poetry to this sort of thing should be disgusted with Donne and embarrassed to discover in itself a liking for Shakespeare.

[86] *The Works in Verse and Prose of William Shenstone, Esq.* (London: R. and J. Dodsley, 1764), II, 333.

Hopkins' Discovery

In this picture of the poetic heritage of Hopkins' world lies the answer to the question, What did Hopkins find? Hopkins found a tradition in English poetry which was older and stronger than the one in possession in his day. He found a rhythmic tradition which could cut under and around the "running" or "common" rhythm of the nineteenth century, not because his new rhythm was the ancient rhythm of English—this would be a fact of no value in itself—but because it was a rhythm still inherent in the language and only suppressed by an artificially sustained tradition. It is indeed strange that between the period when we find Shakespeare's "cabined, cribb'd, confined" and

> If it were done, when 'tis done, then 'twere well
> It were done quickly, ...

and the later period which finally brought Hopkins' "hearts' charity's hearth's fire" or "And the sea flint-flake, black-backed in the regular blow," there is almost nothing to compare with these passages. The place in poetry where such things fit was kept tightly locked. Certainly such expressions were not entirely foreign to speech—though they may have been more foreign to it than we suspect—but the kind of poetic rhythm in favor left them no room. Hopkins opened a place for them.

In opening this place, Hopkins' achievement was not quite alone. After the dramatists and the wit poets, there had remained tendencies to maintain in English poetry the strength of the sense-stress rhythms. (We must remind ourselves continually that these are not *entirely* unlike those of the "smooth" or "reformed" numbers of running rhythm, and hence only rarely will verse be free of at least equivocal instances of them.) There was the case of Milton, who as a young man had, in *Comus*, trafficked in the livening rhythms of the stage, but who—as he himself later acknowledged, telling Dryden that Spenser was his "original"—had turned away to the rhythms of the non-dramatic tradition.

With, however, a scholarly sophistication unknown to Spenser, he had overlaid the Spenserian numbers with a heavy counterpoint and had finally in his *Samson* choruses gone so far as to sacrifice almost completely the rhythm of the alternating stress. But life was gone: under the spell of the epic theory, Milton had fallen upon a coagulating poetic idiom which passed stiff and unyielding to the hands of his successors. Nevertheless, Milton being an approved author, his work came to Hopkins' attention.

The eighteenth century, after Pope, had been pretty destitute of sense-stress rhythms, but latterly there had come Burns, cultivating the habit of direct address, and the sense-stress counterpoint revives once more with the life of the declamatory verse. Burns' strength, which lies in his satirical pieces, is apparent in *To a Louse*:

> Ha! whare ye gaun, ye crowlin' ferlie!
>
> . . . .
>
> My sooth! right bauld ye set your nose out,
> As plump and gray as onie grozet;
> O for some rank, mercurial rozet,
>   Or fell, red, smeddum.[87]

With its three successive stresses tempting the rhythm far from an alternating stress, the last line here is as much a surprise as the first.

Burns is followed by Blake, with his "rhymeless pindarics" and *The Fairy*, which is in genuine skeltonics:

> Sŏ ă Fáirў súng.
> Frŏm thĕ léaves Ĭ sprúng;
> Hĕ léap'd frŏm thĕ spráy
> Tŏ flée ăwáy;
> Bŭt ĭn mў hát cáught,
> Hĕ sóon shăll bĕ táught.[88]

[87] *The Complete Works of Robert Burns*, ed. by Alexander Smith (New York: Thomas Y. Crowell and Co. [no date]), p. 74.

[88] *The Poetical Works of William Blake*, ed. by John Sampson (London: Oxford University Press, 1914), p. 122.

And there was Southey's *Thalaba* and Shelley's *Queen Mab,* done in what was much later to be called free verse, as well as other pieces like those noted by Hopkins, or like Shelley's *A Dirge* ("Rough wind that moanest loud") interesting for a tendency toward juxtaposed stresses. There are stirrings, too, of a new life in Byron, a defender and imitator of Pope. And the Keats of the mature odes picks up a kind of counterpoint verse unknown since the Elizabethans. Lines in the *Ode on Melancholy* can be divided to expose the Old English antiphonal pattern:

> Nó, nŏ, gŏ nŏt tŏ Léthĕ,   nĕithĕr twíst
> Wólf's-bàne, tíght-ròoted,   fŏr ĭts póisŏnŏus wíne;

or

> Ănd féed dèep, déep   ŭpŏn hĕr péerlĕss éyes.[89]

In the *Ode on a Grecian Urn* there is this heavy counterpoint:

> "Béauty̆ is trúth,   trŭth béautў," thăt ĭs áll
> Ye know on earth, and all ye need to know.[90]

The whole nineteenth century witnessed a general movement toward this "rougher" verse, a movement which culminated perhaps in Browning, where a revival of counterpoint brings in again sound echoes. Certain lines in *The Ring and the Book,* for example—there are plenty of others—might be halved as four-stress lines:

> Flúng with ă flóurish!   Bŭt rĕpéntănce, tóo.
> Bŭt púre ănd símplĕ   sórrŏw fŏr láw's brèach
> Rather than blunderer's-ineptitude?
> Cardinal, no!   Abate, scarcely thus!

[89] *The Poetical Works and Other Writings of John Keats,* ed. by H. Buxton Forman and Maurice Buxton Forman (New York: Charles Scribner's Sons, 1938), III, 184. Italics mine.
[90] *Ibid.,* p. 157.

'Tĭs thĕ *fáult, nót*　　　thăt Ĭ dáred trỳ ă *fáll*
With Law and straightway am found undermost,
But that I failed to see, above man's law,
God's precept you, the Christians, recognize?

Cóllỹ mỹ *ców!*　　　Dŏn't fĭdgĕt, Cárdĭnăl! [91]

Apart from the lines divided here, the verse, as is usual with
Browning, is not smooth. Had Browning's idiom been more genuine, less pretentiously offhand, its gawkiness less "flung with a
flourish," his achievement might have partaken of Hopkins'. As
it is, Hopkins says discerningly of Browning's verse, "I greatly
admire the touches and the details, but the general effect, the
whole, offends me, I think it repulsive" (B 137. Sept. 17, 1881),
and he has little patience with "the scarecrow misbegotten
Browning crew" (B 111. Oct. 26, 1880).

Songs, Saws, Nursery Rhymes, Other Special Survivals

While these developments were taking place, sense-stress
rhythms had persisted here and there in out-of-the-way places
where the tradition of smoothness in verse was not enforced: in
songs, including the ballads, where because the verse was subordinated to music great regularity had never been demanded
(musical measure has always been able to salve errancy in syllabic count); and in weather saws and nursery rhymes, for
which no one had bothered to construct metric containers. But
there were other odd places, for wherever departure was made
from the usual running rhythm, the sense-stress pattern had a
chance to assert itself. The various attempts to reproduce Latin
or Greek quantitative meter in English seem to fall back in
reality on a sense-stress rhythm. George Canning pays unconscious tribute to the methods of sense-stress verse when his

[91] XI, "Guido," *The Complete Poetic and Dramatic Works of Robert
Browning* (Boston: Houghton Mifflin and Co., 1895), p. 577.

lampooning attack on Southey's experiments in quantitative meter slips into alliteration and a movement not unlike Old English four-stress verse:

> Needy *K*nife-grinder! *wh*ither are you going?
> *R*ough is the *r*oad, your *wh*eel is *ou*t of *o*rder—
> *Bl*eak *bl*ows the *bl*ast; your *h*at has got a *h*ole in't,
> So *h*ave your *br*eeches.[92]

The same tendency to support with characteristic sense-stress devices the irregularity of pattern which these "classical meters" attempt is found in Tennyson's *Ode to Milton* done in "alcaics":

> O *m*ighty *m*outh'd inventor of harmonies,
> O *s*killed to *s*ing of *T*ime or E*t*ernity.[93]

The same thing had been observable in the "classical meter" of the Renaissance, as in Richard Stanyhurst's *A Prayer to the Trinity*:

> *Bl*essed I iudge *h*im that in *h*ert is *h*ealed,
> Cursed I know *h*im, that in *h*elth is *h*armed.[94]

But here one notes a more marked tendency to reproduce the Old English four-stress line so noticeable elsewhere in the poetry of Stanyhurst's contemporaries.

In turning from the verse of the simple alternating stress, the nineteenth-century writers were all in one way or another falling back on the sense-stress patterning which is so much the bone and sinew of English rhythm. Evidence of the revival of the

[92] "Sapphics: The Friend of Humanity and the Knife-Grinder," *Poetry of the Anti-Jacobin,* with notes by Charles Edmonds (London: G. Willis, 1854), p. 20. Italics mine.

[93] *The Poetic and Dramatic Works of Alfred, Lord Tennyson* (Boston: Houghton Mifflin Co., 1898), p. 267. Italics mine.

[94] "A Prayer to the Trinity," *Translation of the First Four Books of the Aeneis of P. Virgilius Maro: With Other Poetical Devices Thereto Annexed* [1582], ed. by Edward Arber ("The English Scholar's Library of Old and Modern Works," No. 10[London: 1880]), p. 133.

pattern is often in individual instances equivocal, but the evidence in the whole body of English verse toward the end of the nineteenth century as against the middle of the eighteenth is unmistakable. Moreover, there are such signs as the alliteration to be found here and there. This is probably for the most part entirely unconscious, it is not uniform throughout the poems, and yet it comes in quite too persistently to be accidental. It is the old functional alliteration asserting itself again, as it had asserted itself in Old English and was to assert itself in Hopkins' sprung rhythm. It is the alliteration which poets fall back on as a natural help to heighten stress for sustaining a rhythm not built on a regularly pulsing beat.

After Hopkins

But the current of the tradition in which the gaunt and lovable figure of Hopkins stands even managed to flow around him and move ahead before he was discovered in mid-stream. For with the "free verse" which appeared some decades following his death but before the publication of the *Poems,* sense-stress rhythm was pretty thoroughly revived. It is difficult indeed to see anything else in the movement of this verse, which it used to be the fashion to call "strophic." Certainly the rhythm is looser than is usual with Hopkins, and perhaps than is usual with Old English, but in the absence of a regular alternating-stress beat, the sense stress remains as the core to which the movements of the verse are attached. Bridges' remarks are again in place here:

Immediately English verse is written free from a numeration of syllables, it falls back on the number of stresses as its determining law: that is its governing power, and constitutes its form.[95]

Thus in the typical free verse of H. D.'s *Pear Tree,* the lines are loosely organized Old English half-lines:

[95] *Milton's Prosody,* pp. 72–73.

Silver dust
lifted from the earth,
higher than my arms reach,
you have mounted.
O silver,
higher than my arms reach
you front us with great mass;
no flower ever opened
so staunch a white leaf,
no flower ever parted silver
from such rare silver!
O white pear,
your flower-tufts,
thick on the branch,
bring summer and ripe fruits
in their purple hearts.[96]

The pattern here is somewhat flexible; the next-to-last line, for example, might perhaps be read with more stresses. But despite such possible variations, a two-stress pattern survives. Again, in Ezra Pound's *Dance Figure* we find the same movement:

I have not found thee in the tents,
In the broken darkness.
I have not found thee at the well-head
Among the women with pitchers.[97]

These are instances of free verse done in a plain two-stress design, which is extremely common and at the same time exhibits sense-stress patterning more clearly than the complex forms. The latter are too varied for separate treatment here.

T. S. Eliot's *Murder in the Cathedral* asserts once more the claims of structural alliteration (I break the lines to show the tendency to an Old English four-stress pattern):

[96] H[ilda] D[oolittle], "Pear Tree," *A Book of Poems for Every Mood,* ed. by Harriet Monroe and Morton Dauwen Zabel (Racine, Wis.: Whitman Publishing Co., 1933), pp. 84–85.
[97] *Selected Poems,* ed. by T. S. Eliot (London: Faber and Faber, Ltd., 1934), p. 73.

THOMAS

Nó! Shăll Í   whŏ kéep thĕ kéys
Ŏf héaven ănd héll,   sŭpréme ălŏne ĭn Éngland,
Whŏ bínd ănd lóose,   wĭth pówer frŏm thĕ Pópe,
Dĕscénd tŏ dĕsíre   ă púnĭer pówĕr?
Délĕgăte tŏ déal   thĕ dóom ŏf dămnátiŏn,
Tŏ cŏndémn kíngs,   nŏt sérve ămŏng thĕir sérvănts
Ĭs mў ópĕn óffice.   Nó!   Gó.

TEMPTER

Thĕn Ĭ léave yóu   tŏ yŏur fáte.
Yŏur śin sóars súnwărd   cóvĕrĭng kíngs' fálcŏns.[98]

Before this, the direct influence of Old English could of course be felt in Ezra Pound's near-literal translation of *The Seafarer* and elsewhere.

IV

THE AMBIT OF HOPKINS' ACHIEVEMENT

Hopkins, then, had found the tradition of a sense-stress rhythm, which we may also call the declamatory rhythm or the interpretive rhythm of English—a rhythm inherited from Old English as one of the bases of verse until the "reform" and "smoothing" of English numbers, principally under the influence of Edmund Spenser and his followers. Basically, this sense-stress rhythm is a rhythm which grows not from the tendency of English to stress every second or third syllable (whether sense demands this stress or not), but from the tendency of each sense-stress, especially in emotional utterance, to constitute itself a kind of rhythmic unit, either alone or together with a varying number of slack syllables which may precede and/or follow it. These

[98] (London: Faber & Faber, Ltd., 1935), p. 30. Italics mine.

rhythmic units can be of more or less equal weight while retaining great variety of movement—falling, rocking, or rising—and various lengths.

Perpetuated largely in the playwrights and in the line of wit poets, who preserved the tone of direct address in their verse and with this the pre-eminence of sense stress associated with stage delivery, this sense-stress rhythmic tradition persisted quite noticeably as a secondary or "counterpointed" rhythm until Pope, and was, indeed, never quite eliminated even at the height of the Spenserian influence during the eighteenth and nineteenth centuries. During these lean years, sense-stress rhythm survived after a fashion in out-of-the-way places such as songs and popular saws and nursery rhymes (more genuinely, it seems, in the songs than in the saws or rhymes—but this would take long to show). Hopkins notes it in these places. It also persisted in a way in various metrical experiments. Always different from and always somewhat like the "running" or "common" rhythm of English, this sense-stress rhythm is ready at all times to assert itself in English verse, especially when syllabic count is neglected. In Hopkins' day it was reviving to some extent in places other than his own verse.

The rhythm had existed all the time in prose, in the rhythms of speech where the restraint of reformed numbers was not felt. Hopkins himself finally came to understand this. Even before he did, he realized the hold of the rhythm on the language ("I do not claim to have invented *sprung rhythms* but *sprung rhythm*," he tells Bridges—B 45. Aug. 21, 1877), but the reading menu which his age prescribed kept Hopkins from ever knowing how much the forces back of sprung rhythm had normally made themselves felt in English verse.

This limitation of his knowledge did not stop accomplishment, for Hopkins' rhythmic achievement was primarily the work not of theory but of an extremely keen ear aided by a singularly open and objective mind, and it was made possible by the unusually true and consistent sensibility reflected in Hopkins' understanding that "a perfect style must be of its age" (D 99. Dec. 1, 1881 —Dec. 16, 1881).

Hopkins' achievement in reviving sense-stress rhythms is largely traceable to this understanding. On the strength of it, he turned in his poetry to language which is the normal tender for emotion, a currency heavy with the Anglo-Saxon small change of the English tongue. Hopkins' preference for the short word is apparent in every line of his verse.

General neglect of the longer Latin derivatives is indeed not essential to sense-stress rhythm. "Free verse" has never been remarkable for Anglo-Saxon preferences, and its rhythm is no less sense-stress because the stresses consequently occur at a greater distance from one another than is usual in Hopkins, who is able to say of his own sprung rhythm verse that it uses more than three successive slacks only "for particular rhythmic effects" (D 40. Jan. 14, 1881). Moreover, an Anglo-Saxon vocabulary is, conversely, quite consonant with the smooth rhythms of Gray's *Elegy,* which in many stanzas can be convicted of no more Latinity than Hopkins' "That Nature Is a Heraclitean Fire."

And yet, beyond the shadow of a doubt, Hopkins' diction does make the characteristic movements of his verse more unmistakable. By and large, the number of sense stresses in English decreases as words become longer, since each word, no matter how long, ordinarily is ready to receive no more than one sense stress. Filled with short words, and thus adaptable to a high proportion of sense stresses, Hopkins' verse moves so as to underline heavily the principles on which it is based. Stresses are packed close together to form a kind of condenser which gives each stress a higher charge than other diction might do. This is eminently stress verse. And it is stress verse all the more because of Hopkins' revivification of the alliteration and other sound echoes which make the verse of high stress live. Hopkins succeeded in reaching to the very "inscape" of his medium. His achievement is its "clearest-selved spark."

The focal point in Hopkins' own view of his work is his recognition of the occasional co-existence of two patterns in English verse, a phenomenon which he calls "counterpoint." For this is implicit recognition of the fact that, since two distinct rhythms can be attended to, the one rhythm which, isolated, is sprung rhythm, is based on a different thing in the language than is running rhythm—not entirely different, but different enough.

Hopkins' rhythm will be understood only when this fact is appreciated. It will not be understood by being explained in terms explicitly or implicitly those of a rhythm which depends on components of language on which it itself does not depend. It will certainly not be understood by being explained merely in terms of the "feet" which, borrowed in an unfortunate hour from classical prosody, have generally trod under any adequate understanding even of English running rhythm.

Hopkins himself has been charged with such short-sighted comment. Dr. Richards speaks of his explanation of sprung rhythm as a "curious way . . . of eluding a mischievous tradition and a spurious question, to give them a mock observance and an equally unreal answer." [99] But it is a serious mistake to judge the terms in which Hopkins explains his sprung rhythm apart from his own discussion of them in his lecture notes, a discussion which inoculates his whole terminology with a distinction and subtlety sufficient to immunize it against the usual suppositions of the "mischievous tradition." The more valid criticism of Hopkins' explanation is not that it is unreal, but that it is undeveloped; the consistency of its manifold implications is not made clear.

It is this consistency which the present study has attempted to point out and explain in connection with Hopkins' verse itself.

Neither will Hopkins' sprung rhythm be understood by concentrating attention on his "atrocious rhymes," or his "over-reaving" or his other "peculiarities" without regarding his rhythm as a whole. This is Bridges' mistake, and it ends only in bickering. For the apparent incidentals of Hopkins' echoings, stretched lines

[99] Richards, *op. cit.*, p. 203.

(outrides and burden lines), neglect of perfect end-rhyme, and "over-rove" lines are all part of the rhythm Hopkins employs, and at least in germ are likely to be associated with this rhythm in other poets.

Rhythmic integrity makes for great complexity, and hence Hopkins' "sprung rhythm" will be understood first by being heard. Explanation had better wait on love. If it does, the reader will be more than receptive, for he will know that, however great Hopkins' rhythmic achievements, he has others to his credit, too.

GERARD MANLEY HOPKINS, POET OF ASCETIC AND AESTHETIC CONFLICT

CHESTER A. BURNS, S.J.

Every Catholic poet of a religious order has known of conflict between those two opposing elements in his life: the poetic urge and religious discipline. The conflict is not grave; but to the poet concerned it will seem far from trivial. Certainly it was no trivial matter in the mind of Gerard Manley Hopkins, English priest, member of the Society of Jesus of half a century ago, and poet of now eminent and still gathering fame. Indeed Father Hopkins may be said to typify in his person, if not the gravity, then the acuteness of such conflict.

A religious order, the religious poet quickly discovers, is not a society consecrated to a dainty worship of aesthetic sanctities. It is an organization of rugged purpose seriously bent upon serving God as its proper constitutions require. No order comes to mind at the moment whose aims call for the honoring of God through a formal fostering of the poetic spirit. Perhaps some such order may one day be founded. Perhaps; but it is doubtful. And what one doubts is not the possibility, so much as the feasibility of the venture. An order of poets would be an order of dynamic, delicately-geared personalities who in no short time would find their noble experiment in common life crowned with—disillusionment. Such, after the first few weeks of ecstatic general confusion, would to an accompanying loud peal as of thunder shatter to nothingness and be dissolved forevermore. For each member of an idyllic order of this sort would come to demand— would, no doubt, begin by demanding—that he be a law unto himself. And with this method of procedure sinking rapidly

175

into gentle anarchy, common life would revert to private, wherein each individual would go his merry way blithely free with the freedom of the sons of men.

Such a pleasant path of decadence, of course, even under normal conditions, the poet who is a religious is, absolutely speaking, not prohibited from following. Only in those cases in which a sense of honor and the binding force of conscience are looked upon as a check on liberty may he be said to be restrained. Otherwise he is as free as the most unbound of men, since no ties save those of his personal making keep him bound to God and the religious life. His word (in this case a vow solemnly given) is quite literally his bond.

But if he would live in community, he must follow rule, in which eventuality sacrifices of individual preference will be a natural sequel. Now necessarily to be listed among the particular renunciations here included will be the unrestricted exercise of poetic impulse. This for the reason that, while a religious order may make special concessions to special temperaments, it cannot, save at peril of its constitutional integrity, grant unqualified freedom of choice in every matter to any of its members. For if to some, why not to all? And if to all, why—and incidentally, how—a religious order at all? Religious orders would be in a bad way surely if constitutions had to be recast every time a poet hove in sight. Were this the case, the pillars of "religion" would be forever trembling and tottering; for the very essential note of religiously ordered life stands firmly fixed only on the supposition of foundation upon a constant common rule. This failing, there is simply no religious order.

Let it be plainly stated then at the outset: Religious orders have no crying need of poets; nor, yet again, craving for the honor of their company. Be the poets of major, minor, or mediocre attainments, religious orders flourish grandly like the cedars of Lebanon without them. With them they continue so to do provided the poets in question rest content with their chosen common lot.

Poets therefore may not be granted indiscriminate concessions, amounting to mild license, by religious orders—despite what poetic license be conceded them by those loosely-linked bodies called poetic societies. As operating in practice, the religious plan of living calls for poets conducting their day elbow to elbow with scientists, historians, men of letters, scholars, teachers, preachers, and men generally of earnest, if prosaic, pursuits. Their poetry they must learn to take as the bird takes wing— casually and when occasion offers; for, seriously speaking, there is work to be done. They may not seek, and to their credit be it said, they do not (when they are poets of an authentic quality) ask for special favors. Not infrequently the glory of their poetry appears to suffer thereby; but the glory of God is increased, and that is the root reason why they joined a religious order.

On the other hand, the poet who commits himself to such a religious system does not find his personal perplexities so simply solved. He carries with him into his new manner of life an inalienable endowment: his poetic temperament. This he did not leave behind as he left his earthly effects behind when he entered religion. This for good or ill is part and parcel of his native temperament, a concentrated unyielding substratum, upon which neither time nor ascetic effort seems to produce marked change. Time and effort may, of course, and in all probability will, help fashion his character; but temperament persists; for like nature expelled by the fork, it keeps constantly recurring. As he was born a poet, a poet he remains, regardless of what constitutions, what rule added to rule, stands surety for the permanence of the religious order it was his vocation under God to join.

This is not strange, for temperaments, all in all, are not matters of free choosing, nor yet again matter for group-moulding. They are, we well know, gifts of Nature; Nature, that is to say, more correctly spoken of as God; and only God can put asunder what He has put together—something He seems seldom to do.

Therefore the poet on becoming a religious is a poet still; and herein lies the crux of his conflict. His temperament seems always inclined to tend one way when his innate sense of duty must insist that he go another. Train himself as he will by dint of stern discipline, relentless and inexorable, his temperament is always ready to — shall we say? — play him false. Whereas others of more pliant personality have taken on a clock-like regularity which enables them, with almost imperceptible effort, it would seem, to harmonize with formulated rule, he finds after years and years of ascetic endeavor, that he is, alas, no clock! Or if one, is at best one of variable habits, being ever in process of failing the hour by the hour. Wherefore the conflict, having arisen, persists.

What to do? Ah, that is the question! The religious poet so circumscribed faces a dilemma, either horn of which promises small hope of solution. Should he, on the one hand, renounce for the moment his religious obligations (minor ones only, be it understood) and pause as by instinct to contemplate some sunset glow of ideal smouldering on his poetic horizon, there will arise remorse of conscience, dejection of soul, and heart-sadness; his sensibilities shaken and stricken at thought of having failed his Lord. For failed Him he has; briefly, it is true, and in small matter, but failed Him nonetheless. And what is worse, lost time and perhaps grace, in so doing; dreaming gently in the meadow of aesthetic indulgence, when he should be up and about in the field of duty, his hand to the plough of prosaic task with never a glance behind.

Contrariwise, should he spurn the bounties of temperament, the painful reaction will be hardly less acute; for Nature has an artful way of taking revenge for contempt of her gifts. Caught thus between two extremes, the poet in harassed anxiety thinks to walk some golden, middle, and prudent path; but this he finds impractical, his not being what we call a moderate temperament.

Hence he comes, as did Gerard Hopkins at the opening of his religious career, to regard poetry with misgivings, and the obligations of religious life as (at times, let us say) more stringent than in reality they are. Yet with them he cast his lot and to them he cleaved, leaving the culture of poetry to whomsoever it might properly concern. There was to be, as who would doubt, a retracing of steps, a timid prodigal's return, to poetry; but this only after a lapse of seven years, when on occasion of a suggestion by his superior, he took the same almost literally, not to say eagerly, for a positive command. As he advanced in age, a grudgingly peaceful settlement of claims seems to have been established between these rivals; but his heart, even while it embraced poetry appears always to have leaned away from it over towards the reassuring strictures of religion. He apparently was never completely satisfied that in paying tribute to poetry he was not in effect paying tribute to some worldly aesthetic Caesar, and thereby denying God part at least of what was rightfully His. "I cannot find it in my conscience to spend time on it [poetry]," he once wrote a friend who had remonstrated with him for neglecting his talent (D 15. Oct. 5, 1878).

It was not that Gerard Hopkins doubted the intrinsic worth of poetry. That were to doubt the God who had made him—a poet. Besides, such point is past dispute. Poetry is unquestionably good before God, and gives Him honor as do the lilies of the field and the birds of the air. Rather, the question which vexed him was, not whether poetry was good, but whether here and now composition of it was more ill than well advised; and whether by giving time and trouble to it, he might not be rendering himself an unprofitable servant in the eyes of his one true Lord. Father Hopkins was not singular in his uneasiness. Plato had argued a like question at great dialectic length some twenty-four centuries previously, finally concluding from the viewpoint of a statesman that for the moral welfare of citizens, poets must be rigidly excluded from the confines of his ideal state.

The focal point of Gerard Hopkins' anxiety is not hard to lay finger on. There was, no doubt, a generous measure of, so to term it, aesthetic Platonism innate to his sensitive temperament; but his specific difficulty regarding poetry was not the difficulty of Plato. He had no ill-founded apprehensions of moral danger lurking in poetry as such. He was, in consequence of his formal scholastic training, too well grounded in the basic persuasions of Aristotelian-Thomism to see anything but good—and even God —in good poetry. His difficulty in brief was not theoretic. The issues were clearly drawn and free of dialectical embarrassments. His was a severely practical problem and lay in a practical consideration, which, were it to be formulated, might reduce itself to the query: How may one reconcile the erratic fluctuations of inspiration with the steady dictates of duty?

That he should have such a problem may be readily appreciated. Poetic inspiration comes at unpredictable moments. Licit poetic moments in an ordered life, on the other hand, are largely regulated by the clock. Poets must shave, bathe, eat, drink, and sleep, as other men—not to speak of praying, studying, and preaching, things every Jesuit must do. Also he must perform those radically necessary, if unromantic, duties which bring sweat to the brow and bread to the mouth. Yet despite these proletarian demands of life, the urges of inspiration keep coming to poets at all hours, unwooed and unsought. They come at intervals, the exact clock-hour of whose coming no man can foretell: they come in the dark of night and in the full light of day; they come when duty calls away and when no duty whatever calls. Their coming, as stated, is unpredictable.

Now the peculiar difficulty of dealing with inspiration is this: When it comes, it must be utilized instantly, for it is a passing thing, which once passed will not return. Delay is fatal. "One hour from now," it whispers alluringly to the poet busily and necessarily otherwise engaged, "will be too late. Now is the acceptable moment." Inspiration is no respecter of rights at variance with its own; hence moral considerations, such as reverence for duty, may scarcely be said to inhibit its promptings. Either you follow inspiration, and, if you are a poet, poetry results; or you set it aside, and the "light that never was on land or sea" fades and dies and is no more. Whatever else the gain, the poetry is lost.

Being a member of the Society of Jesus, a Jesuit in popular parlance, Gerard Hopkins found in the volatile nature of inspiration a vexing problem. A Jesuit's day (particularly that of a young Jesuit) is not mapped out with tender concern for individualistic promptings, those of inspiration perhaps least of all. His day is for God, and there is small concession made in it to personal preference. What self-development is provided for (and there is much) is of a kind that will be conducive to the common end of the Order, which, when all is said and done, is nothing other than the common end of life itself, heightened to a degree and brought to sharp focus: that is to say, the giving to God at all times an ever and ever greater glory. This, rather than any slight, self-canonized purpose, forms for the individual, and the body corporate as well, the specifying Jesuit ideal.

Poetry as envisioned in the Society's educational perspective is not a way of life. It is an incident along the way; which is all that it should be in any rational presentation of liberal studies. Hence a Jesuit who turns up poet when his days of intellectual and ascetic formation are accomplished, has more than the gay foam of phosphorescent poetic experiences flowing in his wake. Admitted that such a manner of training is rigid, it is far from foolish; and poets are forever dying of folly and their poetry with them.

Still the fact remains that for one of Gerard Hopkins' temperament, the problem of proper reconciliation of inspiration with duty was bound to be perplexing. He solved it quite simply, of course, as he who runs may read, in the first seven years of his Jesuit life; that is, by religiously ignoring inspiration and giving duty his total devotion. Poetry became for him a thing renounced. Which, let it be said, was in practice the safest, if not the theoretic best, thing to do. It tended to make of him a whole man, rather than one of brilliant but disparate parts. Later he worked out a more generous plan, which gave to poetry the time remaining when work of duty was done; time which, as it happened, was hardly a bare sufficiency. Therefore, while in general more satisfactory to his poetic temperament, this solution was not satisfactory in full.

For inspiration, after the manner of clamorous passions, has a propensity for intruding more and more boldly upon a poet's time and attention; and until it has won these for itself does not rest content. But Gerard Hopkins was in the main content. He gave to inspiration (and thereby to poetry) what he counted its due, and to God what seemed to him was His. If God's due in practice far exceeded that of inspiration, Gerard Hopkins was glad. He had entered the Society of Jesus to render God glory; and if in the process of so doing, either quantity or quality of poetry was lost, was not such an outcome best looked upon as, let us say, a matter of poetic justice? Not even for the gaining of the whole world might a man imperil his soul. Poetry surely was not in any scale of values of greater consequence than the whole world, not to speak of it as weighed against the incalculable worth of the immortal soul! No, Gerard Hopkins, poet and ascetic of the Society of Jesus, was not to be deluded on any such specious grounds by the aesthetic wiles of inspiration.

There was quite naturally, as a result of such an intransigent attitude, a regrettable loss. It was a loss tempered indeed by what he unshakenly held to be a greater gain; but loss there was nonetheless, positive, undeniable. No one will ever know in this world of many veiled uncertainties what multitudinous cloud-banks of inspiration, with accompanying train of rich images and brilliant inchoate word-formations, gathered, and to great extent gathered in vain, about the head and heart of Gerard Hopkins, as through the years he went his dutiful, conscientious way, giving glory to God. But to all such promptings when they conflicted with duty he uttered a decisively firm and unequivocal: "Nay." The loss to poetry is great. Perhaps no more justly famed "mute inglorious Milton" is to be found in the annals of literature than this same Gerard Hopkins in these moments of inspiration heroically discarded.

Yet there is palliation and to spare for his unflinching refusal to deal in compromise. One old Master of Novices of the Society of Jesus used to call humorous attention to the fact that uncounted poems of aspiring young Jesuit versifiers were undoubtedly annihilated by the bell summoning to examination of conscience twice daily; yet this same spiritual director warned quite seriously that for a Jesuit it were incomparably more fatal to have the examination of conscience brought to nought by ill-timed poetic composition than to have poetry stilled in the heart by loyal adherence to duty. From which it may be deduced that Jesuits are not with formal intent reared to be poets. "Duty before Beauty" becomes rather their instinctive ideal.

This is as it should be. Art has no law, moral or ascetic, rendering it sacred, and artists no privileges uncommon to the generality of men. A Jesuit poet in last analysis is no more than any given Jesuit, supposing such talent, giving God glory through the exercise of his poetic gifts. When there is question of poetry setting up court for itself, and danger thereby of God's glory being impinged on, danger in fact of that glory being not at all sought, the Jesuit poet must draw swiftly back: else he is in so far no true Jesuit, no authentic follower of Him Whom he has proposed to himself as his leader supreme in life: Christ the Lord.

For a Jesuit, Christ may never be separated from Art, as neither may He be sundered from science, history, teaching, preaching and all laudable life pursuits. Once granted that the "Word was made flesh and dwelt amongst us," a strictly otherworld standard of judgement attaches to human effort, human achievement. What Christ cannot approve of, no Jesuit may dare set seal of approval to, either in his own life or in that of another.

Of this Gerard Hopkins was most vividly aware. Christ was at once his spur and his check. When Christ nodded "Yes" to

Gerard the poet, said Gerard was off with his impetuous rush of scurrying words to heights of poetic achievement:

> But how shall I . . . make me room there:
> Reach me a . . . Fancy, come faster—
> Strike you the sight of it? look at it loom there,
> Thing that she . . . there then! *the Master,*
> *Ipse, the only one, Christ, King, Head:*
>   (*The Wreck of the Deutschland,* St. 28)

When Christ said "No," Gerard, perhaps regretfully but still unquestioningly, gave poetry his simple gesture of negation.

> What do then? how meet beauty? Merely meet it; own,
> Home at heart, heaven's sweet gift; *then leave, let that alone.*
> Yea, wish that though, wish all, God's better beauty, grace.
>   (*To What Serves Mortal Beauty*)

Thus it has come to pass that the poetry we know today as that of Hopkins, G.M., S.J., is confined to a single small volume of comparatively few poems, all of exquisite worth. It might have been of greater bulk. It might even have been of more flawless perfection. Conceivably. Who knows? But one thing it could hardly have been: more to God's glory. That, if one may say so, is its distinguishing quality, its Jesuit hall-mark.

Let there be then the merest modicum of tears shed for the conjectured loss of the Hopkins poetry; and these tears quickly, even joyously, dried. All is not lost when poetry is lost. Those who understand Gerard Hopkins' ideal of life to the full will shed no tears at all. They will know only too well that the world is in the main more nobly enriched by a good man's life than by any product whatever of his head or heart. Poetry—no question of it—has its due place in life, rendering those who read it an unique enjoyment and the poet who writes it the thrilling gladness that comes with poetic creation. Such are its proper functions. But poetry is not life: it is one of life's adjuncts. Not all the tremulous rhetoric in the world need move one by so much as one inch into accepting poetry for what it is not—a thing transcending, if so it might be, life itself.

Gerard Hopkins assuredly was not of such mind. He neither shed, nor, were he alive today, would he shed, great fund of disconsolate tears for the comparatively small bulk, and even, if you will, the flaws of his poetry. Father Hopkins was never dismayed that he did not produce more poetry and greater poetry. His regrets were of quite another order. He regretted only what fault he might conceivably have been guilty of in devoting to poetry that which was more than poetry's right. He enumerates in a letter to a friend a short list of these regrets, a list detailing with conscience-keen accuracy a few of those heart-pangs a sensitive spirit will wince under at thought of real or fancied infidelities to God (D 88. Nov. 2, 1881):

For the backward glances I have given with my hand upon the plough, for the waste of time the very compositions you admire may have caused and their preoccupation of the mind which belonged to more sacred or more binding duties, for the disquiet and the thoughts of vain-glory they have given rise to. . .

Such openly-avowed expressions of compunction represent the living mind of Gerard Hopkins. Softly-muted insinuations of a contrary nature, scattered among the appraisals of critics who admire but do not love him, represent the purest of sheer, not to say unwarranted, conjecture. Nowhere will such expressions be found in writings of Gerard Hopkins' own hand. Nor should such be expected of him. His character was not only too un-worldly, it was of too heavenly a cast for him to be so minded. He was vividly alert to the summons of sanctity. He felt, one may safely assume, as Léon Bloy felt, that: "There is only one tragedy in life, not to become a saint."

Poetry, after all, was not his life-calling. Gerard Hopkins had not sought place in the ranks of the Society of Jesus to become a poet. That he knew well might have been accomplished more effectively (though it is doubtful if so characteristically) in the world from which he emerged. He had embraced the religious life for a transparent twofold reason: to assure, as far as was humanly possible, through working for God's greater glory, his own soul's salvation and sanctification, and to help others towards the same. Poet as he was, he was no vacuous dreamer where deepest realities were concerned. Never did he waver in his firm Jesuit conviction that it is beyond all question preferable to become a saint than to become a poet; and where the two ideals are compatible, again preferable to become more of a saint than more of a poet.

> Ah! there was a heart right!
> There was single eye!
> (*The Wreck of the Deutschland,* St. 29)

these are his admiring, his holily-envious, exclamations apropos of the "tall nun" who called "Christ to her" in the midst of the storm and wreckage that spelled doom to the *Deutschland*. And, all in all, it was the sheer sanctity in the unrivaled heroism of both the woman and the moment that drew him and held him enthralled.

Religious as he was, he was entirely open-eyed to, strictly if somewhat apprehensively conscious of, the fact that if only he had the courage for it, there well might be by God's grace a nobler someone altogether than Gerard Hopkins the poet—Gerard Hopkins the saint!

His sense of a call to a life in union with God as intimate as possible, the implications of a supernatural "noblesse oblige" inherent in the law, letter, and spirit of his vocation weighed seriously on his mind. "My vocation sets before me," he writes decisively, "a standard so high that a higher can be found nowhere else" (D 88. Nov. 2, 1881). Christian, which is to say Catholic to his heart's core, he took his Master Christ as the essential criterion of a genuinely successful career. As he grew in the spirit and, as far as was consonant with his temperament, in fidelity to the letter of his religious life, Christ became more and more his mind's invariable preoccupation; until as once for Saul of Tarsus, changed in a lightning-flash to Paul of the Christians (*The Wreck of the Deutschland,* St. 10), one motto might spell all: "To live is Christ and to die is Christ. Who shall separate me from the love of Christ?"

All through his poetry may be seen (and felt) the gathering and growth of this devotion to Christ. From *The Wreck of the Deutschland,* where "brimming in a flash full," men, as by uncontrollable impulse, go to "Hero of Calvary," on through *The Windhover,* specially dedicated to "Christ our Lord," and still further and further on through *The Loss of the Eurydice, The Bugler's First Communion,* and *The Soldier,* the devotion mounts at increasing tempo, until at length it is caught up and incarnated in the grand burst of paeonic song marking the close of the *That Nature is a Heraclitean Fire and of the comfort of the Resurrection.* Here, in this last of his great poems, written somewhat less than a year before his death, the realization of Christ's victory over sin, and all the implications held therein, burst from his heart almost with a shout of joy as he triumphantly proclaims Christ's emergence from the tomb on Easter morn!

Enough! the Resurrection,
A heart's-clarion! Away grief's gasping, joyless days, dejection.
 Across my foundering deck shone
A beacon, an eternal beam. Flesh fade, and mortal trash
Fall to the residuary worm; world's wildfire, leave but ash:
 In a flash, at a trumpet crash,
I am all at once what Christ is, since He was what I am, and
This Jack, joke, poor potsherd, patch, matchwood, immortal dia-
 mond,
 Is immortal diamond.

Altogether Christ looms large in his work. His hallowed Name, rising like the crest of a wave-swell, breaks again and again above the ever-moving waters of his sweeping emotions—by count over forty times. This, of course, is only natural; for as He was ever vividly present to the mind of Gerard Hopkins, He was of sheer necessity intimately interwoven with the Hopkins verse. So much so, in fact, that with justice it may be said: Who knows not Christ, knows not Gerard Hopkins.

For a man then so vivified by the love of Christ, who will wish to say that the prospect of loss of something as evanescent, albeit so naturally noble, as poetry were subject for tears of an inconsolable grief?

Yet there are those who think it was; or if not, should have been. The critics have spoken; and over the lovely remains of their fancied loss have poured out expressions of a most poignant sadness. But such are best taken lightly. Though representing, let it be granted, the honestly conceived concern of honorable men, such representations are still too ephemeral in substance to be regarded as setting forth a serious sorrow we all should share. "God changeth never," it is true, but critics have been known to do so. Which is as it should be; for as "there lives the dearest freshness deep down things" (*God's Grandeur*), truth is there as well, and the truth should be found and should prevail.

Therefore all sad portraits of Gerard Hopkins "cramped by the stern discipline of Jesuit life" and living out dismal days of broken-hearted frustration among the Jesuits, may be viewed with a smile of gentle, not to say profound, incredulity. As may also those further canvasses of him, purporting to represent his sad lot as he is sent off mercilessly to Ireland, there to die at last immaturely "from a typhoid infection acquired from working in the Dublin slums." [1]

For as facts stand, such things simply are not true. Yet like alligators to Pantheists, Jesuits seem strangely provocative of per-

[1] Paul Engle, "Biography of Poet Reveals His Personality's Richness" (Rev. of Ruggles' biography), *Chicago Tribune*, July 30, 1944.

plexity to a certain type of critic.[2] Just why may be left to the critics to determine. Could it by any chance be the innocent hard logic, the unqualified Catholic insistence of the Jesuits on the simple polar truth that God, not man, is the "measure of things"?

Whatever the reason, Jesuits in the present instance would point out that God has right to a word—even the last word— on such matters as the timeliness of what are popularly—should we say, unthinkingly?—called "untimely" or "immature" deaths;

[2] At times the perplexity assumes amazing proportions, as witness the following arraignment, which, were it not for its grotesque bias, might be taken for a mild misrepresentation of, perhaps even insult to, the Jesuits!

"Humanly speaking he [Gerard Hopkins] made a grievous mistake in joining the Jesuits for on further acquaintance his whole soul must have revolted against a system which has killed many and many a noble soul; but what matters the means compared with the undoubted result. Any wood will do for the cross, when God's perfection is thereby reached. To get on with the Jesuits you must become on many grave points a machine, without will, without conscience, and that to his nature was an impossibility. To his lasting honor be it said he was too good for them. . . ." (F 249. Letter from C. N. Luxmoore to Arthur Hopkins.)

Apart from the matter of truth, to which Jesuits presumably have no right, being, as they are so patently, "without conscience" (something their traducers so easily have—warm and reassuring!), it is difficult to understand how a man of average intelligence, to say nothing of common courtesy, could calmly set forth such judgement and permit its display to the public eye. Even granted that the judgement was hasty, need it have been nasty? Such indictment is a large one and affects a large body of men, and MIGHT be hard to substantiate. Has the memory of Newman's *Apologia* and the hapless Kingsley slipped so completely from mind? At any rate it would seem that here we have Kingsley out-Kingsleyed! One is forced to the conclusion that any wood will do for the Jesuits' cross, when a critic's satisfaction is thereby attained.

The strangeness of the diatribe grows the more one recollects the character of the men who in Father Hopkins' day went to make up what are indifferently labeled "Jesuits," as if one were speaking of hippopotami, rhinoceri, and animals generally of a repulsive sort! Are we to assume that in the writer's conviction Gerard Hopkins was "too good" for association with men of the stamp and achievement of, say, Fathers Bernard Vaughan, Henry Schomberg Kerr, John Morris, Peter Gallwey, Daniel Considine, William Leslie, Sidney Smith, George Porter, Henry Coleridge, John and Joseph Rickaby? These even the casually-informed would recognize as names to be conjured with, or as some would say, honored. Yet these are the "Jesuits" against whom Gerard Hopkins' "whole soul" is presumed to have revolted. Of course, the simple plain truth is that if there were great men before Agamemnon, there were great men, great Jesuits, within arm's reach of Gerard Hopkins as he lived out his days in the Society of Jesus. To his lasting honor be it said Father Hopkins recognized this.

and likewise right to pronounce judgement—even last judgement—on what are again popularly spoken of as "cramped," "frustrated" lives. As exemplification of such word, they (the Jesuits) would call attention to the widely known fact that Jesus Christ, God's very own Son and Himself God, has gone on record as saying that not a sparrow falls to the ground, or a hair from any head, but the heavenly Father of all of us knows it.

Could it possibly be then that by some wholly unprecedented cosmic indifference, this otherwise ever-watchful and solicitous Lord was impelled to lose sight of Gerard Hopkins as he passed his "dismal," "frustrated" days in the Society of Jesus; allowing him with fitting climactic denouement, as he came to his final earthly hours, to slip from life unnoticed and uncared for, and that immaturely? DID THEN THE DARK SIDE OF THE BAY OF GOD'S BLESSING NOT VAULT HIM, THE MILLION ROUNDS OF GOD'S MERCY NOT REEVE— Gerard Hopkins, the dismal and the frustrated—EVEN HIM IN? (cf. *The Wreck of the Deutschland*, St. 12.)

Could such event come to pass under God? "Absolutely, emphatically, no!" would say the Jesuits. "For such is decidedly not God's way!" And though even by self-admission, Jesuits may be mistaken on many points, it will not be, they would insist, on matters such as these. These are as certain and fixed as the ground under our feet and the vault of heaven over our heads.

Wherefore let it modestly be suggested that critical appraisers of literature are best suited to humble labor on their narrow literary lasts. Not theirs to render what only God All-Knowing is qualified to render: authoritative pronouncements on such primal and final matters as life and death. Indeed it would seem advisable that all who touch such topics should, from the outset bow reverently to that which in Ireland, the land of Father Hopkins' death, is with faith-founded reason called: The Blessed Will of God.

But if discussion of what might have been is on the whole futile, plain statement of what actually transpired is not. Father

Hopkins did die at the age of forty-five, as many a worthy man before him had done; and dying piously in the Lord, passed to that land of human heart's desire, where "God shall wipe away all tears from their eyes, and death shall be no more, nor mourning nor crying, nor sorrow shall be any more, for the former things are passed away." But before death he expressed himself to an effect that should with finality lay to rest any valid doubt concerning himself and his happiness.

For after being duly prepared for his passage into eternity by the comforting rites of the Church, he broke in upon the hush of his sickroom with a whisper of words that tendered lucid witness to the serenity of his contented soul. "I am so happy," he said. "I am so happy." Unlike many a brother-poet of morally carefree habits, he sounded strangely unfrustrated. Which stated, need anything further be added, any more conclusive period put to the idly controverted subject of the life, lot, and death of Gerard Hopkins, priest of the Society of Jesus and poet after Christ's own Heart?

AN INTERPRETIVE GLOSSARY OF DIFFICULT WORDS IN THE POEMS

Raymond V. Schoder, S.J.

By Way of Introduction: Hopkins' Diction

The worst stumbling block in the path of the curious or intently earnest reader who is trying to gain a firsthand knowledge of Hopkins' poetry is, beyond doubt, the frequent obscurity of his diction. Confronted on all hands by words which convey little or no clearly defined meaning, many a new reader only too naturally withdraws in uneasy dismay to other fields where his good will runs a better chance of being more considerately received. And even the persistent student often feels that his patient efforts to pluck the meat from these obviously rich poems are being fruitlessly shattered against the adamant shell of an unmeaning vocabulary. Frequently, too, quite false interpretations of a poem are arrived at because the reader has by-passed or misapprehended some important word or words in the text.

All this is a great loss, for Hopkins' thought is always valuable and distinctive. To grasp it in its fulness, with clarity and empathy, is a poetic experience of an uncommonly high and satisfying order. Such an understanding requires, of course, more than a knowledge of words. One must draw upon adequate acquaintance with the complex religious, philosophical, literary, and personal background of Hopkins' highly wrought expression. But the first and most crucial requirement is a reasonably accurate awareness of the intent of his words and of their connotative background, however unusual the language may be. For Hopkins' diction is something apart, as characteristic and distinctive as his rhythm or prose style. As Dr. Pick says, "He uses almost a new language, and doesn't provide a dictionary." [1]

Two factors render his diction difficult: coinage of new words or new senses for old words and employment of provincial or dialectical usage. What appear at first to be archaisms are usually not so. They are but borrowings from the living dialect of the common people or of particular regions whose speech Hopkins had made booty of in his eager chase for the precise, the living, the more colorful word. They are very seldom studied revivals of truly archaic language, and even then find place in his poems only because Hopkins believes their disappearance a great loss to the vigor and expressiveness of artistic English: "I am learning Anglosaxon and it is a vastly superior thing to what we have now. . . . It makes one weep to think what English might have been . . ." (B 163, 162). For Hopkins was ardently convinced that the key to a restored vigor in poetry was to break away from artificial Victorian poets' cant (Bridges' "continuous literary decorum") and write one's thoughts straight out in the natural rhythm and vocabulary of living popular English: "I cut myself off from the use of *ere, o'er, wellnigh, what time, say not* (for *do not say*), because, though dignified, they neither belong to nor ever cd. arise from, or be the elevation of, ordinary modern speech. For it seems to me that the poetical language of an age shd. be the current language heightened, to any degree heightened and unlike itself, but not (I mean normally: passing freaks and graces are another thing) an obsolete one. This is Shakespeare's and Milton's practice and the want of it will be fatal to Tennyson's Idylls and plays, to Swinburne, and perhaps to Morris" (B 89). In accordance with this belief, we find Hopkins perpetually interested in words and in the common speech. Both the *Notebooks* and the *Letters* are full of this eagerness. We find him jotting down apt words or phrases, noting

---

[1] John Pick, *Gerard Manley Hopkins, Priest and Poet* (Oxford Univ. Press, 1942), p. 101. The reference is primarily to Hopkins' *Commentary on the Spiritual Exercises,* but it fits the poems with slight qualification.

local dialect and phonetics, reporting expressions he has heard a lay brother or a farmer or a workman use, dabbling in Maltese, Welsh, Egyptian, and comparative philology, asking experts for aid in determining the precise technical term for something or in defining dialectical equivalents. On the other hand, he often tries his hand at coining just the right expression for some act or object, using this in a poem or making a memorandum of it for possible future use.[2] What he is always seeking is the *mot juste.*

That this often led to obscurity is only natural. Hopkins was aware of the danger and admitted it: "This is a terrible business about my sonnet 'Have fair fallen', for I find that I still 'make myself misunderstood.' "[3] "No doubt my poetry errs on the side of oddness. . . . But 'inscape' is what I above all aim at in poetry. Now it is the virtue of design, pattern, or inscape to be distinctive and it is the vice of distinctiveness to become queer. This vice I cannot have escaped. However, 'winding the eyes' is queer only if looked at from the wrong point of view. . . ."[4] "I can well understand that 'what there is unusual in expression in my verse is less pleasant when you are in that sort of weak state', for I find myself that when I am tired things of mine sound strange, forced, and without idiom which had pleased me well enough in the fresh heat of composition. But then the weaker state is the less competent and really critical" (B 136–137). "I am sure I have gone far enough in oddities and running rhymes . . . into the next line" (B 250). The misunderstanding with which his poems so often met, for reasons of rhythm and content as well as diction, pained and disappointed him, but could not force him to abandon his convictions. He bursts out

[2] Sometimes his memory betrayed him in this, as when he wrote to Dixon of his poem 35: *Ribblesdale,* "*Louched* is a coinage of mine, and is to mean much the same as slouched, slouching" (D 109) ; but, as Bridges says in his note, the word had recognized standing in the dialect dictionaries. Hopkins had probably picked up the word somewhere, then forgotten about it and thought he had created it.

[3] B 174; the sonnet mentioned is 21, *Henry Purcell.*

[4] B 66; the reference is to *Poems* 10.9.

on Bridges: "You give me a long jobation about eccentricities. Alas, I have heard so much about and suffered so much for and in fact been so completely ruined for life by my alleged singularities that they are a sore subject" (B 126).

Admitting his obscurity, he will not abjure it. He protests that the trouble lies not in his words but in the reader's unawareness of their meaning. He is ready to explain terms when asked, and even proposed writing brief prose 'arguments' for each poem, or at least the harder ones. As he says of his poem 49, *Rodriguez,* "The sonnet (I say it snorting) aims at being intelligible" (B 293). Even so, obscurity is not wholly evil: ". . . that is the main thing, to be correct; if I am that, that is the great point gained" (B 213). He even defends apparent obscurity: "Granted that it [the *Wreck of the Deutschland*] needs study and is obscure, for indeed I was not over-desirous that the meaning of all should be quite clear, at least unmistakable, you might, without the effort that to make it all out would seem to have required,[5] have nevertheless read it so that lines and stanzas should be left in the memory and superficial impressions deepened, and have liked some without exhausting all. I am sure I have read and enjoyed pages of poetry that way. Why, sometimes one enjoys and admires the very lines one cannot understand, as for instance 'If it were done when 'tis done' sqq. [*Macbeth* 1.7.1-], which is all obscure and disputed, though how fine it is everybody sees and nobody disputes" (B 50). Hence, what seems at first sight meaningless will yield up its sense when one brings to it the requisite background and analytic study. Then it will be seen to have hidden something too definite and important to the whole to have been sacrificed for mere simplicity of diction: "Obscurity I do and will try to avoid so far as is consistent with excellences higher than clearness at a first reading" (B 54). "Epic and drama and ballad and many, most, things should be at once intelligible; but everything need not and cannot be.

[5] It *is*, then, Hopkins implies, clear in itself if only the reader will work it out.

Plainly if it is possible to express a subtle and recondite thought on a subtle and recondite subject in a subtle and recondite way and with great facility and perfection, in the end something must be sacrificed, with so trying a task, in the process, and this may be the being at once, nay perhaps even the being without explanation at all, intelligible" (B 265–6). "One of two kinds of clearness one shd. have—either the meaning to be felt without effort as fast as one reads or else, if dark at first reading, when once made out *to explode*" (B 90).

Scheme of the Glossary

It is the aim of the following glossary to break down as much as possible the mystery which overclouds many of Hopkins' words. This will allow the general reader to understand more fully the basic meaning of the poems. Unless one knows the intent of the words it is hopeless to try to fathom the further problems of thought, metaphor, or religious-philosophical background. But if the words are clear, one is at least building on solid and objective ground when attempting an analysis of the higher meaning. To proceed otherwise is to theorize in a vacuum.

Some of the difficulties of diction have been explained by Bridges, mostly through citation of Hopkins' own exegesis. A few more have been clarified by various critics, others misinterpreted by them. The present glossary is the result of first-hand analysis of the whole *corpus* of Hopkins' writings, prose as well as poetry, to allow the poet's own explanations and parallel usage priority of appeal. All words were then traced down in the great *Oxford English Dictionary*,[6] *Webster's New International*[7] and Halliwell's *Dictionary of Archaic and Provincial Words*[8] to discover their full connotative range and historical develop-

[6] *The Oxford English Dictionary*, ed. by Murray & Onions, new edition, 13 volumes (Oxford Univ. Press, 1933).

[7] G. and C. Merriam Co., 1932.

[8] James O. Halliwell, *A Dictionary of Archaic and Provincial Words* (Routledge, 1924).

ment. The meanings are arranged so that the one(s) which the context seems to demand come first. Meanings which are practically synonymous with one another are divided by commas; groups of somewhat different meanings are set off by semicolons; and where sometimes very remote meanings for the particular context are cited so that all the word's possibilities may be clear, these unlikely connotations are set off from the preceding by a dash. The words are cited in the order of the poems in which they occur, but an alphabetical index is also appended.

Since this is an interpretive glossary, comments and argumentation are introduced where necessary, but in general the meanings given are directly based on the various sources above cited. In the case of coined words or senses, the interpretation is of course my own deduction from considerations of context and Hopkins' usage. The meanings given are not set forth as definitive for a particular passage, but only as the objective evidence of what the word does mean in accepted usage. If Hopkins misunderstood a word, or used it in an unrecognized sense, or gave it some new twist and technicality of meaning, it is the province of literary criticism to determine so by authentic methods. But at least here is what the word *should* mean, and the necessary starting point for deciding on its actual force in context.

One essays a task like this glossary with some misgivings. Echoing in the ears is Hopkins' parenthetical cry when interpreting for Bridges some puzzling words in an early draft of 11, *The Sea and the Skylark:* "Rash-fresh more (it is dreadful to explain these things in cold blood) means a headlong and exciting new snatch of singing . . ." [9] Then too, some words will not co-operate and yield up any definite sense which wholly satisfies; we can only list their possibilities for private preferential choice. But there is consolation here, for we find that Hopkins himself did not always know what some of his rare words meant! In the *Journal* for June 12, 1874 (N 196) we find: "Much

[9] B 164. Note, however, that Hopkins himself *does* explain.

sense of growth in bare oaks and much cast (so I have written: I hardly understand it) in the boulder." Finally, if anyone feels a bit exasperated with Hopkins for sometimes going too far in his search for the secret word to hit off his intention precisely, and instead burying the sense in the senseless,[10] let him recall Hopkins' friendly plea for reconciliation: ". . . propitiate Lang, set me right with him; not in the literary way but personally; make him understand that those snags that are in my style are not in my heart and temper" (B 158-159).

GLOSSARY

The * indicates a dialectical, provincial, or archaic word or sense; the # signifies that the word or sense is coined by Hopkins; a dash precedes unlikely meanings. Numerals preceding the titles of poems indicate their numbering in *Poems*. Numerals preceding words in glossary indicate line numbers of the poem. (In the case of *The Wreck of the Deutschland* numerals before words indicate stanza and line.)

3 THE HABIT OF PERFECTION
    11 *Ruck:* heap, throng; general run of things; rubbish, nonsense. (Contrast *ruck,* 36.12.)
    11 *Reel:* noise, tumult; whirling movement, stagger; dance.
    12 *Coils:* wrap in coils, ensnare; constrain; * thrash.
    13 *Hutch:* hut, pen, confining abode; small box.
4 THE WRECK OF THE DEUTSCHLAND
    2.8 *Laced:* confine, as the waist, by drawing laces tight; bind; —beat, punish.
    3.2 *Hurtle:* clashing sound, clatter; dashing together, collision, conflict; rush (Cf. 49.8).

[10] Cf. B 163, on an early draft of *The Sea and the Skylark*: "The sonnet you ask about is the greatest offender in its way that you could have found. It was written in my salad days, my Welsh days, when I was fascinated with *cynghanedd* or consonant-chime, and, as in Welsh *englyns*, 'the sense,' as one of themselves said, 'gets the worst of it.'"

3.4 *Spell:* (noun) time, period of anguished struggle; as a verb, *spell* could mean: * signify, import ("that spells ruin"); * utter, declare, tell.

4.4 *Combs:* (of a wave, etc.) break with white foam, roll over, form crest; (trans.) divide into ordered grooves, rake (Cf. 51.6, where Bridges, without authorization, substitutes *moulds* for MS *combs*).

4.6 *Roped:* fed by, connected by twirling trickles to the spring (see Bridges' note).

4.7 *Fells:* hill, small mountain; upland moor; field on side or top of a hill (Cf. 15.3).

4.7 *Voel:* (Welsh) bare hill. The reference is to the hill near St. Beuno's college: ". . . with Fr. Morris up the Voel" (*Jnl.,* Sept. 8, 1874: N 211).

4.7 *Vein:* * rivulet, streamlet (a different use than 4.33.5).

4.8 *Proffer:* (a substantive: gospel-proffer; viz., grace).

5.5 *Damson:* small dark purple plum (prunus damascena).

5.7 *Instressed:* # to feel a vivid impact of something with concentration and many associations, to dwell on, realize, emphasize (cf. N 349: "a dwelling on his own beauty, an instressing of his own inscape" —referring to Lucifer); often akin to *Einfuehlung,* empathy; the forceful impression made on a beholder by the inner energies of a thing's being. (Cf. B 88; D 37, 63, 68; N 98—a still different sense. Contrast also *outstress* in N 344, meaning God's activity outward, 'ad extra.') See on 27.7 (*The Handsome Heart*), and for further prose uses the index to N.

8.3 *Sloe:* the dark purple, sharply sour tasting fruit of the blackthorn (prunus spinosa).

9.3 *Wring:* rack, afflict, vex, distress; twist. (Cf. 17.62 for the intransitive sense.)

11.8 *Cringe:* (trans.) distort, contract, draw in; (intrans.) cower; here probably # causative: make to cringe, cower.

12.3 *Tell:* count, enumerate. (Cf. 32.13; 34.3; 53.2.)

12.7 *Bay:* (architectural metaphor) large partially enclosed space. (Cf. *Jnl.,* Nov. 20, 1869: ". . . in opposite bays of the sky." N 125.)

12.8 *Reeve:* tie fast, attach to something, by passing rope through holes (a nautical metaphor, to which Bridges, in his note *ad loc.,* p. 100, strangely takes exception); —* gather in the folds of a garment. (Cf. on 39.10.)

14.3 *Combs:* crest, ridge, long narrow hill. (Not to be confused with the *comb* of 33.3 which = *coomb*). Cf. N 164: "the comb or crest" of a wave.

14.8 *Wind:* (nautical technical term) guide course, make turn about for some goal. (A different word from the *wind* of 10.9, 17.28, 32.3.)

16.8 *Burl:* # noun from * verb, to bubble up (as a fountain or spring); to rotate, spin with a whizzing noise (=Scotch verb *birl*); —as a noun, *burl* properly means a knot in wood. (Cf. 54.12; also N 135: "the burly waterbacks which heave after heave kept tumbling up." At N 201, 208, 332–5, 338, *burl* = vortex, twirl.)

19.3 *Hawling:* #, not a recognized word; probably intended as equivalent for 'howling'; —old spelling for 'hauling.'

19.4 *Rash:* (Scotch), a wind-driven rainfall; crash; as verb, * to rush, dash violently; as adjective, vigorous, urgent, quick. (Cf. *rash-fresh,* 11.6; rash, 58. 109.)

19.4 *Sloggering:* to strike hard, assail with blows.

19.6 *Fetch:** stretch, reach; trick, stratagem; deep, painful breath.

20.2 *Coifed:* with close-fitting cap.

21.6 *Unchancelling:* #; 'chancel' means sanctuary, the part of a church near the altar and closed off from those not officiating by a lattice or screen.

22.1 *Sake:* * sign, mark, outer meaning, as in 'name-sake,' 'for the sake of.' (See on 21.10.)

23.4 *Lovescape:* # the very pattern, heart, essence of love, viz., Christ. See appendix to glossary on *scape* and *inscape.*

24.6 *Quails:* If 'throng' refers to the other passengers, this word has its common intrans. sense: cower; if to the throng of snowflakes, *quails* will be trans.: cause to quail, daunt, terrify; or * overpower, destroy.

27.8 *Burly:* (cf. hurly-burly): tumult, disturbance.

29.3 *Shock:* probably a substantive in opposition to "night," hence meaning: conflict, crashing struggle; —as adjective, *shock* means only: shaggy, with thick hair.

32.2 *Yore-flood:* #, probably the Deluge; perhaps the primal waters of Genesis, divided by the Creator when land was brought forth at His will.

33.5 *Vein:* * inclination, desire; natural tendency, talent; trait, mood; —a deposit, as of minerals. Note B 170: 'he had a real vein' (i.e., talent); 'vein of beauty' 54.4, B 250; contrast *vein* at 4.4.7.

34.8 *Shire:* district, county; town; as Bridges notes, 'it is the special favoured landscape visited by the shower.'

35.5 *Cresseted:* #, from the cresset-light, a blazing oil in a hollow of stone, a beacon.

5 PENMAEN POOL

    5 *Dart:* hurl, send out swiftly.

    8 *Sculls:* oar at stern, twisted from side to side; a boat so propelled.

11 *Hobs and nobs:* to drink together, be on intimate
terms (= 'give and take'; derived from 'have and
have not').

27 *Roundels:* hollow ring, circle.

8 . THE STARLIGHT NIGHT

4 *Delves:* pit, den.

6 *Whitebeam:* the *sorbus aria,* a tree with white silky
hair under its leaves.

6 *Abeles:* white poplar. (A two-syllable word.)

11 *Sallows:* low, brush-shaped willows ('salix').

9 SPRING

10 *Strain:* inherited quality from ancestors; tune (Cf.
27.14).

10 THE LANTERN OUT OF DOORS

9 *Wind:* * for 'wend,' go, especially in wandering
course. ". . . I mean that the eye winds / only in
the sense that its focus or point of sight winds and
that coincides with a point of the object and winds
with that. For the object, a lantern passing further
and further away and bearing now east, now west
of one right line, is truly and properly described as
winding. That is how it should be taken then."
(B 66–67.) (See above, on 4.14.8, for distinctions
between this and other words.)

11 THE SEA AND THE SKYLARK

2 *Trench:* touch, encroach on; make a groove in.

2 *Ramps:* rush about in rage; as of a horse: to rear on
hind feet as if to climb the air.

4 *Wear:* (technical sense, of the sun and moon) go
on, move slowly; endure, resist attrition.

6 *Rash-fresh:* "headlong and exciting new snatch of
singing" (B 164).
Stanza 2 is explained at length by Hopkins in B 164
(quoted by Bridges in his note to this poem).

12 THE WINDHOVER

    1 *Minion:* sovereign's favorite, darling, pet, 'creature.'

    4 *Rung:* (technical term of falconry) to rise spirally in flight; go about in rings or circles.

   10 *Buckle:* (intrans.) come to close quarters, grapple with, engage, join in close fight (cf. *I Henry VI,* 1.2.95; 5.3.28); — put on armor for contest, buckle on armor; crumple, collapse under pressure (these senses do not seem to fit the context. See the analysis of *The Windhover* in this volume).

   12 *Sillion:* (* spelling for 'selion') a strip or ridge of land between two furrows dividing plots in the open-field system, a 'narrow land.'

13 PIED BEAUTY

    2 *Brinded:* * for 'brindled'; tawny or brownish surface streaked with other hues or spotted.

    3 *Moles:* * spot, stain, as on cloth.

    5 *Fold:* plain earth, ground; enclosed yard, farmstead; the ridge of a field. Cp. N 123: "Br. Sidgreaves has heard the high ridges of a field called *folds* and the hollow between the *drip*."

14 HURRAHING IN HARVEST

    1 *Stooks:* shock, stock, cock, sheaf of hay or corn. Cf. *Jnl.* for Aug. 8, 1874: ". . . the sheaves were scattered and left in the rain, not made into stooks (which by the by the Devonshire people call shocks)." (N 200)

    3 *Sack:* a flowing silk cape attached to the shoulders of the 18th Century French gown, and falling down to form a train. (The clouds are cirrus, the 'meal-drift' cirro-cumulus.)

    4 *Meal-drift:* soft, powdery. Cf. *Early Diary,* 1866 (N 53): "Mealy clouds with a not brilliant moon."

    4 *Moulded:* mix, blend; form, shape. Cf. "moulded clouds" at N 141, 143, 147.

15 THE CAGED SKYLARK
>   1 *Scanted:* confine, restrict.
>   3 *Fells:* elevated wild field, down, moor; * hill. (Cf. 4.4.7.)

16 IN THE VALLEY OF THE ELWY
>   9 *Combes*: * for *coomb:* a hollow steep valley closed in at the head in crescent form by scooped out hill; (in S.E. England) a ravine. (See on *comb* in 33.3.)

17 THE LOSS OF THE EURYDICE
>   6 *Furled:* "How are hearts of oak furled? Well, in sand and sea water. . . . You are to suppose a stroke or blast in a forest of 'hearts of oak' (=, ad propositum, sound oak-timber) which at one blow both lays them low and buries them in broken earth. *Furling (ferrule* is a blunder for *furl,* I think) is *proper* when said of sticks and staves." (B 52.) Cf. F 133: "*Ferrule*—I have heard this pronounced *furl.*"
>   16 *Bole:* stem, trunk. (Cf. 43.9.)
>   28 *Wind:* move sinuously; * writhe, squirm; * leap. The idea intended seems to be 'swirl.' (For distinctions, see on 4.14.8.)
>   29 *Keep:* strong-hold, fortress within a castle. Carisbrook is a famous hill-top castle, with a keep, in the city of that name on the Isle of Wight.
>   61 *Gullies:* #, meaning: engulf, swallow (built either on the 'gully' meaning 'ravine' or 'gully' the * form of 'gullet').
>   62 *Wrings:* (intrans.) writhe and struggle in anguish; suffer. (Cf. the trans. use of the word at 4.9.3.)
>   64 *Sea-swill:* #, from the verb *swill:* to swish and dash about water to clean something.
>   68 *Rivelling:* * wrinkle, shrivel (either intrans. or causative).

94 *Wilaworth:* #, probably referring to the daring courage of the crew, hence: virtue or character all about us, as though springing up wild in the soil of human nature.

99 *Riving:* tear away from; rend, tear asunder, split apart.

119 *Fresh:* (substantive) flood, tide, rush of new water in a river or sea.

Hopkins explains much in the poem in B 52–54 (part in Bridges' note).

18 THE MAY MAGNIFICAT

21 *Bugle:* a blue plant growing in English fields (ajuga reptans). See on 83.15.

25 *Sizing:* assume size, increase, swell. (Cf. Keats, *Endymion* 3.206: 'size and swell'.) See also on 47.11.

39 *Thorp:* hamlet, village.

42 *Brakes:* thicket, clump of bushes. (Cf. 50.9.)

20 DUNS SCOTUS'S OXFORD

2 *Rook-racked:* #, probably referring to rooks sitting in rows on the trees; —the noun * *rack* = a thin cloud; or possibly 'tormented (racked; cf. 32.13) by noise of rooks.'

4 *Coped:* with monk's garb; fought against, matched; vaulted.

21 HENRY PURCELL

6 *Nursle:* to nurse, foster; * to nuzzle.

10 *Sakes, Moonmarks:* see B 83 (quoted in Bridges' note).

13 *Wuthering:* ". . . a Northcountry word for the noise and rush of wind: hence Emily Brontë's 'Wuthering Heights'" (B 83).

Some further points of meaning, especially of the first line, are explained at B 170–174. For lines 7–8, "forgèd feature . . . abrupt self" see appendix to glossary, on *inscape.*

22 PEACE

     4 *Own:* " 'Own my heart' is merely 'my own heart,' transposed for rhythm's sake and then *tamquam exquisitius,* as Hermann would say." (B 196.)

     6 *Daunting:* (noun) intimidation, dispiriting, discouraging; vanquishing.

     7 *Reaving:* " 'Reave' is for rob, plunder, carry off." (B 196.) (Cf. 35.12.)

     9 *Plumes:* preen, dress feathers; —pluck feathers.

23 THE BUGLER'S FIRST COMMUNION

     10 *Fain:* eager, quick (* construed with 'of').

     12 *Housel:* consecrated Species of the Eucharist (wafer form).

     18 *Squander:* scatter, disperse, drive off pell-mell.

     30 *Fretted:* adorned with intricate interlaced pattern, as carved or wrought work; ringed. (Cf. 37.101; 48.9.)

     39 *Brow and bead of being:* = small upshoot of being.

     42 *Rankle:* fester (as a wound); chafe, fret.

     43 *Backwheels:* #, probably an allusion to the Wheel of Fortune, or to a military manœuvre.

     46 *Brandle:* * shake, rock, make totter.

     46 *Ride:* probably referring to the motion of overlapping slabs, as in an earthquake.

24 MORNING MIDDAY AND EVENING SACRIFICE

     Last stanza explained in B 97–98 (quoted in Bridges' note).

25 ANDROMEDA

     1 *Time's Andromeda:* probably the Church.

     8 *Rife:* * quick, ready, disposed to act; abundant, rich.

26 THE CANDLE INDOORS

     4 *Trambeams:* silk threads used in weft or cross-threads of finest silk and velvet are called *trams,* hence the idea here is probably of wavy silk-like beams of light flickering in the dark and fog; — *tram,*

also means rail of a miners' cart or of a street-car; also the shafts or handles along the sides of a barrow.

4 *Truckle:* quail, cower, yield to timidly; be servile, obsequious. Hence probably: bashfully draw back, timidly flee on contact with the eye (note "to-fro"), for they are so weak and gossamer that in the haze one now sees them, now does not; further, such beam effects in optical phenomena are best noted with half-closed squinting eyes and tend to vanish when the vision is fully open ("at the eye," i.e., face-to-face with, in the presence of, the eyes, as in "at the sight").—*Truckle* also means: * to roll; * traffic, deal, barter (with 'with').

27 THE HANDSOME HEART

7 *Self-instressed:* #, here = impelled by its own inner impulse or natural dynamism (equivalent to Aristotle's *energeia*); a different sense than that in 4.5.7.

14 *Strain:* tenor, tone of conduct; mood, temper; inherited quality; effort. (Cf. 9.10.)

29 FELIX RANDAL

1 *Farrier:* blacksmith, horse-shoer (from Lat. ferrarius).

8 *Road:* way, manner; course of action; path.

14 *Fettle:* * arrange, make ready, prepare.

30 BROTHERS

16 *Byplay:* (theatrical metaphor) action aside from main events on the stage.

34 *Give tongue:* to bark, give forth hunting cry when on scent or in sight of quarry. "It means, so to say, 'And by George, sir, when the young dog opened his mouth at last he did make a noise and no mistake.' " (B III.)

31 SPRING AND FALL

8 *Wanwood:* # = unwooded trees, which seem to have lost their essence. Wan- is an old prefix paral-

leling un- or dis- (as in 'wanease,' 'wanworth');
—as an adjective, *wan* means gloomy, dark, sad,
dismal; pale; weak (as of smiles).

8 *Leafmeal:* # leaf by leaf (Cf. 'piecemeal').

32 SPELT FROM SIBYL'S LEAVES

1 *Attuneable:* probably intended to mean: harmonizing, blended.

3 *Hornlight:* # soft yellow evening glow, as of light
through scraped-horn shield of old type lantern (cf.
Rich. III. 1.12.2 'lantern hornes'; *Silas Marner,*
opening of Chap. V). So Hopkins notes, *Jnl.,* Oct.
25, 1870: "In the sunset all was big and there was
a world of swollen cloud holding the yellow-rose
light like a lamp" (N 136), and for May 24, 1871:
"It was a glowing yellow sunset." (N 147.) It is
not likely that *hornlight* here means 'horned moon,'
as it is generally assumed, partly because the crescent
moon is visible in the *evening* only one or two days
each month, hence is not characteristic; furthermore, the *hoarlight* below is in evident parallelism,
as the bleak gray tone of the upper sky when the
blue has left and black has not yet taken over.

7 *Round:* * counsel; —whisper, address.

9 *Damask:* adorn with variegated pattern, etch, especially in black on steely white as in Damascene sword
designs. Cf. *Jnl.* for Apr. 22, 1871: "But such a lovely
damasking in the sky as today I never felt before."
(N 143.) Also for Dec. 19, 1872: "Where the snow
lies as in a field the damasking of white light and
silvery shade may be watched indeed till brightness
and glare is all lost in a perplexity of shadow."
(N 171.) For a closely related passage to this line
see N 186, "Two beautiful sights . . ."

12 *Reckon:* * consider; enumerate, count over.

12 *Reck:* heed, regard; be aware of, know.

13 *Tell:* matter, be of account; have marked effect, be striking, emphatic; count, enumerate; tally; proclaim, announce (intrans.); *tell off* strictly is a military term, to count off some of a group and set apart for a special function, or (intransitively) to number selves off in succession, as ranks of troops. The point here is that these two basic principles, right and wrong, divide all reality among themselves into two opposing groups. The word has various different senses in 4.12.3; 34.3; 53.2.

33 INVERSNAID

1 *Burn:* * (Dialect of North England) spring, brook, fount of water (= 'bourne'). Note that the word is synonymous with *brook* below, in line 10.

3 *Coop:* cage, prison, place of confinement.

3 *Comb:* narrow valley, end-closed ravine (South England, for *coomb*); see on 16.9. Perhaps with an overtone reference to the verb *comb*: to break in white foam, roll over and form crest (of a wave); see this usage at 4.14.3.

4 *Flutes:* form into flutings, channels; sing, make music.

6 *Twindles:* # as a verb, from the * noun 'twindle': twin; thus, to form twin parts, break up into two sections.

9 *Degged:* * sprinkled, dampened.

10 *Braes:* (Scotch) bank, slope, steep side of hill or valley.

11 *Heathpacks:* #, patches of heath (the shrub erica).

11 *Flitches:* slice, strip (strictly of a tree-trunk cut lengthwise, with bark as one of the surfaces).

12 *Beadbonny:* #; bonny = fair, beautiful (Cf. "bonniest," 48.10).

34 "As Kingfishers Catch Fire . . ."

   3 *Tucked:* * pluck, pull; contract; — draw up into pleats.

   3 *Tells:* proclaim, broadcast, announce (intrans.); i.e., sounds out clearly. (See on *tell* at 4.12.3; 32.13; 53.2.) Cf. N 342: "All things are charged with God . . . ring and tell of Him."

   9 *Justices:* used here in special theological sense: to act in a godly manner, live fully energized by grace, justness, sanctity; also, radiating the divine life of grace. In ordinary usage, the verb *justice* is archaic, meaning: bring to justice, administer justice.

35 Ribblesdale

   1 *Throng:* "I mean 'throng' for an adjective as we use it here in Lancashire." (D 109; quoted in Bridges' note.)

   2 *Louchèd:* ". . . a coinage of mine and is to mean much the same as slouched, slouching" (*ibid.*). But as Bridges notes, the word is recognized by the dialect dictionaries.

   6 *Dealt, deal:* bestow on;— * divide, apportion.

   7 *Down:* probably metaphor from duck's down, referring to the fluffy grass (the "louchèd low grass" of line 2); —*down* as a noun also means: an upland pasture.

   7 *Reel:* * dash about wildly; move irregularly, move to and fro.

 10 *Dogged:* obstinate, persistent;—cruel, malicious, sullen.

 12 *Reave:* plunder, pillage, despoil, rob. (See note on 22.7.)

36 The Leaden Echo and the Golden Echo

 12 *Ruck:* crease, fold, wrinkle. (Contrast *ruck* at 3.11.)

 27 *Fleet:* fly, move swiftly; * glide away like a stream,

vanish, * disintegrate, waste away, fade; * float, drift with current.

42 *Fashed:* weary; worried, troubled.

42 *Cogged:* deceived, cheated; loaded (of falsified dice).

The meaning of lines 38–39 is explained in B 159: ". . . means 'Nay more: the seed that we so carelessly and freely flung into the dull furrow, and then forgot it, will have come to ear meantime,' etc."

37 THE BLESSED VIRGIN COMPARED TO THE AIR WE BREATHE

5 *Flixed: flix* means fur, down, hair. Cf. N 124: "flix or fleece" of cloud.

79 *Shot:* metaphor from shot silk, whose woof and warp are of different colors, so that the whole takes on various tints according to the angle and the light.

100 *Flecks:* spot of light, speck, patch, as of sun or fire. (Cf. Longfellow, *The Building of the Ship* 89: "shadows . . . broken by many a sunny fleck.")

101 *Fret:* * ring, ferrule; ornamental interlacing net pattern. (Cf. 23.30; also "fretting" at N 143, 140, 125, 155.)

39 THE SOLDIER

6 *Dears:* *, for 'endears.'

10 *Handle:* the MS has only *reave* here, which Bridges has replaced with handle (see his note). But there seems to be no difficulty with the original word, for it means 'to pass a rope through holes' as in several nautical operations (cf. 4.12.8), hence here stands for competency as a sailor, 'knowing the ropes,' just as the preceding line refers to skill in soldiering. The word, however, is usually spelled *reeve* in this sense; note the different word and meaning at 22.7; 35.12.

41 "NO WORST, THERE IS NONE . . ."

8 *Fell:* savage, cruel, fierce; deadly, dire; * shrewd,

cunning. *Fell* is a noun in its other occurrences; see on 4.4.7; 15.3; 45.1.

42   Tom's Garland

2 *Fallowbootfellow:* #, = now-idle-companion, from adj. *fallow*: idle, unworked; also * brownish or reddish yellow color, as of withered leaves.

12 *Mammocks:* break up, cut into shreds; here "disfigure" (see Bridges' note).

15 *Undenizened:* #, from verb *denizen,* here meaning: unnaturalized, alien, without citizen-rights; disenfranchised.

Much of the poem's meaning is explained by Hopkins in B 272–274 (quoted in Bridges' note).

43   Harry Ploughman

1 *Hurdle:* wattled grating as temporary fence-section or mat to be laid on marshy ground for support; frame, cross-bars.

1 *Flue:* floating particles of down, wool; fluff;—fishnet. Cf. N 110: "a slender race of fine flue-cloud . . ."

6 *Barrowy:* from *barrow*: a hill, small mountain, mound (cf. 65.4);—a carrying-frame.

7 *Curded:* knotted, formed into lumps or curds.

9 *Beechbole:* beech trunk or stem (cf. 17.16).

10 *Features:* (verb) portray, outline.

16 *Churlsgrace:* #, *churl* meaning: man, peasant; villain.

See Bridges' note on the meaning of the last few lines.

45   "I Wake and Feel the Fell of Dark . . ."

1 *Fell:* * gall, bitterness (cf. the *gall* of line 9; also, *Faerie Queene* 3.11.2: 'bitter fell'); *fell* also means: hill, upland moor; skin, pelt; (as adj.) savage, cruel; piercing, painful. Distinguish the word here from the *fell* in 4.4.7; 15.3; 41.8.

46   "PATIENCE, HARD THING . . ."

   14 *Combs:* honeycombs. A different use than at 4.14.3; 33.3; 56.5.

47   "MY OWN HEART . . ."

   11 *Size:* assume size, grow, increase. (Cf. 18.25.)

   14 *Betweenpie:* #, = make pied, produce varicolored contrast with and between (Bridges suggests 'inter-variegate'). Cf. Hopkins' comment on a poem of Canon Dixon's: ". . . I admired it as a happy medley: I thought the fusion or rather the pieing was less happy in the opening of the poem." (D 97.) The verb *pie* has no recognized standing in this exact sense, but only 'to heap up, jumble,' as of type.

48   THAT NATURE IS A HERACLITEAN FIRE

   1 *Flaunt:* (of flowers) wave so as to display beauty; (trans.) display ostentatiously; wave gaily.

   1 *Chevy:* race away, scamper; pursue, chase.

   4 *Shivelights: shive* = splinter, mote; * particle of thread on surface of cloth, fluff. (Cf. 72.38.)

   6 *Peel:* rind (hence here, the surface of the earth);— the word sometimes means: * palisade, rampart; * pillow.

   9 *Footfretted:* #, = stamped into intricate interlaced pattern or fretting. (Cf. 23.30.)

   11 *Firedint:* #, *dint* means: blow, stroke; impression, dent from blow. (In Chaucer, *Troilus* 5:1505, 'thonder-dynt'= crash or stroke of thunder.)

49   IN HONOUR OF ST ALPHONSUS RODRIGUEZ

   8 *Hurtle:* clashing sound, noise of collision. (Cf. 4.3.2.)

50   "THOU ART INDEED JUST, LORD . . ."

   9 *Brakes:* thicket, clump of bushes. (Cf. 18.42.)

   11 *Chervil:* an aromatic herb with curved leaves (anthriscus cerefolium).

51 To R. B.

> 6 *Moulds:* the MS has here only *combs,* for which
> Bridges has substituted the present reading, as an
> easier synonym. *Combs* would mean: put into or-
> der, as by combing. (See on 4.4.4.)

53 "What Being . . ."

> 1 *Rank:* (adj.) * full-grown, nature; copious, abun-
> dant, luxuriant in growth; * stout, strong.
>
> 2 *Tells:* * proclaim, publish, announce; count off.
> Cf. on 32.13.

54 On the Portrait of Two Beautiful Young People

> 4 *Vein:* see on 4.4.7; 4.33.5; cf. B 250, of Canon
> Dixon's poetry: "there is in him a vein of truly
> matchless beauty: it is not always the whole texture
> but a thread in it and sometimes the whole web is
> of that."
>
> 8 *Heft:* weight, bulk, substance; strain; * need, press
> of circumstances. The verb *heft* = to lift up, heave;
> and is sometimes merely a different spelling of *haft*:
> * to use deceit or trickery; * hold off, demur.
>
> 12 *Burling:* * bubbling up. (Cf. 4.16.8.)
>
> 12 *Barrow:* a river in S.E. Ireland, flowing into Water-
> ford estuary. Cf. B 306: "The river is the Barrow,
> which the old Irish poets call the dumb Barrow. I
> call it the burling Barrow brown. Both descriptions
> are true."
>
> 30 *Banes:* harm, woe, what causes ruin; * slayer, mur-
> derer.

56 Ashboughs

> 5 *Lashtender:* #, = tender as eyelash; or as thong,
> cord.
>
> 5 *Combs:* splays, as in hair-comb or cock's crest. A
> different word from the comb of 4.14.3; 33.3; 46.14.

58 St. Winefred's Well

> 15 *Bines:* flexible shoot of a vine or shrub.

34 *Mock:* sham, pretended, counterfeit.

75 *Fleecèd:* "I mean the velvetiness of roseleaves, flesh, and other things, *duvet.*" (B 215.)

96 *Rushy:* producing rushes.

106 *Dene:* * dell, valley (North England dialect); a low bare sand hill near the sea, a dune. (Cf. introduction to Act II, p. 75; also 72.4.)

109 *Rash:* * rushing, dashing; vigorous, quick (Cf. 4.19.4; 11.6).

61 CHEERY BEGGAR

5 *Lime:* lime tree, linden (with fragrant heart-shaped yellow leaves).

63 "THE FURL OF FRESH-LEAVED DOGROSE . . ."

15 *Campion:* a rose-like flower (lychnis or agrostemma coronaria).

65 MOONRISE

4 *Barrow:* * mount, mound, long low hill. (Cf. 43.6.)

71 "STRIKE, CHURL . . ."

1 *Heltering:* #, = helter-skelter-going, in random headlong flight.

72 EPITHALAMION

4 *Dene:* * dell, valley; low bare sand hill near the sea, a dune. (Cf. 58.106.)

4 *Clough:* ravine, steep valley. (Rimes with 'plough.') So N 145.

4 *Cleave:* = *cleve*: a cliff.

9 *Cover:* = *covert*, a shady thicket (so Bridges' note).

10 *Dither:* * tremble, quiver, quake.

28 *Dings:* dash, hurl, thrust.

36 *Coffer:* a box-like space within a wall or pier filled in with rubble.

37 *Selfquainèd:* quain is * for quoin (= coign): an external angle of a wall, corner; wedge-shaped block; cornerstone; internal angle, corner. Cf. N 141, 143 "quaining and squaring."

38 *Shives:* * splinter, particle, tuft. (Cf. 48.4.)

38 *Shoots:* (the noun; so Bridges, in note).

77   A VISION OF MERMAIDS

15 *Strook:* = *struck.*

40 *Gorse:* the prickly shrub ulex europaeus; = furze, juniper.

79 *Purfled:* 'purfle' = a border, ornamental fringe, as in embroidery.

106 *Prankèd:* pleated, arranged in folds; adorned.

79   THE NIGHTINGALE

6 *Hurst:* copse or grove (cf. *copse,* line 45); a wooded hill; sand-bank.

83   WINTER WITH THE GULF STREAM

15 *Bugle:* horned, as wild ox or * bugle; or blue, like the plant *bugle* (as in 18.21).

28 *Brindled:* streaked, brinded.

86   MARGARET CLITHEROE

18 *Clinching:* * for *clenching*: close gripping.

88   O DEUS, EGO AMO TE

10 *Cumber:* distress, burden, encumbrance; * destruction. (Cf. 36.43.)

APPENDIX

On *Scape* and *Inscape*

These two words do not occur in the *Poems,* but are very common in the prose works, and both so bothersome and so frequently referred to that it seems well to indicate here their meaning.

Scape: strictly only a suffix, as in 'landscape,' with the force of '-ship' (friendship, guardianship) = state of being something, condition, office; etymologically derived from Old English '-schap' (whence '-ship'; cf. German -*schaft*), and used in new combinations by artificial back-formation or analogy with 'landscape' (where it has the force of 'view, vista; sketch, outline, design'). Thus G. White, quoting letters of Selbourne (1773): "Mr. Ray . . . was so ravished with the prospect that he mentioned these scapes in his book"; (1776); "He first of all sketches his scapes with a lead pencil"; *Daily News*, Sept. 3, 1868: "Some of these cloud-scapes are extremely grand"; E. W. Coleridge, *Christabel* 3: "Here was one of those moon-scapes which the poet should depict in verse."

Hopkins uses *scape* in the latter way, but as an independent word; also in the gerund form, *scaping*. Bascially, he intends: external outline or form, harmonious pattern or design of parts and lines; in some passages, the sense is shifted to designate an optical illusion of design, a mere appearance or image of some ordered pattern. Note *scapeless* at N 197, and N 193 ("scapeless aimless background" of a picture). For a list of the word's occurrences see the Index to N. The only occurrence in the poems is in the compounded form *Lovescape*, 4.23.4.

Inscape: #, formed on 'scape' as = 'pattern,' with prefix to emphasize the intrinsic and individual aspect which is in the foreground of the word's connotation. The general distinction between *scape* and *inscape* is brought out in the *Journal* entry for May 23, 1874 (N 194), describing his impression of Alma Tadema's painting *Vintage Festival:* ". . . a master of scaping rather than of inscape. For vigorous rhetorical but realistic and unaffected scaping holds everything but no arch-inscape is thought of." The word, then, stresses the internal scaping or design in things, their very soul as beautiful. Out of this basic meaning grow various further connotations, for the deciding of which the context must be studied.

The divisions of meaning are these: (1) the intrinsic *form* or activating principle of an object, whether native, as in natural bodies like bluebells or trees, or intellectually super-imposed by artistic arrangement of parts in an art-work like speech, a poem, or a painting; i.e., the philosophers' *forma informans,* the 'soul' or form actuating particular matter and giving it distinct individual existence outside the mind. In an artifact, this means the essential unifying form or design worked into the material by the artist to produce a *new thing (poiēma)* which will be distinctive and a perfect expression of his thought and mood. "Now it is the virtue of design, pattern, or inscape to be distinctive . . . (B 66); ". . . inscape (the very soul of art)" (D 135); "It is the forgèd feature finds me; it is the rehearsal of own, of abrupt self" (21.7–8); etc. (2)—the most common meaning— the *intrinsic beauty* of a thing, the shining forth or effulgence of its form (this is the Scholastic definition of beauty: *splendor formae*), the glory of its translucent being or "selfbeing" (N 309, etc.). For the true experience of beauty arises only from penetrating, by the mediation of the outer form which is its sensible revelation, to the inner form, the *in-scape*, of the object and drinking in its radiant and abundant reality or truth. For "It is certain that in nature outward beauty is the proof of inward beauty, outward good of inward good. Fineness, proportion, of feature comes from a moulding force which succeeds in asserting itself over the resistance of cumbersome or restraining matter. . . . The moulding force, the life, is the form in the philosophic sense . . ." (F 158–159); ". . . what I call *inscape*, that is species or individually-distinctive beauty . . ." (F 225). It follows that not all objects perceived in their innermost reality are in the strict sense beautiful, but only where the reality is striking, radiant, over-flowing: ". . . beauty is the virtue of inscape, not inscape only" (N 250). Nevertheless, "All the world is full of inscape . . ." (N 173), but "I thought how sadly beauty of inscape was unknown and buried away from simple people and yet how near at hand it was if they had eyes to see it and it could be called out everywhere again" (N 161); for "Unless you refresh the mind from time to time you cannot always remember or believe how deep the inscape in things is" (N 140), etc. (3) By an extension of meaning, *inscape* comes to signify primarily the *outer form* in some passages, the shape or harmonious lines of an object, with little explicit reference to the underlying intrinsic nature of the object. Here the thing in focus is the *accidental* form, the non-essential structuring, and the word differs hardly at all in connotation from *scape*: ". . . chance left free to act falls into an order as well as purpose: looking out of my window I caught it (inscape) in the random clods and broken heaps of snow made by the cast of a broom" (N 173–174), etc. (4) Sometimes the word is equivalent to a *subjectively imposed Gestalt* which random lines assume as one suddenly discovers a pattern in them after close looking. E.g., "Another night from the gallery window I saw a brindled heaven, the moon just marked by a blue spot pushing its way through the darker cloud, underneath and on the skirts of the rack bold long flakes whitened and swaled like feathers, below / the garden with the heads of the trees and shrubs furry grey: I read a broad careless inscape flowing throughout" (N 158).

Further passages where the word occurs, in one or other of the above meanings, may be found by aid of the indexes to the prose works. Two passages are of special worth for their sensitive beauty: "I looked at some delicate flying shafted ashes—there was one especially of single sonnet-like inscape . . ." (N 211); "I do not think I have ever seen anything more beautiful than the bluebell I have been looking at. I know the beauty of our Lord by it. Its inscape is mixed of strength and grace, like an ash." (N 134.)

INDEX TO THE GLOSSARY

References are to the poems, by number and line

Own 22.4

Peel 48.6
Plumes 22.9
Pranked 77.106
Proffer 4.4.8
Purfled 77.79

Quails 4.24.6
Quained 72.37

Ramp 11.2
Rank 53.1
Rankle 23.42
Rash 4.19.4; 58.109
Rash-fresh 11.6
Reave 22.7; 35.12;
  (39.10)
Reck 32.12
Reckon 32.12
Reel (noun) 3.11
Reel (verb) 35.7
Reeve 4.12.8
Ride 23.46
Rife 25.8
Rivelling 17.68
Riving 17.99
Road 29.8
Rook-racked 20.2
Roped 4.4.6

Round 32.7
Roundel 5.27
Ruck 3.11; 36.12
Rung 12.4
Rushy 58.96

Sack 14.3
Sake 4.22.1; 21.10
Sallows 8.11
Scanted 15.1
Scape: Appendix
Sculls 5.8
Self-quained 72.37
Shire 4.34.8
Shive 72.38
Shivelights 48.4
Shock 4.29.3
Shoots 72.38
Shot 37.79
Silk-sack 14.3
Sillion 12.12
Size 47.11
Sizing 18.25
Sloe 4.8.3
Sloggering 4.19.4
Spell 4.3.4
Squander 23.18
Stooks 14.1
Strain 9.10; 27.14
Strook 77.15

Swill 17.64

Tell 4.12.3; 32.13;
  34.3; 53.2
Thorp 18.39
Throng 35.1
Tongue, give 30.34
Trambeams 26.4
Trench 11.2
Truckle 26.4
Tucked 34.3
Twindles 33.6

Unchancelling 4.21.6
Undenizened 42.15

Vein 4.4.7; 4.33.5;
  54.4
Voel 4.4.7

Wanwood 31.8
Wear 11.4
Whitebeam 8.6
Wildworth 17.94
Wind 4.14.8; 10.9;
  17.28
Wring 4.9.3; 17.62
Wuthering 21.13

Yore-flood 4.32.2

HOPKINS: POET OF NATURE AND OF THE SUPERNATURAL

MAURICE B. MCNAMEE, S.J.

Since God first poured Himself forth in creation there have always been souls, enamored of His reflected beauty, who have been moved to give voice to their ecstasy in song. The inspired writer of the book of *Ecclesiasticus* scans the myriad beauties of God's creation: the dazzling splendor of the sun, the moon "shining gloriously in the firmament," "the glory of the stars," "the brightness of the rainbow encompassing the heavens with the circle of its glory," "clouds that fly out like birds," the majesty of mountains, the power and might of thunder and lightning and whirlwinds, snow that is scattered like "birds lighting upon the earth," frost touching everything with down "like the tops of thistles," and ice "clothing the waters with a breastplate of crystal." And yet, in spite of all this manifold beauty of God's visible creation the author is forced to say (*Ecclesiasticus* 43, 32 and 36):

There are many things hidden from us that are greater than these: for we have seen but a few of his works. . . . Glorify the Lord as much as ever you can, for he will yet far exceed, and his magnificence is wonderful.

Like this chapter of *Ecclesiasticus,* many of the psalms are mere litanies of the varied beauties of God's creation, or hymns of praise to God the Creator for His beauty and power manifested in the myriad works of His hands. Thus psalm 103 runs through the whole hierarchy of being, and discovers the hand of God on every round of the ladder. The instinctive reaction of the Psalmist to the pageantry of natural beauty is a song of praise (*Ps.* 103, 33):

> I will sing to the Lord as long as I live:
> I will sing praise to my God while I have my being.

The Natural Revelation of God

The primary purpose that God had in view in creating the world was to communicate, to manifest, to share with men some of His infinite truth, and goodness, and beauty. Thus it was that He made man to His own image and likeness, giving him an intellect and will like His own, that there might be someone to recognize the divine manifestation, someone who could consciously enjoy the generous revelation of His own infinite riches. Man's only reason for being, therefore, is to know, to love, and to enjoy God. In this life, he sees that for which he was made "only darkly as through a glass"; but even through that glass he catches glimpses of God's beauty. It flashes forth upon him suddenly, overwhelmingly at times, from the blazing pageantry of a sunset, from the solemn grandeur of a snow-capped mountain, or from the endless expanse of the surging sea. Here in the grander aspects of nature God speaks to man in unmistakable accents; but He reveals something of Himself, too, through the delicate beauty of a snowflake, or through the fragile iridescence of a dewdrop. At times the very image of God is flashed to him from the countenance of a beautiful and holy character. If man will not blind himself to "the many-splendored thing," God will reveal Himself in hierarchical glimpses from the lifeless pebble on the beach, on up through the living, sentient, thinking ladder of being; for, as St. Paul says (*Rm.* 1,20), "the invisible things of him are clearly seen, being understood by the things that are made."

Through the infinite and gratuitous generosity of God man is destined at last to know God in a face to face vision of His infinite perfections. In this life, however, he must be content with the indirect communication of these perfections through creatures. At times, when this revelation of God through the works of His hands is borne in upon man with peculiar suddenness, freshness, and fulness, he is beside himself with a unique pleasure. He has anticipated a bit of the beatitude for which he was created—the contemplation of the truth and the beauty of God. His faculties for a fleeting moment rest in the possession of that for which they were made. In these moments man captures from the truth and beauty of creatures a flash of the truth and beauty of the Word of God in whom resides the fulness of truth and beauty. Conscious of the goodness of even this refracted ray of God's beauty which he has caught in the prism of his own experience, man feels the unselfish instinct to diffuse, to manifest, to share that beatifying experience with his fellowmen. This is the impulse which prompts men to become creative artists, the impulse to create a new reality which will bring to others what the beauty of a fragment of God's creation has brought to them.

Man will be successful as an artist if he succeeds in incarnating his genuine and worthy inspiration in a medium that will convey to his fellow human beings his own experience with all its richness, fulness, and vitality. No explanation of his experience is wanted; no theorizing is needed. His task as an artist is to embody his living experience in a new medium in order that others may share his apprehension and enjoyment of the resplendence of truth, his grasp of the beautiful. If his medium is harmonious metrical language, the artist is a poet, who has learned to impress his inspiration on the unwilling matter of words. If he is a good poet, then his poem will be capable of engendering in others the richness and pleasure of his own experience.

The Poet of Nature

There have always been poets who have embodied their experience of the beauties of creation in beautiful language. Many have not been conscious of the fact that it was God's beauty they were enamored of in nature, and communicated to others in their poetry; but if they succeeded in carrying their own vital grasp of reality into the medium of their verse, they have, whether they knew it or not, been communicating something of God's reflected beauty in the product of their art. Some poets, like Wordsworth, were vaguely conscious of the fact that, when they sang of the beauties of nature, they were really singing of the beauty of a being behind nature, or, as they dangerously preferred to say, *in* nature

> Whose dwelling is the light of setting suns,
> And the round ocean, and the living air,
> And the blue sky, and in the mind of man.[1]

Francis Thompson was very much aware of this natural revelation of God in the beauties of creation, and made this the frequent theme of his poetry. The burden of much of his song is an enlargement on two lines which occur in his poem, *From the Night of Forebeing* (ll. 104–5):

> From sky to sod,
> The world's unfolded blossom smells of God.

It was for this reason that he preferred to call himself not the poet of the return to nature, but "the poet of the return to God." [2] He recognized that really to return to nature is to discover it to be what God planned it to be—a revelation of Himself. "She is God's daughter," he says, "and lends her hand but to His friends." [3]

Hopkins: Poet of Nature

To sing of God's beauty revealed in creatures is to be a poet of the natural. If God had never given any other revelation of

[1] Wordsworth, *Tintern Abbey*, ll. 97–99.
[2] Everard Meynell, *Life of Francis Thompson* (Scribners, 1916), p. 205.
[3] Thompson, *Of Nature: Laud and Plaint*, ll. 68–9.

Himself than this indirect one in the visible things of creation, there would always have been individuals enamored of even this manifestation of the divine who would have shared their experience with others through the medium of verse. In other words, there would always have been poets of nature.

Gerard Manley Hopkins was deeply aware of this divine communication in the multitudinous variety of visible creation. The two most profound influences on his thought and character, the *Spiritual Exercises* of St. Ignatius and the philosophy of Scotus, both tended to deepen his appreciation of nature as the channel of divine communication, and to sharpen his interest in the particular, individualized aspects of nature through which that communication is realized. The *Spiritual Exercises* begin with a clear statement of the purpose of man's creation and the end of creatures; they close with an act of the love of God motivated by a sweeping survey of the continual and varied communication of God in His visible creation. Hopkins himself, in his *Commentary on the Exercises*,[4] well expresses this function of the visible universe:

God's utterance of himself in himself is God the Word, outside himself is this world. This world then is word, expression, news, of God. Therefore its end, its purpose, its purport, its meaning, is God, and its life or work to name and praise him.

It was in the *Exercises*, therefore, that Hopkins found a justification for his remarkable sensitivity to the beauty of the world about him.

Hopkins was always keenly alive to all those distinctive details of a particular landscape which make it absolutely different from every other one. His interest in painting made him very alert to delicate variations in color, contour, and shape. The subtle changes of light and color which make the same scene contribute new beauties at each consecutive moment always fascinated him.

[4] Unpublished Manuscript, quoted in John Pick, *Gerard Manley Hopkins, Priest and Poet* (Oxford, 1942), p. 49.

Even the earliest entries in his journal show him to have been aware of all the distinctive individualities of everything he encountered during his travels on the continent; they also reveal him as already at pains to capture that distinctiveness in an equally distinctive expression. Hopkins was never content with vague emotionalizing about scenic beauty; he took infinite pains to find the exact word and the perfect comparison to convey the impression of the precise tinge of color of a cloud or of the sea at sunset, or the very feel and texture of a bluebell or a primrose.

Hopkins very early learned to look for that design or pattern in nature which he called "inscape," and which he felt lay at the very heart of ontological beauty. "Inscape" or external pattern he took to be the outward expression of inward pattern or form. Thus in a letter to Patmore, he says (F 158–9):

It is certain that in nature outward beauty is the proof of inward beauty, outward good of inward good. Fineness, proportion of feature comes from a moulding force which succeeds in asserting itself over the resistance of cumbersome or restraining matter. . . . The moulding force, the life, is the form in the philosophic sense.

This feeling for the external pattern expressive of the inward form of things came to be a pivotal point in his thought to which he returns again and again in his journal and in his poetry. He is constantly speaking of the "inscape" in things. We shall cite but one from among the many instances in the journal. It is a passage in which he gives one of his very detailed descriptions of a sunset, but notes it as particularly significant that he had succeeded on this occasion in "inscaping" the sun itself with the rest of the scene. Because it illustrates his powers of description and indicates as well what he meant by "inscape" in a scene, it is worth quoting in full (Jnl. 129):

A fine sunset: the higher sky dead clear blue bridged by a broad slant causeway rising from right to left of wisped or grass cloud, the wisps lying across; the sundown yellow, moist with light but ending at the top in a foam of delicate white pearling and spotted with big tufts of cloud in colour russet between brown and purple but edged with brassy light. But what I note it all for is this: before I had always taken the sunset and the sun as quite out of gauge with each other, as indeed physically they are, for the eye after looking at the sun is blunted to everything else and if you look at the rest of the sunset you must cover the sun, but today I inscaped them together and made the sun the true eye and ace of the whole as it is. It was all active and tossing out light, and started as strongly forward from the field as a long stone or a boss in the knop of the chalice-stem: it is indeed by stalling it so that it falls into scape with the sky.

With these interests, it is not surprising that Hopkins became so enthusiastic about the philosophy of Scotus. In Scotism he found philosophic justification for his longstanding preoccupation with "inscape" or pattern, and with the sharply individualized features of things. In 1872 he wrote in his journal (Jnl. 161):

After the examinations we went for our holiday out to Douglas in the Isle of Man Aug. 3. At this time I had first begun to get hold of the copy of Scotus on the Sentences in the Baddely library and was flush with a new stroke of enthusiasm. It may come to nothing or it may be a mercy from God. But just then when I took in any inscape of the sky or sea I thought of Scotus.

Scotus helped him to see, too, that it was through the experience of the particular patterns or forms of things that the natural manifestation of God to man is realized.

Under the influence of Scotus and the *Spiritual Exercises,* it became habitual for Hopkins to think of God when he "took in any inscape of sky or sea." Thus, when he saw the northern lights for the first time, he wrote in his diary (Jnl. 135):

This busy working of nature wholly independent of the earth and seeming to go on in a strain of time not reckoned by our reckoning of days and years but simpler and as if correcting the preoccupation of the world by being preoccupied with and appealing to and dated to the day of judgment was like a new witness to God and filled me with delightful fear.

And again he records (Jnl. 204–5):

As we drove home [from Ugbrooke at Lord Clifford's] the stars came out thick: I leant back to look at them and my heart opening more than usual praised our Lord to and in whom all that beauty comes home.

With his remarkable sensitivity to all the varied and distinctive beauty of visible creation, and his fresh realization of the function of nature as the channel of God's natural revelation of Himself, it is not surprising that Hopkins made this natural revelation of God's beauty the frequent theme of his poetry.

He gave beautiful and distinctive expression to the general truth of God's manifestation of Himself through visible creation in one of his early sonnets called *God's Grandeur*. The sonnet opens with a new statement of the fact which the poet had experienced so often and expressed so tellingly in his journal—the fact that the world is shot through and through with the beauty of God as with an electric charge.

The world is charged with the grandeur of God. This grandeur flashes out suddenly upon the mind like the light flashed off a crinkled, scintillating piece of tinfoil.

It will flame out, like shining from shook foil. The wonder and splendor of God's beauty, he insists, is trembling at the brink of man's consciousness, pressing in upon him from the whole hierarchy of created being. But thousands of men have been insulated against that revelation by artificiality and convention, by industrial ugliness and squalor.

Generations have trod, have trod, have trod;
And all is seared with trade; bleared, smeared with toil;
And wears man's smudge and shares man's smell: the soil
Is bare now, nor can foot feel, being shod.

But for all that, the beauty of nature is still there to speak to man of God's grandeur, if men will but listen.

> And for all this, nature is never spent;
> There lives the dearest freshness deep down things.

Even though the sun of God's natural revelation has set for many in the murky clouds of industrial squalor, that sun is ready to rise again in the East and flash forth the beauty of God once more, if men will but look to the East. The creative Spirit of Love that was present when the world was first given being and beauty still hovers over it, preserving and fostering that being and beauty.

> And though the last lights off the black West went
>   Oh, morning, at the brown brink eastward, springs—
> Because the Holy Ghost over the bent
>   World broods with warm breast and with ah! bright wings.

In *The Wreck of the Deutschland,* the first major poem Hopkins wrote as a Jesuit, he expressed his deepening conviction of God's natural revelation of Himself in the beauty of creation. He greets God familiarly "wafted" to him in His stars, His thunder, and His sunsets.

> I kiss my hand
> To the stars, lovely-asunder
> Starlight, wafting him out of it; and
> Glow, glory in thunder;
> Kiss my hand to the dappled-with-damson west:
> . . . . he is under the world's splendour and wonder.
>   (Stanza 5, 1–6)

He came to feel more and more that it was precisely in the distinctive and contrasting features of individual beautiful things that God was most clearly "wafted" to him. The idea of the communicability of God through the particular and the individual is beautifully expressed in the octet of poem number 34.

> As kingfishers catch fire, dragonflies draw flame;
> As tumbled over rim in roundy wells
> Stones ring; like each tucked string tells, each hung bell's
> Bow swung finds tongue to fling out broad its name;
> Each mortal thing does one thing and the same:
> Deals out that being indoors each one dwells;
> Selves—goes itself; *myself* it speaks and spells,
> Crying *What I do is me: for that I came.*

Each individual thing in creation by being itself as well as it can, and by revealing itself to man as fully as it can, reveals to him a bit of God's beauty that nothing else in the universe can reveal to him. Therefore, if man wants to catch the full natural revelation of God, he must learn to be sensitive to the particular, individualized aspects of "each mortal thing." God multiplied species, and individuals in the species, precisely that from the contemplation of the many, man might come to know something of the One.

Hopkins reveled in that variety and multiplicity, in everything that is "counter, original, spare, strange," because he knew that the more distinctive a thing is, the more unique a revelation of God it gives. That is why he so loved the "sweet *especial* rural scenes" [5] and all the variegated and contrasting features of those scenes. That is why he felt, as he tells us in *Pied Beauty,* particularly grateful for "dappled things," for "couple-colour skies," for "rose-moles all in stipple" upon the bellies of trout, for the flashing contrast of jetblack wings on golden finches, for rural landscapes stitched together from blocks of pasture and plough and meadowland as variegated as a crazy quilt, and for the distinctive gear and tackle of all the trades that are.

[5] *Binsey Poplars.*

> Glory be to God for dappled things—
>   For skies of couple-colour as a brinded cow;
>   For rose-moles all in stipple upon trout that swim;
>   Fresh-firecoal chestnut-falls; finches' wings;
>   Landscape plotted and pieced—fold, fallow, and plough;
>   And all trades, their gear and tackle and trim.

He was drawn especially to whatever was rife with contrasts, to whatever is

> . . . fickle, freckled (who knows how?)
>   With swift, slow; sweet, sour; adazzle, dim;

because he knew that the beauty in all these contrasts

> He fathers-forth whose beauty is past change:
>   Praise him.

Scattered throughout all Hopkins' poetry we find fresh and original descriptions of the endless variety of created beauty which in the medium of his distinctive verse "flame out, like shining from shook foil" and suddenly flash forth to us a bit of that grandeur of God which enkindled the soul of the poet. A complete catalogue of those flashes of natural beauty which he has captured in his poetry would give us some appreciation of how much of God's splendor he had found "fathered-forth" in the work of God's hands. That catalogue would include: stars that course through the air like "flake-doves sent floating forth at a farmyard scare"; [6] "the moon, dwindled and thinned to the fringe of fingernail held to the candle"; [7] "the dappled-with-damson west"; [8] "silk-sack clouds"; clouds like "meal-drift moulded ever and melted across skies"; [9] "sheep-flock clouds like worlds of wool"; [10] "cloud-puffball, torn tufts, tossed pillows"; clouds that "flaunt forth, then chevy on an air-built thor-

[6] *The Starlight Night.*
[7] *Moonrise.*
[8] *The Wreck,* Stanza 5, 5.
[9] *Hurrahing in Harvest.*
[10] *Penmaen Pool.*

oughfare"; [11] the "wild air, world-mothering air," that "goes home betwixt the fleeciest, frailest-flixed snowflake"; [12] evening with "her fond yellow hornlight"; evening that unbinds earth's being, puts her dapple to an end, dismembering and disremembering all her beauties, burying them in the damasked black of night; [13] the candle-light that "puts blissful back with yellowy moisture mild night's blear-all black"; [14] "raindrop-roundels looped together"; [15] "wiry and white-fiery and whirlwind-swivelled snow"; [16] the river with its "wind-wandering weed-winding bank"; [17] the "gluegold-brown marbled river, boisterously beautiful," that "between roots and rocks is danced and dandled, all in froth and water blowballs"; [18] "a windpuff-bonnet of fawn-froth" that "turns and twindles over the broth of a pool" pitch-black; [19] "the tide that ramps against the shore; with a flood or a fall, low lull-off or all roar"; [20] "a darksome burn, horseback brown," with a "rollrock highroad roaring down"; [21] "aspens dear, whose airy cages quelled, quelled or quenched in leaves the leaping sun"; [22] "glassy peartrees" that "brush the descending blue"; [23] "the groins of the braes that the brook treads through"; "wiry heath-packs, flitches of fern, and the beadbonny ash that sits over the burn"; [24] "rafts and rafts of flake-leaves" that hang motionless as if "painted on the air," "still as hawk or hawk-moth, as the stars or as the angels"; "silk-beech, scrolled ash, packed sycamore, wild wychelm," "hanging honeysuck, dogeared hazels"; [25] "thrush's eggs" that look like "little low heavens"; [26] the song of the thrush that "through the echoing timber does so rinse and wring the ear, it strikes like lightnings to hear him

---

[11] *Nature, a Heraclitean Fire.*
[12] *The Blessed Virgin Compared to the Air,* ll. 1, 4, 5, 6.
[13] *Spelt from Sibyl's Leaves.*
[14] *The Candle Indoors.*
[15] *Penmaen Pool.*
[16] *The Wreck,* Stanza 13, 7.
[17] *Binsey Poplars.*
[18] *Epithalamion.*
[19] *Inversnaid.*
[20] *The Sea and the Skylark.*
[21] *Inversnaid.*
[22] *Binsey Poplars.*
[23] *Spring.*
[24] *Inversnaid.*
[25] *Epithalamion.*
[26] *Spring.*

sing"; [27] the lark that pours and pelts music from the sky "till none's to spill nor spend"; [28] the woodlark with his "tiny a trickle of song-strain"; [29] the mastery of the windhover rolling, striding, hurling, and gliding through the air on "a wimpling wing" in an ecstasy of achievement; [30] and then Old Oxford "branchy between towers; cuckoo-echoing, bell-swarmed, lark-charmed, rook-racked, river-rounded; the dapple-eared lily below thee." [31]

Hopkins was ever aware that all this pageantry of natural beauty "he fathers-forth whose beauty is past change." "Nature is never spent"; it is ever ready to fulfill its purpose of revealing God to man. When man allows himself to catch that revelation he is beside himself with a unique pleasure and satisfaction.

These things, these things were here and but the beholder
Wanting; which two when they once meet,
The heart rears wings bold and bolder
And hurls for him, O half hurls earth for him off under his feet. [32]

It is man alone who can know and enjoy all this beauty and thank the giver. "Earth," Hopkins says in another of his poems, "with no tongue to plead, no heart to feel, . . . thou canst but be."

And what is Earth's eye, tongue, or heart else, where
Else, but in dear and dogged man? [33]

Since man has a heart, he must feel grateful to God for all this wealth of beauty "charged with the grandeur of God"; and since he alone has a tongue, he should voice the gratitude of all creation.

What do then? how meet beauty? Merely meet it; own
Home at heart, heaven's sweet gift. [34]

[27] *Spring.*
[28] *The Sea and the Skylark.*
[29] *The Woodlark.*
[30] *The Windhover.*
[31] *Duns Scotus's Oxford.*
[32] *Hurrahing in Harvest.*
[33] *Ribblesdale.*
[34] *To What Serves Mortal Beauty?*

Hopkins recognized, too, that more of God is flashed off man himself than off any of God's other visible creatures. Thus in *To What Serves Mortal Beauty?* he says:

> To man, that needs would worship block or barren stone,
> Our law says: Love what are love's worthiest, were all known;
> World's loveliest—men's selves.

And again in *Nature is a Heraclitean Fire* he declares that "million-fuelèd, nature's bonfire burns on," but that man is her "bonniest, dearest to her, her clearest-selvèd spark." It is his realization of man's high place in the hierarchy of being that made Hopkins so much interested in all things human. *Nil humanum a me alienum puto.* He was interested in men's trades, their hobbies, their physical appearance, and their character—in everything that made them distinctive individuals. This interest in nature's "clearest-selvèd spark" is revealed in his poetry. He gives us glimpses of quite a variety of these distinctive "sparks" of human nature here and there in his poems. We hear of a "bugler boy from barrack"; [35] of Marcus Hare, Captain of the *Eurydice*; [36] of Sydney Fletcher "Bristol-bred"; [37] of a "seacorpse cold," "all of a lovely manly mould, every inch a tar, of the best we boast our sailors are"; [38] of Henry Purcell, the musician, "so arch-especial a spirit," who with his "air of angels" "fans fresh our wits with wonder"; [39] of a boy with a "handsome heart" and "a gracious answer"; [40] of an elder brother whose life was all laced, "love-laced," in the life of his younger brother; [41] of little Margaret "grieving over Goldengrove unleaving"; [42] of a lad with a torn straw hat; [43] of boys from the town bathing, hurling their "bellbright bodies" through "earthworld, airworld, waterworld"—"all by turn and turn about"; [44] of "Felix Randal the farrier," "big-boned and hardy-handsome,"

[35] *The Bugler's First Communion.*
[36] *The Loss of the Eurydice*, 1.45.
[37] *Ibid.*, 1.57.
[38] *Ibid.*, ll. 73-6.
[39] *Henry Purcell.*
[40] *The Handsome Heart.*
[41] *Brothers.*
[42] *Spring and Fall.*
[43] *No. 63.*
[44] *Epithalamion.*

who "at the random grim forge, powerful amidst peers, didst fettle for the great grey drayhorse his bright and battering sandal"; [45] of Harry Ploughman with his "hard as hurdle arms," his "rack of ribs," and "scooped flank"; [46] and of "the tall nun" on the *Deutschland* who was "first of a five and came of a coifèd sisterhood." [47]

In all physical beauty, but very particularly in all human beauty of body and soul, Hopkins saw a revelation of the beauty of God Himself. He was as exact in his observation of all the distinctive details of nature as was Tennyson; he was even more deeply aware of nature's sacramentalism than was Francis Thompson; he was an eminently successful poet of the natural revelation of God. But Hopkins' chief claim to distinction lies in the fact that he was more than that. He was preeminently a poet of the *supernatural*.

The Supernatural Revelation of God

It was a wonderful condescension on the part of God to manifest Himself to man in the majesty and beauty of creation, but His condescension went much further. He would not only tell man about Himself as the Maker and Master of the universe; He would reveal to him the intimate secrets of His inner divine life. He would tell man what man could never have gathered from the language of creation—the fact that the life of God is like a family life. He would do even more than that; He would reach down and make man a member of that family; He would adopt him into the family circle of the Godhead—where God the Father would be his Father; where God the Son would be his Elder Brother; and where the Holy Spirit would dwell within his soul, giving testimony to his spirit that he was, indeed, the

[45] *Felix Randal.*
[46] *Harry Ploughman.*
[47] *The Wreck*, Stanza 20, 1–2.

adopted son of God. Man would be made to feel at home even at the divine hearthside.

God's generosity was so great that when man had shown himself an ungrateful son, when he, a prodigal, had wandered off and squandered his inheritance in a far country, He did not leave him to his own devices. On the contrary, He sent His only-begotten Son to lower Himself to man's level, to take on Himself the burden and limitations of human flesh, that He might regain for man that share in the divinity which he had thrown away by sin. By becoming man, the Son of God, the Eternal Word of God, was translated into a language that all men could understand. The words that He spoke were the words of eternal life. Because the Son of God really became man, He had a real human mother; henceforth for all eternity there would be a human mother in man's heavenly home. Because the Son of God had become man, it would be eternally true that God could speak to man with a human voice and love him with a human heart. And when Christ had gone home Himself, and even after He had brought His Mother home to Him, He did not leave men orphans. In His Church He gave His brothers of adoption a Holy Mother on earth; and in His Sacraments He gave them the means of receiving, repairing, and nourishing in their souls the divine life which He had purchased with His own death. This is the supernatural communication of God to men which not only speaks to man of God as sunsets and snowflakes speak to him, but which brings the throbbing triune reality of the Godlife into his soul. It gives man not merely the privilege of piecing together hints of God's love and life refracted in the beauty of His creation, but gives him the power and right to know Him as He is, and to share His life—still darkly and imperfectly here through the light of faith, but one day perfectly and eternally through the light of glory. In this supernatural manifestation and communication of Himself, God, in His divine unselfishness, has kept back nothing that He could give to man.

He deigned to share with him the triple richness of His own inmost life.

The Poet of the Supernatural

If even the natural manifestation of God in the works of creation has found continual voice in the songs of poets, we would expect that the astounding condescension and generosity of this supernatural communication of God in the works of grace would be a perennial source of limitless inspiration to Christian poets. But the strange fact is that seldom has this been the sustained theme of a poet's song in any language. Dante has sung of it extensively and incomparably well in his *Divine Comedy;* Milton sang of it coldly and erroneously in *Paradise Lost* and *Paradise Regained;* Patmore sang of some phases of it in *The Unknown Eros;* other English poets, Crashaw for instance, have made it the subject of an occasional poem; but Hopkins sang of it more consistently and beautifully than any other English poet.

Hopkins As a Poet of the Supernatural

High achievement as a poet of the supernatural demands two things of an artist: he must have a profound understanding of supernatural truths and experiences, and be capable of communicating to others the fruits of that understanding in appropriate metrical language. The following pages are meant to show how firm was Hopkins' grasp of the great central truths of revelation. Only when we recognize that these supernatural truths and values do form the leitmotif of the greater part of his poetry, can we appreciate the genuine appropriateness and true artistry of his expression of them.

The heart of the whole supernatural order is the revelation of God as a triangle of personal life rather than merely the being of power and wisdom manifested in the order and beauty of

creation. It is this triune God that we find Hopkins apostrophiz-
ing in his poetry. Thus in *Summa:*

> The best ideal is the true
> And other truth is none.
> All glory be ascribèd to
> The holy Three in One.

And in *The Wreck of the Deutschland* (Stanza 9, 1–2) it is
again the triune God that he invites men to adore:

> Be adored among men,
> God, three-numberèd form.

There is hardly a single one of his poems in which the father-
hood of God, the brotherhood of Christ, or the creative love of
the Holy Spirit does not confront us.

The fullest supernatural revelation of God to man was realized
in the Incarnation when the very "Word of God became flesh
and dwelt amongst us." The Word-made-flesh was the perfect
Evangelium, the perfect news of God. If Hopkins was so enthusiastic about the natural revelation of God in visible creation,
we would expect him to have had a like enthusiam for the
marvellous manifestation and communication of God in the Incarnation. He did. That enthusiasm permeates practically all
his poetry.

To God the Son, the Incarnation was an inconceivable condescension and humiliation; for man, it was an equally inconceivable exaltation. Hopkins had come to appreciate both aspects
of this central mystery of his faith, and never tired of speaking
and writing of them. In a letter to E. H. Coleridge, he says that
no man could ever consider life trivial if he realized what hu-
miliations and limitations the Second Person of the Blessed
Trinity took upon Himself to raise the lives of all men above the
trivial (F 9, Jan. 22, 1866) :

I think that the trivialness of life is, and personally to each one, ought to be seen to be done away with by the Incarnation . . . (the greatness of which no saint can have ever hoped to realize) that our Lord submitted not only to the pains of life, the fasting, scourging, crucifixion, etc. or the insults, as the mocking, blindfolding, spitting, etc., but also to the mean and trivial accidents of humanity. It leads one naturally to rhetorical antithesis to think for instance that after making the world He shd. consent to be taught carpentering, and, being the eternal Reason, to be catechised in the theology of the Rabbins.

Hopkins embodies one of those "mean and trivial accidents of humanity" to which the Incarnate Word of God submitted in *The Wreck of the Deutschland* where he speaks of the Word after His conception as abiding in a "warm-laid grave of a womb-life grey" (Stanza 7, 3). Compared to the glory of the life that was His in the bosom of the Trinity, of which He "emptied" Himself when He became man, the limitations of the life in the womb of His mother, were, indeed, like the darkness of a grave. In another poem Hopkins expresses one of those antitheses which he says the condescension of the Incarnation naturally suggests. He speaks of God's "infinity dwindled to infancy," and of the Son of God becoming dependent upon a human mother for a

> Welcome in womb and breast
> Birth, milk, and all the rest.[48]

But God the Son assumed these limitations willingly because He wanted to bring men news of God as He really is. It was one of the purposes of the Incarnation to reveal God's lovableness to man in a human form. According to Scotus, Hopkins' favorite theologian, this was so much a part of God's plan for man that the Son of God would have become Incarnate even had man never needed a redeemer. He would always have needed the revelation of God's love for him shining out through

[48] *The Blessed Virgin Compared to the Air*, ll. 20–21.

human eyes and throbbing in a human heart. In any event, it was indeed a *felix culpa* that brought God so close to man in the Incarnation. The God of the Old Testament, Hopkins reminds us in one of his poems, was a God of majesty and power striking awe and a holy fear into the hearts of men. The glory of God laid bare to man's gaze would blind him; it had to be "sifted to suit our sight." It was the Incarnation that stepped down God's glory to the capacities of men. The beauty of "our day-star" is not clouded nor dimmed in the Word-made-flesh; it is rather made sweeter and "much dearer to mankind."

> A mother came to mould
> Those limbs like ours which are
> What must make our day-star
> Much dearer to mankind;
> Whose glory bare would blind
> Or less would win man's mind.
> Through her we may see him
> Made sweeter, not made dim.[49]

This grasp of the marvelous implications of the Incarnation so steeped the very atmosphere of Hopkins' thought that he came to see everything in the world as touched and tinged by the Word-made-flesh. In his comments on the *Contemplation for Obtaining Love,* he speaks of the color which the Incarnation lends to all things, in these terms:

Suppose God showed us in a vision the whole world enclosed first in a drop of water, allowing everything to be seen in its native colours; then the same in a drop of Christ's blood, by which everything whatever was turned to scarlet, keeping nevertheless mounted in the scarlet its own colour too.[50]

One has only to read his diaries and poetry to realize that Hopkins saw all things, even natural beauty, transfused with a new

[49] *Ibid.,* ll. 104–11.
[50] From Unpublished Manuscript quoted in John Pick, *Hopkins, Priest and Poet* (London, 1942), p. 45.

significance because of the Incarnation. Stars and bluebells remind him now not merely of God but of Christ. After surveying the beauty of an Autumn sky in *Hurrahing in Harvest,* he continues:

> I walk, I lift up, I lift up heart, eyes,
> Down all that glory in the heavens to glean our Saviour.

Thus Hopkins came to invest everything with a double sacramentalism. He had learned not only to see nature "charged with the grandeur of God"; he had also learned to "inscape" it with the Incarnate Word.

The Son of God was given to the whole human race in the Incarnation. Through the marvellous instrumentality of grace, He may be given to every single member of the human race. Christ was conceived at Nazareth and born at Bethlehem only once; He is conceived and born in the souls of men through grace times without number every day. This is a vital truth of the supernatural order which fascinated Hopkins the religious poet, and he returns to it again and again in his poetry. In *The Wreck,* he recalls the Feast of the Immaculate Conception, "Feast of the one woman without stain," and reminds us that she was conceived immaculately, and conceived her Son but once. "For so conceived, so to conceive thee is done" (Stanza 30, 5). Christ remained in the "warm-laid grave" of Mary's womb for nine months before He was born; He is conceived and born simultaneously now wherever a soul cooperates with His grace. It was such a birth of grace that took place in the soul of the "tall nun" in the floundering Deutschland. She, even though "the rash smart sloggering brine blinds her," "she that weather sees [but] one thing, one; has one fetch in her: she rears herself to divine ears"; and calls on her Master, *"Ipse,* the only one, Christ, King, Head"; "the cross to her she calls Christ to her, christens her wild-worst Best." "Here was a heart-throe, birth of a brain, word, that heard and kept thee [Christ] and uttered thee outright" (Stanzas 19, 24, 28, 30). The nun cooperated with the grace of God that came to her amidst the "buck and flood of the wave," and gave birth once more to a fuller life of Christ within her soul. "She has thee for the pain, for the patience" (Stanza 31, 1). Because the nun like Mary at the Incarnation had said her *fiat,* Christ, a living flame was once more enkindled in the world. Hopkins addresses Him reincarnated in the soul of the nun (Stanza 34, 1–5):

> Now burn, new born to the world,
>   Double-naturèd name,
> The heaven-flung, heart-fleshed, maiden-furled
>   Miracle-in-Mary-of-flame,
> Mid-numberèd He in three of the thunder-throne!

This spiritual conception and birth of Christ goes on in countless souls every moment of the day through the mysterious operations of grace. In these spiritual conceptions and births Mary still "plays in grace her part" because she "holds high motherhood towards all our ghostly good." She, as the mediatrix of all graces,

> . . . mothers each new grace
> That does now reach our race.[51]
>
> .   .   .   .
>
> Of her flesh he took flesh:
> He does take fresh and fresh,
> Though much the mystery how,
> Not flesh but spirit now
> And makes, O marvellous!
> New Nazareths in us,
> Where she shall yet conceive
> Him, morning, noon, and eve;
> New Bethlems, and he born
> There, evening, noon, and morn—
> Bethlem or Nazareth,
> Men here may draw like breath
> More Christ and baffle death;

[51] *B. V. Compared to the Air,* ll. 47–8, 22–3.

> Who, born so, comes to be
> New self and nobler me
> In each one and each one
> More makes, when all is done,
> Both God's and Mary's Son.[52]

"Breathing in Christ like air" and Christ's becoming man's new self" sound like St. Paul's "I live, now not I, but Christ liveth in me." The incorporation of the individual, "each one," in Christ through grace is the exaltation of human nature resulting from the Incarnation. It runs through the thought and poetry of Hopkins like a refrain. Thus in the octet of poem 34, he says that "each mortal thing does one thing and the same"; it "deals out that being [that] indoors each one dwells"; "*myself* it speaks and spells." By being itself it reveals itself; and by revealing itself it reveals what it is, a reflection of God. Therefore, Hopkins goes on to say, the man in sanctifying grace, incorporated as he is in Christ, being in fact another Christ, reveals to God and men what he really is—Christ, "a nobler me." Thus it is that Christ now born a thousand times by grace "plays in ten thousand places, lovely in limbs, and lovely in eyes not his."

> I say more: the just man justices;
> Keeps grace: that keeps all his goings graces;
> Acts in God's eye what in God's eye he is—
> Christ—for Christ plays in ten thousand places,
> Lovely in limbs, and lovely in eyes not his
> To the Father through the features of men's faces. (No. 34)

He had said in his notes on the *Spiritual Exercises* that Christ's grace operative in the soul of man might be expressed in this fashion (N 332):

> It is as if a man said: That is Christ playing at me and me playing at Christ; only that it is no play but truth; That is Christ *being me* and me being Christ.

[52] *Ibid.*, ll. 55–72.

Hopkins had really grasped the Pauline concept of oneness with Christ.

The Christ-life born in the soul by grace may be clouded or killed by sin. Thus Hopkins, in the poem *Spring*, bids men "have, get" "all this juice and all this joy" of spring as a "strain of the earth's sweet being in the beginning in Eden garden," before sin "cloud Christ" in the soul, and sour "innocent mind and Mayday in girl and boy." The life in Christ must be protected, too, by purging out the poison of concupiscence, the residue of the fall. As the blood is purged of impurities by the flood of fresh pure air in the lungs, so concupiscence is purged by the flood of God's grace shed upon the soul through the azured atmosphere of Mary, Mediatrix of all Graces.

> [She] plays in grace her part
> About man's beating heart,
> Laying, like air's fine flood,
> The deathdance in his blood;
> Yet no part but what will
> Be Christ our Saviour still.[53]

The Christ-life, born in the soul by grace, and protected by grace, is also brought to vigor and maturity by grace. By cooperating with every movement of that divine action in the soul, man grows to his full stature in Christ—"more makes, when all is done, both God's and Mary's Son." "Grace," Hopkins says in his commentary on the *Spiritual Exercises* (N. 337), "lifts the receiver from one cleave of being to another, and to a vital act in Christ; this is truly God's finger touching the very vein of personality, which nothing else can reach." And again he says (N. 332) that grace is

. . . any activity on God's part by which, in creating or after creating, he carries the creature to or towards the end of its being, which

[53] *B. V. Compared to the Air*, ll. 49–54.

is its self-sacrifice to God and its salvation. It is, I say, any such activity on God's part; so that so far as this action or activity is God's it is divine stress, holy spirit, and, as all is done through Christ, Christ's spirit.

It is by cooperating with this divine activity in the soul, by being docile to the "divine stress," that the soul can "flash from the flame to the flame then, tower from the grace to the grace," [54] and thus reach the fulness of its life in Christ.

It is one of the generous mercies of Christ that He allows men to share in the distribution of the graces He purchased by His suffering and death. He made Mary, through whom He received His human life, the channel of His divine life into the souls of men. Hopkins has sung incomparably well of her function as Mediatrix of All Graces in the most penetrating and beautiful Marian poem in our language, *The Blessed Virgin Compared to the Air We Breathe*. She is the blessed, spotless atmosphere through which comes "each new grace that does now reach our race." What His Blessed Mother is in a pre-eminent way, Christ has allowed other souls to be in a lesser way—channels of divine grace. Thus the nuns on the *Deutschland,* because they were incorporated in Christ, because they had become the very "cipher of suffering Christ," were used by "lovely-felicitous Providence" to "be a bell to, ring of it, and startle the poor sheep back," those "comfortless unconfessed of them," back to the fold of God's mercy and love. God made these five sisters a "vein for the visiting of past-prayer," a channel of grace to "the-last-breath penitent spirits" (Stanzas 22, 31, and 33). Hopkins expresses the same idea in *The Loss of the Eurydice:*

> And the prayer thou hearest me making
> Have, at the awful overtaking,
>   Heard; have heard and granted
> Grace that day grace was wanted. (ll. 113–16)

[54] *The Wreck,* Stanza, 3, 8.

This channeling of Christ's grace to sinners through the interces-
sion of a saint is possible because "the just man justices," [55] because, being another Christ, what he does is a "Christ-done
deed." [56]

One of the deepest mysteries in life is the inescapable problem of mental and physical suffering. There is absolutely nothing
in the natural order to explain it, and it remains a mystery to
man even in the supernatural order. It is only in the order of
grace, however, where it is illuminated by the light of faith, that
it becomes even tolerable. It is easy to accept God revealed to
us in the beauties of creation; but it is hard to see His hand
in the sufferings and sorrows of life. It is exhilarating to accept
God in the more pleasant communications of His grace; but it
tests the soul to the quick to have to greet Him in His sterner
visitations. It is only when the mystery of suffering has been
"inscaped," brought into focus with Christ on the cross, that
men see it in its one true perspective. It is only when suffering
has been transformed into sacrifice by being united with the
sacrificial suffering of Christ that it begins to take on meaning
and value. Hopkins had pondered this mystery long and prayerfully, and he put his meditations into his poetry.

The whole *Wreck of the Deutschland* grapples with this problem of suffering and misfortune and throws it into proper supernatural perspective. God is under the world's "splendor and
wonder"; He is wafted out of the stars, and "the dappled-with-
damson west"; but "his mystery [of suffering] must be instressed,
stressed," precisely because it is not easy to see God's stress there
(Stanza 5). We often fail to recognize the hand of God in the
storms of life. The greatest graces of our lives, however, frequently come to us not in the blissful manifestations of God, but
in these very strokes and storms that bring us to our knees. When
nothing else will move or melt us to repentance or love, suffering
will often succeed (Stanza 6, 1–7):

[55] No. 34.
[56] *The Soldier.*

> Not out of his bliss
> Springs the stress felt
> Nor first from heaven (and few know this)
> Swings the stroke dealt—
> Stroke and stress that stars and storms deliver,
> That guilt is hushed by, hearts are flushed by and melt.

Suffering is as inescapable as life itself. Confronted with it, even "the faithful waver"; but "the faithless fable and miss" (Stanza 6, 8). The only source of stability in the face of suffering is at the feet of the "hero of Calvary" (Stanza 8, 7). By His suffering Christ gave all suffering a new value and meaning. He elevated it to the dignity of redemptive and reparative sacrifice. From Calvary every other sacrifice forever derives its meaning and value. Like the sufferings of the five nuns on the Deutschland, the sufferings of all men can be joined with the sufferings of Christ, and take on some of their reparative and redemptive value (Stanza 22, 1–6).

> Five! the finding and sake
> And cipher of suffering Christ.
> Mark, the mark is of man's make
> And the word of it Sacrificed.
> But he scores it in scarlet himself on his own bespoken,
> Before-time-taken, dearest prized and priced.

This does not explain suffering, but it does elevate and enrich it. Where there is great love of God, and suffering is seen to be His will, it will be accepted wholeheartedly and generously. "The lingerer with a love glides lower than death and the dark." And once this complete surrender is made to God, that "stanching, quenching ocean of a motionable mind"; to God, the "ground of being, and granite of it"; to God, "throned behind death with a sovereignty that heeds but hides, bodes but abides"; then a matchless calm and confidence comes in which the soul can pray (Stanza 9, 5–8):

Beyond saying sweet, past telling of tongue,
  Thou art lightning and love, I found it, a winter and warm;
    Father and fondler of heart thou hast wrung:
Hast thy dark descending and most art merciful then.

Hopkins had learned by personal experience the bitterness of physical and mental suffering. "God's most deep decree bitter would have me taste: my taste was me"; "self-yeast of spirit a dull dough sours" (No. 45). But he had also learned to unite those sufferings with Christ suffering, and then discovered that even in them the "dark side of the bay of God's blessing" was vaulting him in.[57] He found that in his sufferings God was fanning and winnowing him in order "that my chaff might fly; my grain lie, sheer and clear" (*Carrion Comfort*). The moment that he surrendered to God he discovered that he was filled with a peace and joy that no suffering or failure could destroy.

Nay in all that toil, that coil, since (seems)
      I kissed the rod,
Hand rather, my heart lo! lapped strength, stole
      joy, would laugh, cheer.
Cheer whom though? the hero whose heaven-handling
      flung me, foot trod
Me? or me that fought him? O which one? is it each
      one? That night, that year,
Of now done darkness I wretch lay wrestling with
      (my God!) my God.

Because in his own life he had "inscaped" the mystery of suffering with the cross, he was able to cast them both into beautiful perspective for us in his poetry.

To be "inscaped" with Christ suffering here means to be "inscaped" with Him triumphant hereafter. That is the significance of the last lines of *That Nature is a Heraclitean Fire and of the Comfort of the Resurrection.*

[57] *The Wreck*, Stanza, 12, 7.

> the Resurrection,
> A heart's-clarion! Away grief's gasping, joyless days, dejection.
>   Across my foundering deck shone
> A beacon, an eternal beam. Flesh fade, and mortal trash
> Fall to the residuary worm; world's wildfire, leave but ash:
>   In a flash, at a trumpet crash,
> I am all at once what Christ is, since he was what I am, and
> This Jack, joke, poor potsherd, patch, matchwood, immortal
>   diamond,
>   Is immortal diamond.

Made one with Christ by grace, man, even in his body, will be one with Christ hereafter in the glorious triumph of the resurrection.

Hopkins, we have seen, highly esteemed natural beauty, and was extraordinarily sensitive to its subtlest revelations; but, in the light of his profound penetration of the supernatural verities, it is not surprising that he thought far more of "God's better beauty, grace." [58]

But merely having the supernatural truths as one's theme does not make a successful *poet* of the supernatural. No one knew that better than Hopkins himself. He remarks in a letter to Canon R. W. Dixon (D 133):

> This is the artist's most essential quality, masterly execution: . . . the begetting one's thought on paper, on verse, on whatever the matter is; the life must be conveyed into the work and be displayed there, not suggested as having been in the artist's mind.

To be a *poet* of the supernatural it is not only necessary to penetrate deeply the supernatural truths; it is also essential that the poet's living apprehension of those truths be "conveyed into . . . and displayed" in his verse. If there was ever a poet who succeeded in doing this, Hopkins is that poet. His very experiments in prosody were partially motivated by a desire to get a

[58] *To What Serves Mortal Beauty?*

verse-medium flexible enough to express all the nuances of his intellectual and emotional response to the overwhelming fact of God's manifold sharing of Himself with the creature of His hands.

Once the supernatural truths Hopkns is trying to convey in his poems have been grasped and meditated, then his rich apprehension and fresh, masterly expression of them become almost as rooted in the mind as the very words of Scripture themselves. One can hardly think of those truths without recalling his expression of them. "Wetness to water is not more wed" than the thought of Hopkins' poetry is wed to his expression of it. This fact can be appreciated only when the thought of his poetry has been mastered, because then only is one in a position to appreciate the inevitableness of its expression. It is precisely in his apt use of meter and choice of language that Hopkins the *poet* is revealed. He did succeed in wedding his thought to its expression. From that marriage has come a wealth of new poetic being capable of engendering in other minds all the poet's rich appreciation of the natural and supernatural revelations of God. This is only another way of saying that Gerard Manley Hopkins was an eminently successful *poet* of nature and of the supernatural.

THE THREE LANGUAGES
OF POETRY

WILLIAM T. NOON, S.J.

> One cannot reach Parnassus except by flying thither.
> Yet from time to time more men go up and either perish
> in its gullies fluttering "excelsior" flags or else come down
> again with full folios and blank countenances (N 9).

Even as a young student, Gerard Manley Hopkins could not help talking about poetry like a craftsman. He knew about words the way a woodsman knows about timber. He understood language from the technician's point of view. He was himself a *poet* in the primitive sense: a *maker* of words.

At the same time, Hopkins is far from considering poetry on its technical side alone. No amount of learned theory will help a man to write a poem well, or to read a poem well, unless he understands more about poetry than theory can teach him. Poetry is literature, and as such we may apply to it the definition of literature that Hopkins works out in one of his earliest notebooks: Language that is deeply penetrated by idea (N 95). By the language of poetry we are then to understand not simply the words themselves, but the life principle that animates the words, that gives to the words the breath of life.

In a long letter written to Mowbray Baillie, while both men were still undergraduates at Oxford, Hopkins has a full treatment of what he calls "the three languages of poetry" (F 68–76. Sept. 10, 1864). Here we discover valuable clues why the language of poetry is a living language, and not words alone. A short summary of the pertinent portion of the letter will indicate what it is, as Hopkins sees it, that gives to poetry its life.

1. There is the *language of inspiration.* This alone is poetry proper, and it can be written only by poets, and by them only while they are in a mood of great mental excitement.

2. There is *Parnassian,* which may be divided into:

(a) Parnassian proper, the language of the poet, spoken at the poet's level best, but not under the spell of great inspiration; and,

(b) *Castalian,* a higher sort of Parnassian, but still the lowest kind of inspiration.

3. There is the *language of poetry used (or sung) on the Delphic Plain,* that is, the language of poetry only in so far as poetry is not prose.

In the letter to Baillie, Hopkins also brings into his scheme *Olympian,* "the language of strong masculine genius which suddenly forces its way into the domain of poetry, without naturally having a right there." Rossetti's *Blessed Damozel* is offered as an example of *Olympian,* but beyond this, the term is not developed nor is it strictly included to describe or subdivide any one of "the *three* languages of poetry" (*Ibid.,* p. 73). *Castalian,* although it is included as a division of *Parnassian,* is likewise left almost altogether undeveloped. It is set down briefly as language "too characteristic of the poet, too so-and-so-all-over-ish, to be quite inspiration" (*Ibid.,* p. 72).

Throughout this scheme, we cannot fail to notice that Hopkins' division of the languages of poetry into three main classes is made solely on the grounds of inspiration. One may have all the technical skill in the world and be adept at all that pertains to the craft of writing poems, but unless he have in addition this special something that we call inspiration, Hopkins maintains, he will never write poetry. If he is a genius, what he writes, without inspiration, may rise to *Parnassian,* or to *Castalian* perhaps. If he is not a genius, he will never do better than write verse. Preconceived theories make no difference to the poet when he comes to write his poems. So Hopkins found it was in his

own case,[1] and so, he avers, one who has written any real poetry
will agree. "The effect of studying masterpieces is to make me
admire and do otherwise. So it must be on every original artist
to some degree" (B 291. Sept. 25, 1888).

THE LANGUAGE OF INSPIRATION

Hopkins does not leave us up in the air, moreover, as to what
he understands by this word *inspiration,* a term which has been
so freely and often so loosely used. In words that come deftly
to the point, he tells us what this term means (F 69. Sept. 10,
1864):

I mean by it a mood of great, abnormal in fact, mental acuteness,
either energetic or receptive, according as the thoughts which arise
in it seem generated by a stress and action of the brain, or to strike
into it unasked. This mood arises from various causes, physical
generally, as good health or state of air, or prosaic as it is, length of
time after a meal.

The latter part of this quotation recalls A. E. Housman's remark when he was asked to define poetry. He said that he "could
no more define poetry than a terrier can define rat," but added
"We both recognize the object by the symptoms which it provokes
in us." The symptoms that Housman then describes, symptoms
that constitute his reaction to an authentic poem, come close to
what Hopkins has just said about the experience of the poet
himself, as he goes through the first emotion, or inspiration,
which is to be transfused into poetry. The poetic symptoms, as
they are enumerated by Housman, are as follows: a bristling of
the skin, a shiver down the spine, a constriction of the throat,
and a precipitation of water to the eyes.[2] To which Housman
significantly adds: "Experience has taught me, when I am shav-
ing of a morning to keep watch over my thoughts, because if a

[1] John Keating, "Impressions of Father Gerard Hopkins, S.J.," *Month,*
CXIV (Sept., 1909), p. 249.
[2] A. E. Housman, *The Name and Nature of Poetry* (Macmillan, 1933),
pp. 46–50.

line of poetry strays into my memory, my skin bristles so that the razor ceases to act!" (*Ibid.*)

Emily Dickinson similarly writes: "If I read a book and it makes my whole body so cold no fire can ever warm me, I know it is poetry. If I feel physically as if the top of my head were taken off, I know this is poetry. There are no other ways I know it." [3] Cecil Day-Lewis states in comment on these words (*Ibid.*, p. 251):

There can be little doubt that this emotional disturbance in the reader is a reproduction of the disturbance which was the poetical impulse of the writer; and this reproduction is the first aim and effect of poetry. The first test of poetry is an empiric one.

With this testimony of a contemporary poet that "the first test of poetry is an empiric one," we are brought back again to Hopkins, who makes the same admission in the dialogue *On the Origin of Beauty* when he remarks (in the person of the Professor) that he does not object to being called a Positivist too in a way (N 81).

"The peculiar quality of intense inspiration," which Father Feeney recognizes in Hopkins' own poetry,[4] is precisely what Hopkins himself demanded of all poetry that is worthy of the name. Without this intense inspiration, the poet cannot with heart set to work. The poet is always to be *struck with lightning,* so to speak, every time he is inspired. So it had been with Wordsworth, Hopkins writes to Dixon, when Wordsworth wrote the *Ode on the Intimations of Immortality* (D 147. Oct. 23, 1886). So it has been with all poets always who have written poetry that is authentically great (*Ibid.*):

There have been in all history a few, a very few men, whom common repute, even where it did not trust them, has treated as having

[3] Quoted by C. Day-Lewis, "A Hope for Poetry," *Collected Poems* (Random House, 1935), p. 250.

[4] Leonard Feeney, S.J., "A Further Comment," *America*, LXI (Jan. 23, 1937), p. 320.

had something happen to them that does not happen to other men, as having *seen something,* whatever that really was. . . .

Human nature in these men saw something, got a shock; wavers in opinion, looking back, whether there was anything in it or no; but is in a tremble ever since.

One of the distinctive delights of reading Hopkins' own poetry is this electrical shock of beauty, a steady current of inspiration, "live and lancing like the blowpipe flame" (*To R.B.*). *The Wreck of the Deutschland* is charged with it from beginning to end (e.g., ll. 20–21):

> I whirled out wings that spell
> And fled with a fling of the heart to the heart of the Host.

The Leaden Echo and the Golden Echo opens with this same impulsive breathlessness, a taut eagerness to find words that will keep pace with the thoughts, which, even as he writes, are rushing on ahead (ll. 1–2):

> How to keep—is there any any, is there none such, nowhere known
>   some, bow or brooch or braid or brace, lace, latch or catch or
>   key to keep
> Back beauty, keep it, beauty, beauty, beauty, . . . from vanishing
>   away?

The last lines of *Hurrahing in Harvest* may also be evidenced as *the language of inspiration,* the way a poet talks while still under the influence of a great stress of feeling:

> These things, these things were here and but the beholder
>   Wanting; which two when they once meet,
> The heart rears wings bold and bolder
>   And hurls for him, O half hurls earth for him off under his feet.

There is also an entry into his *Journal* for December 23, 1869 (N 128), which helps us to understand better how Hopkins believes this inspiration works. He tells us how during his Long Retreat, Sister Emmerich's account of the Agony in the Garden was being read in the refectory, and at one point, of a sudden, he was seized by an unlooked-for flood of emotion and began to sob and weep. Why at this point were the flood-gates let down? Why is the poet of a sudden *inspired* by something that he has known and seen for a lifetime perhaps, but which only this moment takes on meaning in his eyes?

There is always one touch, something striking sideways and unlooked for . . . which pierces, and this may be so delicate that the pathos seems to have gone directly to the body and cleared the understanding in its passage.

This release of strong emotion does not always lead, however, to the composition of a poem. "Everybody has like moods," Hopkins tells Baillie, "but not being poets what they then produce is not poetry" (F 69. Sept. 10, 1864). Nor is the poet himself always successful in turning such moods to poetical account. Indeed, there may be times when the intensely personal nature of the mood, or its sacredness may forbid the poet to make capital of it. "It would be sacrilege to do so" (B 66. Feb. 15, 1879). Setting these important exceptions aside, it still remains true that the highest poetry wants "the one rapture of an inspiration" (*To R.B.*), and without it the poet works in vain.

Does this mean that the poet can write only while the spell of great, intense inspiration is upon him? Does Hopkins differ here from Wordsworth, who claimed that "poetry is the spontaneous overflow of powerful feeling recollected in tranquillity"? Although Hopkins prescinds from Wordsworth's notion of *tranquillity,* nevertheless, he too teaches that a time of recollection in most cases is required. The birth of a poem is not a matter of the few moments of its conception, but of a long period of travail and gestation. As he tells us, in the sonnet to Robert Bridges (*To R.B.*), which stands as a sort of epilogue to the published poems:

> The fine delight that fathers thought . . .
> Leaves yet the mind a mother of immortal song.
> Nine months she then, nay years, nine years she long
> Within her wears, bears, cares and moulds the same.

Hopkins advises against trying to compose when the mood has altogether spent itself. Revision of what one has written he holds, for this reason, dangerous in the poet's case. "The worst is," he warns Bridges, "that one seasons over a thing and one's first verjuice flattens into slobber and sweet syllabub" (B 146. June 7, 1882). Verbal alterations at most are all that are possible, "and even verbal alterations will be hazardous, for the stress of the mood which dictated and justified the word or image has passed away" (F 165. Sept. 28, 1883).

Better to keep the excellence of inspiration, Hopkins advises Patmore, than cause this to perish by trying to improve on a poem, when the inspiration itself has weakened. "Some flaws are flies in amber" (F 153. Sept. 23, 1883). The poet ought not to look on his moods or his inspirations from the outside. These ought always to be intensely personal, subjective if you will, so long as the effort of composition is still being made (F 165. Sept. 28, 1883):

> For a time we keep the connection with our past feelings open; they recede, but still we have an insight into them; then something comes between and a long while after looking back, like the tail of a train going round a sharp curve, you see your own self quite from outside.

No one could give more attention to the technical aspect of poetry, when he chose to, than Hopkins. Yet it is evident that he would be among the first to admit that the poet cannot and ought not to give his mind chiefly to this aspect when he is at work. "The rise, the roll, the carol, the creation" (*To R.B.*, l. 12) must come first and impel the spirit to song. The *thoughtfulness* that Hopkins looked for in poetry is a *spontaneous thoughtfulness*, which is utterly free from *poetical fashion and cant* (F 188.

Nov. 23, 1883). All poetry, in one sense, is love poetry, Hopkins tells us, and he who is very much in love does not think a great deal of how he is expressing that love in words. "Feeling, love in particular, is the great moving power and spring of verse" (B 66. Feb. 15, 1879).

PARNASSIAN

From the way that Hopkins stresses the necessity of inspiration, we might at first conclude that without this lightning stroke of feeling, it were useless for the poet to set down a single line. This would be an exaggerated view. Hopkins has been speaking of the *highest poetry,* poetry that is "the virtue of its own kind of composition," as "eloquence, for example, is the virtue of oratory and not oratory only" (N 250). Hopkins knew that it is not possible that the poet will always be able to work in this "mood of great, abnormal in fact, mental acuteness" (F 69. Sept. 10, 1864). Nor is it, indeed, necessary that every line of a poem be able to trace its origin back to a mood of such intense emotional stress and mental excitement.

The term, *Parnassian,* which Hopkins uses to describe poetry that is less than *inspired* and yet more than verse, is not necessarily a term of reproach. *Parnassian* is that language "which genius speaks as fitted to its exaltation, . . . but does not sing in its flights" (*Ibid.*). A genius like Shakespeare rarely needed, says Hopkins, to speak in *Parnassian* (F 70. Sept. 10, 1864), but this is not the case with most poets, with most geniuses. Sometimes they must come down out of the heights; in a long poem especially, it is impossible that every line should, as it were, take our breath away and every fresh beauty take us by surprise (*Ibid.*).

Tennyson is the poet whom Hopkins instances as the great writer of *Parnassian,* although he tells us regretfully that he had once thought "that Tennyson was always new, 'touching,' beyond other poets, not pressed with human ailments, never using *Parnassian*" (*Ibid.,* p. 72).

It is the poetry that genius writes when it is working on the plains, and not soaring in the heights, that is our best lead, says Hopkins, to individual style. The language of inspiration has, properly speaking, no style of its own. But each poet, Hopkins maintains, has his own dialect of *Parnassian* (*Ibid.*, p. 69). Then he adds: "In a poet's particular kind of *Parnassian* lies most of his style, of his manner, of his mannerism, if you like" (*Ibid.*, p. 70). Each poet must be allowed to have his own way of looking at things, his own way of putting things. Each poet has characteristics and peculiarities of his own. These will be sure to stand out when he is writing, not on the heights, but on the level of his own mind. It is on the basis of these that the reader first discovers and afterwards recognizes a writer's style (*Ibid.*, p. 71).

One of Hopkins' uncompleted poems will illustrate what he says about *Parnassian*. In the fragment, *Ash-boughs,* we find (in one variant) the following lines:

> May
> Mells blue and snow white through them, a fringe and fray
> Of greenery: it is old earth's groping towards the steep
> Heaven whom she childs us by
>
> (*Ash-boughs,* variant a, ll. 8–11).

Several of Hopkins' own mannerisms are evident in these lines. There is, to begin with, the double alliteration in "May" and "mells," "fringe" and "fray." There is the internal rhyme of "blue" and "through." There is the novelty of "mells," which requires investigation or reflection on our part before we are certain of the image we are trying to bring into focus. Finally, there is the figure at the end, the abrupt change of metaphor. In this case, Heaven and earth are represented as the parents of men. The loveliness of the ash-boughs reminds Hopkins of their creator. It is a spiritual image, one characteristic of the Jesuit poet-priest who could write into his *Journal* in the first years of his religious life: "I do not think I have ever seen anything more beautiful than the blue bell I have been looking at. I know the beauty of our Lord by it" (N 134).

Hopkins makes a great deal of allowance for the individual differences that genius takes. He is very far, however, from basing his whole concept of style upon individual differences alone. No poet ought to be too persistent in his own way of looking at things, as for example, Hopkins claims, Wordsworth was "too essentially Wordsworthian." Wordsworth's sonnets, Hopkins tells Bridges, "have an odious goodness and neckcloth about them which half throttles their beauty" (B 38. April 3, 1877).

As late as 1882, nearly twenty years after the letter to Baillie, where Hopkins first set down his notions on "the three languages of poetry," he writes to tell Bridges that a poem Bridges has submitted to him for criticism is written in *Parnassian*. Then he endeavors again to define style. It is, he tells Bridges, a nameless quality, something that he himself sometimes called *bidding*:

I mean the art or virtue of saying everything right *to* or *at* the hearer, interesting him, holding him in the attitude of correspondent or addressed or at least concerned, making it everywhere an act of intercourse . . . and of discarding everything that does not bid, does not tell (B 160. Nov. 4, 1882).

Whenever a writer's peculiarities interfere with this attitude of intercourse, whenever he begins talking, as it were, to himself and not *to* and *at* his hearer, his *style* is really no style at all, and, in Hopkins' view, he ought to try to change it. Hopkins, we see, cannot be brought to the defense of any theory of *private poetry*. At all costs, the poet, if he is to be articulate at all, is faced with the necessity to communicate, and this means to transmit thought and emotion to others.

ODDITY AND OBSCURITY

In the light of this principle of *bidding*, it does not appear at first sight that Hopkins could have had much toleration for either oddness or obscurity in a poem. This interests us since it is precisely this charge of *oddity* and *obscurity* that has been consistently leveled against Hopkins' own poems ever since their first publication in 1918. Robert Bridges, at that time poet-laureate of England, their first editor, was the earliest to sound this criticism in the *Notes* appended to the first edition; [5] and the criticism has been echoed and re-echoed ever since. But may we not inquire what were Hopkins' notions on "oddness" and "obscurity"? Other writers have held theories from which they most strenuously departed in practice. Is this also true in Hopkins' case?

The fact of the matter is that Hopkins did not regard "obscurity" and "oddness" necessarily as defects. Neither should be sought for its own sake, but there are "higher excellences," Hopkins writes to Bridges, "than clearness at a first reading" (B 54. May 30, 1878). Someone may be talking right *to* and *at* us, but it does not follow that we must be able at once to see through everything that is being said. The *active communication* may continue even when we need further reflection, or perhaps a repetition, to understand fully what has been spoken. Moreover, if we are in conversation with genius, we should anticipate this need. "Most things should be at once intelligible, but everything need not and cannot be" (B 265. Nov. 6, 1887).

If the poet has a profound thought to express, or again, if he is striving for some complex emotional reaction in his hearer, is it to be expected that everything he says will be on first hearing transparently clear? The poet must at times sacrifice something, and Hopkins holds that "this may be the being at once, nay perhaps the being without explanation at all intelligible" (*Ibid.*, pp. 265–66).

In an article in *The Dial* for September, 1926, I. A. Richards develops this point much as we have seen Hopkins previously develop it. "Modern verse is perhaps more often too lucid than too obscure," Richards tells us. He continues:

[5] *Poems*, pp. 97–98.

It passes through the mind (or the mind passes over it) with too little friction and too swiftly for the development of the response. Poets who can compel slow reading have thus an initial advantage. The effort, the heightened attention may brace the reader, and that peculiar intellectual thrill which celebrates the step-by-step conquest of understanding may irradiate and awaken other mental activities more essential to poetry. It is a good thing to make the light-footed reader work for what he gets. . . . What is a distraction in a first reading may be non-existent in a second.[6]

What Richards is saying here seems to be much what Hopkins means when he talks about "excellences higher than clearness at first reading." The meaning of a poem cannot always be "felt without effort as fast as one reads," Hopkins explains to Bridges, nor is this kind of clearness in every instance an asset to a poem (B 90. Oct. 8, 1879). There is an altogether different kind of clearness in which the meaning, "if dark at first reading," when once made out, will "explode." This *explosion out of the darkness* may, in the long run, give to the poem's meaning a clarity and right temper that more than compensate the reader for the initial obscurity that he must work to dispel.

A modern critic, David Daiches, traces the whole theory of *sprung rhythm* to Hopkins' endeavor to establish this second kind of clearness, this "explosion out of darkness" as a poetic principle: communication, as it were, on several different levels at once.[7] "All the devices which for the casual reader produce only obscurity are really intended to prevent the reader from understanding anything until he can understand everything." [8] This is, as Daiches points out, the force of the term "explode," for "it conveys the sense of everything happening at once."

Anyone who has read Hopkins seriously cannot but realize

[6] I. A. Richards, "Gerard Hopkins," *Dial,* LXXXI (Sept., 1926), pp. 195–203.

[7] For another, and to me more cogent, explanation of Hopkins' development of sprung rhythm, see the study in this volume by Fr. Ong.—Editor.

[8] David Daiches, *Poetry and the Modern World* (Chicago University Press, 1940), p. 32.

what this "explosion out of darkness" means. The reader of a
Hopkins poem for the first time finds himself sometimes at a
loss to make out the meaning of the words. There is an impression
of vitality and masculinity created by the language, but the impact of the idea is not at first felt. You patiently work out the
collocation of phrases, you look up the meaning of unfamiliar or
uncertain words, you determine the exact sense of other emphatic
words in the passage or poem. Somewhere in this process, you
abruptly become aware of what the poet is telling you: the idea
strikes home. There is an inrush of feeling, "a melting, a madrigal
start!" [9] You are never let down! After you have made the
effort, you are rewarded. Hopkins never asks this labor for the
sake of *fool's gold*.

The fourth stanza from *The Wreck of the Deutschland* may
be offered as evidence of what we mean:

> I am soft sift
> In an hourglass—at the wall
> Fast, but mined with a motion, a drift,
> And it crowds and it combs to the fall;
> I steady as a water in a well, to a poise, to a pane,
> But roped with, always, all the way down from the tall
> Fells or flanks of the voel, a vein
> Of the gospel proffer, a pressure, a principle, Christ's gift.

"Sift" in the first line holds us up. Then we see that it refers
clearly to the sand of the hourglass. In "Fast" and "motion,"
there appears to be some play on words. An instant's reflection
enables us to see that "Fast" means "fixed" or "secure." "Combs"
is unfamiliar. We look up its meaning, and we find that "to
comb" is "to curl over and break into foam, as waves." So far,
then, we know all that we need to know to arrive at the meaning
of the first four lines. It might be stated something like this: To
all outward appearances, my life is peaceful, but I am aware
interiorly of conflict.

[9] *The Wreck of the Deutschland*, stanza 18, l. 6.

The fifth line stops us for a while. Then we see that the obscurity vanishes by our supplying the verb "am" in second place: "I *am* steady as a water in a well." Again a comparison is being used to suggest the evident serenity of his life. "Poise" gives us no trouble. "To a pane" is, at first, questionable. The ambiguity clears up, however, when we fit this piece in with the rest. What do you see when you look down into a well? The surface is still, clear, steady like a sheet of glass, like a window-pane.

"Voel," "fells," and "flanks" in the next two lines all require clarification before we may go on. Bridges' note tells us that "voel" is a word used in Wales for a "bare hill." (The poem, we recall, was written at St. Beuno's College in North Wales.) "Fells," we find, are waste-lands, barren upland levels, and "flanks" are stretches of land situated at the side of hills. "Roped with" still confuses us, until we see that its meaning here is "fed with." In other words, there is activity deep down in the well. Somewhere from the hill-top's barren summit, water is trickling down through the earth and comes into motion as a spring from which the well gets its water. Beneath the surface calm, hidden from view in the well's innermost depths, unremittent activity goes on.

All of this brings us to the last line. Here it is necessary to understand "proffer" not as a verb but as a noun, an "offer." What, then, is this offer, this "proffer" from the Gospel, this gift of Christ that is the "principle" of life for Hopkins? To answer this question, we must depend to a certain extent on the rest of the poem. *The Wreck of the Deutschland* shows how we find Christ in suffering, in combat. Christ came not to bring peace, but the sword. "If you will come after me, you must take up your cross daily and follow me." This is "the Gospel proffer"; this is the *vein,* the narrow, trickling stream that gathers force and pressure, that wells up constantly beneath the tranquillity of the surface. My life possesses the steadiness of my convictions, of my faith, Hopkins tells us: it is at the wall fast, like the hour-glass. But beneath the visible calm and quiet, there is a great tension, a great struggle going on. It is the struggle that Christ promised to his followers. It is the "principle" of the Cross.

Not everyone, perhaps, will be willing to follow every detail of this explanation. The interpretation of any poem is to a certain extent subjective and dependent on one's previous associations. All that is claimed for the interpretation here is that it follows the text of the poem, that it "makes sense," that it fits in perfectly with the rest of the work, and that the discovery of the meaning not only brings an intellectual thrill, but that we are put into contact emotionally with the way Hopkins felt as he groped for words to express his idea, as he actually experienced the need for expressing, transmitting his thought in language.

Has a poet the right to ask for so much effort on the part of his readers? If his thoughts are commonplace, his emotions ordinary, then he has no right to compel us to work so hard to find out what he has to say. This is not the case with Hopkins. He does not disappoint us. The initial effort is not easy, but once this effort is made, the meaning is unlocked for us for good; and we come back again and again, not to read poetry that palls from repetition, but to delight in a permanent possession, a golden gift, whose value grows with time. It is hard work the first time over to learn the combination; but once we have mastered the combination, it is no trick at all to use it time and again. Great riches remain ours for the asking.

POETRY AS SPEECH

Another factor that must be taken into consideration when we look into the so-called obscurity of Hopkins' poetry is that he wrote it primarily to be listened to, to be heard by the ear, rather than to be read (or scanned) by the eye. Very much of the initial difficulty clears up when we take time out to pronounce the words; and a little practice in reading Hopkins aloud is a wonderful help to understand what the words are all about.

Hopkins is convinced that modern poets make too little of the sound element of poetry. A poem must be heard with the ears, he insists, not simply read with the eyes. Eye-rhymes he cannot for this reason abide (B 35. April 3, 1877). The poet must compose with a view to the sound and not to the sense alone. This attention to the sound element, he tells Patmore, is primary in his own case: "Such verse as I do compose is oral, made away from paper, and I put it down with repugnance" (F 231. May 12, 1887).

This preoccupation with the sound value of a poem is evident in the early *Note-books*. In one fragment, "Poetry and Verse," poetry is thus defined (N 249):

Poetry is speech framed for contemplation of the mind by way of hearing, or speech framed to be heard for its own sake and interest even over and above its interest of meaning.

In other words, poetry is meant for the ear; the sound element is paramount; it must be heard or read aloud, or at least *listened to* by oneself; the *spoken sound* of it must be dwelt upon and understood.

Finally, to answer the objection of obscurity, one further principle must be accepted before approaching the poetry of Hopkins. Hopkins always takes it for granted that his reader is mentally alert. Activity is always assigned to the mind contemplating the spoken sound. It is the *energy*, not the passivity, of contemplation that Hopkins makes much of, that he understands as a prerequisite of artistic enjoyment and appreciation. The mind must be continually making acts of comparison to perceive the likeness and unlikeness patterns. In the case of the *spoken sound* of poetry, the mind contemplating finds the patterns in the sound, in what Hopkins characteristically calls the "oftening, over-and-overing, aftering of the inscape" (*Ibid.*).

The second line of *The Windhover* appears at first glance to be self-contradictory:

Of the rolling level underneath him steady air, and striding . . .

How, we ask ourselves, can the air be at the same time "rolling" and "level"? If we read the line aloud, we discover that the collocation of words is this:

Of the rolling pause
   level underneath him pause
        steady air

The air *is* rolling, but the Windhover takes it in stride. It is all the same to him. It is level, so far as he is concerned. Evidently the obscurity of the line is not very great when an intelligent reading of the line aloud completely clears up the difficulty.

All that Hopkins says, however, on the necessity of an artificial structure in poetry, on the pattern of sound, must not be exaggerated. The "exquisite artifice" he speaks of does not destroy but rather requires and builds on the simple, natural expression of thought, as he is careful to point out early in the dialogue, *On the Origin of Beauty.* "A perfect style," Hopkins is never tired of repeating, "must be of its age" (N 88).

THE DELPHIC PLAIN

Hopkins' description of *Delphic,* or the language used (or sung) on the Delphic Plain, is quite sketchy in itself. By this term, he signifies, as we have already pointed out, the language of poetry only in so far as poetry is not prose. "Poetry when spoken is spoken in it, but to speak it is not necessarily to speak poetry" (F 72. Sept. 10, 1864). Look at it, listen to it off-hand, and you may imagine that you are reading or listening to a poem. Focus your attention on it, and you discover that except for poetic form, the excellences of poetry are not present.

Here, of course, Hopkins says nothing new. What makes Hopkins' observations of interest to us at this point is the evident distinction that he takes for granted between the language of poetry and the language of prose. The style of prose is a positive thing, just as the style of poetry is a positive thing, Hopkins writes from Dublin to explain to Coventry Patmore his criticism of a prose work of Patmore's in the *Fortnightly Review* (F 232. Oct. 20, 1887). The distinction between the two languages, between poetry and prose, consists, Hopkins notes, in far more than the mere presence or absence of verse forms; but Hopkins does assume that prose lacks these verse forms, while poetry, or what even superficially looks like poetry, possesses them. In other words, Hopkins assumes that the ordinary reader at first glance distinguishes what looks like poetry from what looks like prose by the quick test of apparent verse forms.

Now all this raises at least *two* questions in our minds:

(1) What is the radical difference, as Hopkins sees it, between poetry and prose; and

(2) How would Hopkins explain *free verse*: that is, poetry lacking in strict verse forms?

PRINCIPLE OF PARALLELISM

To answer the first of these questions, that is, to determine the difference between poetry and prose, we must first of all keep in mind Hopkins' great principle of parallelism.

Literature, like every art, aims at strict beauty, and is distinguished from the other arts because of the medium it employs, the medium of words. The use of words with order and arrangement is that which differentiates the language of literature from the language of ordinary use. The literary artist must have a sense for, and pay conscious attention to, the arrangement of the words he uses. Gradation, intensity, climax, tone, *chiaroscuro,* emphasis—all of these effects, according to Hopkins, are illustrative of what he calls a "chromatic parallelism" (N 93). Literary prose partakes of these effects, as much as does poetry. Indeed, it is by means of these effects that the prose of literature differs from the prose of common speech (N 82, 93).

Over and above these effects, this "chromatic parallelism," however, there is also what Hopkins calls a "marked parallelism."

Here the opposition between words is more pronounced, the contrast is more striking, the transitions are more sudden, more abrupt. Metaphor, simile, parable, antithesis, contrast, are the effects produced by this "marked parallelism." Such effects are, it must be noted, more likely to be found in poetry, where, according to Hopkins, "likeness is sought in unlikeness" far more than in prose (N 93).

In an essay, *Poetic Diction,* Hopkins points out how decisively modified must be Wordsworth's view: "The most interesting parts of the best poems will be found to be strictly the language of prose when prose is well written" (N 92). If this is so, asks Hopkins, "if the best prose and the best poetry use the same language, why not use unfettered prose of the two?" To answer this question, Hopkins reverts to his great principle of parallelism.

It is plain, Hopkins observes, that poetry differs from prose not only because of its having a far more "continuous and regular artificial structure" but also because it employs throughout a more strictly regular parallelism, both in diction and in thought (N 93). For this very reason, "poetry tasks the highest powers of man's mind" far more than prose. A concentration, or an intensity, of thought is called into play in order to follow the artificial structure, and to see through the other parallelisms as one goes along. Since Hopkins founds his ideal of beauty on the principle of order, of unity in variety, it is not difficult to see why he should yield to poetry a pre-eminence of beauty that he does not give to prose.

FREE VERSE

Hopkins' distinction of poetry from prose on the grounds that poetry possesses a more pronounced, more "marked" parallelism both in diction and in thought puts us on the right track to answer our second question: How would Hopkins explain free verse?

Historically this question has a peculiar interest. Hopkins far more than any other of the Victorians has been claimed by the school of free verse poets. Indeed, there are many free verse poets of our own day who speak not without pride of a literary ancestry that goes back to the Jesuit poet-priest. Certainly it cannot be denied that Gerard Manley Hopkins anticipated more than a few of the techniques employed by the modern free verse poets. Yet a point of difference arises precisely on the use of free verse itself.

A careful analysis of Hopkins' own prosody, such as Father Lahey gives in his chapter entitled "The Craftsman," [10] or as Herbert Read gives in *English Critical Essays* for 1932,[11] proves convincingly, it seems, how painstaking a metrician Hopkins was in the composition of his own poetry. Once you have found the scansion key, this poetry scans with exactness. Hopkins radically modified the conventional metrical forms, it is true, but his own break with the standard prosody of English verse by no means led him to throw all the rules of prosody overboard when he wrote his own poems. Rather, he strove to perfect a metrical theory of his own.

"Outrides," "paeans," "counterpoint feet"—the words themselves which Hopkins chooses to describe his metrical discoveries reveal a poet uncommonly sensitive to the sound pattern of his verse, one who is eager to get the verse forms right. Do not use the sonnet form at all, Hopkins advises his friend, Canon Dixon, unless you know how to follow perfectly the sonnet's structural exactions (D 71. Oct. 12, 1881). Merely to modify the rhyming scheme of the sonnet he labeled "literary licentiousness." "A downright prolapsus or hernia takes place and the sonnet is crippled for life" (*Ibid.*).

A parting glance at one or two of Hopkins' own definitions of poetry may clarify his own concept of verse. At the outset, it must be remembered that these definitions are from his early

[10] G. F. Lahey, *Gerard Manley Hopkins, A Life* (Oxford University Press, 1930), pp. 87–106.

[11] Herbert Read, "The Poetry of Gerard Manley Hopkins," *English Critical Essays,* 1932 (Oxford University Press, 1932), pp. 361–368.

writings. However, the testimony of the letters written later on and the evidence of the poems themselves indicate, that much as Hopkins may have developed his ideas as time went on, he did not retract his concept of poetry and poetic form as he worked this concept out for himself at Oxford. The notes, *Rhythm and the Other Structural Parts of Rhetoric,* written at least seven years after the last Oxford note-book, are of a piece with the earlier declarations. As Humphrey House says of these notes, "They explain the seven years' silence" (N xv). They prepare us, at least remotely, for the appearance of Sprung Rhythm, which, considered structurally, is a vastly different thing from free verse.

At the beginning of a set of lecture notes intended, it would seem, for use during the period that Hopkins was Professor of Rhetoric at Manresa House, Roehampton, 1873–1874, there stands the following definition of verse: "Verse is speech having a marked figure, order/ of sounds independent of meaning and such as can be shifted from one word or words to others without changing" (N 221). It is this "order of sounds" that Hopkins had in mind, as we have already noted, when he said in the *Dialogue* that poetry differs from prose "by having a continuous and regular artificial structure" (N 249). In the fragment, *Poetry and Verse,* which belongs to the same period as the Roehampton lecture notes, poetry and verse are distinguished thus: "Poetry is speech couched in a repeating figure and verse is spoken sound having a repeating figure" (N 231).

"Repeating figure," "order of sounds," "continuous and regular artificial structure"—these and similar phrases invariably occur when Hopkins has the language of poetry in mind. He speaks of prose rhythms at times, for example, toward the end of the lecture notes to which we have already referred (N 221); but when he does so, it is always clear that it is the rhythm of prose and not of prose poetry that he is discussing.

Walt Whitman writes good "rhythmic prose," Hopkins admits in a letter to Bridges, but "it is rhythmic prose and that only"

(B 156. Oct. 18, 1882). It is not poetry! Moreover, Hopkins is anxious that his friend should see that there is a world of difference between this "savagery" of Whitman's art and the careful elaboration of his own compositions. Whitman's rhythm, the outstanding, perhaps the unique example of free verse rhythm that Hopkins had a chance to know among the poets of his own generation, strikes Hopkins as no more than common prose, no more, in fact, than "rhythm run to seed" (*Ibid.*, p. 157). Moreover, this criticism of Whitman on the metrical score strikes us all the more forcibly when we remember Hopkins' warm sympathy with the spirit of the few Whitman poems he had read (*Ibid.*, 155):

I always knew in my heart Walt Whitman's mind to be more like my own than any other man's living. As he is a very great scoundrel this is not a pleasant confession. And this also makes me the more desirous to read him and the more determined that I will not.

The fact that the poet must work under the constraints of an artificial structure does not strike Hopkins as being in any sense a liability. "Genius," he points out in the *Dialogue,* "works more powerfully under the constraints of metre and rhyme and so on than without, is more effective when conditioned than when unconditioned" (N 83). Again, a little later on he remarks, "Greatness is measured by the powerful action of mind under what we look on as difficulties" (N 84). Only inferior minds, then, whose resources are meagre, find it hard to go on within an artificial structure, and Hopkins views it as a great advantage that such minds should be brought to an end of what they have to give, of what they have to say.

Concentration and intensity are necessary alike for the poet and for those who read what the poet writes. So far as an artificial structure involves concentration and intensity, it is, as Hopkins views poetry, a distinct asset. The intellectual element is never minimized in Hopkins' view of any art. We may or may not agree with this view, but so far as we accept it, much of free verse represents a movement, a trend with which Hopkins is not merely out of sympathy, but one to which he is actually opposed.

From everything that we have said here and have tried always to allow Hopkins to say for himself, there emerges, we believe, a poet-critic who is temperate, liberal, honest, fair. "No one ever wrote words with more critical deliberation than Gerard Hopkins," [12] his old friend and lifelong correspondent, Robert Bridges, could write of him forty years after his death. The Jesuit priest of Farm Street and St. Stephen's Green knew that it was a good work, and one pleasing to God, to write good poetry and to write of poetry well (B 231. Oct. 13, 1886):

A great work by an Englishman is like a great battle won by England.

[12] Robert Bridges, *Three Friends* (Oxford University Press, 1932), p. 104.

WHAT DOES THE WINDHOVER *MEAN?*

Raymond V. Schoder, S.J.

The Windhover is one of the most discussed, and it would seem least understood, poems of modern English literature. To borrow a phrase from the sestet, "no wonder of it." For the poem was bound to attract the attention and admiration of critics, so remarkable is it for freshness, originality, and power. It admirably manifests Hopkins' characteristic style, his wealth and depth of ideas, his vigorous, tense diction, vivid imagery, and marvelous rhythmic sense. Hopkins himself felt this, for he wrote Bridges in 1879 that he considered *The Windhover* his masterpiece, "the best thing I ever wrote." [1] The fact that poems equally great were to follow does not detract from its praise, and the piece rests secure in its excellence.

But it also remains a subtle and evasive problem. Critics who harmonize in the chorus of its praises part company when offering an interpretation. And none of them seems to have really sounded the poem's depths, because not building on an adequate consideration of the poem's complex religious and philosophical background in the author's mind, and on a sufficiently minute examination of certain factors in the text.

The aim of the present study is to submit the text to a fuller analysis in the two-fold light of the dynamically Jesuit cast of Hopkins' mind and of the basic critical principle – stemming from Plato [2] – that any fine work of art is like a living organism: unified throughout its diversified parts by a single dominant principle or soul, with each part contributing its special func-

[1] B 85 (June 22, 1879).
[2] *Phaedrus* 264c.

275

tion to the perfect operation of the whole and subordinated to it, while being harmoniously suited to all the other members. For no explanation of a poem's meaning can claim to be valid unless it fits without violence each word of the text; conversely, it must draw from each word a very definite and objective signification naturally blending into a single import for the integrated whole. Only where this inter-coherent intelligibility emerges from an explanation of a poem may we be confident that we have grasped its meaning substantially, even though perhaps unaware of some of the complementary implications it holds for the poet himself.

On the other hand, because of Hopkins' unique poetic style and outlook, there is danger of forming an *a priori* judgment of this poem—that it cannot, for instance, have as theme an idea common to other poets, but must be more subtle, more full of implications than appears on the surface, wholly unusual and original. But perhaps it is *not*. The only way to find out is to take the text as it stands and make it give up its own meaning. It suffices to know beforehand that whatever the theme or 'point,' Hopkins will treat it in a wholly personal way, and give it a deep-felt, authentic expression it has never received elsewhere. He will give us, for certain, a new and striking poetic experience.

THE WINDHOVER

To Christ Our Lord

I caught this morning morning's minion, king-
  dom of daylight's dauphin, dapple-dawn-drawn Falcon, in his
   riding
  Of the rolling level underneath him steady air, and striding
High there, how he rung upon the rein of a wimpling wing
In his ecstasy! then off, off forth on swing,
  As a skate's heel sweeps smooth on a bow-bend: the hurl and
   gliding
  Rebuffed the big wind. My heart in hiding
Stirred for a bird,—the achieve of, the mastery of the thing!

Brute beauty and valour and act, oh, air, pride, plume, here
　　Buckle! AND the fire that breaks from thee then, a billion
Times told lovelier, more dangerous, O my chevalier!
　　No wonder of it: shéer plód makes plough down sillion
Shine, and blue-bleak embers, ah my dear,
　　Fall, gall themselves, and gash gold-vermilion.

What the Critics Say

The difficulties—and differences—in understanding this sonnet are unusually numerous. A brief summary of the published interpretations will make clear how varied are the problems which the poem raises and how necessary it is to re-examine the text carefully if we wish to be objective in interpreting it.

The reasons for considering these other explanations inadequate or in some matters misleading and unfounded will come into focus in the course of the positive analysis which will follow. Most of the authors mix good points with bad, but in varying proportions.

The interpretation given by Father Thomas J. Grady [3] stresses the positive, joyful, dynamic spirit of the poem and its splendid rhythmic art. The main point is placed in the octave's direct presentation of the bird as achieving glory and ecstasy by energetic natural activity. The poem is seen as an enthusiastic statement of Hopkins' sacramental view of nature, that "Each thing by being itself proclaims God" through exerting itself to the full. The dedication "To Christ Our Lord" implies nothing special, in Father Grady's view. It is practically hopeless, he feels, to try to make much sense or poetry of the sestet. "Buckle" merely states that all the elements listed *are* fused in the bird himself, to whom the "here" and "chevalier" refer exclusively. The falcon is definitely not an allegory or symbol, yet can be made such to suit the reader. The important comma after "plume" in line 9 is omitted both times the line is quoted.

[3] Thomas J. Grady, *"Windhover's* Meaning," *America* 70 (Jan. 29, 1944), pp. 465–466.

Eleanor Ruggles, in a sensitive but only partial explanation of the sonnet,[4] sees in the falcon "one facet of nature reflecting and declaring God's immanence" by its instinctive fulfilment of its natural destiny, thereby asserting its selfhood and making the poet see how far he and his fellow men fail to live up to this ideal. The whole is a re-statement of the theme of the *Deutschland,* of Loyola's Exercises, and of the religious life—that our best praise of God is to fulfil our destiny, even if this entail trial and distress. Christ's passion best shows His majesty; and the windhover is Christ. Just what "buckle" is meant to signify Miss Ruggles will not say.

Elsie E. Phare's analysis [5] is somewhat similar, but timid and very incomplete. She reads several disparate meanings into "buckle," explains the sestet as spoken by Our Lord to the poet, or even to the bird, and thinks it likely that "the poet is still envious of the beauty of the bird," and a bit pouty about the painful implications of the plough- and ember-image.

Bernard Kelly's interpretation [6] is at first sight brilliant and profound, but without much foundation in the text. The poem is explained as being a concrete presentation of the psychological process of knowledge, whereby the external object is assimilated through the operation of the 'agent intellect' and its abstracted form impressed upon the passive intellect until the two become one thing in the act of knowing. As he says, "The peril and beauty of the windhover inform, are one with, the peril and beauty of the poet's mind, who sees and knows the bird. . . . Behind the poem will always be the knowledge . . . of the mind in its act of knowing, . . . explaining that the intelligibility of things is in their act." "The achieve of, the mastery of the thing!" are taken as the poet's exclamation at "grasping the valiant

[4] Eleanor Ruggles, *Gerard Manley Hopkins, A Life* (W. W. Norton, 1944), pp. 155–157.

[5] Elsie Elizabeth Phare, *The Poetry of Gerard Manley Hopkins* (Oxford University Press, 1933), pp. 130–133.

[6] Bernard Kelly, *The Mind and Poetry of G. M. Hopkins* (Pepler and Sewell, London, 1935; not paginated).

beauty of the bird in his mind" or achieving at last identity with it by way of concept. "Buckle" is explained as meaning a command to the bird "to lock in the embrace of the mind; to be itself in its own power and act present in the image of it." One questions, though, whether the psychological mechanics of knowledge are in themselves an apt subject for poetry. Surely they are not the subject of this poem.

A far more common interpretation is the one rather widely established by the reputation of I. A. Richards, F. R. Leavis, William Empson, and W. H. Gardner. These critics agree on a basic reading of the poem as one of renunciation, stoic sacrifice, indecisive inner conflict, and defeat. In the *Dial* for September, 1926,[7] Richards expounds the poem in this fashion, and proposes several other interpretations of individual words which do not hold up under minute analysis. Such is making "daylight's dauphin" mean that the bird is a miniature sun flashing on high, while "more dangerous" and "gall" and the "weary, exhausted rhythm of the last line" are said to indicate the poet's unappeased discontent and jealousy at having to renounce the easier and more glamorous outer activity represented by the falcon.

In a later study of the poem,[8] Richards develops this idea, and after denying that the piece has any parable-value or moral, explains that "The poet's heart has been in hiding, from the life of the senses, from the life of imagination and emotional risk, from speculation. . . . It has been hiding in the routine of meditation, in doctrine taken as understood or left unexplored . . ." until shocked out of this lethargy "with a pang of regret for the renunciations of physical adventure imposed by his choice of life." In the *Dial* article he goes so far as to claim that "the poet in Hopkins was often oppressed and stifled by the priest. . . . (His was) an asceticism which fails to reach ecstasy and accepts the failure. All Hopkins' poems are in this sense poems of defeat."

But this is a travesty of Catholic asceticism, a misconception

[7] I. A. Richards, "Gerard Hopkins," *The Dial* 81 (Sept., 1926).
[8] Quoted in Phare, *The Poetry of G. M. Hopkins*, pp. 133–136.

of religious life as though inevitably dull, crushing, a timorous blinking of the real issues of life, an irrational throwing away of natural talents on a visionary cause. As though Jesuits could not be joyous, hard-headed realists, living a most active and positive life in the midst of the world! Hopkins is not a Carthusian; and even the Carthusian's renunciation of the world is happy and triumphant, utterly different from such imaginary accounts.

The nadir of this way of reading the poem is probably reached in Empson's analysis.[9] Here again, the whole is made out to be a groan of patient, negative renunciation, a jealous envy of the bird's freedom for conspicuous external activity. The ash falling in is taken as a symbol of a life whose precarious order is again and again shattered by internal collapse, while "the gold (which) painters have used for the haloes of saints is forced by alliteration to agree with the gash and gall of their self-tortures." In fact, this poem is selected to illustrate what Empson calls the ambiguity of indecision, where two admitted meanings of the same word are in unresolved conflict, so that "in the first three lines of the sestet we seem to have a clear case of the Freudian use of opposites, where two things thought of as incompatible but desired intensely by different systems of judgments are spoken of simultaneously by words applying to both: both desires are thus given a transient and exhausting satisfaction, and the two systems of judgment are forced into open conflict before the reader."

The artistry of the piece appears to Empson negligible: "Such a process . . . could tap the energies of the very depths of the mind. At the same time one may doubt whether it is most effective to do it so crudely as in these three lines: this enormous conjunction standing as it were for the point of friction between the two worlds conceived together affects one rather like shouting in an actor and probably to many readers [seemingly Empson himself] the lines seem so meaningless as to have no effect at all." Poor Father Hopkins!

[9] William Empson, *Seven Types of Ambiguity* (Chatto and Windus, 1930), pp. 284–286.

The same general view of the poem, though without these extravagances, is taken by F. R. Leavis,[10] who sums it up, after referring the reader to Richards' and Empson's "admirable" analyses, as a poem of inner friction and dejected renunciation of the active life. Similarly, W. H. Gardner[11] can see in the poem only resignation, appeasement of grieved sense of ambition, the sheer plodding priest's sacrifice of the 'knight of Christ' glory he so admires in the falcon. The asceticism of the poem is wholly negative, a repression of impulsive desire to share the dangerous mortal beauty revealed in the falcon.

John Pick's reading of the poem [12] is similar. "Rung" is explained by Richards' reference to the *manège*, and it is the sillion itself (defined as 'furrow'), which gleams when the plodding plough breaks it up. "Buckle" is taken as meaning collapse, and the theme of the whole is summed up thus: "It is in the act of 'buckling' when the windhover swoops down, when its flight is crumpled, when 'brute beauty and valour and act, oh, air, pride, plume' in an act of self-sacrifice, of self-destruction, of mystical self-immolation send off a fire far greater than any natural beauty." This is to be understood as a "sacrifice transmuted by the Fire of Love into something far greater than any mere natural beauty." The central idea of the whole is: "Here is Christ upon the Cross and Hopkins the *alter Christus.*"

Daniel Sargent, in his brief summary of the poem,[13] follows Leavis and Richards. The basic point is that "the bird is all 'air, pride, plume,' as we all wish to be, as he, Hopkins, has chosen not to be."

Professor McLuhan's interpretation [14] is involved and puzzling,

[10] F. R. Leavis, *New Bearings in English Poetry* (Chatto and Windus, 1932), pp. 181–182.

[11] W. H. Gardner, "The Religious Problem in G. M. Hopkins," *Scrutiny*, June, 1937.

[12] John Pick, *Gerard Manley Hopkins, Priest and Poet* (Oxford University Press, 1942), pp. 70–71.

[13] Daniel Sargent, *Four Independents* (Sheed and Ward, 1935), p. 148.

[14] H. Marshall McLuhan, "The Analogical Mirrors," *Kenyon Review* 6 (Summer, 1944), pp. 322–332.

because largely subjective. The sillion shines, because "this 'Jack, joke' plodding behind the plough makes the trash and mud of earth shine like diamond." "The underlying image in the last three lines is that of mortal *clay* transformed. It is made to shine and to fructify by the humble service of the plough (the obedient will). The 'blue-bleak' earth provides the transition to the embers covered with clay-like ash." Again, "the shining armor of the falcon's imitation of Christ's mastery is to be buckled in the hidden heart of the poet," for 'buckle' implies 'buckler,' and as the falcon's actions mirror Christ, the poet says "let us take this mirror (St. Paul's 'armour') and buckle it here in my hidden heart . . . Christ's fire will burst on and from the second mirror 'a billion times told lovelier' than from the falcon." The key to Hopkins' meaning "is, of course . . . the basic mirror images of his analogist vision." "Buckle means that the 'brute beauty' of the bird as mirror of God's grandeur is to be transferred or flashed to the 'heart in hiding,' just as the burnished surface of the plow in action is hidden in the earth." The poem's theme is passive: "Just as 'the fire that breaks from thee then, after the mirror of mortal beauty has been buckled to the hidden heart, is not a fire produced by any direct action or valor, so the fire that breaks from the 'blue-bleak embers' is not the effect of *ethos* but *pathos,* not of action but of suffering or patience."

Finally, Herbert Read [15] draws a wholly different conclusion. He asserts that Hopkins had scruples over the intense activity of his senses in this poem, which he tries to palliate by dedicating the piece to Christ our Lord; "but this is a patent deception. It does not alter the naked sensuality of the poem. There is no asceticism in this poem."

The Critic's Task and Technique

Still further problems, not touched by the critics, are latent in the text and must be faced. Is the grammar of "Brute beauty. . .

[15] Quoted in Phare, *op. cit.,* p. 139.

Buckle!" to be taken as a series of nominative nouns with an exclamatory indicative "Buckle!" or are the nouns in the vocative, and the verb a plural imperative? Why is AND so written and stressed? Why exactly "minion" and "dauphin"? What does "rung" mean in the fourth line? Again, "bow-bend" and "my heart in hiding" could admit of various connotations. And what is the structure of the argument—does the sestet apply the action in the octave positively, by way of analogy and moral, or is it negatively contrasted to the first part? Again, do the two concluding images of the plough and embers recapitulate that of the falcon, or rather provide an opposing parallel, setting the sestet against the octave?

Hopkins is forever teasing us by this almost unconscionable ambiguity, a fault we would not easily put up with in a lesser poet. Clearly, however, Hopkins does not intend both alternatives in these ambiguous words. The fad in certain schools of recent criticism, of reading all possible connotations into every word of a poem, is surely unsound and dangerous. It is true that the Metaphysical poets seek their effect by way of ambivalent words intended to suggest two or more simultaneous but different levels of meaning—what they call "wit." But one should not force other types of poetry into this mould. The words may bear, indeed, a wealth of associated and secondary meanings clustering around the basic intention and lending it fullness of content, like grace notes playing about a musical theme. But to say that they mean both this thing and that, its opposite or even contradictory, is to confess ignorance of the real meaning, and to weaken the concentrated vigor and directness of the poet's thought.

Where opposing interpretations seem possible, then, the critic must strive to determine which one of them the poet intended, by light of context and the integrated structure of the whole. Hopkins, more than most poets, has something very precise in mind. An explanation of one of his poems that ends up in confusion or counter-balanced alternatives simply has not yet found the clue to its meaning.

That the meaning of the *Windhover* is hard to find is sufficiently apparent from the evidence of the preceding pages. Clearly, too, a different critical technique ought to be tried, since the customary approach has yielded so little agreement and persuasiveness. What is needed is a close objective analysis of all details of the text against the full background of Hopkins' thought and work. What this poem calls for is *exegesis* part by part, a running commentary. If I propose, then, to essay this here, the reader will understand that the fulness and length of the discussion are not to be ascribed to a love of belaboring the obvious. (Obviously much in the poem is *not* obvious!) It is simply necessary to reason things out explicitly, to put down all the evidence, whether new or common, if we wish to do full justice to the poem and to Hopkins. Such an analysis of this key poem might also serve as a general introduction to the whole of Hopkins' outlook and technique, and as a suggestion of the careful study which much of his work requires if it is to be properly appreciated.

The Theme in Summary

The structure and meaning of the *Windhover* can, I suggest, be stated thus: the sudden vision of a hawk pluckily and joyfully battling with the elements seizes upon the poet's mind and, becoming a symbol of the Christian knight valiantly warring against evil, stirs him from a timid and reluctant state of soul to resolutions of heroic deeds in the more active service of Christ in advancing His Kingdom among men; for he sees that this will make his life more noble, more glorious and exciting than the cautious reserve of a self-nursing and commonplace Christian existence. He then confirms his resolution to brave the wounds of more aggressive crusading for Christ by noting further natural instances, analogous to the energetic bird, where toil and pain also result in augmented splendor.

Kingdom of Christ Motif

The sentiments and imagery of this poem are basically a poetic re-statement of the great meditation on the Kingdom of Christ in the *Spiritual Exercises* of St. Ignatius.[16] For the intention of that stirring consideration is to enflame the Christian soul with determination to follow in the laborious steps of the Divine Leader in His thrilling battle with all the forces of evil, to uplift and beautify the souls of men for His Father's glory. The dramatic scene which St. Ignatius here draws is as famous as it was familiar to Hopkins: Christ, the eternal King, noblest and worthiest of leaders, whose very aspect and example move the soul to deepest loyalty and reverence, summoning His subjects individually and announcing to them His intention to subdue the whole world and all His enemies, and thus enter into the glory of His Father. He Himself will set the example, and bear every hardship, labor, and suffering of the campaign, so that His follower has only to share with Him the toil, if he would also share with Him the fruits of the inevitable victory—and this in proportion to his valor and services.

Any man, exclaims the soldier-saint, who turned a deaf ear to this remarkable enlistment, would surely be worthy of contempt as a coward and slacker. But "all who have any judgment and sense" will offer themselves wholly to the task, while the knightly soul will hasten to proclaim its unrestricted dedication to the cause, and its resolve to be *outstanding* in its promotion. Such will promise with firmest determination to perform any service asked, and in complete dismissal of self-comfort and private inclinations imitate this great Captain in bearing all attacks, contempt, and sacrifice of wordly goods 'for the duration,' i.e., throughout life.

This is a burning proclamation, a cry of selfless heroism and undaunted valor in deep-set conviction of the nobility and splendor

[16] Text in *The Spiritual Exercises of St. Ignatius of Loyola*; translated by Father Elder Mullan, S.J. (P. J. Kenedy and Sons, 1914), pp. 55–58.

of Christ's cause. It is all positive, a call to action and to battle, whatever the cost to selfish interests. It is a challenge to offer one's all to Christ, to *do* something, do something more, do everything in one's power for the triumph of His Kingdom in one's own soul and in all other men. This is the trumpet-call to energetic action, to be a Crusader of Christ. These ideas are basic in any Jesuit's mind, and they were, we know, a perpetual and dominant attitude of Hopkins' outlook and life.[17]

The Octave: First Half

These, then, seem to be the sentiments running through the poet's mind when in the fresh splendor of the dawn his eye suddenly is attracted and held by the sight of a soaring kestrel hawk battling through the day-break winds: [18] "I caught this morning morning's minion, kingdom of daylight's dauphin, dapple-dawn-drawn Falcon . . ." The suddenness, surprise, and joyful triumph

[17] Note, for instance, how the image of Christ the King comes up in the *Wreck of the Deutschland* (1876), several times;

  st. 10: "Make mercy in all of us, out of us all
        Mastery, but be adored, but be adored King."

  st. 28: "The Master,
        Ipse, the only one, Christ, King, Head."

  st. 35: "Our King back, oh, upon English souls!"

Also in poem 39, *The Soldier* (1885):

"Mark Christ our King. He knows war, served this soldiering through."

And the idea breaks forth spontaneously in the midst of a sermon on the Holy Ghost (1880 or 1881): "Did not he (Christ) cry men on? Not only by words . . . not only by standards and signals . . . but best of all by deeds, by his own example: he led the way, went before his troops, was himself the vanguard, was the forlorn hope, bore the brunt of battle alone, died upon the field, on Calvary hill, and bought the victory by his blood. He cried men on; he said to his disciples . . . Follow me; they did so; he warned all: He that would come after me let him deny himself and take up his cross and follow me; but when they would not follow he let them go and took all the war upon himself. . . . For though Christ cheered them on they feared to follow, though the Captain led the way the soldiers fell back; he was not for that time a successful Paraclete" (N 287-288).

[18] For a parallel in Hopkins to this poem's theme and title compare the entry in his *Journal* for Aug. 14, 1874: ". . . a wedge of sunlight streamed down through a break in the clouds upon the valley: a hawk also was hanging on the hover" (N 203).

of the stirring sight are all implied in the word "caught." This also arouses an image of hunting, so that the bird is as it were snared by the far-reaching, invisible meshes of the mind, which is itself so struck by the contact that its attention is wholly concentrated on its catch. The intensity of the experience starts the mind working quickly, until the whole chain of associations, reflections, and development which comprises the rest of the poem has worked itself out to completion.

The falcon is described, most strikingly, as "dapple-dawn-drawn," that is, drawn up by the dappled dawn into the air. The "drawn" may also mean etched against the dawn in silhouette, but rather as a secondary reflection and a sort of word-play, for the basic meaning demanded by the entire context is that the bird has been called forth from slumber into action by the arrival of dawn, its familiar friend and accustomed associate in the new day's exploits.

This epithet "dapple" is one of Hopkins' favorites, and a perpetual delight in varicolored beauty is a striking characteristic of his poetic interests. In the *Wreck of the Deutschland* (st. 5), he cries "I kiss my hand to the dappled-with-damson west," while in *Pied Beauty* the whole poem is a paean on this very theme, "Glory be to God for dappled things"; and in *Spelt from Sibyl's Leaves,* he expresses the utmost grief that "earth her being has unbound, her dapple is at an end." The presence of this epithet, then, at the opening of the *Windhover* is a sign that the experience is irradiated by the glow of a quality most pleasing to the poet's mind. It is part of the total beauty of the bird in flight which overwhelms the poet's soul.

The bird is characterized as "morning's minion, kingdom of daylight's dauphin" with significant intent. For its bearing shows it to be the favorite, the half-spoiled darling of the dawn, the heir-apparent of daylight's kingdom, ever to be found near it as its closest follower and pet. Moreover, by reason of this special relationship to the monarch, a minion and dauphin is usually inclined to carry himself with a certain self-assurance and haughti-

ness, fearless and self-willed in his consciousness of relative im-
punity for his actions because of the king's protecting benevolence.
This is why the falcon flies so confidently, so boldly into the gusts
of air, and makes the rounds of his demesne with such regal
show and independence, to the admiring applause of the poet.

Moreover, the entire poem is pervaded by an air of medieval
chivalry, like the meditation on the Kingdom of Christ which it
is re-expressing. "Minion," "dauphin," "chevalier," and other
words are obviously meant to give this archaic flavor, and to call
up a pageant of colorful feudal imagery and associated ideals.
Furthermore, the bird seems on reflection and by a sudden illumi-
nation to become for the poet a symbol, a reminder of Christ—
the Crusading King in question. This appears to be implied in the
poem's explicit dedication "To Christ Our Lord," and in its
consistent echoing of the Kingdom of Christ motif.

Supplementary meanings such as these constitute a second level
of the poet's thought, lying not on the poem's surface but in its
inner context. They will at least give us the right approach and
overtones; for the experience is clearly sublimated in Hopkins'
deeply religious and Ignatian mind into a vision of spiritual combat under the leadership of Christ. We, then, must stress these
background ideas even more explicitly than the poet himself,
merely to come to the poem with the right mood and imagery.

The falcon is further pictured now "in his riding of the rolling
level underneath him steady air, and striding high there . . ." He
"rides" the billowing air as a ship the waves, and as a crusading
knight his swaying, powerful charger. For the air at dawn is commonly rough and boisterous, since the growing heat of the sun
stirs currents of warm rising air while the colder portions rush in
to take up the vacated place. But the bird by his spirited, energetic
exertion subdues its rolling turmoil into steadiness and level calm,
or rather treats it in his strength as though it were but steady and
calm, turning its wildness to submissive support underneath *him*,
its master. The line is evidently intended to be read as though
hyphenated into one composite idea: "rolling, level-underneath-

him, steady air," for this alone removes the difficulty of such opposite adjectives as "rolling," and "level," "steady" applied to the same subject at once.

The gallant bird, however, not only rides over opposition, but does it with a fling of joyous, conscious power: "and striding high there." It is the princely, the royal favorite's stride, the determined, fearless, justifiably confident bearing of one aware of his dignity, his rights, and his power. A thrill of admiration is the natural reaction of the onlooker, and this very aspect of the bird's flight is one of the major causes of Hopkins' delight.

In Christ, too, one is reminded of its counterpart. For the falcon is not only a vividly real natural object, but becomes on meditation a symbol, a revelation of Christ, Who also stirs the mind to admiration with His utterly intrepid comportment in the face of opposition. He not merely went up to Jerusalem in the teeth of His foes, but walked thither so resolutely that the disciples were amazed: "They were on the road, going up to Jerusalem, and Jesus was walking ahead of them, and they were astounded and followed in fear." [19] As Hopkins said elsewhere, in admiration, "his [Christ's] heart was brave . . . . He found the thought of His Passion past bearing, yet He went through with it" (N 264). He goes forth to His death firmly, of His own accord: "Arise, let us go! Behold, he who shall betray me is at hand." [20]

For Hopkins, Christ is the supreme Hero of all time, Who of His own free choice undertook the greatest, most painful and terrifying mission ever laid on man's shoulders, and with inexpressible heroism flowing from infinite love and selfless dedication carried through the mighty struggle unto death, even death on a cross, to the final triumphant "It is consummated!" In the imagery of the Easter liturgy, *Vita et Mors duello conflixere mirando; Dux vitae mortuus regnat vivus!* [21]

[19] *St. Mark* 10.32.
[20] *St. Matthew* 26.46.
[21] "Life and Death grappled in wondrous battle; the Captain of Life, though slain, lives triumphant!"
Hopkins often speaks of Christ as a hero in this sense, as in *Wreck of the*

Such are the inspiring aspects of his Captain, Christ, which seem recalled to Hopkins' mind as he watches in awed admiration the plucky, gallant, spirited bird wrestling with the wind. Nor is the closing touch, "high there," without significance. The heights up to which the bird fights his way by sheer mettle are a large part of the thrill and inspiration of the sight. Exalted and lofty too are the regions to which Christ's example and divine challenge call the soul. The whole experience is one of being dared to higher levels of action.

The Octave: Second Half

"How he rung upon the rein of a wimpling wing in his ecstasy!" Once more the theme of this first movement is re-stated with variations. The bird is soaring in glorious rhythmic circles, ever driving upward with a thrill of achievement, of gratifying approach to its goal in the heights. The word "rung" is, characteristically, the exact technical term for the occasion, called up from Hopkins' remarkable vocabulary of old and rare words still fresh to his mind with all their original meaning and color, "with the sap still in them." "Rung" is here intransitive, the technical term from falconry defined by the *New (Oxford) English Dictionary*

Deutschland (st. 8): "To hero of Calvary, Christ's feet"; *ibid*. st. 35: "Hero of us, high-priest"; *ibid*. st. 33: "Our passion-plungèd giant"; *Carrion Comfort*: "the hero whose heaven-handling flung me, foot trod me"; *Loss of the Eurydice* (ll. 109–112):

> "But to Christ lord of thunder
> Crouch; lay knee by earth low under:
> 'Holiest, loveliest, bravest,
> Save my hero, O Hero savest.' "

And he has an entire sermon of glowing earnestness on this very concept: "Our Lord Jesus Christ, my brethren, is our hero, a hero all the world wants. . . . He is a warrior and a conqueror. . . . He is a King. . . . He is all the world's hero, the desire of the nations. But besides he is the hero of single souls . . . all his servants take up their cross and follow him. And those even that do not follow him, yet they look wistfully after him, own him a hero, and wish they dared answer to his call. . . . Make him your hero now. . . ." (N 260–266).

as used "of a hawk: to rise spirally in flight." [22] It means, then, to fly about in rings or circles, and should not be confused with the transitive parallel forms such as 'ring a bell,' 'ring the changes,' or 'ring in the reins.'

I. A. Richards' interpretation,[23] that it is taken from the vocabulary of the manège, to mean making a horse go about in a circle under the control of a rope, clearly gives only a secondary meaning, to be thought of subsequently to the basic image from falconry; it is brought in, if at all, by the implications of "on the rein of a wimpling wing," which is primarily to remind us again of the crusading-knight-motif which underlies the whole poem as a second level of meaning. The word seems also to imply Hopkins' marveling at the control of such power by so tiny and flimsy a fulcrum as a wing, which here serves to "rein in" the bird's flight.

The falcon's wing is described as "wimpling" [24] because of the way the feathers appear in graceful folds when seen from below (as Hopkins recalls from closer observation before), and also because the mechanics of banked flight require the pivotal wing to be contracted so that its shortened span forces the surface into little bulging ripples. Hopkins' sharp eye delights in noting such details of nature lore, and his ability to express the observation so acutely indicates high poetic power.

The fact that the bird is shown soaring about so joyously, "in his ecstasy!" [25] is crucial to an understanding of the poem. Hop-

[22] *The Oxford English Dictionary*, vol. 8, p. 692, col. 2.

[23] "Gerard Hopkins," *The Dial* 81 (Sept. 1926).

[24] Compare *Morning Midday and Evening Sacrifice:*
"The dappled die-away
Cheek and wimpled lip."
Also *The Leaden Echo and the Golden Echo* (l. 25):
"the wimpled-water-dimpled, not-by-morning-matchèd face."

[25] Hopkins has an interesting entry in his *Journal* for Nov. 8, 1874, which parallels the present passage: "We saw a vast multitude of starlings making an unspeakable jangle. . . . They would sweep round in whirlwinds — you could see the nearer and farther bow of the rings by the size and blackness . . . then they would fall upon a field and so on. . . . I thought they must be full of enthusiasm and delight hearing their cries and stirring and cheering one another." (N 215.)

kins is gripped and inspired by the sight not merely because it is a manifestation of such graceful beauty and thrilling valor, but also because it is a revelation that spirited action is a key to happiness.[26] The joy of function, the thrill which compensates noble exertion, is a major chord in this poem's central theme. It will ring out again, and sweeten all the harder notes of the personal challenge in the finale.

This ecstasy of valiant endeavor applies also to Christ. Did He not "exult as a giant to run His course," [27] and proclaim His eagerness for the struggle: "I am come to cast fire on the earth, and what will I but that it be kindled?" [28]

Now the bird turns from his steep climb to glide down defiantly into the teeth of the wind: "then off, off forth on swing, as a skate's heel sweeps smooth on a bow-bend." After circling about in ascending spirals, the falcon suddenly levels off, swings outward and down in the opposite direction in a neat, swift curve, then tilts his wings to the other side and executes a reverse curve. The whole motion looks like a figure-eight or the contours of a ribbon tied in a bow. It is just what one sees a hawk do occasionally as it coasts back and forth over a chosen area of inspection. In its graceful beauty and impression of controlled power, it reminds Hopkins, most aptly, of a skater sweeping powerfully yet easily around in smooth curves, while the *heel* of the skate scrapes up a spray of ice flakes in a flurry of power. The simile is remarkable, and like all of Hopkins' comparisons strikingly fresh and original.

"The hurl and gliding rebuffed the big wind." The bird shows a sort of defiance for his antagonist, a disdainful attitude not based on contempt but on fearless trust in his own proved strength. He shows this not merely by pitting his forces counter

[26] Aristotle had shown that happiness lies in activity, as the crowning bloom of properly ordered function, the perfection of operation. Pleasure, too, is nothing else than the natural consequence and reward of due exercise of the faculties on their proper objects. (*Nicomachean Ethics* 1174b–1175a.)

[27] *Psalm* 18.6.

[28] *St. Luke* 12.49.

to the wind and "hurling" himself through it, but also by "glid-ing" along with it or down on it from his height with an air of yielding for a moment to its will until he decides to terminate its permitted control. The "gliding" probably refers to the "off, off forth on swing . . ." downwards, after the upward spiralling by counter-thrust or "hurl."

There is a parallel to this too in Christ's struggle. His mastery of every situation is shown not only by energetic counter-action, as when He denounced the Pharisees or hurled His captors back-ward to the ground by a mere word, but also by His majestic free submission to their will: "But this is your hour, and the power of darkness." [29] He is master still.

Transition

The pivotal line of the poem now sums up the significance of all that has gone before and leads into the dominant thought of the sestet: "My heart in hiding stirred for a bird—the achieve of, the mastery of the thing!" [30] Hitherto, the poet has been lost in the thing itself, the vision which has been dominating his atten-tion. Now he adverts reflexly to his own reaction. He realizes that all along his emotions and will have been stimulated to act, as well as his mind. This has been almost unwitting, secret, "in hiding" from his attention. But more than that—his heart itself has been, consciously enough, "in hiding" from something it fears, from the bitter implications of life and from Christ's insistent challenge to a more heroic plane of activity. It has been shrinking from the cost and pain of doing great things, somewhat in the mood of Francis Thompson's *Dread of Height*,[31] in which the

[29] *Ibid.*, 22.53.
[30] Compare the very similar passage in *Henry Purcell:*
"so some great stormfowl, whenever he has walked his while
The thunder-purple seabeach plumèd purple-of-thunder,
If a wuthering of his palmy snow-pinions scatter a colossal smile
Off him, but meaning [only] motion fans fresh our wits with wonder."
[31] *The Poems of Francis Thompson,* edited by Rev. Terence L. Con-nolly, S.J. (Century Co., 1932), pp. 161–163.

very realization of fragile man's sublime goal and calling terrifies the soul and makes it want to forget the noble challenge. We hear an echo here of the theme worked out by Hopkins earlier in the *Wreck of the Deutschland,* stanzas 2 and 3, especially the lines:

> I did say yes
> O at lightning and lashed rod;
> Thou heardst me truer than tongue confess
> Thy terror, O Christ, O God;
> Thou knowest the walls, altar and hour and night:
> The swoon of a heart that the sweep and the hurl of thee trod
> Hard down with a horror of height . . .

It is the same sort of experience as St. Augustine describes in the *Confessions: Et reverberasti infirmitatem aspectus mei radians in me vehementer, et contremui AMORE ET HORRORE: et inveni longe me esse a te in regione dissimilitudinis, tamquam audirem vocem tuam de excelso: "Cibus sum grandium: cresce et manducabis Me."* [32]

Hopkins is not hiding, of course, from the world or reality but from Christ's challenge to follow Him all the way to heroic heights of selfless crusading for God, to be perfect even as his heavenly Father is perfect. For although in his daily life as a Jesuit he is dedicated to the greater glory of God, nevertheless he realizes that he could exert himself to still more valorous deeds for the triumph of Christ in his own soul and in other men. It is only that he dreads the price this would entail, and is already weary from the long and ruthless struggle against self. His present mode of service is noble and satisfactory, or at least sufficient; must he rise still higher, be *outstanding* in the ranks of his Captain Christ? He knows he ought to. In the spirit of St. Ignatius' cry in the *Exercises:* "What have I done for Christ? What am I doing for

[32] "And in the strength of Thy radiance upon me my weak vision was smitten back, and I trembled WITH LOVE AND WITH FRIGHT: and I discovered that I was far from Thee, in the region of unlikeness, as though I heard a voice from on high: 'I am the food of the great: grow, and thou shalt eat Me.'" (*Confessions* 7.10.)

Christ? What *ought* I do for Christ?" [33] he feels that more is expected from him, that his own self-respect demands it. Yet he shrinks from the thought and tries to hide from it under the cover of an uneasy complacency in his already more-than-average service.

In this frame of mind, he implies, he has come upon this falcon, and while watching it discovers that his timid heart has been increasingly stirred with admiration. A mere bird! Yet what valor, what energetic achievement, what mastery of its own well-disciplined powers and through them of the buffeting wind! The beauty of perfect function, the manifest joy in the perilous, triumphant activity, the reckless abandon to the nobility of the deed in forgetfulness of all toil and pain to self have aroused in him a sudden envy, a pang of remorse for his own slackness in the battle, a renewed impulse to go and do likewise. The sublimation of the plucky bird into a symbol and reminder of Christ the supreme hero, the King Who is ever beckoning to press closer to Him in the very center of the fray, intensifies the impulse a hundredfold. He has seen now more clearly that nobility and beauty of life lie, by the very nature of things, in brave action, in exertion of will to ever greater deeds of dedication and sacrifice. He is on the verge of an heroic decision.

There is a tensely dramatic pause, then he bursts out, in the sestet, into an expression of his resolve to do as the falcon has done, to be a more gallant crusader with Christ.

The Sestet, First Half: challenge accepted

The transition from the bird to self, from the objective ideal to its personal application and realization is admirably direct and definite. He calls on all the factors of the bird's inspiring achievement to come and put themselves in operation here in *his* life too: "Brute beauty and valour and act, oh, air, pride, plume, here buckle!"

[33] *The Spiritual Exercises of St. Ignatius,* translated by Fr. Mullan, p. 39.

This line is the crucial one of the whole poem. On its interpretation depend the meaning and structural integration to be attributed to the entire piece. Here all interpreters, however closely agreeing on individual points of the poem, must part company on the meaning of the whole if they differ on this one line. Intriguingly enough, an important clue to the poet's own intention lies locked in an unobtrusive comma. Not that this is all, for the context and the required meaning of the words themselves would seem to clamor for one interpretation against all others; but the grammatical logic revealed by the final comma of the line strongly supports the same view.

Although on less careful analysis the nouns of this line seem to be equally susceptible of construction as nominatives or vocatives, and the verb "buckle!" as indicative or imperative, a close scrutiny of the text shows that only the latter alternative in each case seems to be intended. And this at once rules out any reading of the poem as one of defeat, despair, jealous pining, passive resignation, or anything other than the spirit of the Kingdom of Christ meditation.

One hardly puts a comma *at the end* of a series of nominatives, separating the final member from the common indicative verb; nor does one properly leave it out after a series of vocatives, before their common imperative. Neither can "air, pride, plume," be taken as a merely parenthetical aside or counterpart, to be set off by commas. The scansion is against it, and the words are too important to the sense and effectiveness of the line as turning point. Despite the tantalizing ambiguity of the structure, then, where even the ",oh" and the exclamation point conspire against us by remaining noncommittal, open to either acceptation of the nouns and verb, it seems clear that "buckle!" must be taken as a challenge, in the direct imperative, not as an assertion of fact.

As an imperative, its force can scarcely be a despondent "collapse," as we say that auto fenders 'buckle' in a collision—one doesn't invite an admired agent to come here now and collapse in a fiasco! Nor will it mean "buckle on" as armor for protection or aggression, with the imperative addressed to a single person (the poet) outside the series of nouns from "beauty" to "plume," for this too (apart from not making good sense) would require the omission of the comma, which has no place between an imperative and its *object*.

"Buckle," then, as an imperative addressed to all the nouns in the series, must have here its intransitive sense, which is given by the dictionaries as: "to prepare self for a contest or undertaking; hence to apply self with vigor to a task; to come to close quarters, grapple, engage." [34] This is the meaning the word has, for instance, in Shakespeare's "In single combat thou shalt buckle with me." [35] Today, we are more familiar with this sense of the word when used with the preposition, as "buckle to" a hard task.

As will be more apparent later, the whole context of the poem corroborates this interpretation, that "buckle" here signifies ✓ "grapple," "engage."

Hopkins' meaning, then, in this line is definite. He calls upon all the elements which went to make up the engrossing vision of the falcon gloriously exerting its energy and by its valor and fulfilment of natural function bringing delight to the beholder and praise to its Maker. They are invited to come and re-enact their struggle "here," in the poet's heart; and the new field of battle is designated with courageous, even triumphant emphasis by its metrical position. With admirable vigor and economy, he sweeps the whole scene with his gaze and fastens on the very aspects of the octave's description which most essentially express its significance: the "valor and act" which have thrilled him and which result in "brute beauty," that is, natural, spontaneous, indelib-

[34] *The Oxford English Dictionary*, vol. 1, p. 1151, col. 3; *Webster's New International Dictionary of the English Language* (Merriam, 1929), p. 286, col. 1.

[35] *I Henry VI* 1.2.95; cf. *ibid.*, 5.3.28:
    "My ancient incantations are too weak
    And hell too strong for me to buckle with."

erate beauty flowing from the very function rather than consciously elaborated art; the "pride" or high-spirited mettle and
display of the wheeling bird [36] and charging knight; the "plume"
of feathered wing, of dauphin's cap and crusader's crest; and the
"air" which by opposing the rest has brought out their splendor,
and which here in this summary functions as the surest hint that
the whole line is intended to recall everything that has gone
before.

What will result from the acceptance of this challenge is very
clear to the poet: "AND the fire that breaks from thee then, a
billion times told lovelier, more dangerous, O my chevalier!" The
very way in which the "AND" is emphasized reveals its importance in the development of the thought. It is the "and" of consequence, equivalent to "and as a certain result . . ."; for the
preceding line is really a protasis, to which this is the apodosis—
if this struggle is re-enacted in the poet's soul, *then in consequence*
a glory, a "fire" will break forth from him too. (The address has
been shifted by the "here" from the elements to the poet himself:
'thee'). His soul will acquire in his own eyes and in Christ's a
new splendor, the glow of active virtue and valor and love proved
by deeds.[37]

The bird sitting on a limb had stirred no excited admiration,
but only when in difficult activity; so too the radiance of divine
grace will flame out from the poet's soul, roused from complacency to brave exertion, "a billion times told lovelier" because
"more dangerous," more daring than in the case of the falcon, as
much as grace surpasses nature and spiritual struggle outshines

[36] As in Shakespeare's: "A falcon towering in her pride of place" (*Macbeth* 2.4.12). The word "pride" seems to be used by Hopkins with some of
its other connotations also: "feeling of elation, pleasure, or high satisfaction
derived from some action"; "pomp or display"; "mettle or spirit in a horse"
(*Oxford English Dictionary*). For the last meaning, which certainly fits our
context well, cf. Shakespeare's "Your Uncle Worcester's Horse came but
to-day, And now their pride and mettal is asleepe" (*I Henry IV* 4.3.22);
"The colt that's backt and burthend being yong, Loseth his pride, and neuer
waxeth strong" (*Venus and Adonis* 420).

[37] This thought is elaborated by Hopkins himself in the sestet of poem 39,
The Soldier.

physical combat. For if "Honour is flashed off exploit," [38] the nobler the exploit the more lovely is the glory.

Hopkins addresses his heart in all this as "O my chevalier," that is, as crusading knight of Christ. The word is not a colorless equivalent to our 'cavalier' but an intentional echo of medieval crusading terminology; it admirably brings back into the mind's focus those significant words of the octave: "minion," "dauphin," "riding," "rein," etc., and reiterates the imagery of the Kingdom of Christ meditation on which the whole poem is based.

It is indeed possible, by taking "buckle" as an indicative, to explain these lines somewhat differently, and understand the "here," "thee," and "chevalier" as referring to the bird, and only indirectly to the poet himself. Either way, the poem's point and logic are the same. But there are several considerations which seem, especially when taken together, to show that Hopkins is explicitly applying to himself the lesson he has noted in the falcon's acts.

If the octave has made anything clear it is that the *reason* Hopkins admires the scene is the gallantry of the struggle, and that the cause of the bird's splendor, perfection, and exultation is its energetic "act," which reveals its "valor" and explains its "brute beauty." Hence it would be very weak and inept for the poet to *state* that which he has already made clear: "Why look, the reason I admire this bird is because here it is grappling with the wind!" That fact should be obvious from the mere dramatic description in the octave, particularly from the words "striding," "in his ecstasy," "rebuffed the big wind," and the expressed admiration for the masterly achievement. But if "buckle" is taken as imperative, and "here," "thee," and "chevalier" made to refer to the poet himself, the lines immediately assume great poetic intensity and give a much more artistic structure and a fuller meaning to the poem, by opening up fresh veins of thought on the spiritual and personal level. All thus becomes a parable, charged with profound significance.

[38] Poem 49.1 (*In Honour of St. Alphonsus Rodriguez*).

This is fully in Hopkins' manner, as when in *Hurrahing in Harvest* while contemplating the beauty of an autumn sky he suddenly reverts to himself:

> I walk, I lift up, I lift up heart, eyes,
>   Down all that glory in the heavens to glean our Saviour . . .

Similarly, in *Spelt from Sibyl's Leaves*, while immersed in pondering the mystery of advancing evening, he twice bursts out into personal soliloquy: "Heart, you round me right /With: Our evening is over us; our night . . ." and later: "Our tale, O our oracle!" This self-address is of course common poetic usage, especially in a sonnet, and very frequent in Hopkins.[39] The transition here from the falcon to self has been artfully prepared for by the sudden personal cast of thought at the end of line seven: "My heart in hiding . . ." And it seems clear at the end that the poet has been addressing his own heart in the sestet, for the "ah my dear" of line thirteen can hardly have any other object.

Above all, the comparatives in line eleven support this view, indeed appear to demand it. For the glory can scarcely be said to be "a *billion* times told lovelier, more dangerous" when the bird is in action than when it is resting; but to say that a corresponding struggle in Hopkins' own soul will be a billion times lovelier and more dangerous than it is in the bird, since it will be on the supernatural plane, makes excellent sense. Indeed, how can the struggle, if confined to the bird, be called *more* dangerous, if only contrasted to the state of ease, which holds no danger at all?

Furthermore, in this personal application of the bird's lesson—

---

[39] For instance Poem 45: "What sights you, heart, saw; ways you went!" *Wreck of the Deutschland*, st. 3: "My heart, but you were dovewinged . . ."; *ibid.*, st. 18:
> "Ah, touched in your bower of bone
> Are you! turned for an exquisite smart,
> Have you! make words break from me here all alone,
> Do you!—mother of being in me, heart."

See also the conclusions to *The Candle Indoors* and *On the Portrait of Two Beautiful Young People.*

which is certainly implicit anyhow, even if "buckle" is taken as indicative, since the line together with the two following then implies a universal principle, applicable to Hopkins also—lies the deeper explanation of the poem's dedication "To Christ our Lord." For the whole piece is really a votive offering to Christ, a sort of written deed or document proclaiming Hopkins' consecration of himself to Christ's more active service, his acceptance of his Captain's challenge as mysteriously revealed to him in the action of the bird, which, like the stormfowl in *Henry Purcell,* "meaning [only] motion fans fresh our wits with wonder."

In the light of Hopkins' fondness for repeating ideas and images which have struck him forcibly, strong confirmation for our interpretation is afforded by recalling that in an early poem, of October, 1865, he wrote (N 52):

> Let me be to Thee as the circling bird . . .
> That shapes in half-light his departing rings.

In that poem, the bird teaches him love of God; in the *Windhover,* valorous exertion in Christ's cause. A closer parallel could not be asked. Let Hopkins be his own interpreter.

The Sestet, Second Half: Corroboration

All is now rounded off with a concluding appeal to two other natural analogies which enforce the same lesson as the falcon, and which serve to confirm or 'clinch' the resolution which the poet has taken. If he too submits all his faculties and energy to Christ's work, heedless of the cost to self, his life will be thereby the more glorious. Like the sailor he has described in the *Loss of the Eurydice* (line 78), he too will be "strung by duty" and therefore "strained to beauty."

Now, he muses, in an undertone of self-consolation for the anticipated suffering, this is, after all, a natural law, to be observed in operation in many other cases also: "No wonder of it," be not surprised at this dependence of splendor on beyond-the-average exertion and suffering; it is a law of things. For instance, "shéer plód makes plough down sillion shine": the ploughshare, rusty and drab in a corner of the barn from idleness or disuse, once put to work at its lowly task in "sheer," unmitigated, unrelenting toil, begins to gleam and "shine" all down the furrow, its soft, smooth brilliance glowing with a beauty that often flashes from one end of the row to the other.[40]

"Sillion" is not a color-tone, but the archaic spelling for 'selion,' which means the ridge or strip of land between furrows dividing plots in the open field system.[41] And although the freshly turned earth also glows for a time on its damp, packed surface, this is surely not referred to in the line, as some would insist. Hopkins does not write 'plough-down sillion' or 'ploughed down sillion,' which would be required if "sillion" were to be the subject of the verb "shine." Nor would this image be nearly as powerful, since the earth's gleam is weak and fleeting and not due to its own exertion or "sheer plod."

A further example comes to the poet's mind: "and blue-bleak embers, ah my dear, fall, gall themselves, and gash gold-vermilion." The coals of a dying fire, so finely characterized as "blue-bleak," blaze out into a sudden final glory if they fall from their place of inert obscurity and suffer a "galling" wound which makes them burst into an orange splendor, as though "gashed" and bleeding. The compensatory refulgence of their symbolic agony has not only the painful red of spilt life-blood, but the glorious gold of nobility, quasi-martyrdom, and that generous sacrifice which is "precious in the sight of the Lord." [42]

The law of glory through struggle, he thus reminds his heart ("ah my dear"), prevails not only when the struggle is one of joy, as with the falcon, but also when it implies pain and the wearisome cross of undiversified drudgery, as in the galled ember and plodding plough. Perhaps, after all, his ardent resolution

[40] This is the precise point of Vergil's description of the plow:
   Incipiat sulco attritus splendescere vomer. (*Georgics* 1.46)
[41] For illustration of the word's history, usage, and various forms, see the *Oxford English Dictionary.*
[42] *Psalm* 115.15.

to do great things for Christ, in the crusading spirit of the knight and dauntless bird, will bring him, not to their plane of external activity before the eyes of an admiring world, but rather to the hidden, unglamorous, less adventuresome struggle of patient plodding in his duties as a priest, or (as it actually did) to a slow martyrdom in the dying fires of undermined health.[43]

The heavy, weary movement of the closing lines reflects this sobering and realistic thought. But what of it? In Christ's eyes the lowly role can be just as glorious, though the glory be hidden from men's notice.[44] So he rises yet higher in his heroic resolve, and accepts even this. After all, did not his Leader say, *"Ought* not Christ to have suffered these things, *and so* enter into His glory?"* [45] Such is the law of supernatural life. As Hopkins once wrote of Christ's life and example, ". . . through poverty, through labour, through crucifixion his majesty of nature more shines" (N 264). Just so, even the humble plough "shines" from its toil, and the gashed embers can make one last total expenditure of their powers and glow in a sunset glory.

The very air of triumph in the rhythmical swiftness and energy of the words "shine" and "gold-vermilion" echoes his consolation and his trust. And thus the poem ends in a blaze of spangled color which reflects the very first image with which it began—the bird exultantly soaring among the clouds as the golden sun creeps up on the flame-red glory of the dappled dawn.

The Spirit of the Poem

A true concept, then, of Catholic asceticism and Jesuit spirituality, so admirably expressed in the Kingdom of Christ medita-

[43] The late sonnets (Nos. 40, 41, 44-47, 50, and *Spelt from Sibyl's Leaves* —for which last Bridges gives the wrong date; it should be 1884|85; see N 425) give moving testimony to the anguish of this spiritual martyrdom with which Christ honored the poet's offer, and to the nobility of loyal faith with which Hopkins bore the struggle. I show this more fully in my analysis of *Spelt* in *Thought* 19 (Dec. 1944), pp. 633–648.

[44] The best commentary on this truth is Hopkins' poem 49, *In Honour of St. Alphonsus Rodriguez*.

[45] *St. Luke* 24.26.

tion, will enable us to see that the momentous resolve the poet takes under the stimulating example of the windhover is not one of dour self-repression but of eager, positive dedication to action. He will do more and braver things for Christ, first in the fuller and more energetic adhesion of his own will to Christ, then, in consequence, on the plane of active ministry for souls by labor, example, and suffering offered up in Christ's cause. Whether this will mean the joy and glory of the falcon's soaring or the hidden struggle with monotonous duties or wasting fires of pain, he conquers his natural repugnance at the cost in a generous, selfless, supernaturally joyful casting of his services at the feet of his Captain Christ.

All this is in the spirit of St. Ignatius' prayer: "Dearest Lord, teach me to be generous: to serve Thee as Thou deservest, to give and not to count the cost, to fight and not to heed the wounds, to toil and not to seek for rest, to labor and not ask for reward— save that of knowing that I am doing Thy will." Another Jesuit poet, Father James J. Daly, in his *Grand Review* of forebears in the Society, has admirably expressed Hopkins' theme and the Jesuit spirit:

> We have brave fathers: high-strung men who poured
> Their youth, strength, natural hopes, dreams of renown,
> *Lightly into the lap of Christ,* their Lord.[46]

This gallant fling of the hand as the knight lays all at his King's service is not done in sorrow or regret. Nor is the aim of true Catholic self-discipline and asceticism repression of activity, but the pruning away of disordered and parasitical impulses so that activity may be all the more vigorous and telling along those channels most worthy of man. Unless one understands these things, there is no hope of rightly appreciating Hopkins.[47]

[46] J. J. Daly, S.J., "The Grand Review," in *Boscobel and Other Rimes* (Bruce, 1934), p. 84.

[47] Dr. Pick has well explained the place and function of Catholic asceticism in Hopkins' achievement, both in his book, *G. M. Hopkins, Priest and Poet*, pp. 37–38, 51, 55, 117–118, and in a fine article "The Inspiration of Hopkins' Poetry," *America* 68 (Jan. 23, 1943), pp. 437–438.

Poetic Artistry of the Windhover

Most of the poetic merits of this splendid sonnet are so obvious and striking as not to require comment. But we may briefly list the main points, to complete our analysis. The opening lines show remarkable power in re-creating the vision of the falcon in flight—the bird is not merely described, but made to live in our consciousness because the words have such dramatic and representative force that their object is acted out before us. As Richards justly remarks,[48] we participate in the bird's flight, and empathy could hardly be carried further in verse. The very rhythm tells the story, after the fashion of descriptive music.

The octave is almost instrumental in its movement, rushing, whirling, soaring, gliding in its flight. How clearly lines 2, 3, and 4 echo the movement they relate! "Rebuffed the big wind" has all the snap and defiance it describes, while the final line of the octave has a swift, triumphant rhythm most suited to the poet's expressed mood. There is again, a heroic ring about that decisive "Buckle!" So too, the slow, weary movement of lines 12 and 14 is perfect musical accompaniment to the theme, while the sudden explosion of the final "gold-vermilion" by itself should reveal the air of joy and triumph, *not* of depressing renunciation, which dominates the whole.

We see clearly in this poem Hopkins' characteristic energy of thought, the "power and velocity of his mental creation and that joy of the senses which is the unmistakable Hopkins," as Bernard Kelly has put it.[49] The sonnet has a wonderful integration of structure, a unified "inscape" whose interacting parts are perfectly blended in function. As usual with Hopkins, the imagery is remarkable for originality, fresh vigor,[50] and colorful life. Great strength and independence of poetic expression mark the han-

[48] "Gerard Hopkins," *The Dial*, Sept., 1926.

[49] *The Mind and Poetry of G. M. Hopkins*; not paginated.

[50] Contrast, for instance, the description of the falcon whirling in the dawn with Shelley's romantically over-colored and superficial handling of an equivalent theme in *Lines Written Among the Euganean Hills*, ll. 71-85.

dling of the sonnet form (among other things, the first eight lines all end in "-ing"!), which here reaches the perfection of Hopkins' fearless revision of its metrical structure.

Above all, we delight in the characteristic Hopkins mastery of the word. In sound and sense, every word is highly effective, filled with living energy and instinct with beauty, rich in implications, a challenge to the mind's minutest scrutiny. Grammar, image, rhythmic function all reflect the inspired intensity of true poetic utterance, as, before our eyes

> The fine delight that fathers thought; the strong
> Spur, live and lancing like the blowpipe flame,
> Breathes once and, quenchèd faster than it came,
> Leaves yet the mind a mother of immortal song. (*Poems* 51)

By virtue of his remarkable command of language, Hopkins has been able, somehow, in this poem to get the subtlety, the intuitive vigor, the depth, and the noble religious coloring of his thought into words. He has succeeded in communicating his highly complex reaction in nearly all its fulness to its material representation in language. We cannot but admire the high art by which he has accomplished it; "the achieve of, the mastery of the thing!"

THE LOSS OF THE EURYDICE
A CRITICAL ANALYSIS

"It is best to read the *Eurydice* first, which is plain sprung rhythm and will possess you with the run of it" (D 26. March 29, 1879). This essay on the *Eurydice* ought, therefore, to be of particular interest to readers who have not yet found for themselves deep in Hopkins' poetry its "dearest freshness." On the other hand, the St. Georges who have long ago overpowered the dragon on guard at the entrance to Hopkins' realm of beauty,[1] those who are "at home . . . to his truth and grace," may not reckon the *Eurydice* as beneath their special concern, for did not Hopkins agree with Bridges that this poem "shews more mastery in art" than even the *Deutschland*?[2]

Relative Simplicity of the Poem

The *Eurydice* is a much simpler poem than the *Deutschland*. "Short and easy," Hopkins calls it (B 51. May 21, 1878). Of course, this last assertion must be taken relatively. The more ready intelligibility of the *Eurydice* is not, however, as might be at first supposed, due to its greater "mastery in art." Hopkins corrects this facile mistake when he tells us: "The further in anything, as a work of art, the organisation is carried out, the deeper the form penetrates, . . . the more effort will be required in apprehension" (N 96). At all events, one would make a grievous error were he to believe that Hopkins' frequent intricacy of

---

[1] See Bridges' note on the *Deutschland* in *Poems*, 2nd ed., p. 104.
[2] B 119 (Jan. 26, 1881). But he adds: "still I think the best lines in the *Deutschland* are better than the best in the other. One may be biassed in favour of one's first-born though."

thought and expression was an affectation. "Obscurity," he wrote to Bridges, "I do and will try to avoid so far as is consistent with excellences higher than clearness at a first reading" (B 54. May 30, 1878). This implied bid for rereading was, as a matter of fact, occasioned by difficulties which Bridges had with the *Eurydice*. In a previous letter Hopkins had been quite explicit (B 50–51. May 13, 1878):

When a new thing, such as my ventures in the *Deutschland* are, is presented us our first criticisms are not our truest, best, most homefelt, or most lasting but what come easiest on the instant . . . Same of the *Eurydice*—which being short and easy please read more than once.

Even after we have "understood" Hopkins' poems we must still reread them to accustom the mind to their ruffling originalities. Otherwise we shall not be able to enjoy them, as Coventry Patmore expresses it, "without much interruption from the surprise of such novelties" (F 205. March 20, 1884)—understood, of course, that to an old familiar, Hopkins' poetry has wholly cast off all repellent strangeness, or rather that what was thought odd has at length been seen to fit into the pattern, to be part of the design or "inscape" of the work of a rare and distinctive genius.

Its Rhythm

The *Eurydice* is written in sprung rhythm. Now it might well be imagined by the uninitiate that this unusual metrical scheme of Hopkins would be the source of special difficulties in reading his poetry. That this fear is groundless can easily be shown. Sprung rhythm is most adequately discussed elsewhere in this volume. For our purposes here we have merely to recall its general character. "To speak shortly, it consists in scanning by accents or stresses alone, without any account of the number of syllables, so that a foot may be one strong syllable or it may be many light and one strong" (D 14. Oct. 5, 1878). Hopkins considerately adds a special note on the rhythm of the *Eurydice*: "Written in sprung rhythm, the third line has 3 beats, the rest 4. The scanning runs on without break to the end of the stanza, so that each stanza is rather one long line rhymed in passage than four lines with rhymes at the ends."[3]

By way of illustration let us consider the scansion of the first two stanzas of the poem.

> The Eurýdicé—it concérned thee, O Lórd:
> Three húndred soúls, O alás! on boárd,
>   Some asleép unawákened, áll un-
> wárned, eléven fáthoms fállen
>
> Whére she foúndered! Óne stróke
> Félled and fúrled them, the heárts of oák!
>   And flóckbells óff the aérial
> Dówns' fórefalls beát to the búrial.

As will be seen partly from this brief consideration, but much more from each one's experience, sprung rhythm is far from offering serious obstacles to the reader. On the contrary, as Hopkins declares, it "is the most natural of things," being "the rhythm of common speech and of written prose, when rhythm is perceived in them."[4]

Our brief review of the nature of sprung rhythm has been necessary if for no other purpose than to emphasize the importance of stress in the poem under consideration here. "To do the *Eurydice* any kind of justice," Hopkins insists (B 51–52. May 21. 1878),

you must not slovenly read it with the eyes but with your ears, as if the paper were declaiming it at you. For instance the lines 'she had come from a cruise training seamen' read without stress and declaim is mere Lloyd's Shipping Intelligence; properly read it is quite a different thing. Stress is the life of it.

[3] Cited by Bridges. See *Poems*, p. 107.
[4] *Poems*, p. 5. Citations are from "Author's Preface."

On a later occasion he came back to the same point (B 79. Apr. 22, 1879):

When on somebody returning me the *Eurydice,* I opened and read some lines, reading, as one commonly reads whether prose or verse, with the eyes, so to say, only, it struck me aghast with a kind of raw nakedness and unmitigated violence I was unprepared for: but take breath and read it with the ears, as I always wish to be read, and my verse becomes all right.

Circumstances of Its Composition

The *Eurydice* like the other shipwreck piece came after a period of poetic inactivity, though this was very much longer in the case of the *Deutschland.* Hopkins, who at the time was stationed at Mount St. Mary's College, Chesterfield, writes to Bridges (B 48. Apr. 2, 1878): "My muse turned utterly sullen in the Sheffield smoke-ridden air and I had not written a line till the foundering of the Eurydice the other day[5] and that worked on me and I am making a poem. . . ." Thus the first draft of the poem was dated "April '78"; however, Hopkins later made various corrections, some even years later.[6] Shortly after he had written it, Hopkins offered the poem to the *Month* for publication, but the editors of this periodical rejected it as they had previously rejected the *Deutschland.* Hopkins simply says, "They did not like it" (D 15. Oct. 5, 1878).

Summary of Thought Development

A careful analysis of the poem should illuminate and strengthen our own convictions on its merits and demerits. But as a preliminary to a more thorough, stanza-by-stanza study we shall, beyond doubt, find it helpful to summarize the thought movement of the whole.

[5] March 24, 1878, as the subtitle of the poem tells us.
[6] See note on the *Eurydice* in *Poems,* p. 107.

In the very first two lines the religious character of the poem is manifest. The shipwreck of the Eurydice is a matter for God's special Providence—the salvation of souls is involved. In lines 1–44 Hopkins describes the ship, the storm that overtook it, and the sudden foundering. The Eurydice was no richly cargoed merchant vessel, but a ship of Her Majesty's Navy. It was returning from a training cruise for young seamen when a storm moving from off the southern coast of England struck and quickly capsized it. Lines 45–72 deal with the fate of certain individuals aboard. Marcus Hare, the captain, went down with his ship, feeling this to be his duty. Only two of the crew were rescued. The harrowing experience of one of these, named Sydney Fletcher, is related. The striking aspect of a corpse recovered from the sea inspires three further stanzas (ll. 73–84).

However, the pathos surrounding this one dead sailor is to Hopkins merely an instance of a vaster woe: the spiritual shipwreck of multitudes of his countrymen as a result of England's abandonment of the Catholic Faith. The first evil that Hopkins sees in the English Reformation is the despoiling and theft of the ancient Catholic cathedrals and places of pilgrimage. This "curse" he could, indeed, overlook were it not for the ruin caused the living temples of the Holy Spirit,[7] the damnation of many souls, occasioned by this sad cleavage from the unity of the true Church.[8] The greatness of the spiritual loss is accentuated by the poet's dwelling for one stanza (ll. 99–104) on the rich Catholicism of mediaeval England; but he speedily breaks off this train of thought, as though aware it is digression from his special theme: the story of the Eurydice and its crew.

In the stanzas which follow (ll. 105–120) he brings before us the loved ones of the dead sailors. He approves their grief, but

[7] Cf. St. Paul, 1 Cor. 3.16; 6.19.

[8] Hopkins was well aware of the universal Catholic teaching that Protestants in good faith—and certainly multitudes of them are in good faith—may save their souls, but he knew too that it is considerably more difficult to do this without the aid of those sources of grace which the Catholic Church puts at the disposal of her members, and notably without the Sacrament of Penance ("Confession").

he urges them rather to fall on their knees and pray Christ to save the souls of the drowned men. The concern of these last stanzas is the spiritual after-fate of the shipwrecked crew. Were their souls lost? Did they lack that sanctifying grace without which there is no salvation? The odds, so to speak, were against them, "unconfessed" heretics [9] as they were; yet hope is by no means excluded: God's foreknowledge of the prayers to be offered up after the disaster may have led Him to make extraordinary provision for the spiritual rescue of these poor seamen.

Detailed Analysis of the Poem
The Tragic Theme (ll. 1–8)

The poem opens at a pitch of intense emotion. The poet is about to make some statement about the Eurydice when a rush of feeling interrupts his thought and inspires him to call upon the "Lord of living and dead." "It concerned thee," that is to say, this boat and its fate were of intense interest to you, O Christ —and why? because there were souls on board, and you, Lord, are the Shepherd of souls.[10] The cry to God is not a complaint— as though God were not about His proper business—but rather a fleeting meditation on the mystery of God's Providence. There is implicit, moreover, a petition recommending the unfortunate crew to Christ's care, "care and dear concern."

The pathetic mood of the poem is fixed in the moan "O alas!" Alas, for the sudden wreck! Alas, for the unprepared men! The unpreparedness lamented is directly the physical and mental unreadiness, but symbolically it is the lack of spiritual preparation in the sailors. Many of the men will die "cut off even in the blossoms" of their sin,[11] "unhouseled, disappointed, un-

[9] Cf. *The Wreck of the Deutschland*, stanza 31, line 4 and *Henry Purcell*, stanza 1, and the explanation of the latter given in a letter to Bridges. See B 170–171 (Jan. 4, 1883).
[10] In the first draft of stanza 1 the second line read "Three hundred hearts," which is certainly stirring; but then the poem loses a key word.
[11] *Hamlet* I. V. 76.

aneled." [12] There is here not even such a mercy as was vouchsafed the crew of the Deutschland, no prophetic-tongued daughter of St. Francis to be a bell to Providence,

> . . . ring of it, and
> Startle the poor sheep back! [13]

Deeper than Prince Ferdinand's father in Ariel's song the bodies of the men go down with the ship—a physical descent which can suggest to the mind the sinking of souls into Hell: and so it does here, though this latent fear is not clearly expressed until the last stanza of the poem.

Illustrative of the complex images created by Hopkins' ingenious imagination are the next words:

> . . . One stroke
> Felled and furled them, the hearts of oak!

We are so fortunate as to have the poet's own explanation (B 52. May 30, 1878):

How are hearts of oak furled? Well, in sand and sea water. The image comes out true under the circumstances, otherwise it could not hold together. You are to suppose a stroke or blast in a forest of 'hearts of oak' (ad propositum, sound oak timber) which at one blow both lays them low and buries them in broken earth. *Furling* . . . is *proper* when said of sticks and staves.

To explain the obvious, as the trees are felled and bury themselves in the soft ground by their own weight and the momentum of their fall, so the men are knocked down by the storm blast and wrapped round in swirling water and sand (the wreck took place not far from shore).

"To every word," wrote Hopkins (N 95), "meaning a thing and not a relation belongs a passion or prepossession or enthusiasm which it has the power of suggesting or producing. . . ." What was Hopkins' precise enthusiasm that led him to compare the

---

[12] *Ibid.*, l. 77. The words are quoted from Hopkins (N 91) who uses them to illustrate the antithetical force of negative words.

[13] *The Wreck of the Deutschland,* stanza 31.

shipwrecked sailors with oak trees? Of course, a rough appropriateness would be apparent to anyone, but Hopkins was a poet
of exceptionally fine sensibilities; his comparisons are not lightly
or casually selected. In the mouths of the characters in his dialogue "On the Origin of Beauty" he puts what is doubtless his
own sentiment. "The oak," says Hanbury in the dialogue, "is
quite a rugged boldly-irregular tree: and this I should say was
one of the things which make us invest it with certain qualities
it has in poetry and in popular and national sentiment." [14] But
as the dialogue goes on it becomes clear that there is also in the
oak a less obvious but truly amazing symmetry. So that for Hopkins the oak tree could aptly serve as metaphor for the "hardy-
handsome" man.

"To every word meaning a thing . . . belongs a passion or
prepossession. . . ." Doubtless, "thing" is here to be taken
broadly enough to include not only substances, but also actions
and states, since we cannot get the most from a poet until we
know his "prepossession" in regard to the words which signify
these. Now Hopkins, as it happens, had a very distinctive prepossession toward tree-felling. If we can come to share his particular reaction, the lines on the "hearts of oak" will heighten
in significance.

We are all, no doubt, familiar with Hopkins' eloquent plaint
against the desecrators of Binsey.[15] We can compare with this
what he wrote in his journal for April 8, 1873 (Jnl 174):

The ashtree growing in the corner of the garden was felled. It
was lopped first: I heard the sound and looking out and seeing it
maimed there came at that moment a great pang and I wished to
die and not to see the inscapes of the world destroyed any more.

Again, under December 18, 1873, he wrote (Jnl 187): "Felling
of trees going on sadly at Roehampton."

As Hopkins himself indicates, the prepossession of a word may

[14] N 58. In one of his early diaries he had written (N 49): "Oak roots
are silvery, smooth, solid and muscular."
[15] *Binsey Poplars.*

not be the same for all. To a woodcutter the chopping down of a tree is an altogether desirable event; to most of us it is a more or less regrettable but commonplace occurrence; to Hopkins, however, it was sheer tragedy.

The meaning of the last two lines of the stanza:

> And flockbells off the aerial
> Downs' forefalls beat to the burial

may not be clear to all. They are undoubtedly to be taken quite literally. The bells of the sheep grazing on the seaward slopes of the lofty downs (on the southern coast of the Isle of Wight, near which the ship foundered) sounded a sort of funereal music for the drowning men.[16] Strange dirge tinkled out by sheepbells! Truly admirable is the poetic contrast between the idyllic pastoral scene conjured up by the gentle sheep and the violent storm, "Havoc-pocking" the sea with corpses!

The Ship and Her Crew (ll. 9–12)

The next two stanzas do not require quite so much comment. The *Eurydice,* epic-like, had opened with an excursion *in medias res.* Now the poet goes back to tell the story from the beginning. In the first of these stanzas (ll. 9–12), we observe a beautifully wrought antithesis, and in this, as indeed throughout the poem, an immense care for structural parallelism. In the "Origin of Beauty" [17] cited above, the youthful Hopkins in the person of the "Professor" dogmatized as follows:

Hebrew poetry, you know, is structurally only distinguished from prose by its being paired off in parallelisms, subdivided of course often into lower parallelisms. This is well-known, but the important part played by parallelism of expression in our poetry is not so well known. I think it will surprise anyone when first pointed out.[18]

[16] Cf. N 163, where Hopkins speaks of rocks hidden by the "fall of the hill." In N 118 he describes a "sheepflock" on the downs.

[17] See also the statements of Hopkins on parallelism in general as noted in Fr. Noon's study in this volume, pp. 252.

[18] N 80. Modern scholars, to be sure, now hold for other elements in Hebrew verse structure.

In a different paper written about the same time, he has a further remark on this subject which happens to apply very strongly to his own poetry (N 93): ". . . the more marked parallelism in structure," he writes, "whether of elaboration or of emphasis begets more marked parallelism in the words and sense."

The thought antithesis in the lines (9–12) is between the bales or bullion on the one hand and the men on the other. Hopkins was always aware of the tremendous worth of a human being, and the incalculable superiority of man over any inanimate or non-human values. This matter comes forward once more in lines 89–96 of this poem, and the same thought "flushes" other poems, as *To What Serves Mortal Beauty* and *Ribblesdale*.

The crew of the vessel—so lines 12 and 14 tell us—were grown men and brave young lads approaching manhood. The epithet "bold" is typical not only of young men in general, but also of Hopkins' ideals. Though frail and sadly sensitive to pain, Hopkins was by no means a physical coward. As a boy, he used to climb high into the perilously swaying treetops (Cf. L 8). Likewise he did not hesitate to "cheek" a birch-fond headmaster (Cf. F 2. May 7, 1862). All his life long he retained a great admiration for bravery, which manifests itself time and again in his poetry; to give but a few instances, in line 95 of the poem under analysis, in the *Deutschland* (stanza 16), in *The Bugler's First Communion,* where a lad blessed for his many virtues is first of all "dauntless," and expressly and emphatically in No. 39 (*The Soldier*). Hence "boldboys" is high compliment on this poet's lips.

But for all their daring the youths, flower of human life, and the men, its sturdy hardened trunk, are alike to be destroyed by the tempest.

The Storm (ll. 17–32)

Hopkins' genius for contrast dexterously exploits the fact that the boat was wrecked not by a storm arisen on the high seas (ll. 17–18),[19] but by a savage gale off land, and their own land, England (ll. 19–20)! That which should have been their refuge becomes their ruin. They are in a manner betrayed.

In these lines that "beat and breathe in power" even such strong alliteration as "Home was hard at hand" passes without note, is natural and effective. The special function of alliteration in Hopkins is explained in another essay of this book; here it will be enough to say that he had no inhibitions in regard to its use. Alliteration, even "thickly" used, he considered not vulgarity, but a "grace" (N 242–243). "One may indeed doubt," he wrote in his lecture notes (N 243), "whether a good ear is satisfied with our verse without it."

Pure beauty (which, moreover, owes nothing to alliteration!) is line 21: "And you were a liar, O blue March day." It is not original, certainly, to address a personified day; practically every poet has done this early or late in his career. It is, however, sufficiently unusual to address a day with such a splendid insult— to give it the lie.[20]

This and the following line "haunted" Canon Dixon on his own admission. They seemed to him "more English-Greek than Milton." However, he misread the second line as "Bright, sun-lanced fire of the heavenly bay" (D 32. March 1, 1880). Hopkins answered:

In one point I seem to have your admiration on false pretences. What I wrote was

Bright sun lanced fire in the heavenly bay, etc.—that is/

a bright sun was darting fire from the bay of heaven, but that was of no avail, for did not a fatal north wind . . . and so on.[21]

[19] "Overwrought" in l. 17 is a happy choice. The squall is pictured as capable of wearing down the strength of a ship, of exhausting it with wrestling and "ruinous shock."

[20] The deceitful character of weather at sea has been stigmatized by poets from classical times down. Cf. Lucretius' "subdola cum ridet placidi pellacia ponti" (*De Rerum Natura*, Bk. II, l. 559).

[21] D 33 (May 14, 1880). Hopkins' own version of l. 22 contrasts better with l. 24 and is more dramatic, but Dixon's blunder version beautifully supports the otherwise isolated l. 21.

In the last two lines of this stanza (ll. 23–24) "Boreas" is a pleasing use of a proper name in an indefinite sense. *"Black Boreas"* also evokes the image of black clouds, but directly that of a black wind—a breath-taking vision! Yet the detail really crying out for comment in these lines is the rhyming of "wrecked her? he C" with "electric." [22] "Some of my rhymes," Hopkins confides to Bridges (B 180. May 11, 1883),

I regret, but they are past changing, grubs in amber; there are only a few of these;
Others are unassailable;
Some others again there are which *malignity may munch at* but the Muses love.

We wonder how he would have classified the rhyme in question here.

It would be out of place in this essay to go into a lengthy discussion of Hopkins' views on imperfect rhymes. We must content ourselves with one immediately applicable quotation. "There is more licence," he tells us, "in double rhymes [where two syllables rhyme with two] and when there are several consonants instead of one, as *balance, talons, gallants,* which are almost as good as perfect rhymes." [23] Many of his malignity-munched rhymes were justified to his own satisfaction by this principle; thus in the *Eurydice* "England" and "mingle? and" (ll. 25–26), "thither" and "with her" (ll. 43–44), "captain" and "wrapped in" (ll. 45–46), etc.

The "offending" rhyme in lines 23–25 has at least this one important merit: it speeds the tempo of lines 23–24, leads the reader to begin the next stanza too ("A beetling,") at a rapid clip, and so puts one at once into the feel of the onrushing tempest. This is now driving over England in the form of a lowering cloud topped

[22] There are in this same poem two other examples of "rove over" rhymes (ll. 67–68 and ll. 91–92), but in them the rhyming sounds more nearly approximate each other.
[23] N 245. Double rhymes are defined on p. 244.

with gleaming white.[24] Soon, however, not one storm alone is involved, but, as it would seem, a veritable conspiracy of them.
High in the heavily charged air, roped hail clouds [25] are energeti-
cally producing their pebble-shaped missiles,[26] while dry, hard,
biting storm-snow, great quantities of it, winds itself there in the
wild sky—winds itself, that is, coils itself like snakes prepared to
spring, or gathers itself as if on a giant windlass in order that
when the doom hour strikes it may "off wild winch whirl, and
pour And pelt *death,* till none's to spill nor spend." [27]

The above interpretation may not be in every detail precise,
but mindful of Hopkins' dictum (N 286) that it is "contemptible
. . . to give up at the first hearing of a hard passage," we have
made what we think a proper effort at unraveling this teasing
air-tangle.

The next stanza (ll. 29–32) on the contrary, offers little
difficulty to the intellect, though it calls for a few topographical
notes.[28] All the places named by Hopkins are to be found on the
Isle of Wight off the southern coast of England. Carisbrooke
Castle is situated one mile from Newport. It is an ancient Norman
structure, famous particularly as being the place where Charles I
was imprisoned for almost a year. The lofty keep is besides of
special architectural interest. Appuldurcombe [29] is famous for its
park, long the seat of the Worsley Family. In a line with the other
two places, but on the southern coast of the island is Ventnor, a

[24] Perhaps, though, Hopkins is saying that the whole cloud was shiny in
its smoothness. Squall clouds can be *light* gray, especially when they break.
[25] Cf. N 150, where Hopkins describes a cloud "roped like a heavy cable."
On the other hand, in his early poem *A Voice from the World* he speaks
of "strings of rain" (N 17). The hailropes may have been not clouds or cloud
parts but "shadowtackle" within the cloud.
[26] That the "Heavengravel" is for a sinister purpose may be gathered from
the poet's previously chosen word, "grimstones" (Cf. B 54. May 30, 1878).
[27] *The Sea and the Skylark,* which, of course, has "music" in place of
"death." (Cf. Glossary in this book, *ad loc.,* for somewhat different interpretation.—*Editor.*)
[28] The information in this paragraph is taken from *The Blue Guides:
England.* Ed. by Findlay Muirhead (London, Macmillan, 1930), pp. 88–91.
[29] Hopkins' spelling is more quaintly suggestive. Hopkins' sketch of a
beech at "Appledurcombe" appears in N facing p. 48. It is dated July 25.

town of something over 6,000 inhabitants. This is a celebrated health resort charmingly perched on slopes overlooking the sea and just below the towering height of St. Boniface Down. This latter is the highest point on the Isle and so justifies Hopkins' epithet of "aerial" (l. 7).

The Capsizal (ll. 43–44)

In lines 33–34 there is a hint of *hybris*, preparing us for tragedy; then in 35–36 begins a terse but marvelously vivid description of the actual foundering of the ship. We cannot but be struck by the dramatic directness of

> Sharp with her, shorten sail!
> Too late; lost; gone with the gale.

However, we may have overlooked the fact that Hopkins is continually thus capitalizing on the vividness of conversation and direct address. To illustrate from the *Eurydice* alone: in line 1 he addresses himself to God; lines 9–10 and 15–16 are rhetorical questions; in line 21 he addresses the personified day; lines 26–28 contain rhetorical questions; lines 35–36 contain an imperative and the equivalent of an answer; there are direct quotations in lines 42, 52, and 55; the "Oh!" of line 71 is felt to be the exclamation of the rescued lad; line 77 has another imperative; lines 85–104 draw vividness from their shift to the first person; lines 101–104 have besides an indirect quotation and an imperative; in lines 105–106 the poet addresses first the mother of a drowned sailor, then the wife of the same or of another, then the sweetheart of another; in lines 111–116 he puts into their mouths a prayer addressed to Christ. Not surprising, then, that Hopkins should say that the *Eurydice* ought to be read "as if the paper were declaiming at you!" Hopkins, as was said in another of these studies, writes declamatory poetry, poetry in which strong stresses come naturally.[30]

[30] Cf. the studies in this volume by Fr. Ong. (p. 93), and Fr. Noon (p. 252).—*Editor.*

In lines 39–40 occurs another example of Hopkins' "counter-pointing" imagination: water is death and Death is a person. Most poets would have been content either to personify the water or to personify death, but Hopkins combines or counterpoints the two sets of harmonizing images.[31]

Line 41 is manifestly onomatopoeic:

Then a lúrch fórward, frígate and mén [32]

Onomatopoeic and climactic as well is line 44 in which the rhythmic fury of the gale and the "beat of endragonèd seas" blend with the symmetry of pathetic feeling. In lines 43–44 the idea is that the ship which so far had been a kind shelter for the crew had now become their prison, their bonds, deadly cooperator in their destruction.

Story of the Captain (ll. 45–56)

This and the two following stanzas (ll. 45–52) are a revelation of the potentialities of sprung rhythm in the hands of a master craftsman. In these verses Hopkins opens all stops, so to speak, and as a result what a richness of rhyme, of assonance and alliteration, of onomatopoeia; and yet "How all's to one thing wrought!" Surely verse could not go much further.

It will be good to recall here that each foot, more or less like a bar of music, should have the same time value, though, of course, the equivalence is not to be pressed too rigidly.[33] We might

[31] Abbott is undoubtedly wrong in his conjectures about "mortholes" (see B 53. May 30, 1878, and note). It is merely Hopkins' euphonic spelling of "mortals" pronounced so as to rhyme with "portholes." The Latinism of "mortholes" would, besides, be most unlike Hopkins.

[32] Hopkins himself gives this scansion in B 52–53 (May 30, 1878). Another verse which can cause trouble on first reading is l. 37. Hopkins scans this as follows:

Thís was thát féll capsíze

See B 52 (May 30, 1878).

[33] "In Sprung Rhythm, as in logaoedic rhythm generally, the feet are assumed to be equally long or strong and their seeming inequality is made up by pause or stressing." Hopkins in "Author's Preface," Poems, p. 4.

represent the "time" of ll. 45–52 as follows, letting either syllable
of a two-syllable foot constitute unity. However, the second
"beat" of syllables marked "2" is really a pause before going on,
rather than a prolongation of the sound. The stress, according to
Hopkins, is for convenience' sake always put on the first syllable
of a foot, and is strongly marked.[34]

> Marcus Hare, high her captain,
> Kept to her—care-drowned and wrapped in
>   Cheer's death, would follow
> His charge through the champ-white water-in-a-wallow,
> All under Channel to bury in a beach her
> Cheeks: Right, rude of feature,
>   He thought he heard say
> 'Her commander! and thou too, and thou this way.' [35]

---

[34] Cf. *idem,* pp. 1–2, and the reference given in note 12 above.

[35] The rhythm of the *Eurydice,* like that of many of Hopkins'
poems, has a tendency to become dipodic, and, in any case, has marked resemblances to dipodic verse. At least this much appears proven by Harold
Whitehall in a recent article ("Sprung Rhythm," *Kenyon Review,* Summer
1944, pp. 332–354). Moreover, his general remarks on the central position in
Hopkins' poetic consideration of the "pattern of sound," and the analogies
of this with music seem to me very well said. Using Professor Whitehall's
system of notation (S indicates strong stress; L, light stress; o, zero stress,
P or p, pause) I think the rhythm of ll. 45–52 could be represented more or
less as follows:

```
S O L p/ S  O L  O/
Marcus Hare, high her captain,
   S   O O L p/ S   O   L   O/
Kept to her—care-drowned and wrapped in
   SpPp/ S   O L O
Cheer's death, would follow
O/  S   O  O  L  O/ S O O O L O/
His charge through the champ-white water-in-a-wallow,

S  O O L O O/ S O O O L  O/
All under Channel to bury in a beach her
   Sp   Lp/ S  O L O
Cheeks: Right, rude of feature,
     O/  SpP O/ Sp  Lp
He thought he heard say
 O  O/ S  O  O   L  O O/ Sp O Lp
'Her commander! and thou too, and thou this way.'
```

In lines 45–56 we have the incident of Marcus Hare. The details of these two stanzas, dexterously twined to beauty, seem to call for explication. Hare, the ship's chief officer, stuck to his boat; and, although overwhelming sorrows, surging higher than the seas, had already drowned his hope, and despair had cloaked his heart of courage, he determined to follow the vessel committed to his care down through the tumbling, swirling, wallowing waves,[36] white like the foam from the mouth of a charger. The Channel is, of course, the English Channel; the cheeks of the boat are the sides of the prow.

The commander is an upright man, though physically and even mentally he is rough, unrefined. His conscience tells him that he ought to go down with his ship, that he too should go the underwater way of his vessel to a sandy grave. The rightness or wrongness of the objective action, the trueness or falseness of the captain's conscience would depend on circumstances and need not detain us here. In any case, he had the personal obligation of following his conscience, and this he did.

In the following stanza (ll. 53–56) Hopkins moralizes: " 'even' those who seem unconscientious will act the right part at a great push." This brief paraphrase is an explanation by the poet himself given to Bridges. (B 53. May 30, 1878.)

Story of Sydney Fletcher (ll. 57–72)

There follows the anecdote concerning the rescue of Sydney Fletcher. The whirlpool formed by the sinking ship sucks him also down into its gully. He wrestles for his breath with the brownish water,[37] with the brown "Death," which is surging and spouting everywhere around him, till through the Providence of God a

---

[36] "Water-in-a-wallow" is probably to be taken as structurally similar to the common slang expression "in-a-spin."

[37] One suspects that Hopkins is fond of brown water. In *Inversnaid* the water is "horseback brown," in *On the Portrait of Two Beautiful Young People* we have "burling Barrow brown," while in *Epithalamion* the river is "gluegold-brown."

life preserver buoys him up to safety from the all-swallowing sea. Lines 65–68 tell us that after rising to the surface, to the "round air," [38] he searches in vain for sight of land or rescue ship, his vision blinded by the snowstorm, which seems to wrinkle and shrink the atmosphere. However, after an hour of suffering he and a fellow crewman are rescued. For his part, he is so overcome with joyous emotion that he loses consciousness.

The Sea-corpse (ll. 73–84)

The next three stanzas (ll. 73–84), beginning with "they say who," constitute the most beautiful passage in the poem.[39] The inscape, or inner order apparent to the poet in the drowned man, is brought before us with splendid clarity, the principal means being the selection of the salient characteristic, the quasi-essence of everything named.

The dead man was "every inch a tar." Perhaps the connotation of "tar" to some readers may be such as to break down the delicate growing pathos. Yet to a seafaring people like the British the word would doubtless arouse pleasant associations and thoughts of honor; the context would clinch this reaction.

Remarkable always is the diction of Hopkins, teeming with homely Anglo-Saxon monosyllables, that give his poetry its realism, its vigor, its telling power "home at heart." The role of monosyllables in rhythm based almost entirely on *sense* stress (as opposed to the arbitrary stresses found in poetry made up largely of polysyllabic words) is described in another essay of this book.[40]

Line 77 "Look, foot to forelock, how all things suit!" is comparable to the opening lines of *Morning Midday and Evening Sacrifice:*

[38] Pleasing variant for "round sky" and accurate, for what but air is the hollow-seeming hemisphere of blue which we call the "sky"?

[39] This too is the opinion of Claude Colleer Abbott. See his note on B 48 (Apr. 2, 1878).

[40] Cf. Fr. Ong's study, p. 93.

> The dappled die-away
> Cheek and wimpled lip,
> The gold-wisp, the airy-grey
> Eye, all in fellowship—

This suiting of parts, this shining order in the dead sailor's being is the inscape which takes Hopkins' heart with beauty. His faithful performance of life's tasks has strung the man, has tensed him to the point where he will as readily flash off beauty as a tuned violin string will emit exquisite notes.

Hopkins held that there is in everything a principle of order, of design, which, however, meets resistance from recalcitrant matter. Rough handling may conceivably help subdue the forces of opposition so that the order may more completely dominate the whole being. A man living a hard, vigorous life would thus be "strung," that is brought to the highest pitch of perfection his being could reach, and all the imperfections, the dross stemming from the resistance of the matter to its information or "flushing" by the spirit (which in man is the ultimate principle of order or pattern) could in this way be strained out.

Part of the pattern or inscape of the sailor was his handsome tan, his "brown-as-dawning" skin. It is somewhat more conventional to think of the dawn as rose, but golden brown dawns, bronze dawns, russet dawns are, as anyone knows, not uncommon. In the first draft of these lines Hopkins had written "And russet-of-morning-skinned," for which color he had the authority—if authority were needed—of Shakespeare himself.[41]

In his fragment No. 63 Hopkins tells of a lad whose cheeks
> . . . the forth and flaunting sun
> Had swarthed about with lion-brown
> Before the Spring was done.

[41] We have only to recall the familiar "morn, in russet mantle clad" of Hamlet I.1.166. In regard to the word "forelock" at the beginning of this stanza, we should note that the forelock was in itself a symbol of beauty to Hopkins. Cf. *On the Portrait of Two Beautiful Young People*.

But the sailor's brown was due not alone to the beating sun rays, but came about "With brine and shine and whirling wind." This line, like the similarly constructed line 44, is imitative and should be read whirlingly, so to speak.

In the following stanza we reach the climax of this section of the poem, the part dealing with the external and visible shipwreck. Deep, intensely deep emotion charges these restrained verses. With his customary fineness of insight Hopkins picks out those precise features of the dead man which best illustrate his peculiar worth and merits. His fingers are, more than most men's, quick and dexterous from tying and untying knots; his hand is roughened by toil but, far from disfigured, it reveals new and unexpected harmonies of flesh and muscle and bone as it closes in manly firmness over a sea rope. He has mastered the art of sailing, he has acquired golden experience, glorious capacities for future success in his life's calling. Future? Ah, there shall be now no future, not one more mile of joyous sailoring. His talents sleep in his soul-forsaken body—in his bones, sturdiness, in his muscles, "sinew-service"—sleep "and will not waken."

Thoughts on Spiritual Shipwreck (ll. 85–96)

Sad as is the fate of this poor boy, his story is but a type of a far greater tragedy: the shipwreck of English souls—truly a call to constant mourning. What disastrous thing has brought about this harm to his countrymen? It is the Protestant Reformation of Henry, Edward, and Elizabeth.

How many sad results from this: the confiscation of the magnificent old cathedrals and abbeys, the failure to preserve them and their consequent falling into ruin and decay, or else preservation and care not by the true owners, the priests and nuns, but by looting nobles, who put these holy places to profane uses. Glorious shrines, goal of pilgrimages,

And not from purple Wales only nor from elmy England,
But from beyond seas, Erin, France and Flanders, everywhere [42]

[42] *St. Winefred's Well*, ll. 11–12 fr. end of fragment; *Poems*, p. 79.

are now sadly abandoned, if not desecrated. Such the fate of Canterbury, such the fate of Walsingham.

All this, indeed, is a dreadful consequence of the Reformation in England, but it is an ancient evil and the poet would willingly forget it, but there is something worse which he cannot forget, a catastrophe borne in upon him and recapitulated by the loss of the Eurydice. Not alone temples built with hands, but the God-erected temples of the Holy Spirit, men, human beings, are coming to spiritual ruin, like these daring sailormen and lads so dear in their natural value and selfworth. Ruined because they lacked —too, too many of them—the grace by which they would have "put on Christ," the "Christing" grace; for this, if they had still possessed it at the moment of death, would have spelt for them eternal salvation. Not that many, perhaps, of these unfortunate men were not saved, although "listed to a heresy here" [43] and so cut off from the true Church, the mother of grace; but saved with how much greater difficulty and by what devious ways.

Glories of the Past (ll. 97–104)

Surely a theme for deep lament. Why did the all-mastering Christ permit it? the tearing of the seamless robe, the rending of his countrymen from the unity of the Mystical Christ. These Englishmen, moreover, in the olden days were steeped in Catholic Truth and alert to the stimulus of divine inspirations. A token of this would be the fact that "in Catholic times Walsingham Way was a name for the Milky Way, as being supposed a fingerpost to our Lady's shrine at Walsingham" (B 53. May 30, 1878). These are Hopkins' own words. In another letter to Bridges he explains the "And one" of line 103 and shows the unity of the stanza. "The One of the Eurydice," he writes,

[43] *Henry Purcell.* Cf. note 20 above. For a description of grace and its effects by Hopkins, see N 332 and 337. It is appropriate to cite here the words which Hopkins put into the mouth of the "Professor" in his dialogue *On the Origin of Beauty*: ". . . almost all works of art imply knowledge of things external to themselves in the mind of the critic—in fact all do . . ." (N 68).

is Duns Scotus, on whom I have a sonnet lately done which I will
send you. The thought is: the island was so Marian that the very
Milky Way we made a roadmark to that person's shrine and from
one of our seats of learning (to wit the above) went forth the first
great champion of her Immaculate Conception, now in our days
made an article of faith.[44]

Founded in the time of Edward the Confessor, this Walsingham
of which Hopkins speaks was from the first a celebrated place of
pilgrimage until its destruction by Henry VIII in 1538. To it
came pilgrims from every quarter of Europe, kings and com-
moners, rich and poor. Hither from Cambridge in the year 1511
came Erasmus with pious offering of Greek verses. In July 1538
this rich shrine was seized, and its treasures were carried away.
Later a private residence was built on the spot where the shrine
had stood.[45]

In line 103 the poet interrupts himself: "Let be, let be." Do
not waste time bewailing withered glories. God, who never
permits evil except that He may draw good therefrom, would not
have allowed this sundering of England from the unity of Christ-
endom had He not planned in some way to restore it with
splendors on a yet grander scale.[46]

[44] B 77 (Apr. 8, 1879). The letter is headed "Oxford." Hopkins rejoices
in these manifestations of English piety because he is at once both an ardent
Catholic and a great patriot. On his patriotism cf., e.g., the *Deutschland,*
stanza 35, No. 44, No. 59, B 131 (June 16, 1881), B 231 (Oct. 13, 1886),
and L 140–142.

[45] Joseph Clayton, *The Catholic Encyclopedia.* Special ed. (Encyclopedia
Press, copyright 1913), article, "Walsingham Priory," p. 543.

[46] This, we think, is the answer to the "why" of l. 98. W. H. Gardner's self-
rejected hypothesis of a "veiled rebuke to the Deity" has no real probability
at all. See W. H. Gardner's essay "The Wreck of the Deutschland" in *Essays
and Studies* of English Association, 21 (Oxford, Clarendon Press, 1936),
p. 147. The "hoar-hallowed" shrine of Walsingham is again the object of
pilgrimage. S/Sgt. Albert J. Hebert, Jr., whose home is in New Orleans,
Louisiana, writes from the British Isles: "On my leave I not only saw Glasgow
and Edinburgh, but was privileged to make a rather modern, train-transferring
pilgrimage by myself to the little ancient town of Walsingham. . . . Of the
once magnificent Augustinian Priory only a few ruins remain . . . the church
of the original shrine is not in Catholic hands but is well preserved, and the
grounds are in good care. Thru the town of little streets and old walls and

Lament and Prayer for the Crew (ll. 105–120)

The poem at this point returns to its original theme, the foundering of the Eurydice. However, not directly to the ship or its crew, but rather to the loved ones mourning their loss. The two stanzas (ll. 105–112) beginning with "O well wept, mother" are condensed to the very edge of intelligibility. A defect, no doubt, but the poet does not want the poem to become emotionally slack at this strategic point; in fact he wants a new tensing of emotion, to last until the final stanza brings a satisfying resolution.

To Bridges, who had difficulty with the meaning of the first two of these lines (105 and 106), Hopkins explained: " 'O well wept' should be written asunder, not 'wellwept.' It means 'you do well to weep' and is framed like 'well caught' or 'well run' at a cricket-match" (B 53. May 30, 1878). Of course, the relative "who" is understood after "mother" and after "sweetheart." The idea of the last two lines is clearer: Though grieving for the dead will not help them, yet mother, wife, and sweetheart are bid to shed the tears which are a fitting expression of genuine love. Perhaps Hopkins had in mind the image of Christ weeping at the death of His friend Lazarus. At least, his thoughts are on Christ at the opening of the next stanza, in which the poet urges these sorrowful women to bend in reverence to the majestic Christ, to kneel before Him in prayer. And what means the prayer? The first line addressing Christ with beautiful appellations is easily appreciated. Not so line 112; Hopkins gives the key (B 78. Apr. 22, 1879):

---

ancient stone houses I went out past the Franciscan ruins about a mile or so to the present shrine, the remodeled Slipper Chapel. This is a rather small building, but its walls enclose space that has been the kneeling ground of uncounted kings, husbandmen, saints and scholars. Inside was a lovely altar and to the left the statue of Our Lady of Walsingham, modeled on the representation of her on the seal of the Augustinians, and attended by candles, flowers and the occasional pilgrim." (Letter to the writer of this essay. Dated September 18, 1943.)

The words are put into the mouth of a mother, wife, or sweet-heart who has lost a son, husband, or lover respectively by the disaster and who prays Christ, whom she addresses 'Hero savest,' that is, 'Hero that savest,' that is Hero of a Saviour, to save (that is, have saved) her hero, that is, her son, husband, or lover: 'Hero of a Saviour' (the line means) 'be the saviour of my hero.'

As John Pick points out in his *Gerard Manley Hopkins: Priest and Poet,*[47] this stanza springs from the thought sequence that Hopkins developed much more fully and with great beauty some-what over a year later in a sermon preached at Bedford Leigh. Its topic sentence is: "Our Lord Jesus Christ, my brethren, is our hero, a hero all the world wants." [48]

Since Christ is a Hero who saves, it is with confidence that the prayer goes on: O Christ, at the time when the storm overtook the ship, and death the men, have (already) heard the prayer which you now hear me making to you. May you, who foresaw this prayer would be made, have heard this prayer ere it was yet spoken. "Have," according to Hopkins, "is the singular imperative (or optative, if you like) of the past, a thing possible and actual both in logic and grammar, but naturally a rare one" (B 174. Feb. 3, 1883). Here the poet is directly explaining a similar passage in his sonnet on Purcell, but at the end he adds: "The same thought (which plays a great part in my own mind and action) is more clearly expressed in the last stanza but one of the *Eurydice,* where you remarked it."

The last stanza of the poem justifies this "past optative" prayer. Truly, a soul which has actually descended into hell is thereupon beyond hope of redemption, past possibility of salvation; the case is not the same with souls whose lives and deaths would lead our frail and fallible human judgment to conclude that they must be damned. These can still be prayed for as long as we do not know

[47] John Pick, *Gerard Manley Hopkins: Priest and Poet.* (Oxford University Press, 1942), p. 85.
[48] This sermon may be found in N 260–266. The sentence quoted occurs on p. 260.

for sure—as we shall know only after the conflagration of dooms-day—that they are locked in damnation, since the eternal God, above and beyond the limitations of time, foresees and in His sweet mercy can hear our prayers and all prayers fresh sprung from the heart, no matter whether or not the thing these prayers petition be in relation to them past, present, or future.

Unity of the Poem

In our detailed discussion of so many minute points we may have lost sight of the fast unity of the whole. As we draw near the end of this essay it will be good, then, to indicate this once more. The unity, we say, lies in the priestly anxiety of the poet.

Hopkins, a priest to the tips of his thought, is throughout concerned with the salvation of the crew of the Eurydice. The *"awful overtaking"* is such primarily because the men are spiritually

. . . asleep unawakened, all unwarned.

In view of the possible everlasting damnation of most of the crew the tragedy of the shipwreck is darkened beyond measure. However, what distresses the heart of Hopkins more by far is that these sailors are but a few of the thousands of his people who are foundering spiritually, that is, losing their souls, as a result of England's break with the true Church. What can be done for these sailors? Prayer alone can move the Divine Mercy. It is not expressly said, but is surely implied that the same remedy will work for the whole mass of his countrymen.

Conclusion

"Prayer shall fetch pity eternal." A great thought, appropriately expressed, and a worthy ending of a deeply religious poem. When we have arrived thus far, we no longer wonder that this work of

Hopkins should have aroused the usually unresponsive Bridges to "monstrous and indecent spiritual compliments" (B 52. May 30, 1878), and led Canon Dixon to express in his own way the admiration of us all: "The Eurydice no one could read without the deepest and most ennobling emotion" (D 32. March 1, 1880).

THE THOUGHT STRUCTURE OF
THE WRECK OF THE
DEUTSCHLAND

ROBERT R. BOYLE, S.J.

In 1877 Sidney Lanier was distressed by a problem that has troubled the minds of most men at one time or another (*To Beethoven*):

> Th' indifferent smile that nature's grace
>   On Jesus, Judas, pours alike;
> Th' indifferent frown on nature's face
>   When luminous lightnings strangely strike
>
> The sailor praying on his knees
>   And spare his mate that's cursing God . . .

Hopkins had given his answer to that problem just a year or so before in *The Wreck of the Deutschland*. Perhaps Lanier would not have understood the answer even if he had had access to Hopkins' expression of it. But it is Christ's answer. It is St. Paul's answer. It is the answer of the Catholic Church. The mystery lies not in nature but in man. The mystery of God's grace in us, of Christ in us, of the mastery, the power of God in us—that is Hopkins' answer, and the subject of his masterpiece.

Hopkins is not dealing directly with the problem of suffering, but with the answer to that problem. His concern is with the power and the mastery of God. He takes the viewpoint of Christ:

> . . . but thou art above, thou Orion of light;
> Thy unchancelling poising palms were weighing the worth,
>   Thou martyr-master; in thy sight
> Storm flakes were scroll-leaved flowers, lily showers—sweet heaven
>   was astrew in them.

333

This is not a poem of the Passion, but of the Triumph which followed upon the Passion. It is not the lament of those who die, but the paean of those who seize the Life which follows death. It is not a wail expressive of suffering, but a song thrilling with triumphant joy.

The spirit of St. Paul shines through the poem from beginning to end. The power of God which St. Paul celebrated in everything he wrote is celebrated here:

> Thou mastering me
> God!
>
> Melt him but master him still.
>
> Make mercy in all of us, out of us all
> Mastery, but be adored, but be adored King.
>
> Thou Martyr-master . . .
> There then! the Master . . .
>
> I admire thee, master of the tides . . .

The mastery of God, in which all things work together for good, is Hopkins' theme. According to Edith Sitwell, "The whole poem is inhabited by a gigantic and overwhelming power, like that of the element that inspired it." [1] The power of the sea is a symbol, for Hopkins, of the power of God—"Stanching, quenching ocean of a motionable mind." The whole spirit of the poem is positive, not in any sense negative. It is the spirit of the Fourth Week of St. Ignatius' *Spiritual Exercises* where, in the concluding "Contemplation for Obtaining Divine Love," we behold God behind everything, God acting in and with everything, God working out His own transcendent glory in the universe.

The first part of the poem—which I will consider here rather briefly in relation to the poem as a whole, leaving consideration

[1] Edith Sitwell, *Aspects of Modern Poetry* (Duckworth, 1935), p. 60.

of its peculiar difficulties for the last part of my essay—gives the poet's qualifications for writing on this theme. He himself has experienced God's grace, the power of God working in him, and therefore he can know the experience of the nun. God's finger touched him, and almost unmade him. His heart was flushed by that stroke of God's finger, that "stress" of God felt in the innermost depths of his being, and his heart melted. The storm which brought this stress of God's power was not, in Hopkins' case, a physical storm, but a spiritual one, concerned not with "wild waters," but with "walls, altar and hour and night." He experienced it during a period of tremendous spiritual stress—"And the midriff astrain with leaning of, laced with fire of stress." I consider it probable that he refers here to his conversion to Catholicism, which must have cost him his greatest sacrifice up to the time when this poem was written. At any rate, he feared the power of God, he feared the "hurtle of hell," so he "whirled out wings that spell." I take this last phrase to mean that the image spells something, is significant, probably because the bird with extended wings forms a cross.[2] The poet fled to Christ, to the "heart of the Host," and there found his strength and power. Christ gave him the grace to rise to ever new levels of the supernatural realms, sustained and lifted by that gift:

> My heart, but you were dovewinged, I can tell,
> Carrier-witted, I am bold to boast,
> To flash from the flame to the flame then, tower from
> the grace to the grace.

His experience of grace is embodied in two striking figures: he seemed to be drained of himself like sand in an hourglass, and to be sustained from beneath like water in a well.

[2] W. H. Gardner, in his important study of the poem in *Essays and Studies*, Vol. 21 (Oxford University Press, 1936), suggests (p. 136, n. 1) that "spell" is used in the sense of a period of time, as when we say "a long dry spell." In such case, Hopkins would be referring to *"that* spell" as the last in a series of spiritual experiences.

The following rather difficult stanzas are clarified somewhat by a quatrain written many years later (No. 73):

> What I know of thee I bless,
> As acknowledging thy stress
> On my being and as seeing
> Something of thy holiness.

What he can know of God begins with what he sees in nature, in stars and in storms, symbols of Christ's sweetness and power. He blesses and greets Christ, therefore, when he recognizes Him under nature's splendor and wonder. God's instressing of him, His finger's stroke upon his being, is delivered through nature; the stress, the activity of God which he feels within him is mediated by nature. God's grace, which is His power working in us, flows from the Cross of Christ, Who, by redeeming our fallen nature, made it possible for us to know more fully the Power Who lies under the power of nature. Nature speaks to us of God, and we are forced to hearken to her message when she drives us "hard at bay," holding us helpless in a superior power. Then we lash out with the best word, "yes," which is our acceptance of the mastery of that Power behind nature, or with our worst word, "no," which is our rejection of it. By that word the man makes known what side he takes, for or against God, and thus shows what he is (No. 67):

> What makes the man and what
> The man within that makes:
> Ask whom he serves or not
> Serves and what side he takes.

This revelation of his nature which each man experiences in his "yes" or "no" Hopkins compares to the experience of breaking the skin of a sloe which one has put whole into one's mouth. There is no escaping the rush of flavor, the "nature" of the fruit—sour or sweet. The metaphor represents a man's "conversion" or "non-conversion," his acceptance or rejection of God's mastery, in which act the true nature of the man, sour or sweet, appears. Response to Christ's power, His "stress," means life. Christ seeks to evoke that response even from the maliciously rebellious by the exercise of His power and mastery, thus forcing a decision:

> It is even seen, time's something server,
> In mankind's medley a duty-swerver,
>   At downright 'No or yes?'
> Doffs all, drives full for righteousness.[3]

Whether the man accepts or rejects that mastery, he must ultimately submit to it:

> . . . Hither then, last or first,
>   To hero of Calvary, Christ's, feet—
> Never ask if meaning it, wanting it, warned of it—men go.

The first part of the poem concludes with a prayer to God that He should fulfill His glory in men. The apparent paradoxes ("lightning and love," "a winter and warm," "Father and fondler of heart thou hast wrung,") are identified in God, Who when He has His "dark descending" is then most merciful. The poet prays that He should make His mercy and mastery shine out through us by whatever means He will, whether by violence (storms) as in the conversion of Paul or by "a lingering-out sweet skill" (stars) as in that of Augustine. God appears to adapt His means to those with whom He deals. But the purpose of all things—of forces of nature, of the responses of men—is that God be glorified.

The second part of the poem, which illustrates God's use of the violence of nature to achieve His ends, begins dramatically with the cry of Death, and a variant of the dread "Memento homo quia pulvis es . . ." The description of the boat's launching into

---

[3] *The Loss of the Eurydice,* ll. 53–56.

the storm, of the wreck, and of the long terrible hours, is broken by the poet's cry to the "mother of being in me, heart." As in stanza seven, where the "heart" is said to utter truth not conceived before, the heart here finds the truth beneath the appearances. In the face of this seeming tragedy, the heart of the poet gives a gleeful, a "madrigal start." He inquires after the meaning of this glee. Does his heart have some interest there?

Yes, a sister calling their common Master. That is the interest. The flight of the nuns into exile and their seeming desperate loneliness recall Hopkins' sonnet on the Church (*Andromeda*):

> Her Perseus linger and leave her to her extremes?—
> Pillowy air he treads a time and hangs
> His thoughts on her, forsaken that she seems,
> All while her patience, morselled into pangs,
> Mounts . . .

But Christ was watching always; He was "weighing the worth"; the snowflakes in His sight were not cold signs of cruel fate but "scroll-leaved flowers, lily showers—sweet heaven was astrew in them."

"Martyr-master"—that name sounds the note of the next section. Christ is the Martyr Whose five wounds were scored on Him by men. He scores that cipher "himself on his own bespoken," that cipher of his wounds which is the "stigma, signal, cinquefoil token" for the lettering of the fleece of the Sacrificial Lamb, for the ruddying of the divine Rose. Hopkins celebrates the wounds of Christ in similar terms in *Rosa Mystica*. The Blossom referred to here is Christ:

> What was the colour of that Blossom bright?
> White to begin with, immaculate white.
> But what a wild flush on the flakes of it stood,
> When the Rose ran in crimsonings down the Cross-wood.
>   In the Gardens of God, in the daylight divine
>   I shall worship the Wounds with thee, Mother of mine.

How many leaves had it? Five they were then,
Five like the senses, and members of men;
Five is the number by nature, but now
They multiply, multiply, who can tell how.
   In the Gardens of God, in the daylight divine
   Make me a leaf in thee, Mother of mine.

The nuns were daughters of St. Francis, who himself bore the wounds of Christ, and here they share that privilege. The result of this triumph of Christ in them is their coming "to bathe in his fall-gold mercies, to breathe in his all-fire glances."

The poet notes the striking contrast between his own situation and theirs at the time of the wreck. He was at rest in the quiet countryside of Wales, where it was easy to know that Christ the shepherd was watching over him; the nun, helpless amid the wild waters, unfalteringly knew that the Good Shepherd was with her there.

Hopkins calls upon the Holy Spirit, "arch and original Breath," for light to understand the nun's cry. Did it signify that she desired to share the Passion of Christ, her lover? Or did she long for her suffering to cease that she might come to its reward, "the treasure never eyesight got, nor was ever guessed what for the hearing"? Not these. It is not sudden danger but a long period of suffering which "fathers" the plea for relief from the "sodden-with-its-sorrowing heart." Nor in such sudden danger does the Passion make its appeal. The nun has another motive. But it cannot be expressed. It is not a concept, but a vision, and that vision is Christ. She knew His power under the storm. She cries her "yes" and experiences His mastery within her. She is experiencing what Hopkins described of himself in the first part of the poem. She echoes the prayer which concluded the first part, calling upon Christ to ride in His triumph in her as in all the living and dead, to make His glory out of her.

This is the climax. The poet takes satisfaction in dwelling upon the perfect response of this creature to her God. She knew Him under the storm; the storm could not drive her from Him any more than a beacon of light can be blown from its course. She conceived Him, she bore Him within her ("I live now, not I, but Christ liveth in me" [4]), she shared His sacrifice. She saw Christ in the storm and "worded it" by Him, as Simon Peter had seen the Godhead in the man Jesus before him, and had worded his vision for the ages. She was like Peter, too, in being a rock amid the storm, like the Tarpeian rock at Rome.

As a result of her sacrifice the nun shares Christ's glory, as does the "one woman without stain" who gave Christ birth. For the nun too has given Him new birth:

> But here was heart-throe, birth of a brain,
> Word, that heard and kept thee and uttered thee outright.

Christ had said: "If anyone love me, he will keep my word, and my Father will love him, and we will come to him and make our abode with him" (John, 14:23).

The poet turns for a moment to consider the other passengers who perished, "the comfortless unconfessed of them." His heart "bleeds at a bitterer vein" for them, who have also suffered the wreck and the storm and yet have not gained Christ. However, God was working also in these others; He was also their Father. And they heard the cry of the nun too. Perhaps that cry had moved them as it had moved the poet, and had "startled the poor sheep back."

Hopkins ends with passionate and almost incoherent praise of the majesty and mercy of God. He applies to Him various titles rising from the image of the storm: the master of the tides; the recurb and recovery of the gulf's sides, the girth of it and the wharf of it and the wall (an echo of St. Paul's "so that, being rooted and grounded in love, you may be able to comprehend with all the saints what is the breadth and length and height and depth . . .") ; the "stanching, quenching ocean of a motionable mind," that is, God is the ocean which quenches the ever-chang-

---

[4] Galatians, 2.20.

ing desires of the human mind; the "ground of being, and granite of it," He of Whom alone it can be said, "I am Who am."

God is beyond all grasp, throned behind nature and behind death, which seems to us so conclusive. Yet in some measure the poet had grasped Him:

> I kiss my hand
> To the stars, lovely-asunder
> Starlight, wafting him out of it . . .

The nun had grasped Him:

> Ah! There was a heart right!
> There was single eye!
> Read the unshapeable shock night
> And knew the who and the why . . .

God is behind death with a "sovereignty which heeds but hides," that is, sees what is going on but does not clearly force His will upon men; Who "bodes but abides," that is, knows what will happen but does not therefore forestall the free acts of men. He is there with a mercy that will top the flood and be a saving ark to all who will listen to Him; with a love that goes even "lower than death and the dark"; with a vein (that is, a channel) for reaching the hopeless, the sinful, "the-last-breath penitent spirits," those rescued at the "uttermost mark" by Christ, striding across the stormy waters of the world.

The poet now quietly calls upon Christ to blaze in splendor before the world:

> Now burn, new born to the world,
> Double-naturèd name,
> The heaven-flung, heart-fleshed, maiden-furled
> Miracle-in-Mary-of-flame,
> Mid-numberèd He in three of the thunder-throne!

The storm is passed. Christ has reclaimed His own. This "storm of his strides" was not a punishment for the nuns, but a glorious fulfillment, "a released shower, let flash to the shire." He was not "a lightning of fire hard-hurled," as the disciples had wished to call down upon the unfriendly Samaritans: " 'Lord, wilt thou that we bid fire come down from heaven and consume them?' But he turned and rebuked them, saying, 'You do not know of what manner of spirit you are; for the Son of Man did not come to destroy men's lives, but to save them' " (Luke, 9:54–56).

Hopkins calls upon the nun to pray for the English, upon whose shoals she found her glory; to pray that Christ might again be the Sun of Britain, her high-priest, her warming fire.

The essential unity of the whole poem is achieved by a perfect structural parallelism in which part is proportioned to part. The two main divisions of the poem are labeled Part the First and Part the Second. In the former the power of God masters the poet, in the latter the same power masters the nun. Since the peculiar difficulties of Part the First will explain similar difficulties in Part the Second, I will consider here in detail only the problems which rise in relation to the first part.

Hopkins first discusses God's finger touching him, which is "the stress felt, the stroke dealt," of stanza six; in the second and third stanzas he describes his response and its results. In stanza four he expresses metaphorically the destruction of the old man and the support of the new, which is Christ's own life feeding and supporting him like the water from the mountain feeding and supporting the water in the well. The source of that life is the proffer of the gospel; the dynamic pressure of it lifts him; it is the principle of his new being; it is Christ's free gift to him—grace.

In the next stanza the poet points out that Christ speaks to him in all of nature—as in *Hurrahing in Harvest:*

> And, eyes, heart, what looks, what lips yet gave you a
> Rapturous love's greeting of realer, of rounder replies?

As a result of the touch of God's finger, he has been moved to acknowledge Christ behind nature, and this is the grace which

Hopkins shares with the nun. This is Christ's gift (1 Cor., 2:10–12):

But to us God has revealed them through his Spirit. For the Spirit searches all things, even the deep things of God. For who among men knows the things of a man save the spirit of the man which is in him? Even so, the things of God no one knows but the Spirit of God. Now we have received not the spirit of the world, but the spirit that is from God, that we may know the things that have been given us by God.

The action of grace which Hopkins treats in the poem is that which causes the recipients to be "raised to the state when their deeds should be the doing of God in them" (N 338), a statement which clarifies the difficult line of the twenty-eighth stanza, "Let him ride, her pride, in his triumph, despatch and have done with his doom there." So intimate is the union between Christ and the nun that her triumph is His doing, His triumph; her pride is Christ acting in her; the despatch of His doom, His plan, the sacrifice which He demands of her—"But he scores it in scarlet himself on his own bespoken"—this is the doing of God in her.

In his *Comments on the Spiritual Exercises* Hopkins calls this sort of action an activity of that form of grace which is "elevating, which lifts the receiver from one cleave of being to another and to a vital act in Christ: this is truly God's finger touching the very vein of personality, which nothing else can reach and man can respond to by no play whatever, by bare acknowledgment only, the counter-stress which God alone can feel ('subito probas eum'), the aspiration in answer to his inspiration. Of this I have written above and somewhere else long ago." [5]

In this passage, I believe, lies the key to the whole poem, which thus becomes an illustration of that elevating grace. If this is true, the thought-structure of the poem centers about the line "His

[5] N 337. Humphrey House, editor of the *Notebooks*, suggests, I think rightly, that the "somewhere else" is the first part of *The Wreck of the Deutschland*.

mystery must be instressed, stressed," which expresses the inspiration of God and the answering aspiration of man. To understand the full implications of the line, it is necessary to examine the terms "instress" and "stress" and so to derive Hopkins' conception.

Dr. Pick—and in this he agrees with Mr. Gardner—takes the terms as synonyms: "Ordinarily Hopkins uses 'instress' verbally and 'stress' substantively; here, however, the first is an intensive form of the second, and the impact is heightened by the reversal of the expected word order." [6] As Dr. Pick points out, such an interpretation is not in accord with Hopkins' ordinary use of the terms. There seems to be no good reason for supposing that Hopkins employs the terms in a sense different from his ordinary usage, which is here both appropriate and forceful. A consideration of Hopkins' usage of the terms in his other writings will make this clear.

Hopkins defines "stress" thus: "Stress appears so elementary an idea as does not need and scarcely allows of definition; still this may be said of it, that it is the making a thing more, or making it markedly, what it already is; it is the bringing out its nature" (F 179. Nov. 7, 1883). He uses the term to denote emphasis of a word or syllable: "Its principle is that all rhythm and all verse consist of feet and each foot must contain one stress or verse-accent . . ." (D 39. Dec. 22, 1880). He uses it further to denote the bringing out or the emphasis of a thing's or person's nature: "It is as if the blissful agony or stress of selving in God had forced out drops of sweat or blood . . ." (N 344). In this second usage the term "stress" is similar to the philosophical terms "act" and "perfection": "Nevertheless the being it has got has a great perfection, a great stress, and is more distinctive and higher selved, than anything else I see, except other such minds, in nature" (N 312). It denotes activity: "Chance then is the ἐνέργεια, the stress, of the intrinsic possibility which things have" (N 310). "The word inspiration need cause no difficulty. I mean by it a mood of great, abnormal in fact, mental acuteness,

[6] John Pick, *op. cit.*, p. 44, n.

either energetic or receptive, according as the thoughts which
arise in it seem generated by a stress and action of the brain, or
to strike into it unasked" (F 69. Sept. 10, 1864). It is opposed to
"slack," both in the sense of word emphasis—"So that wherever
there is an accent or stress, there there is also so much unaccentuation, so to speak, or slack, and this will give a foot or rhythmic
unit, viz. a stress with its belonging slack" (D 22. Feb. 27, 1879)
—and in the sense of "nature" emphasis:

> Not, I'll not, carrion comfort, Despair, not feast on thee;
> Not untwist—slack they may be—these last strands of man
> In me or, most weary, cry *I can no more* (No. 40).

"Stress," then, is the general term which includes the terms "instress," "outstress," "distress," and "counter-stress."

"Instress" Hopkins defines as "throwing a stress on"—"The
meaning of it is that you can without clumsiness instress, throw
a stress on a syllable so supported which if it were unsupported
would be drawling" (N 226)—or "coming to stress"—"And as
mere possibility, passive power, is not power proper and has no
activity it cannot of itself come to stress, cannot instress itself"
(N 310). When used verbally, "instress" means for him the process of bringing a thing to a state of stress, of actualising a thing:
". . . for the constant repetition, the continuity, of the bad
thought is that actualising of it, that instressing of it, which he refused himself to be guilty of but which is carried out by a power
not his doing him violence" (N 321). In this last passage, it is
clear that the one concerned could instress himself with the bad
thought, that is, could make it actual in himself, put himself in a
state of stress towards it, or he can be instressed by a power other
than his own. It is "active power" which instresses, not "passive
power."

When used substantively, "instress" usually means that quality
in a thing which brings about a state of stress or of act in the
beholder: "Take a *few* primroses in a glass and the instress of—

brilliancy, sort of starriness: I have not the right word—so simple a flower gives is remarkable" (N 142–143); ". . . light beating up from so many glassy heads, which like water is good to float their deeper instress in upon the mind" (N 174); "(there is a simplicity of instress in the cinqfoil)" (N 209); " 'The Wood-pecker' reminds one of Cowper's poems in this metre and has the same sort of 'instress' of feeling but not quite the same satis-factory cadences" (D 63. Sept. 26, 1881). "Instress" in this sub-stantive use might be called the "flavor" of a thing.

Hopkins further distinguishes the general term "stress" by means of the term "outstress," which refers to the act proceeding from the stress of the subject and terminating outside the sub-ject: "The first intention then of God outside himself or, as they say, *ad extra,* outwards, the first outstress of God's power, was Christ . . ." (N 344). "Outstress" is the act of the stress out from the self, as "instress" is the act of the stress, either one's own [7] or the power of another's stress, towards the self.

Hopkins uses "distress" to signify a falling from stress, a de-emphasizing of the nature: "Michael and his angels instressed and distressed them with the thought of their unlikeness to the Most High . . ." (N 351). The bad angels were instressed with the thought (that is, the thought was made actual to them) and were distressed, thrown off from stress, made even less what they should be. If their natures had not been in rebellion against truth, if they had said "yes" instead of "no," they would have been "stressed" as a result of that "instress," that is, their natures would have been emphasized, have been in more perfect act, have been more what they should be.

---

[7] This occurs when by one's own immanent activity one moves oneself to act: e.g.

> "What the heart is! which, like carriers let fly—
> Doff darkness, homing nature knows the rest—
> To its own fine function, wild and self-instressed,
> Falls light as ten years long taught how to and why" (No. 27).

"It is choice as when in English we say 'because I choose,' which means no more than (and with precision does mean) I instress my will to so-and-so" (N 328).

The line from the *Deutschland* states "His mystery must be instressed, stressed." God's mystery must be instressed, that is, made actual in us. After it has been made actual in us, it must be "stressed" by us, emphasized, made more what it already is. Note that as a result of the instress of God's mystery we are not, like the bad angels, "distressed," unless we say "no," refuse to accept and respond to that "instress." By saying "yes" we respond to the instressed mystery, we "stress" it, emphasize it, throw ourselves into act in regard to it. Hopkins refers to such action in the passage: ". . . this is truly God's finger touching the very vein of personality, which nothing else can reach and man can respond to by no play whatever, by bare acknowledgment only, the counter-stress which God alone can feel ('subito probas eum'), the aspiration in answer to his inspiration" (N 337). Here "counter-stress" means our own stress or act as counter or opposed to God's stress or act. "Counter-stress" is distinguished not from "instress" or "outstress," but from the distinct stress of another. Taken in itself, without considering some outside stress, "counter-stress" means merely "stress." The "counter-stress" in this passage results from feeling the stress of God, from being "instressed" or touched by the finger of God. "Stress" refers to immanent activity, and our stress or counter-stress springs from our own being. Therefore, when God's power or stress acts upon us, that power must be responded to or "stressed" within us by our own "counter-stress," our own reaction, our aspiration answering His inspiration.

According to Hopkins' ordinary use of the terms "instress" and "stress," then, the line "His mystery must be instressed, stressed" means: "God's mystery must be made actual in us by his action, and must be responded to by our own." We can respond to His power "by bare acknowledgment only," by "blessing" and by "greeting" Him: "For I greet him the days I meet him, and bless when I understand." To say that God's "mystery must be instressed, stressed" is to say that although God is under the world's splendor and wonder, nevertheless the mystery of His being there must be made actual in me, and, having been made actual, must be responded to by my own response, my "greeting," my "kissing my hand" to Him, my saying "yes."

The sixth stanza states that the stress which we feel, the stroke dealt, does not spring from His bliss; it springs from nature, from time. This stress or stroke brings us to the recognition of Christ in nature. It is the absence of this recognition which terrifies the guilty when the stroke of God swings from the natural objects around us; it is the presence of this recognition of Christ which makes faithful hearts flush and melt. The stroke of lightning is the same for all, but the response to that stroke, the meaning of that stroke, differs with each man. The faithful may waver before the terror of God, as the poet described himself doing in the third stanza, ". . . where, where was a, where was a place." But those in whom Christ lives fully, those who have said "yes," are steady as a beacon of light: "But in all these things we overcome because of him who has loved us. For I am sure that neither death, nor life, nor angels, nor principalities, nor things present, nor things to come, nor powers, nor height, nor depth, nor any other creature will be able to separate us from the love of God, which is in Christ Jesus our Lord" (1 Cor., 1:18).

The key to understanding that stress which we feel in stars and storms lies in the Incarnation of the Second Person of the Blessed Trinity, the God-Man Jesus Christ. From His life and passion swells that supernatural power of grace which carried the poet and the nun to selfsacrifice to God, and to salvation: "For grace is any action, activity, on God's part by which, in creating or after creating, he carries the creature to or towards the end of its being, which is its selfsacrifice to God and its salvation" (N 332). We ordinarily are ignorant of this power acting within us, since it is the very life of our supernatural life (if we have it), the very current in which we move. We should always be ignorant of it unless we were driven hard at bay, knew our own strength as useless, and felt a greater power surging through us. That is the way the "heart, being hard at bay, is out with it." This is the point at which the man knows himself to be slipping away like sand in an hourglass, and feels the upsurge of divine power from underneath lifting him up "from the flame to the flame," towering "from the grace to the grace." In such an hour we lash out with our best or worst word; we "word" ourselves— we say what we are. We are mouthed to flesh-burst, and flooded with the taste of ourselves. In his *Commentary on the Spiritual Exercises,* Hopkins says, ". . . I consider my self-being, my consciousness and feeling of myself, that taste of myself, of *I* and *me* above and in all things, which is more distinctive than the taste of ale or alum, more distinctive than the smell of walnutleaf or camphor, and is incommunicable by any means to another man . . ." (N 309). In one of the later sonnets (No. 45) he develops the same thought:

> I am gall, I am heartburn. God's most deep decree
> Bitter would have me taste: my taste was me;
> Bones built in me, flesh filled, blood brimmed the curse.
> Selfyeast of spirit a dull dough sours. I see
> The lost are like this, and their scourge to be
> As I am mine, their sweating selves; but worse.

Those in hell taste themselves forever, as they have chosen to do, and they are sour. They excluded the stress of God which would have instressed them, brought them to stress. They said "no" to Him, and their "no," when time is no more, is eternal.

The prayer which closes the first part of the poem is that God will master us all, exert His power in all, and in all of us be adored King. Our "yes" is all we can give, and it is the glory of man to give that "yes," the sublime opportunity of man to have a chance to say that "yes," to share the Sacrifice, the infinite "yes" of Christ. The poet was given that chance and "did say yes." The nun was given that chance, and "the call of the tall nun to the men in the tops and the tackle rode over the storm's brawling." It is clear, then, surely, how far this poem is from being one of sorrow, of penitence, of doubt, of suffering. I believe that Canon Dixon, admirable critic though he sometimes was, missed the essence of the poem, which lies far beyond the "elements of deep distress in it" which he mentions: "The Deutschland is enormously powerful: it has however such elements of deep distress in it that one reads it with less excited delight though not with less interest than the others" (D. 32–33. March 1, 1880). The *Deutschland*, as a matter of fact, concerns itself with elements of deep distress only as a prelude to the triumph which follows. It is not a poem of Good Friday; it is an Easter poem. It is the record of the triumphant cry of a Christian who won the good fight, who received the crown of glory, who after glorious combat is dissolved and lives with Christ.

APPENDIX

THE HISTORICAL BASIS OF
THE WRECK OF THE DEUTSCHLAND AND *THE LOSS OF THE EURYDICE*

NORMAN WEYAND, S.J.

> I may add for your greater interest and edification that what refers to myself in the poem is all strictly and literally true and did all occur; nothing is added for poetical padding.
>
> (B 47. Aug. 21, 1877)

The words "what refers to myself" in the above quotation have undoubtedly prompted a question in the minds of numerous readers: "How much of the *non-personal* matter in *The Wreck of the Deutschland* is also based on historical fact?" The contemporary accounts in the London *Times* for December, 1875, provide an interesting answer to the question. As these accounts are not readily available, selections from them may prove helpful to readers curious concerning the full background of the poem's inspiration.

The space which the *Times* gave to the event for a number of days shows the widespread attention which the wreck received. Hopkins, together with all England, was evidently moved. Consequently it is not difficult to appreciate the poet's experience, which he later recounted in a letter to Canon Dixon as follows (D 14. Oct. 5, 1878):

But when in the winter of '75 the Deutschland was wrecked in the mouth of the Thames and five Franciscan nuns, exiles from Germany by the Falck Laws, aboard of her were drowned I was affected by the account and happening to say so to my rector he said that he wished someone would write a poem on the subject.

On this hint I set to work and, though my hand was out at first, produced one.

Even as readers have wondered about the historical basis for such incidents as those of the passengers taking to the rigging and the cry of the tall nun in *The Wreck of the Deutschland,* so they may find themselves with questions concerning the "beetling baldbright cloud," "Sydney Fletcher, Bristol-bred," "Royal and all her royals wore," and various other details in *The Loss of the Eurydice.* The contemporary issues of the *Times* again give much enlightening information; hence, the relevant passages from the March, 1878, issues are also included here.

Anyone who has consulted similar *Times* reports of the period will know how such accounts constantly repeat details in quoting evidence from witnesses, explanations by officials, and the like. Therefore, it would be inadvisable to reprint all of the complete accounts. Although even the reports and passages from reports given below contain repetition of a number of details, the entire matter should prove helpful and interesting to readers familiar with the two poems.

THE WRECK OF THE DEUTSCHLAND

The Times, Wednesday, Dec. 8, 1875, page 5.

LOSS OF THE DEUTSCHLAND

The following telegrams have been received at Lloyd's:—

"SHEERNESS, Dec. 7.

"A boat came ashore this morning from the Deutschland, steamer, with Quartermaster named Beck August and two dead men in her. Had been in boat 38 hours."

"2:30 P.M.

"Quartermaster of Deutschland named August, one named Forsenstein, one not known.

"General cargo and passengers.

"Not known what has become of ship or the rest of passengers and crew.

"Steamer struck on sandbank in North Sea. One boat left ship before him.

"Number of passengers and crew 150. He thinks all the rest are lost."

"HARWICH, Dec. 7.

"The Deutschland, North German steamer, from Bremen for New York, with emigrants, grounded on the Kentish Knock˘ at 5 a.m. on Monday morning. Heavy north-east gale; thick, with snow. Crew and passengers drowned. The Deutschland has beaten over the Kentish Knock, and is now in four-and-a-half fathoms water, apparently parted amidships.

"When Captain Brickenstein left the steamer she was full of water, rising and falling with the tide. Assistance has been sent."

The following telegrams are from our Harwich correspondent:—

"HARWICH, Dec. 7.

"The North German Lloyd steamer Deutschland, of Bremen, Captain Brickenstein, from Bremen for New York, with emigrants, grounded on the Kentish Knock on Monday morning during a gale from the north-east, thick with snow. Part of the crew and passengers were landed here to-day by the tug Liverpool, of Harwich, and placed under the care of Mr. Oliver John Williams, the North German Consul at Harwich. About 50 of the crew and passengers are drowned. The names of the cabin passengers missing are Ludwig Heerman, J. Grossman, Maria Forster, Emil Hack, Bertha Fundling, Theodor Fundling, five nuns, Procopi Kadolkoff, and O. Lundgren."

(Also *The Times*, Wednesday, Dec. 8, 1875, page 5.)

A Special Reporter of the Press Association at Sheerness gives us the following additional particulars which were last night elicited from the Quartermaster, who was then supposed to be the only survivor of the disaster. The Quartermaster said:—

"I am a seaman belonging to the Deutschland. I am Quartermaster of the ship. I am a married man, belong to Bremerhaven, and have two little children. We had 130 in the crew, and I think from 150 to 200 passengers and the mails and cargo. We were going to New York, but should call at Southampton on the way out. We left Bremen on Saturday and when we got beside the lightship we let go anchor. On Sunday morning we weighed anchor and proceeded on our voyage, a regular gale blowing at the time. In the evening, during a storm, we struck on a bank and stuck fast. It had been blowing heavily. We tried to get off, but could not; the sea washed over us fore and aft, carrying away much of our gear. The captain kept very cool, and when the vessel grounded he ordered the lifebelts to be served out to both the passengers and crew. In the morning the ship being about to break up, as we thought, the captain told us to lower the lifeboats. I and two seamen got into one, but in lowering it the heavy seas twice capsized it, and we were each time thrown into the water. We managed to get into the boat, which righted, but dismayed at finding ourselves adrift, as the rope fastening us to the ship had broken. We endeavored to pull to the ship, but were not strong enough in the heavy lifeboat to make head against the heavy sea. The last I saw of the ship they were endeavoring to launch all the boats. The sea was very wild at the time, and the ship laboured heavily. I got up a small sail, and drifted before the wind, but my two mates were soon helpless through the blinding snow and piercing cold. One died the same night and the other on the next morning. On Monday I saw several ships and made signs of distress, but none came near me. On Tuesday I passed a lightship and called out again, but I suppose they did not hear me. I saw a light on shore, and luckily managed to steer my boat to it."

The survivor was too exhausted to give further particulars of the conduct of the captain and crew after the vessel struck, and said, "I hope to have a better night's sleep to-night than I have had these last three nights." A remark having been made that it seemed strange that he was not provided with a lifebelt the same as his two deceased comrades, a smile broke over the poor fellow's face as he replied, "All my thoughts, Sir, were at the time to get the lifeboats out to save the passengers, and I forgot my belt." He seemed anxious to know the fate of the remainder of the crew and the passengers of the ill fated vessel, and appeared disappointed when told that nothing whatever was known there as to their safety or otherwise.

A tugboat has left Sheerness for the spot described by the Quartermaster, who is suffering greatly from exposure, but is progressing more favorably than the medical man anticipated. An inquest will be held on the two bodies found in the boat.

The Times, Thursday, Dec. 9, 1875, page 6.

THE LOSS OF THE DEUTSCHLAND

The wreck of another large German Transatlantic steamer so soon after the disaster of the Schiller—also German, though of a different line—is a coincidence of calamities which at present there is no reason for thinking other than fortuitous. The North German Lloyd Company, to which the Deutschland belongs, has a very large fleet, and claims not to have lost a single passenger's life since the starting of her lines in 1856. The company are their own insurers, and therefore the loss in the case of the Deutschland falls entirely upon the owners, so far as hull and freight are concerned. The Deutschland had eight large boats, of which two or three were lifeboats; and the refuges thus provided were enough for all the 123 passengers—two first cabin, 24 second cabin, and 97 steerage—and 90 or 100 of crew who sailed in her from Bremen. She is said by the owner's agents to have had on board no less than 1,000 life-belts. The 'tween-decks, where the steerage passengers slept, are described as "roofed" with these appliances, and there was a life-belt at the head of every first and second-class passenger's bunk. At Southampton she would have taken on board more passengers and the English mails, which the Company has been in the habit of carrying for 14 years. She had both a Weser pilot and an English Channel pilot on board when she struck; and her master, Captain Brickenstein, had been many years in the service of the company. Benning, the purser, one of the unfortunate men lost, had been in the vessel since the first voyage of the steamship in which he met his death. The Deutschland, though not registered with Lloyd's in London, was

entered in the "Liverpool Underwriters' Book of Iron Vessels." She
was of British build, and was launched by Messrs. Caird, of
Greenock, in 1866. She was 328 ft. long, 26 deep, and 40 beam. Her
engines were two direct action, of 600-horse power in all. Her registered tonnage was 2,690 under deck, 2,898 gross, 1,971 net. She had
five bulkheads—that is to say, she was in six compartments, and
there is therefore room to hope that the ship may be got off,
although no more lives can be expected to be saved. Mr. Wallis, of
Keller, Postlethwaite, and Wallis, agents for the North German
Lloyd's, went off to her with Captain Brickenstein from Harwich
yesterday, and late last night telegraphed to London, respecting
materials which might be useful for the purpose of saving the ship.
The comparative calm which the change of wind to west south-west
brings may be favorable to this operation.

There is as yet no definite explanation (beyond that which the
snow storm may supply) of the deviation from her course which
led the ship, leaving the Knock Edge Light on her port side probably, to ground on the shifting sands of Kentish Knock. This is,
with the exception of the Galloper, the outermost shoal at the
mouth of the Thames, and the steamer must have passed quite close
to the light in reaching the place where she lies with her bows to
the south-west and her stern to the north-east, in 4 to 4½ fathoms
water at high tide and 20 ft. less at low water. As the wind was
blowing strongly from the east-north-east it is perhaps a reasonable
presumption that the numerous shoals of the Dutch coast were
sought to be avoided by a westerly course, with the result that the
ship approached too close to the Thames shoals.

We append, among other things, a singularly clear statement by
a survivor. It will be observed that the propeller was lost at an early
stage, and thus the chance of escape by backing off was lost. The
quartermaster Beck mentioned in the statement is the man who
came ashore at Sheerness. It appears from the narrative that over
200 persons took to the rigging on Monday night, and our Harwich
correspondent sends the list of those saved. In that cold and terrible
night between Monday and Tuesday, many unhappy persons must
have lost their hold upon the rigging and fallen numbed into
the sea.

A survivor has made the following statements:—

"The steamer struck on Monday morning at 5 o'clock. The sea was very rough, blowing hard from the east-north-east, thick with snow. The lead was cast every half-hour. We found 24 fathoms and then 17 fathoms. Immediately afterwards she struck, ship going dead slow. The engines were turned full speed astern, and immediately lost propeller. The ship was then driven further up; two boats were lowered—one in charge of the fourth officer, and containing seven or eight persons, and the second with Quartermaster Beck in which it is believed there were only three or four persons. But both filled. No other boats were launched, the sea being too rough, but the rest were kept in readiness. Ultimately, however, the sea stove in and washed overboard the whole of the boats. During Monday efforts were made by throwing cargo overboard from the forehold to keep the ship's stern to sea, keeping her bows inshore to prevent her getting broad side to the sea; and passengers were sheltered as far as possible in the deck-houses. The pumps were kept going all the day till dusk came on at 4 p.m. As the tide rose the dark came on, the passengers and crew were compelled to take to the rigging. For the decks became awash. Captain Brickenstein, who had not left the bridge, remained there until washed out by the sea; and then he took to the rigging like the others."

The tug Liverpool arrived about noon on Tuesday.

The Times, Dec. 10, 1875, page 10.

THE LOSS OF THE DEUTSCHLAND

HARWICH, Thursday.

An inquest was held here today upon the bodies of two men, seven women, a female infant, two girls, and one boy brought ashore by the steam tug Liverpool. The Coroner was Mr. Codd, the foreman of the jury Mr. Whitmor, ship owner, formerly a captain in the merchant service. Mr. Chapman, solicitor, attended on the part of the owners of the vessel, the North German Lloyd's. Mr. Williams, North German Consul, at Harwood, also attended the inquest. Dr. Christian of Ipswich, acted as interpreter.

Carl Lukermann, chief steward of the screw steamer Deutschland, was the first witness. He identified the bodies viewed by the jury as those of passengers on board the vessel, but did not know any of their names. The Deutschland sailed from Bremen on Saturday, the 4th inst., with emigrants and a general cargo, for New York. The emigrants, he believed, were 111 in number, the crew were 99.

Captain Brickenstein, who gave his evidence in English, said:— I commanded the Deutschland, which left Bremerhaven on Saturday, and, anchoring in the river owing to heavy weather, left the Weser on Sunday morning, December 5, for New York. The register and papers of the ship are lost, and therefore I cannot say exactly how many passengers were on board, but I believe there were about 107 emigrants with other passengers, and 99 crew. It was about 9:30 a.m. on Sunday morning when we left the river, the wind blowing from the north-east pretty freely, with snow falling at intervals. The wind increased to a heavy gale by night time, with a heavy snow storm. Every two hours soundings were taken, and between 4 and 5 A.M. we cast the lead three times. From 4 A.M. also we went half speed. At half speed we should be going about 9½ knots an hour [sic]. The lead was cast about five or seven minutes before the ship struck, and we then found 17 fathoms of waters. Soon afterwards, at a little after 5 o'clock, we saw breakers. I do not think we had gone two miles after the casting of the lead before we saw the breakers. The vessel had no sails set, she was under steam alone. There were at the time four look-out men on the bridge and two in the bows, but the weather was so thick that they were of little use. When we look [sic] the last cast of the lead the vessel was stopped, and was merely drifting with the wind. She was thus sent ahead for about a minute or two, and then we saw breakers. Immediately I ordered the steamer to go at full speed astern, but had hardly given the order when the screw broke and the vessel was left at the mercy of the wind and waves. Then she struck on the sands. It was then nearly high tide. I at once ordered the boats to be cleared away and rockets to be fired. We did not burn blue lights, that being forbidden; it is a pilot signal. The ship touched the sand twice slightly before she became fixed. We had life-belts for more than 500 passengers. I ordered an officer to go below, serve out the lifebelts, and see that every passenger put one on.

By the Jury.—If a lifeboat had been sent out to us from Harwich, with the tug-boat, after our signals were answered from Harwich, nearly all on board might have been saved.

A juryman (Mr. Basham).—We have no lifeboat at Harwich; we want one badly.

Witness continued.—One of the boats was cast off or was dashed away by the sea soon after we struck. Three others were stove in. No help came to us from the time we struck at 5 A.M., on Monday morning, till 10 A.M. on Tuesday morning. As soon as the vessel struck she broached to and was left broadside on in the trough of the sea. It is possible that several people were at that time washed overboard. It was a clear day on Monday, though the sea was high. There were vessels passing, and we made such signals as we could with pistols and otherwise, but none of the passing vessels answered us. On Monday night we sent up rockets again, but received no help.

A Juryman.—The signals were seen and answered from Harwich. Many seamen would have been ready to go out and give help, but the weather being so bad they did not feel that they ought to endanger their lives in the absence of a lifeboat. As it is, the lives of many of these poor people have been lost through the want of a lifeboat at Harwich.

Another juryman.—The want of a lifeboat has often been felt here.

Witness.—It was the Liverpool tug-boat, of Harwich, which came to our help, and it took off 138 people, all who were then left alive. At that time the passengers were able to go below. About 9 a.m. on Monday we hove cargo overboard from the fore end of the ship to try to lighten the ship, and were at that work till Monday afternoon at 5 P.M. We had previously set the foresail to try to force her through the breakers. Afterwards, when we got on to the top of the sand, we let go both anchors. The ship, after striking, was pretty high above water. The people were safe enough at first; some were on deck, some were below, and were tolerably comfortable, though at times a wave would break over fore and aft. All that day the sea was heavy and the wind strong. About 2 A.M. on Tuesday I ordered the passengers on deck, and the aft-cabin filled with water about an hour afterwards. That was when the tide rose.

All came up. Most of the people got up the rigging, but fell off, chiefly from cold and exposure, and some of the bodies were carried through the broken glass of the skylights into the cabin.

By the Jury.—I did not expect to make the Gallopper Sand till 6:30, whereas the ship struck at the sand at about 5:15. We were, therefore, a long way out of our reckoning. We only had an ordinary log, not the patent log.

The Foreman.—If you had had a patent log on board, would you not have been able to check off your course, and probably save the ship?

Witness.—I do not think so. The lead was cast three or four times in the last hour, and we found the ship in deep water each time. I therefore thought myself justified in going at half-speed. The weather was so thick that we could not see the light on the Kentish Knock. I was on deck when the vessel struck, and had been there all night. We had an English pilot, Mr. Harvey, on board, but he had not charge of the ship. He would only take charge when we made the Nab, and would then take us into Southampton. He was on the bridge at the time we struck, but gave no directions. All directions were given by me. After daylight on Monday we did not fire any guns of distress. Our powder got wet and we could not fire.

Dr. Franz Buen, the surgeon of the vessel, gave evidence as to the cause of death. One of the children, a little girl between two and three years old, died in the arms of her mother before the survivors were rescued, and the body was taken by her on board the tug.

Auguste Lauenstein, the chief mate of the steamer, said they started from the river at a speed of 12 knots, with a fresh breeze from the north-east. The captain was on the bridge after dark on Sunday night. The vessel was not slowed till 4 A.M. on Monday, when she was put on half-speed. Witness hove the lead at 5 o'clock, and found 17 fathoms. He then went on to the bridge, upon the starboard side, and in six or seven minutes the captain saw the breakers, and witness saw him telegraph into the engine-room, "Full speed astern." There were a few revolutions of the screw afterwards, but it then started and broke. The screw did not last long enough to influence the course of the ship, which was really drifting ahead when she struck. The wind was right astern. The headway of the vessel was not stopped, and after twice touching gently she struck on the sands. The screw did not break by touching the sand; it broke while the vessel was still drifting ahead. If the screw had not given way, the vessel might have been saved. They did not know where they were when they saw the breakers; snow was falling and the weather was very thick. As to the patent log, you could not use it when you were heaving the lead every quarter or half an hour, for the line would foul the propeller. The English pilot was not in his own waters, and would have no knowledge of the navigation where the vessel struck. His duties would not begin till he got into his own waters.

Mr. Basham.—I think the jury ought to know when the signals were first seen by the Coastguard at Harwich, and at what time the first answering rocket was fired from the Coastguard station.

Witness.—We fired rockets at 5:15 A.M. on Monday, directly after we struck; but we did not see any answering signals (from the Sunk and the Cork lightships) until 6 or 7 P.M. on Monday evening.

Reinhold Schmidt, a chief engineer of the steamer, said he was in the engine-room when the ship struck. The propeller broke about a quarter of an hour before the ship struck; the engines had to be reversed, and were working about four minutes astern before the propeller broke. Witness could assign no reason for the breaking of the propeller. He did not feel the ship touch the ground before the propeller broke. The screw of a steamer does not project below the keel. The engines were stopped altogether for the soundings. Then they went on at half speed as before, and in a very few minutes the order came into the engine-room "Full speed astern!"

The Coroner said the question for the jury to decide was whether the ship was lost through the gross and culpable negligence of the captain, who admitted that he had sole charge of the ship, or whether it was lost by uncontrollable circumstances, such as the state of the weather, the snow-storm, and the breaking of the propeller. The evidence on these points was not likely to receive any material addition, and the jury would probably be prepared to return their verdict.

The jury still pressed an answer to the question when the distress signals were first seen and answered by the Coastguard at Harwich.

The Chief Officer was therefore sent for, and in reply to questions said the Coastguard saw no rockets on the Sunday night, nor yet on Monday morning. Rockets could not be seen in the daytime. No rockets were seen till Monday night. A report was made to him at 5:30, and an answering rocket was fired about 20 minutes to 6 P.M.

At this point the inquiry was adjourned till Tuesday next.

A Correspondent at Ramsgate telegraphed last night:—

"A bottle was washed ashore at St. Nicholas to-day, containing the following:—"Bremerhaven.—We are ashore one hour, every minute terrific thumping. One boat and passengers already gone. D. J. Behring, Bremerhaven. I believe we are lost. I depart in peace with my God and without any anxiety for you. Love to friends, children, and mother-in-law.—D. J. Behring." A case of silk washed ashore at St. Nicholas marked "W.S. and Co., Z." 360 cases of gloves have been washed ashore at Kingsgate. The Champion, lugger, of this port, boarded the vessel this morning and found several bodies."

We published yesterday lists which, on reading them together with the information given by the owners, appear to make the following numerical statements of the loss of life by the Deutschland approximately correct. The London agency of the North German Lloyd's informs us that 123 passengers and 90 or 100 crew sailed from Bremen. Taking the lower number of crew as correct, there were 213 souls on board the Deutschland when she struck. The names of persons saved, according to a revised list, makes the total number of passengers saved to be 85, and the crew 49, or 134 in all. August Beck, who drifted to Sheerness in one of the lifeboats, lives also, and so out of 213 we have 135 survivors. As many human beings' lives as 78 appear, therefore, to have been lost. Doubt and difficulty in the enumeration arise from the different ways in which children may be reckoned, either as persons or as fractions of families. The number in the first and second classes are likely to vary by exchanges, which are made on payment of a higher fare at the last moment or in the course of the voyage. The English pilot is safe, but he probably did not enter into the enumeration of the persons on board. The owners offer to all the wrecked who desire to proceed a passage in their next steamer, the Mosel, which is to leave

Southampton on Monday: and they have now, being uninsured, advertised the Deutschland as she lies for sale by private contract.

The following is a revised list of persons saved among the passengers only. . . .

The Times, Saturday, December 11, 1875, page 7.

THE LOSS OF THE DEUTSCHLAND
(From Our Own Reporter)

HARWICH, Friday.

The bodies of the four German nuns were removed today for interment at a convent of the Franciscan order, to which they belonged, near Stratford. They were from a convent in Westphalia. Most of the surviving passengers and crew left Harwich to-day. One engaging little girl, of German parentage, but American born, passed the terrible night of Monday in her father's arms, but seemed little the worse now for the cold and exposure, and, with the happy forgetfulness of childhood, laughed and chattered as though she had passed through no such ordeal. Two or three passengers are still suffering from cold, and are confined to their beds at the various hotels. There is no serious case of illness, however. The body of one of the saloon passengers brought ashore yesterday has been identified, and will be taken in a shell to Bremen for interment. Mr. O. T. Williams, the German Consul here, has been instructed by the Consul-General in London that the Imperial Foreign Department at Berlin will defray all disbursements for the relief of the survivors, and that everything is to be done which is essential for their maintenance and comfort. They had, however, been well cared for before the receipt of those instructions, though they cannot even now understand how it is that with a big steamer stranded in such a beaten track, in easy reach of passing vessels, and within signaling distance of three lightships—the Kentish Knock, the Sunk, and the Cork lightships—thirty hours should have elapsed before they were rescued.

From the statements of survivors and evidence given by the captain and others, an account of the shipwreck was obtained, the first portion of which was published yesterday. What follows is the continuation of this narrative. Most of the passengers awoke by the breaking of the screw when the ship struck. They hurriedly dressed and came on deck. The danger, however, did not seem imminent, and the assurances of the captain and his officers, added to the intense cold and wet, soon sent them shivering alarmed below. At first some sail was set. The cargo in the forehold was thrown overboard. The male passengers were summoned at daylight on Monday to man the pumps, and worked them cheerily. After some hours' work, however, the vessel made so much water that Captain Brickenstein feared if she slipped off the bank into deep water she would go down like a stone. He therefore anchored. The boats were at first ordered to be cleared away, and the story of one who got away and was borne to Sheerness is already known. It was the captain's opinion, however, that no boats could live in such a sea, and he had confident hopes of a speedy rescue. After daylight the remaining serviceable boats were not used. They were, I believe, three in number, including a lifeboat. And now comes the most remarkable and pitiable chapter in a sad story. Rockets were thrown up directly the Deutschland struck; in the blinding snowstorm, however, they no doubt were invisible to the lightships. But Monday was a tolerably clear day; passing vessels were distinctly seen from the Deutschland's deck, and every effort was made to attract their intention [sic]. The passengers and crew watched those vessels, two of them steamers, hoping that each of them had seen, or must soon see, the signal of distress. But one after another passed by and night came on. All this time the passengers had not suffered materially. It is possible that a few may have been washed overboard as they first hurried on deck after the vessel struck. But after the first shock they kept up their spirits well. Plenty to eat and drink was served out to them, and the work to which the male passengers were put was useful in diverting their thoughts, but it became known that at night the rising tide and rough sea would imperil all on board. At night, therefore, rockets were thrown up once more, and this time they were answered from the Sunk Light, a lightship to the south-east of the wreck. The signals at the Sunk Light were repeated by the men at the Cork Lightship, which is situated still near [sic] to Harwich, and after some time they were answered by the coastguard at Harwich. But there is no lifeboat at Harwich, and whether from this cause or not, although on Monday night it was known at Harwich that a vessel was in distress, no help was tendered till ·daylight on Tuesday morning. Some of the jury on Thursday expressed the belief that if a lifeboat had been stationed it might have been towed out to sea by the steam tug, and the two together might have saved the lives of nearly all on board the wreck. I have talked with the captain of the steam tug, who is represented to me, and no doubt is, a brave fellow, ready to risk his life in any hopeful enterprise. But the Kentish Knock is 25 miles distant from Harwich, and the wreck is 27 miles distant. The Knock is approached from here by a difficult navigation, and Carrington, the captain of the tug, says that in thick weather, with such a sea as was running on Monday night the task of rescuing life at such a distance would have been hopeless even with a lifeboat. I have no doubt both these theories will be amply discussed hereafter. It is sad anyhow to know that these 200 fellow-creatures remained for some 30 hours so close to the English coast, passed by English vessels during the day, and their signals of distress seen and answered from the land at night, and that, notwithstanding, so many of them perished just at the last. I said that their situation first became perilous on Monday night or rather Tuesday morning. At 2 A.M., Captain Brickenstein, knowing that with the rising tide the ship would be waterlogged, ordered all the passengers to come on deck. Danger levels class distinctions, and steerage and first-class passengers were by this time together in the after saloon and cabins. Most of them obeyed the summons at once; others lingered below till it was too late; some of the ill, weak, despairing of life even on deck, resolved to stay in their cabins and meet death without any further struggle to evade it. After 3 A.M. on Tuesday morning a scene of horror was witnessed. Some passengers clustered for safety within or upon the wheelhouse, and on the top of other slight structures on deck. Most of the crew and many of the emigrants went into the rigging, where they were safe enough as long as they could maintain their hold. But the intense cold and long exposure told a tale. The purser of the ship, though a strong man, relaxed his grasp, and fell into the sea. Women and children and men were one by one swept away from their shelters on the deck. Five German nuns, whose bodies are now in the dead-house here, clasped hands and were drowned together, the chief sister, a gaunt woman 6 ft. high, calling out loudly and often "O Christ, come quickly!" till the end came. The shrieks and sobbing of women and children are described by the survivors as agonizing. One brave sailor, who was safe in the rigging, went down to try and save a child or woman who was drowning on deck. He was secured by a rope to the rigging, but a wave dashed him against the bulwarks, and when daylight dawned his headless body, detained by the rope, was swaying to and fro with the waves. In the dreadful excitement of these hours one man hung himself behind the wheelhouse, another hacked at his wrist with a knife, hoping to die a comparatively painless death by bleeding. It was nearly 8 o'clock before the tide abated, and the survivors could venture to go on deck. At half-past 10 o'clock the tugboat from Harwich came alongside and brought all away without further accident. Most of the passengers are German emigrants, and it is only right to add that they have received here from the first the utmost kindness and sympathy.

The Times, Monday, December 13, 1875, page 9, column 4.

The light which has yet been thrown upon the wreck of the Deutschland is still scanty. We must wait for some time before we can form a fair estimate of the responsibilities of those who had charge of the ill-fated vessel when she went ashore. But the judgement which must be passed upon those who left her to her fate during a long winter's night and dismal morning is confirmed by the defence of their advocate, the Mayor of Harwich, whose inadequate excuses we publish in another column. The "painful surprise" with which the Mayor perused our observations upon the conduct of the municipality and seafaring population of Harwich was assuredly not so great as that with which the people of these kingdoms learnt that a wreck could be stranded off the English coast, appealing to English sailors for aid, and for thirty hours should be left without that aid. The Mayor of Harwich does not dispute a single one of the material statements on which the "painful surprise" of the nation has been founded, yet he is angry that we should have ventured to express an opinion on the subject until an inquiry before a Coroner had "brought all the circumstances to light." We do not want to disparage Coroner's inquests, but the facts which have excited universal indignation could hardly have been touched by any conclusions of a local jury as to the causes of the disaster. It is indisputable that there was no lifeboat at Harwich; that the Deutschland lay beaten by the waves on the Kentish Knock for thirty hours without receiving assistance in any shape, and that for one half that time, at least, the signals of distress were seen and recognized by the Harwich seamen. Can any severity of invective carry more condemnation than is involved in these shameful certainties?

Let us look first at the Mayor's excuses for the absence of a lifeboat. He "freely admits that such a necessity exists, and hopes before long that means will be found to supply the deficiency." We have no doubt of it, now that the scandal of the want has been published to the world, and has made Englishmen ashamed of such neglect and eager to remedy it. Indeed, Lord Strafford offers, in a letter we publish this morning, to bestow a lifeboat upon Harwich "provided the authorities of the town guarantee that it shall be properly housed, kept in good repair, and ready for any emergency with a skillful and experienced crew." Other liberal proposals have been tendered to Harwich, and now, we presume, one of them will be accepted. But we trust, if Lord Strafford's offer, or that of any other generous benefactor, find favour with the municipality of Harwich, the experience of "some years ago"—we quote from the Mayor's apology—may not be repeated, when "a lifeboat belonging to the port absolutely rotted to pieces without being once used." Then, it seems, there was a lifeboat and no tug to take the boat out to sea; now there is a tug, but no lifeboat. Nevertheless, according to the Mayor—who is borne out, indeed, by the witness belonging to the tug Liverpool who appeared before the Coroner on Saturday —the combination of appliances would have made little difference, for there was no determination to use them. The Mayor says, "It is not certain that even with a lifeboat the Liverpool or any tug would have proceeded 30 miles on such a night as that of Monday last." What is certain is that the Liverpool did not try; the Captain saw the rocket signals on Monday evening at 6 o'clock, and on Tuesday morning at 8 o'clock he made up his mind to steam out to the wreck. "He chose a prudent time to go out," said the Mate of the tug, without a thought of sarcasm. But, as a Juror remarked, the tug must often have gone out in much worse weather. On the night of Monday, however, the Liverpool was not driven back by stress of weather; she never attempted to stir outside the harbour. Yet the Captain was troubled with no such doubts as those which exercise the Mayor of Harwich about the significance of the rocket signals. "We knew all the previous night, from the rockets," says the Mate, "that there was a vessel in distress." Prudence is an admirable quality in its place and season; but the prudence of the Captain of the Liverpool, for whose services the Mayor of Harwich bespeaks our "thanks and praise," is hardly calculated at the present moment to excite enthusiasm. For the time the Mayor must be content to find his panegyric of the seamen of Harwich rather coolly appreciated.

There remains, however, a circumstance to which the Mayor of Harwich opportunely draws attention, and which, it may be hoped, will not escape close inquiry. In addition to the services of the Captain and crew of the tug Liverpool, the Mayor demands public gratitude and honour for other seamen of the port of Harwich who "have been saving materials and cargo from the ship." He alludes, no doubt, to the crews of the coasting smacks who do a steady business as 'salvors' along the East Coast, but whom it does not 'pay' to save lives when lives only are to be saved. These smacks are provided, it is said, with good lifeboats, and the Captain of the tug Liverpool insisted that they could render quicker and better assistance to a vessel in distress than any lifeboat stationed so far away as Harwich. They may not have seen the signals which were seen at Harwich; but no sooner had the Liverpool taken the survivors on board than a crowd of these 'salvors' descended upon the helpless steamer and revelled in pillage. It is alleged even that the bodies of the drowned did not escape. We are unwilling to pass censure upon a large class for what may have been the work of a few reckless men, but it is too clear that there is a leaven of lawlessness among the seafaring population of this coast which needs stern repression. Those who persisted in plundering and dismantling the vessel on Wednesday, after the owner's agents had boarded her and

given notice that she was not derelict, were simply wreckers, crimi-
nals of a type which we had hoped was eradicated in England. It is
shameful that where men were found in considerable numbers thus
bold enough to defy the law there were none found daring enough
to risk anything for the sake of saving life.

Lord Strafford's offer of a lifeboat will not probably interfere
with the employment of the other proposed benefactions for this
purpose. Some large subscriptions have already been promised, and
more will undoubtedly be forthcoming; nor, in spite of the adverse
opinion of Lloyd's Agent at Harwich, who two years ago decidedly
pronounced that a lifeboat for that port would be a "useless expense," is it likely that even the chance of coping with disasters
such as that of last week by means so simple will be neglected. Not
only at Harwich, but at other parts of the coast—at Clacton or
Walton, for instance—lifeboats might usefully be stationed. But no
mechanical appliances will be sufficient without two qualities in
which we should be sorry to think Englishmen wanting—courage
and common sense. In spite of the seemingly unfavourable evidence
the story of the Deutschland's loss affords, we refuse to believe that
the spirit of English seamen is extinct among the coasting population of Kent and Essex. But even courage by itself will be of little
worth. A lifeboat cannot be posted within sight of every point where
a wreck may happen. A very modest measure of intelligence is, however, enough to make mechanical aid and manly spirit serviceable.
Even on last Monday evening, when the rocket signals of the
Deutschland were perceived at Harwich, there was time to seek
elsewhere the lifeboat the want of which, we are assured, disabled the
Harwich men from going out to sea. If the people at Harwich had
telegraphed to Broadstairs, where a lifeboat was ready for service,
an attempt at all events might have been made to avert the terrible
loss of life which occurred eight or nine hours later. But there was
no mind, it seems, capable of suggesting an expedient so simple.

The Times, Monday, December 13, 1875, page 10, column 1.

. . . I can only record the fact that, while no salving smacks
came near the Deutschland during the 30 hours in which her 200
passengers and crew were in such sore need of help, the steamtug

Liverpool had hardly cleared from the wreck with the survivors before two or three of these smacks came swooping down, and must soon have been followed by others. Next day, when the tug went out again on the part of the owner's agents, 14 smacks and luggers were gathered round the wreck. Up to this time it may be said that the smacksmen had no reason to suppose that the steamer was not a derelict, given up by captain and crew as a total loss, and therefore the legitimate spoil of salvors in their own as well as the owners' interests. But the owners' agent and the third mate of the Deutschland went aboard on Wednesday, and found 50 or 60 men at work in the cabins and on deck, breaking open passengers' luggage, fishing cargo up out of the hold, stripping the saloon and cabins—in short, wrecking the ship. It was in vain that the mate and the owners' representative interposed and warned them off. The work of pillage—it can hardly be called by any other name—went on, and on Thursday, when the wreck was taken in charge by Captain Heathcote on behalf of the Marine Salvage Association, the wreckers had left little in the saloon and cabins worth carrying off, and had stripped the ship of braces, running gear, rigging, leaving, in fact, "hardly a ropeyarn." I wish this were the worst that had to be told. Twenty bodies have now been brought into Harwich by the steamtug. Mr. Guy, the inspector of police here, tells me that, with one exception, not a single valuable was found on the persons of these unfortunate people, and that it was clear their pockets had been turned out and rifled. There were ring-marks on the fingers of women, and of at least one gentleman. The rings themselves had disappeared. One poor fellow wore a second pair of trousers, and in a pocket of the inside pair there was a thaler and two smaller pieces of silver. Another body was brought ashore on Friday night. It was found wedged tight in one of the ventilators communicating with the funnel. The man may have been washed headforemost down the cowl, and his body could only be recovered by ropes used by the crew of the tugs. On his person was found a silver watch, with a pocketbook and papers, showing that his name was Carl Ernst Friedrich Conrad Schnepel. The other bodies were floating in the saloon or cabins, in which the smacksmen had been operating as I have described. No suspicion whatever rests on the crew of the tug. The inference, therefore, is unavoidable, and it is one which must be painful to all Englishmen. One of the bodies is said to have had on it a belt and pouch with a large sum of money and valuables, and, if so, all have disappeared. I have tried to state fairly the case as regards smacksmen, and forbear to give statements which have reached me as to their treatment of the bodies. But enough has been said to suggest whether on these occasions something cannot be done to prevent these scenes of lawlessness, which are only one or two degrees less disgraceful than the wrecking that used to disgrace some parts of our coast. In theory, all property received should, as I have said, be taken to the Receiver of Wreck. In practice, little or none of the valuable and portable salvage finds its way to this official. In the case of a British vessel the Receiver of Wreck is empowered to take immediate measures for the protection of property from wreckers and, I believe that Mr. Wood, who acts in that capacity at Harwich, would have been prepared to afford such assistance here, upon receiving a requisition. The presence in the harbour of a man-of-war, the Penelope, Commander Roberts, would have afforded facilities for such protection, and some of the men and marines of this ironclad, have indeed, since been employed at the wreck by the Marine Salvage Association. But the speediest and most effective means of prevention might have been afforded if the Admiralty had ordered a gunboat to follow the steamtug which was sent from Sheerness upon the first news of the catastrophe. I ought to add that the 14 smacks and luggers already mentioned hailed from the fishing village in the Colne river and from Whitstable, Ramsgate, and Margate. Two Harwich smacks which were also at the wreck have surrendered the property they brought ashore to the Receiver of Wreck, who gives the smacksmen of this port a high character for manliness and fairness of dealing with salvage since he had occasion to proceed against them some 15 years ago, when 17 of them were imprisoned for offences of this description.

The Times, Monday, December 13, 1875, page 10, column 2.

Four of the five nuns who perished by the wreck are to be buried at Leytonstone today. They belonged to a Franciscan nunnery in

Westphalia, and are regarded by their co-religionists in London as having been exiled from their native land in consequence of Falck Laws. When their deaths became known it was resolved by the authorities of the Roman Catholic Church in London to give the bodies solemn burial. For this purpose two Franciscan Fathers were despatched to Harwich, and the bodies were placed in oak coffins lined with white satin, and brought to London on Friday evening. On reaching Stratford they were delivered over to the care of the nuns at the Convent of Jesus and Mary, who assisted by the nuns of the Sacred Heart, prepared their dead sisters for burial. The dead nuns were wearing, with slight variation, the dress common to the order; and as there was found on each dress the number assigned to a nun in making her profession of religion, all will, no doubt, in this way be identified. After being made ready the bodies lay in state in the spacious schoolroom below the Franciscan church at Stratford throughout Saturday and yesterday. The open coffins lay side by side upon a raised dais, lighted candles were placed beside the coffins, while vases of flowers and wreaths of immortelles were grouped at the heads and feet. Upon both days large numbers of people visited the place, the major portion of whom appeared to be prompted by feelings of devotion. The deceased appeared to be between the ages of 30 and 40, and their faces wore an expression of calmness and resignation. Their fingers were clasped upon a rosary and crucifix; upon the breast of each lay a cross of white flowers, the gifts of the Ursuline nuns of Upton. One, noted for her extreme tallness, is the lady who, at midnight on Monday, by standing on a table in the saloon, was able to thrust her body through the skylight, and kept exclaiming in a voice heard by those in the rigging above the roar of the storm, "My God, my God, make haste, make haste." There will be a solemn mass (*coram archiepiscopo*) in the Franciscan church, Stratford, this morning at 11. Cardinal Manning will deliver a funeral oration over the deceased, after which they will be interred in St. Patrick's Catholic Cemetery, Leytonstone.

THE LOSS OF THE EURYDICE

The Times, Monday, March 25, 1878, page 9, column 6.

FOUNDERING OF HER MAJESTY'S
SHIP EURYDICE

Over Three Hundred Lives Lost.

We have received the following sad news from the Admiralty:—
"The Admiralty have received the following telegram from Admiral
Fanshawe, Commander-in-Chief at Portsmouth:—

" 'Have just received the following from coastguard, Ventnor:—[1]
Eurydice capsized off Dunnose, Cuddicombe, first class boy, and
Fletcher saved, Tabor, first lieutenant, very doubtful, Steamer go-
ing immediately.' "

"A further telegram states that she capsized in a sudden squall
at half past 4 this afternoon.

"A subsequent telegram states that Lieutenant Tabor and Colonel
Ferrier, R.E., are dead.

"The Eurydice was commissioned by Captain Hare, in February,
1877, as a training-ship for second-class ordinary seamen, and she
was returning to Spithead after a winter's cruise in the West Indies.

"The Admiral Commanding-in-Chief at Portsmouth has sent
steamers to search the vicinity of the accident, but no further report
has been received.

"Admiralty, Sunday, 11:30 P.M."

(By Telegraph.)
(From our Correspondent.)

VENTNOR, Sunday Evening.

Her Majesty's training-ship Eurydice capsized in a sudden squall off
Dunnose, Isle of Wight, at half-past 4 o'clock yesterday afternoon,
and went down at once. The schooner Emma, which was passing,
picked up five men, but some of these have since died. Cuddicombe,
a first-class boy, and Fletcher were saved, and Tabor, the first Lieu-

---

[1] Geographical location.

tenant, but it is very doubtful whether he will recover. The military engineer officer was drowned. The ship was commissioned at Portsmouth on the 7th of February, 1877, and was ordered to the West Indies. She was bound for Spithead, and was observed passing Ventnor a few minutes before the catastrophe with all sail set. A snow storm then came on very suddenly with very heavy gusts of wind. Probably no more men have been saved than those picked up by the schooner, as a strong ebb tide was running. The sun came out brilliantly after the squall, but nothing could be seen from the shore at Ventnor except a few large boxes being swept down the Channel, and certainly no boats. The schooner has been detained by Captain Roche, R.N., Inspecting Commissioner, St. Catherine's Division of the Coastguard, who went on board immediately with Ventnor doctors, and has telegraphed to the Admiral at Portsmouth to send round a steamer.

LATER.

Lieutenant Tabor is dead, and his body has been brought ashore, so that the only survivors, as far as is known, are Benjamin Cuddicombe of Plymouth, and Sidney Fletcher, of Bristol, first-class boy, aged 19. Cuddicombe states that the ship capsized in a squall and snowstorm five miles off Dunnose, about 4 o'clock. More than three hundred men were on board, all of whom, he believes, are lost except himself and Fletcher. Cuddicombe was among the last on the ship. Captain Hare was near him when the ship went down, sucking many with it. Cuddicombe and a man near him said that a vessel was close by when the squall came on, and, therefore, they would be surely picked up. He was over an hour in the water. Being a first rate swimmer, every one called out to him for help. He tried to assist two or three, but at least four clung to him, and he was obliged to kick them off. Was well taken care of by the master of the schooner and crew. The ship left Bermuda three weeks ago, passed the Lizard yesterday, and expected to anchor at Spithead about 5 o'clock.

These two men are well cared for at the Cottage Hospital, Bonchurch, and are under the care of Dr. Williamson of Ventnor, who considers them to be doing fairly well.

The Eurydice was a training-ship for ordinary seamen, and is officially described as "sixth rate. She was under the command of Captain Marcus Hare." Having left Bermuda on her return trip as recently as the 6th inst., she was not expected to reach Portsmouth for some days. Her consorts, the Martin and the Liberty, have arrived, the former at Portsmouth, and the latter at Plymouth.

The following list of officers aboard is given in the NAVY LIST:—Captain Marcus A. S. Hare: Lieutenants, Francis H. Tabor, Charles Y. Strange, William E. Black, Stanley A. Burney: Staff-Surgeon, James L. Whitney; Paymaster, Frank Pittman; Sub-Lieutenants, the Hon. Edward R. Gifford, Herbert S. Edmonds, Walter S. Smith, Sidney G. Randolph; Surgeon, Robert Murdoch, M.B.; gunner, Frederick Allen; boatswains, William Brewer, Joseph Warren; and assistant clerk, William Lamont.

The Times, Monday, March 25, 1878, page 9.

EDITORIAL

It is with deep concern that we have to announce the loss of one of HER MAJESTY'S ships. The Eurydice, a wooden sailing frigate, fitted out for the training of ordinary seamen, had just returned from her winter cruise in the West Indies, with a complement of more than 300 men and officers, and was on her way to Spithead. Yesterday afternoon she was observed passing Ventnor under full sail on her voyage up the Channel, when a sudden snow-storm came on, accompanied by heavy squalls of wind. When the storm cleared away the Eurydice was nowhere to be seen. She had been taken aback by a sudden shift of the wind or capsized by its unexpected force, and it is officially reported to the Admiralty that she has gone down with nearly all hands on board. A passing schooner picked up five men, among them the first lieutenant, who surv..ed only a short time; two only of those who were rescued are now alive, and there seems little or no hope that the lives of any others of the crew can have been saved. The weather cleared almost as suddenly as it had become foul, but nothing could be seen from Ventnor but a few large boxes rapidly carried away by a strong ebb tide, and no trace of a boat could be discerned. From the accounts which have reached us it is but too certain that there is nothing left of a well-found ship and a gallant crew but one or two survivors picked up more dead than alive.

It would be premature to attempt to divine the causes of the disaster, and very likely we shall never know much more than we do at present. Lieutenant Tabor, the only officer rescued, has since succumbed to the effects of exposure in yesterday's bitter weather, and we cannot hope for much information from the rescued survivors of a ship overtaken by so sudden a calamity. It is the first impulse of human nature, when such a disaster is reported, to throw the blame on some one, or, at any rate, to believe that the catastrophe might have been averted. It would be a grave injustice to a noble and gallant service like that of the British Navy to yield to such an impulse in a case like the present save on the clearest and most decisive evidence. The dangers of the sea are ever present; they come suddenly and unexpectedly, and the utmost vigilance cannot always be on its guard against them. At any rate, this is a case of purely maritime mishap. The Eurydice was not a new-fangled ironclad, whose capabilities and sea-going qualities were unfamiliar to her officers and crew, but a sailing frigate specially fitted out for the training of the ordinary seamen in the duties of ordinary seamanship. It has long been the practice of the Admiralty to send out the boys trained in the stationary training ships for a short cruise at sea in vessels appointed for the purpose. This has generally been done during the summer months, but a few years ago Mr. WARD HUNT determined that this valuable training should be continued during the winter, and the brigs in which it was carried on were sent either to join the Channel Fleet at Lisbon or on an independent cruise to the West Indies, in order to avoid the tempestuous and inclement weather prevalent on the English coasts. The Eurydice, a vessel twice the size of the ordinary brigs in use for this service, was fitted out last spring for a similar purpose, only, instead of being manned with drafts of boys direct from the training-ships, she received a crew of ordinary seamen—that is of youths just above the rating of boys, whom it was judged expedient to submit to a similar course of training in practical seamanship. The necessity for this kind of training is greater now than ever when a larger proportion of seamen in the Royal Navy have to serve much of their time in turret ships and other mastless vessels, where the specific duties of seamen are reduced to a "minimum." Thus manned and suitably equipped the Eurydice, accompanied by two of the ordinary training brigs, was dispatched on a cruise to the West Indies. She was coming home in ordinary course, and was yesterday on her way to Spithead, when, almost in sight of port, she was overwhelmed with sudden disaster. The loss to the country of so many gallant men is severe, and at this juncture especially it will be keenly felt; but our sympathies are first of all due to the friends and relatives of those who in the very moment of buoyant hopes and confident expectations of a happy return to their homes have thus been suddenly swept to their doom.

It is but a trite reflection, perhaps, that the perils of the sea are ever present, but such a disaster as has befallen the country brings the reflection home with a new and real force. Soldiers are only called upon to fight when their country is at war, but sailors the moment they are put to sea are forever face to face with an enemy vigilant, remorseless, and at times, irresistible. It is this, no doubt, that gives the seafaring life its charm for adventurous spirits, but it should also quicken the sympathies of those who stay at home and are tempted to repeat complacently the well-worn burden of "Suave mari magno" as often as the wind howls and the storm rages. Every Englishman who loves his country and is grateful to those who defend it will feel a personal grief at the loss of the Eurydice, and will acknowledge that those who went down with her died at their posts, and were serving their country as if they had been actually fighting in the cause. After all, there is no nobler end for a brave man than to die in the service of his country, and the friends of those who are gone will be consoled, even at this bitter moment of their grief, by the conviction that the country shares their sorrow, and is not unmindful of the sacrifices which those who serve her either in person or through their kith and kin are daily called upon to make in her behalf.

The Times, Tuesday, March 26, 1878, page 6, column 1.

Parliamentary Intelligence.

House of Lords, Monday, March 25th

LORD SUDELEY wished to ask the noble lord who represented the Admiralty in that House whether he could afford their lordships any further information with respect to the foundering of the Eurydice.

LORD ELPHINGSTONE said it was with deepest regret he had to confirm the sad report which had appeared in the morning papers. That account was correct in every particular. Yesterday afternoon, in a snowstorm, the Eurydice foundered within two miles and a half of the Isle of Wight, with over 300 men and boys on board. Only two boys were saved of the entire number of officers and crew. Since he came into the House he had received a statement which enabled him to give their lordships some particulars as to the Eurydice. She was originally a 26-gun frigate, built by Admiral Elliot for the purpose of competing with the well-known ships built by Sir E. Symonds. She was in every respect a most excellent and seaworthy ship. She was first commanded by the present Sir G. Elliot, and subsequently by Captain O. Tarleton, on the West Indian station. When last year it was decided by Mr. Ward Hunt to employ in training-ships the second-class ordinary seamen attached to the reserves in home-ports, the Eurydice, after repairs by White, of Cowes, was fitted out for a training ship, 22 out of her 26 guns having been removed, four having been left for the purposes of exercise. . . . The officers were especially selected. She was commissioned by Captain Hare in February 1877. That gallant officer had been in command of the Boscawen, the training ship for boys at Portland. Lieutenant Tabor had been a lieutenant of the Narcissus from 1870 to 1872, when she was flagship of the Flying Squadron, during which time he kept watch, the ship having been nearly always under sail. He was afterwards first lieutenant of the Cruiser, sailing ship, which was used in the training of ordinary seamen in the Mediterranean, in which ship he served three years and a half. The other lieutenants were selected for their promising characters. The Eurydice had been on a cruise to the

West Indies, for which station she left England in November, 1877. Her crew consisted of her proper complement of officers and petty officers, who were permanent, and of as many ordinary seamen as she could carry with comfort. She carried the same ballast as on former occasions, a rather larger quantity of water, and her rig was the same as before, but she carried two 64-pounder guns on the main deck and none on her after-deck. The wreck lay in 11 fathoms of water, two miles and a half east-north-east from Dunnose, with half of her topsails and rigging above water. From an examination made on the rigging it was concluded that the crew were engaged in shortening sail when the accident occurred, as the fore and main sheets and main-topsail halyards were found let go, and the fore-topmast studding sail was partly taken in. No bodies or wreckage had been found beyond what were picked up at first. What actually occurred at the time of the foundering the Admiralty did not know, and it was doubtful whether any light would be turned on it. He would not be doing justice to his own feelings, nor, he was sure, to those of their lordships, if he did not express deep and sincere regret at the occurrence and sympathy for the friends and relatives —some of whom he feared, were parents—of those who had been lost.

(Hear, hear.)

The Times, Tuesday, March 26, 1878, page 10, cols. 1 and 2.

The wreck of the Eurydice, the training-ship for young ordinary seamen, off the Isle of Wight, and almost within sight of Spithead, for which place she was standing, at the end of a pleasant and successful cruise to the West Indies, is a disaster which calls vividly to mind the loss of the Captain off Cape Finisterre. With this exception, there is nothing to compare with the calamity which occurred on Sunday afternoon, so far as the Navy is concerned, though the loss of life has frequently been exceeded by the sinking of emigrant vessels. . . . So far as can be ascertained the Eurydice had 368 souls on board at the time, though this is very much a matter of conjecture, as, besides her own officers and crew, she was bringing home a number of military officers, supernumeraries, and invalids from the West Indies. Hence considerable uncertainty exists both as to the names and numbers of the officers. The Eurydice was a wooden sailing, fully-rigged ship of 921 tons displacement, and was at one time considered one of the smartest and quickest 26-gun frigates in the service. She was built about 1843. . . .

The Eurydice left Bermuda on the 6th inst., and nothing was heard of her until she was seen by the coastguard at Bonchurch at 3:30 on Sunday afternoon, bearing for Spithead under all plain sail, and with her port stunsails set on the foretopmast and main-topmast, the object being clearly to arrive at the anchorage at Spit-head before night fall. There was an ominous stillness prevailing at this time. A heavy bank of clouds was coming down from the north-west, and the glass was falling rapidly. . . . At ten minutes to 4 the wind suddenly veered round from the west to the eastward, and a gale, accompanied by a blinding fall of snow came rushing from the highlands down Luccombe Chine, striking the Eurydice just a little below the beam, driving her out of her course, which was heading to the north-east, and turning her bows to the east. This is what seems probable, though, from the manner in which the sea was concealed by snow, nothing was seen of her at the supreme moment when she capsized to starboard. The air cleared as suddenly as it became overcast, the wind sinking away at the same time. As soon as anything could be seen, the masts and top-hamper of the ship were discerned above the water about 2¾ miles E.N.E. off Dunnose, a well-known and lofty landmark between Shanklin and Ventnor. The ship lies in 11 fathoms of water, and from her position she appears to have righted in going down. Of the whole number of souls on board, only two persons, as already reported, succeeded in reaching the shore alive. These are an able seaman named Benjamin Cuddiford, a native of Plymouth, and Sydney Fletcher, an ordinary first-class seaman, aged 19, belonging to Bristol. Lt. Tabor died before reaching the shore. . . . Much surprise has been caused at the small number rescued, the more especially as the time being at hand for the changing of the watch a great many men would be on deck at the time. Ordinary seamen are also taught swimming as part of their training for the sea. No doubt numbers threw themselves overboard when the ship capsized and were sucked down by the ship and carried out to sea by the tide; but there is good reason for supposing that the majority succumbed through becoming chilled by the cold.

Captain Langworthy Jenkin, master of the Emma, schooner, bound from Newcastle for Poole with coals, was the means of rescuing the survivors, and has brought his ship into Portsmouth to give particulars. He states that at 45 minutes past 4 on Sunday afternoon, after a heavy squall, the atmosphere cleared and he observed some wreckage and the royals of a ship flapping above the water. He also fancied he heard some one shouting for assistance. He sent a man into the rigging to look out, who reported that he saw a man floating in the water with a cork jacket. He immediately made sail and stood towards him. Having to tack once to fetch him, he hoisted out boats, which picked up four men, and one man was picked up from the ship. . . . The Coastguard boat afterwards came alongside with Commander Roach, who recognized the body of Lt. Tabor. . . .

The boy Fletcher is too weak to furnish full particulars of the sad affair. He states, however, that he was below with the greater part of the crew, when, hearing a noise, he rushed up the hatchway and heard a cry, "All hands for themselves." He caught a life buoy and jumped overboard, as did also the rest who were picked up. A minute afterwards the ship gave a lurch forward and sank, drawing him down to a considerable distance, but the life buoy raised him again. In an account given by Cuddiford it is stated that the ship capsized in a squall and snow storm at as nearly as he can state 4 o'clock in the afternoon, when they were five miles from Dunnose. There were over 300 men on board, all of whom, except himself and Sydney Fletcher, who belonged to the Rover, were, he thought, drowned. He was one of the last to leave the ship. The captain was standing near him at the time the ship went down after capsizing. When she sank she carried down with her a large number of men who were clinging to her. A man near him said that a vessel was close by when the squall came on, and that they were all sure to be soon picked up. He was more than an hour in the water, being a first-rate swimmer, and very many of his messmates called out to him for assistance. He tried to help two or three; but at last, as he found there were four clinging to him, he was eventually obliged to kick them off. The survivors were well taken care of by the master of the schooner and crew. . . .

Prior to leaving Portsmouth, Cuddiford made an important statement to Admiral Foley of the circumstances attending the wreck. He said:—

"At 7 bells on Sunday afternoon, the 24th inst., the watch at a quarter to 4 o'clock was called to take in lower studding sails. I was on deck to tend the lower tack, and let it go. The captain gave orders to take in the upper sails. The wind was then freshening. The captain ordered the men to come down from aloft and then to let go the topsail halliards. The gunner's mate let go the topsail halliards, and another man, Bryant, let go the mainsail. The water was then running over the lee netting on the starboard side, and washed away the cutter. The foretopmast studding sail was set. The wind was about a point abaft the port beam. I caught hold of the main truss, fell, and caught hold of the weather netting and got the ship's side. We could see her keel. She righted a little before going down, bringing the mizzen topsail out of the water. She then went gradually over from forward, the greater part of the hands being at the fore part of the ship outside. She then turned over, bringing the port cutter bottom upwards. I and another, Richards, cut the foremost gripe, and then saw the captain standing on the vessel's side near the quarter boat and the two doctors struggling in the water. I swam some distance, keeping over my head a life-buoy, which I found, and then picked up some piece of wreck, which I gave to some of the men in the water. I then came across the copper punt full of water, five men were in it. The sea capsized the punt, and they all got on the bottom. They asked me if there was any sign of help. I told them the best thing they could do was keep their spirits up. One of them was letting go his hold of the punt. I do not know his name. I next saw Mr. Brewer, the boatswain, with a cork lifebelt on. He was struggling strongly. I then saw Fletcher in the water with a cork belt and breaker. I lost sight of him during the snow. About five minutes afterwards the weather cleared up. I saw Fletcher again, and we kept together. Then we saw land, finding it too rough, we turned our backs to the land and saw a schooner. The schooner bore down on us, sent a boat, and picked up two officers that I had not previously noticed with a wash-deck locker. A rope's end was thrown to me from the schooner, and I was then picked up. I judge that I was in the water one hour and 20 minutes. The officers picked up were Lt. Tabor and a captain of the Royal Engineers who came on board at Bermuda with one corporal, one bombardier, four privates, and the servant of an officer of the Royal Engineers. The ship capsized about 10 minutes before 4 o'clock. The captain was giving orders at the time, and was carrying out his duty. We rounded on the weather beam, and set the lower studding-sail, at 2 P.M. The ship was then going 8½ knots. I don't know who was the officer of the watch, as the captain was carrying on the duty. The Hon. Mr. Gifford went to the wheel to help at the time the water was coming over the lee nettings in consequence of an order being given to put the helm up. There were the following supernumeraries on board: . . . I believe some of the maindeck ports were open to let in the air to the main deck mess. I don't think the hands were turned up; there was hardly time for that. I saw most of the men forward take off their clothes and jump off before I lost sight of them in the squall. When the snow cleared up the ship was gone down."

During yesterday the Commander-in-Chief was in constant communication with Her Majesty and in the course of the day received the following telegrams from the Queen. The first, which came direct from Her Majesty, was in the following terms:—

"The Queen is deeply grieved to hear of the loss of the Eurydice. Her Majesty anxiously asks for further details."

The second was transmitted to the First Lord of the Admiralty, and was to the following effect:—

"The Queen would ask Mr. Smith to make known her grief at the terrible calamity to the Eurydice, and her heartfelt sympathy with the afflicted friends and relatives."

In another telegram to Mr. Smith the Queen said the telegrams had caused her the greatest grief. These telegrams, having been forwarded to Admiral Fanshawe, were promptly posted at the dockyard gates, where they were eagerly read by sympathetic crowds.

. . . Admiral Foley visited the wreck in the course of the afternoon, and from an examination of the rigging and gear of the ship he is firmly of the opinion that the crew were in the act of shortening sail at the time the ship sank. . . . The squall, however, was evidently too sudden and powerful for the crew to relieve the ship in time. There is also reason for concluding that the ports on both sides were open, and that the water rushed in on the starboard side, which prevented the ship from righting and pulled her over. . . . No attempt has yet been made to penetrate below decks. It is expected that a month will elapse before the ship can be raised and brought into harbour. No more bodies have been recovered. . . . There is deep and widespread grief throughout the town.

A profound sensation was created at Chatham . . . as the relatives of several of the seamen on board the ship live in that district. . . .

The Times, Wednesday, March 27, 1878, page 10, column 2.

The inquest on the bodies of Francis Hope Tabor . . . and Bennett, an ordinary seaman, was opened yesterday at 1 o'clock at the Queen's Hotel. . . .

Robert Montague Tabor; of Carshalton, Surrey, has seen the bodies viewed by the jury. One of them was that of his brother, Francis Hope Tabor. He was a naval lieutenant. He last saw him alive about six months ago, in Kent. He was First Lt., and was on his way from Bermuda on board the Eurydice. He was expected home daily when he heard of his death. He would be 30 in July.

Benjamin Cuddeford [*sic*] was next examined. He said that . . . Between half-past 3 and 4 o'clock the port watch was called to take in the lower stunsail, as the weather looked dirty. The captain gave orders to "watch in" lower stunsail. It was just coming on to blow. The sail was taken in, and then orders were given to take in the royals. The royals were lowered, but not furled at this time. The captain gave orders to let go the topsail halyards and the mainsheet. Witness saw this order was done himself. He heard the captain say, "If you can't let it go, cut it." He did not know to what this referred. The water was up to the men's waists on the starboard side. He expected that the order referred to the fore sheet. . . . He climbed to the quarter-deck netting over the ship's side on the weather side. He there could see the ship's keel and the sails in the water. . . . He stuck to the ship, and the captain gave orders to get the fore cutter clear, but we were only able to get one gripe clear by cutting it with a knife. The captain was beside me at the time. A man named Richards who was assisting me was washed away and the cutter was not got clear, because the water was encroaching upon us. Witness then jumped overboard and passed the two doctors who were drowning, but could render them no assistance. There were many others in the water at the time. He swam to a round lifebuoy and then to the aid of the others, taking them pieces of spars and wreck. The vessel went down immediately after he jumped overboard, the captain being on deck. . . . They were not tacking when the gale struck them, the wind being on their beam. This was between half-past 3 and 4. They had had no warning that the storm was coming on. . . . The wind caught them from the same direction it had been blowing previously. . . .

By Mr. Harvey.—As soon as the captain saw the storm coming, he ordered the stunsail, the largest sail in the ship, to be taken in. The men were ordered down because it was feared that the topgallant mast and royal mast might fall upon them. It was necessary for the men's safety that they should come down. . . . It was a sudden gust which sent her over without any warning. As one of the ship's company, he did not expect that any such thing would occur. The captain stood on the ship's side after she heeled over. Everything was done to save the ship and the men's lives by the captain. There was no want of seamanship in the management of the ship. The captain and officers were all able seamen. During the whole time he had been in the service, now 21 years, he had never witnessed so quick a storm. . . .

Sydney Fletcher, just turned 19, an ordinary first-class seaman on board the Eurydice, was next called. He stated he had been with her during the last six months. He was below during Sunday afternoon. He was getting his tea to come on at eight bells (4 o'clock), when he heard a rush of water coming through the port. He had just before felt the ship give a lurch. He lowered the aft por [sic] and ran on deck when he saw the water coming in over her lee nettings. He assisted another man to overhaul the fore topsail halyards. He then got over the weather netting and walked aft on the quarter on the ship's side. The ship was on her side at the time, and he walked below her ports. He could see the keel of the ship out of the water. The wind was blowing and the snow was falling. The main yard was touching the water. The captain was standing on the quarter giving orders. . . . He saw that the sails were set when he came on deck, but he could not tell their state. He did not observe that the weather had changed before the water came in. Of the whole starboard watch only about two men and a boy came up beside himself. They were all making a row, crying and screaming. The reason why he escaped was that he was close to the hatchway. . . . From what he had seen he thought there were about 24 lifebelts on board, but he did not see many of them in use. They could not be readily got at, the majority being kept in the pinnaces. On ordinary occasions when the ship was sailing they could readily be got at, but not on Sunday in the condition the ship was in. (The lifebelts having been painted the day before, they were hanging over the side.) . . .

George Parkinson, able seaman, deposed that he was aboard the schooner. He saw the Eurydice before the storm came on. All the sail was out on the Eurydice, so far as he could see, when he first saw her. He did not consider she had too much sail for her safety. After the squall came on he could not see anything and he never saw the ship again. . . .

The jury, after being absent from the room about half an hour, announced their agreement in the following verdict:—

"We find that Louis J. C. Ferrier, Francis Hope Tabor, and Bennett were accidentally drowned owing to the capsizing of Her Majesty's ship Eurydice by a sudden squall off Dunnose on Sunday, the 24th inst., and the jury consider from the evidence that no blame whatever can be attached to the captain, officers, and men of the ship."

———

The Times, Wednesday, March 27, 1878, page 10, column 4.

To the Editor.

Sir: Perhaps you will allow me, as, doubtless, one of the last to see the Eurydice before she went down to describe her to you as I observed her within half an hour or so of that fatal event. . . . Between 3 and 4 on Sunday afternoon I was walking with a friend along the cliff from Shanklin to Sandown, a stiff gale was blowing at the time, and it was as much as we could do to keep our feet. Some half-dozen vessels were plainly visible in the Channel. One of them especially attracted our attention, a fine-looking ship—the Eurydice, as she has since turned out to be—keeping very close into land, carrying full sail, and bowling along in magnificent style at the rate of some nine or nine-a-half knots. Her royals were set, her studding sails were set; in a word, she had crammed on every stitch of canvas she had it in her power to carry. There was no mistake about this. . . . I remarked to my companion on the vast amount of canvas she was carrying, and observed that I feared, unless she shortened sail, as we observed other vessels doing, she might come to harm. This was about 20 minutes to 4 for by mere chance I happened to look at my watch at the time. We were then near Sandown. A very few minutes afterwards a sudden squall struck us, accompanied by a blinding snow storm, which effectually shut out the vessel from our view. I saw nothing more of her till yesterday morning, when, as I sat at breakfast, I saw her foremast and mainsail with the top spars broken off, and with sails set, standing out of water two miles or so from Sandown beach.

It is very likely that poor Capt. Hare, a gallant officer and one who ever had the credit of being a careful seaman, did not observe in time, through being under the lee of the tall cliffs, the signs of ill-omen in the heavens which were so plainly discernible on land. There is not a doubt that he did observe those signs at last, and that he gave orders to shorten sail accordingly. Those orders however came too late, and result is the record in our naval history of a painful sequel to the story of the Captain.

London, March 26, VIATOR.

The Times, Thursday, March 28, 1878, page 10, column 3.

Although the Coroner's jury has agreed in finding a verdict exonerating the captain, officers, and crew of the Eurydice from any culpability as regards the loss of the ship, it has been noticed that they expressly do so from the evidence that was adduced before them, and as this consisted necessarily of the statements of the able seaman Cuddiford, and the ordinary seamen [sic] Fletcher, a mere lad, who was below at the time the ship was struck, it is thought that further investigation into the circumstances of the wreck is called for. A Naval Court of Inquiry will be held on board the Duke of Wellington at Portsmouth. . . . The great difficulty is to account for Capt. Hare crowding his vessel with canvas at a time when the falling of the barometer showed that bad weather was at hand, and after other ships had shortened sail. There has been no rumours [sic] of panic, but it is thought that the efforts of the officers at the supreme moment of being struck may have been partly arrested by the fact that the ship was manned by ordinary seamen who were comparatively inexperienced. It is also regarded as unusual that a ship with all her canvas spread and cutting through the water at about nine knots should have had her lee ports open. Had the ports been closed, or had they been closed as soon as the squall was noticed, it is thought that the ship would have righted herself after being struck, even had there been no time to lower the halliards and shorten sail.

The Times, April 1, 1878, page 11, column 3.

Saturday was another blank day so far as the clearing of the wreck of the Eurydice was concerned. The wind blew all day strongly and coldly from the north, and the dockyard tugs did not leave their moorings. . . .

The more the matter of the foundering of the training ship is discussed the more necessary seems the holding of a naval inquiry, for the purpose of clearing up questions which were not submitted to the jury at Ventnor and which only a Court of professional and scientific experts will be able to fully appreciate. With reference, indeed, to one very important point, the jury were clearly misinformed. The boy, Fletcher, from what he had heard among his messmates, was under the impression that the ballast of the ship was principally composed of the water which was stored below for drinking and cooking purposes, and of the usual stores of the ship. At the end of the voyage, of course, the weight of the water and stores would be much diminished, and hence had they

constituted the main ballast of the Eurydice, her stability would
have been greatly affected by their exhaustion. To rebut this evidence, the able seaman, Cuddeford [*sic*], was recalled by the Admiralty agent, and he said that the ship had the proper amount of
ballast for her tonnage and that her lower tier of water tanks was
never disturbed. This was considered satisfactory by the jury, but it
has since been discovered from drawings that the ship was not fitted
with a second tier of tanks. It is not, however, believed by professional persons at Portsmouth that the reduction in the weight of
water in stores would seriously lessen the stability of the ship. The
utmost difference which the loss during the voyage would make
in the draught of the Eurydice would be about eight or ten inches,
the only practical result of which would be to make her a little more
"lively." In order to clear up the question of the amount of water
in the ship at the time of foundering Admiral Foley has instructed
the divers to measure the contents of the tanks as soon as they are
reached; but as they have been filled with sea water, it is not considered likely that their present condition will afford any guidance
as to their state on Sunday, the 24th ult.

The midship section of the ship shows that the ports were just
about 6 ft. above the water line, and that the comparatively small
heel of 18 deg. would bring the ports under water and prevent the
vessel righting.

Yesterday, at Portsmouth, reference was made to the sudden
calamity in most of the pulpits, and in several of the churches col-
lections were made on behalf of the friends and relatives of the
seamen.

The Times, Monday, April 2, 1878, page 10, column 2.

Yesterday, the Lord Mayor received over 400 pounds at the
Mansion house in aid of the fund now being raised there for the
relief of the widows, orphans, and relatives of the crew of her
Majesty's ship, Eurydice. . . .

At a meeting of the Town Council of Edinburgh held yesterday,
the Lord Provost said he wished to draw attention to the loss of Her
Majesty's ship, Eurydice, by which numerous families were rendered

comparatively destitute through the death of their bread-winners. It was a matter which called for the sympathy of the public, and he was sure they would have pleasure in using every endeavor to alleviate, as far as possible, the consequence of the calamity. He proposed that intimation should be made that subscriptions in behalf of the widows and orphans would be received by the City Chamberlain or himself. The motion was agreed to.

A CHRONOLOGICAL HOPKINS BIBLIOGRAPHY

NORMAN WEYAND, S.J.

Introduction

The bibliography here presented is intended to be comprehensive but by no means exhaustive. Since it is inevitable that many valuable titles are missing, I shall be happy to receive information on these. The items listed range from those of a definitely scholarly type to others representative of the writing of students, from studies published in highly academic journals to those appearing in periodicals of a primarily devotional character. This variety of entries should manifest, if nothing else, the widespread interest which exists in the poet Gerard Manley Hopkins and the great appeal which he has to readers of varied types.

The entries are arranged in chronological order, as such an order will indicate the noteworthy growth of interest in Hopkins; it should, further, present an historical perspective to the development of the study of Hopkins. For purposes of ready reference, however, an alphabetical index of the authors listed is added.

Unfortunately, I do not possess complete bibliographical information on every title at this time of publication. Yet it seems better to include certain incomplete entries—those, for example, without the page numbers of the journals in which the articles appear—rather than to omit them entirely.

Although the studies in the volume were originally written for publication in 1944, the centennial of the poet's birth, the bibliographical entries extend to items which appeared before the end of 1946. So many valuable writings appeared during the period from 1944 to 1946 that it was evident that with the delayed publication of the volume these later entries should be given.

Some early anthologies which include poems of Hopkins and comment on the same, as well as a few significant later ones, are here listed. To include all such anthologies which have appeared in recent years would have been a useless labor, since the well-known textbooks and general anthologies which present poems of Hopkins with comment are almost innumerable.

The large number of people, both here and in Great Britain, who have contributed entries to this bibliography forbids the naming of most of those who deserve credit. Yet, the names of some who have consistently aided the compilation in various ways cannot be passed over. Father Schoder has sacrificed countless hours to the work. The following three members of religious orders all contributed most valuable help: Sister Marian Raphael Carlson, S.H.N. (whose doctoral dissertation *Gerard Manley Hopkins and His Critics* I was happy to direct); Sister Mary Roberta, S.S.N.D., who, in addition to providing the unusual portrait of Hopkins which serves as our frontispiece, has helped much toward the completeness of the bibliography; and Sister Thomasine, S.S.J., who has ever been alert in submitting references which might otherwise have been missed.

Four of my recent graduate students should also be listed for their services—Sister Ann Carol, O.P., and the Misses Nancy Swarva, Mary Ann Anderson, and Jacqueline Krump—as well as Miss Helen Printy and Fathers Paul Crane (of Oxford, England), Joseph G. Milunas, Edward L. Surtz (who completed a pioneer Master's thesis on Hopkins when material on the poet was very limited), and J. Barry Dwyer, all of the Society of Jesus.

Only one who has done intensive bibliographical work can realize the difficulties inherent in a project of this kind. Fully conscious of the deficiencies of this compilation, I present it as a

working basis for further study in Hopkins bibliography. I trust
that it will be useful to students of the poet until I or another
can offer a more complete work in the field.

In the bracketed comments referring to Hopkins' own published writings and to Father Lahey's life of the poet, the abbre-
viations explained in the beginning of this volume are used; for
example, "B" stands for *The Letters of Gerard Manley Hopkins
to Robert Bridges,* "P" for *Poems of Gerard Manley Hopkins*
and "Life" for the book *Gerard Manley Hopkins, A Life,* by
Gerald F. Lahey, S.J.

WRITINGS BY
GERARD MANLEY HOPKINS

1863

"Winter with the Gulf Stream," *Once a Week* VIII (Feb. 14),
p. 210. [Text in P, pp. 143–44.]

1881

Stonyhurst Magazine I No. II, (July), p. 35. [Latin verse rendering of Dryden's "Epigram on Milton." Text in B, p. 317.]

1882

"A Curious Halo," *Nature* XXVII (Nov. 16), p. 53 [Letter on unusual sunset. Text in D, p. 161.]

1883

[Pen-name Bran], "A Trio of Triolets," *Stonyhurst Magazine* I No.
IX, (Mar.), p. 162. [Three humorous poems. Text of two in B,
p. 317; P, p. 87.]
"Shadow-Beams in the East at Sunset," *Nature* XXIX (Nov. 15),
p. 55. [Letter on recent phenomenon. Text in D, pp. 161–62.]

1884

Nature XXIX (Jan. 3, pp. 222–23.) [Letter on recent remarkable sunset. Text in D, pp. 162–66.]

1885

In Thomas Arnold, *A Manual of English Literature Historical and Critical*, 5th ed., (London: Longmans), pp. 470–71. [Biographical and literary notice of R. W. Dixon. Text in D, pp. 177–78.]

1886

"Songs from Shakespeare in Latin," ("Full Fathom Five"), *Irish Monthly* XIV, p. 628.

1887

"First Fruits" in R. W. Dixon, *Bible Birthday Book* (London: Routledge), entry for May 25. [First stanza of "Morning Midday and Evening Sacrifice." Text in P, p. 45.]
"Songs from Shakespeare in Latin" ("Come unto These Yellow Sands"), *Irish Monthly* XV, p. 92.

1890

"Ad Mariam," *Blandyke Papers* XXVI (May), p. 130. [Text in P, pp. 144–45.]

1893

"Habit of Perfection" [partial text], "The Starlight Night," "Spring," "The Candle Indoors," "Spring and Fall," "Inversnaid," "To seem the stranger . . .," "Justus quidem es . . .," "To R. B.," "Thee, God, I come from . . .," "A Vision of the Mermaids," in Alfred H. Miles, *Poets and Poetry of the XIXth Century* (London: Hutchinson), vol. 8, pp. 161–70. [Texts in P, pp. 8–9, 26–7, 27, 46, 50, 52, 65, 68–9, 69, 91, 130–34.]

1894

"Ad Mariam," reprinted in *Stonyhurst Magazine*, V No. LXXII (Feb.), p. 233 ff.

1895

"Mary Mother of Divine Grace Compared to the Air We Breathe," in Henry C. Beeching, *Book of Christmas Verse* (London: Methuen), p. 121. [Text in P, pp. 56–60.]

"Heaven-Haven," "God's Grandeur," "Morning Midday and Evening Sacrifice," "Barnfloor and Winepress," "Thee, God, I come from . . .," in Henry C. Beeching, *Lyra Sacra*: A Book of Religious Verse (London: Methuen), pp. 313–16, 354. [Texts in P, pp. 8, 26, 45, 135–36, 91.]

1898

"Rosa Mystica," *Irish Monthly* XXVI (May), p. 234. [Text in P, pp. 146–47.]

1900

In Basil Champney, *Memoirs and Correspondence of Coventry Patmore* (London: Geo. Bell), vol. II, pp. 345–55. [Several letters to Coventry Patmore. Text in F, pp. 188–90, 198–202, 210–13, 214–15, 217, 218–20, 231–35, 237–41, 244–45.]

1902

"Mary Mother of Divine Grace Compared to the Air We Breathe," "Rosa Mystica," reprinted in Orby Shipley, *Carmina Mariana*: An English Anthology of Verse in Honour of and in Relation to the Blessed Virgin Mary, Second Series (London: Burns and Oates), pp. 183–89.

1903

"Heaven-Haven," *Living Age* CCXXXVI (Jan. 10), p. 128.

1906–07

"The Diary of a Devoted Student of Nature," *Letters and Notices*, (Apr. 1906; Apr., Oct. 1907). [Extracts from Hopkins' Journal, edited by John George MacLeod, S.J. Text in N., pp. 105, 217.]

1909

In J. Keating, S.J., "Impressions of Father Gerard Hopkins, S.J.," *Month* CXIV (Aug., Sept.), pp. 152–53, 256–57). [Letter to R. W.

Dixon and two letters to Coventry Patmore. Texts in D, p. 1–3; F, pp. 214, 237.]

1916

"The Candle Indoors," "Spring and Fall," "The Habit of Perfection" (first two stanzas), "The Wreck of the Deutschland" (first stanza), "In the Valley of the Elwy," "The Handsome Heart," in Robert Bridges, *The Spirit of Man*: an Anthology for Time of War (London: Oxford U. Press). [Texts in P, pp. 46, 50, 8, 11, 32, 47.]

1918

Poems of Gerard Manley Hopkins, now First Published, Edited with Notes by Robert Bridges, Poet Laureate (London: Humphrey Milford, Oxford U. Press).

1919

"Rosa Mystica," *Month* CXXXIII (May), pp. 339–40. [Printed because omitted by Bridges.]

1920

A Vision of the Mermaids, Prize Poem dated Christmas, 1862, now for the first time printed in full (London: Humphrey Milford, Oxford U. Press). [Reprinted in P, pp. 130–34.]
"Dorothea and Theophilus," *Dublin Review* CLXVII (July), pp. 45–6. [Final expanded text; reprinted in P, pp. 141–42.]
Dublin Review CLXVII (July), pp. 58–66. [Extracts from Hopkins' Journal. Texts in N., pp. 108–9, 114, 118–19, 121, 125, 129, 133–35, 149–50, 155, 175–76, 177, 178, 181, 182, 186, 198.]

1930

Poems of Gerard Manley Hopkins, Edited with Notes by Robert Bridges. Second Edition, with an Appendix of Additional Poems, and a Critical Introduction by Charles Williams (London: Oxford U. Press).

1932

In Robert Bridges, *Three Friends* (London: Humphrey Milford, Oxford U. Press), pp. 103–4, 239–41. [Letter to Robert Bridges and letter to R. W. Dixon. Text in B, 16–17; D, 1–3.]

1935

The Letters of Gerard Manley Hopkins to Robert Bridges, Edited with Notes and an Introduction by Claude Colleer Abbott (London: Oxford U. Press).
The Correspondence of Gerard Manley Hopkins and Richard Watson Dixon, Edited with Notes and an Introduction by Claude Colleer Abbott (London: Oxford U. Press).

1936

"On a Piece of Music," *Month* CLXVII (Feb.), pp. 160–67. [Text re-edited and annotated by G. Bliss, S.J.]
"The Woodlark," *Month* CLXVII (June), pp. 528–35. [Text re-edited and annotated by G. Bliss, S.J.]

1937

Note-Books and Papers of Gerard Manley Hopkins, Edited with Notes and a Preface by Humphry House (London: Oxford U. Press.)

1938

Further Letters of Gerard Manley Hopkins, including his Correspondence with Coventry Patmore, Edited with Notes and an Introduction by Claude Colleer Abbott (London: Oxford U. Press).

1945

Selections from the Note-Books of Gerard Manley Hopkins, Edited by T. Weiss (Norfolk, Connecticut: New Directions Press).

WRITINGS ON OR WITH REFERENCES TO GERARD MANLEY HOPKINS

1873

1. Clarke, Marcus, *Holiday Peak* or *Mount-Might-Ha-Been* (Melbourne, Australia; G. Robertson). [Story in which Hopkins is one of the characters.]

1887

2. Dixon, R. W., *Lyrical Poems* (Oxford: H. Daniel), ["Dedicated to the Rev. Gerard Hopkins, by the Author."]

1889

3. Anon., "Gerard Manley Hopkins," *Freeman's Journal* [Dub-
lin] (June 10), p. 5.

1890

4. Bridges, Robert, "To the Memory of Gerard Manley Hopkins," *Shorter Poems* (London: Geo. Bell and Sons). [Open-
ing ode of Book II.]

1892

5. Boas, Frederick, "Gerard Manley Hopkins," *Modern English
Biography* (London: Truro, Netherton & Worth), vol. 1,
p. 1534.

1893

6. Bridges, Robert, "Gerard Hopkins" in Miles, Alfred H.,
Poets and Poetry of the 19th Century (London: Hutchinson),
vol. 8, p. 161. [Biographical and literary notice.]

1895

7. Beeching, Henry, *A Book of Christmas Verse* (London:
Methuen), p. 173. [Note on Hopkins.]
8. ———, *Lyra Sacra: a Book of Religious Verse* (London:
Methuen), p. 354. [Note on Hopkins.]

1900

9. Champneys, Basil, *Memoirs and Correspondence of Coventry
Patmore* (London: Geo. Bell & Sons), 2 vols. [On Hopkins
passim.]

1902

10. Russell, Matthew, S.J., "Poets I Have Known," *Donohoe's
Magazine* (Apr.).

1905

11. Gosse, Edmund, *Coventry Patmore* (London: Hodder & Stoughton), p. 169.

1909

12. Keating, J., S.J., "Impressions of Fr. Hopkins," *Month* CXIV (July, Aug., Sept.), pp. 59–68; 151–60; 246–58.
13. Brégy, Katherine, "Gerard Manley Hopkins, an Appreciation and an Epitaph," *Catholic World* LXXXVIII (Jan.), pp. 433–47.

1910

14. Saintsbury, George, *A History of English Prosody* (London: Macmillan), vol. 3, p. 391.
15. Brégy, Katherine, "Coventry Patmore," *Catholic World* XC (Mar.) p. 803.

1912

16. Brégy, Katherine, "Gerard Hopkins," *The Poets' Chantry* (London: Herbert & Daniels), pp. 79–88.
17. Lechmere, L., "Oxford 1863–67," *Oxford and Cambridge Review* XIX (May 12), pp. 73–113.

1913

18. Warren, Thomas Herbert, *Robert Bridges, Poet Laureate*, Readings from Poems [public lecture], (Oxford: Clarendon Press), p. 16.
19. Keating, J., S.J., "The Poetry of Fr. Gerard Hopkins," *Month* CXXI (June), pp. 643–44.

1914

20. Kilmer, Joyce, "Manley Hopkins," *Poetry* IV (Sept.), pp. 241–45.

1916

21. Neenan, Sister M. Pius, *Some Evidences of Mysticism in English Poetry of the Nineteenth Century* (M. A. Thesis, Catholic U., Washington).

22. Saintsbury, George, in Ward, A. W. and Waller, A. R., *Cambridge History of English Literature* (N. Y.: Macmillan), vol. 13, p. 234. [Notice on Gerard Manley Hopkins.]

23. Kilmer, Joyce, "Father Gerard Hopkins, S.J.," [poem], *Studies* V (Mar.), p. 106.

1917

24. Hone, J. M., "Gerard Hopkins: A Sketch," *New Statesman* IX (June 9), pp. 231–32.

25. Caine, Hall, "Gerard Hopkins," *New Statesman* IX (June 23), p. 277.

1918

26. Kilmer, Joyce, "Father Gerard Hopkins, S.J.," [poem], *Joyce Kilmer: Memoir and Poems,* edited by Robert C. Holliday (N. Y.: Geo. Doran), p. 138.

27. Hogan, A. J., S.J., "Fr. Hopkins' Poetry," *America* XVIII (Feb. 16), pp. 447–48.

1919

28. O'Neill, George, S.J., *Essays in Poetry* (Dublin: Talbot Press), pp. 117–38.

29. Anon., "Poems of Gerard Manley Hopkins," *Times Literary Supplement* (Jan. 9), pp. 19–23.

30. Guiney, Louise I., "A Recovered Poet," *Month* CXXXIII (Mar.), pp. 205–14.

31. Maynard, Theodore, "Solitary of Song," *America* XX (Mar. 1), pp. 533–34.

32. Anon., "Marianism of Hopkins," *Saturday Westminster Gazette* (Mar. 8).

33. Anon., "Marianism of Gerard Manley Hopkins," *London Universe* (Mar. 14).

34. Anon., "A Prophet Unveiled," *New Statesman* XI (Mar. 15), p. 530.

35. Guiney, Louise I., "Improper Editings," *London Universe* (Mar. 21). [Reply to No. 32.]

36. Harting, E. M., "Gerard Hopkins and Digby Dolben," *Month* CXXXIII (Apr.), pp. 285–89.

37. Anon., "A Medley of Verse," *Spectator* CXXII (May 10), pp. 598–99.
38. Anon., [review of P], *Dial,* No. 66 (May 31), p. 572.
39. McBrien, Peter, [review of P], *Irish Rosary* (June).
40. O'Neill, George, S.J., "Poems of Gerard Manley Hopkins," *Studies* VII (June), pp. 331–33.
41. Murry, J. M., "Poems of Gerard Manley Hopkins," *Athenaeum* (June 6), pp. 425–26.
42. Lappin, H. A., "Gerard Manley Hopkins and His Poetry," *Catholic World* CIX (July), pp. 501–12.
43. B., C., "Reminiscences of Fr. Gerard Hopkins," *Month* CXXXIV (Aug.), pp. 158–59.
44. Russell, Matthew, S.J., "Fr. Gerard Manley Hopkins, S.J., and his Poetry," *Irish Monthly* XLVII (Aug.), pp. 441–48.

1920

45. Murry, J. M., *Aspects of Literature* (London: W. Collins & Sons), pp. 52–61. [Reprint of Essay on Gerard Manley Hopkins, originally in *Athenaeum,* June, 1919.]
46. Feeney, Leonard, S.J., "Father Hopkins' Mystic Songs," *America* XXIII (May 1), p. 41.
47. Page, Frederick, "Fr. Gerard Hopkins: His Poetry," *Dublin Review* CLXVII (July), pp. 40–45.
48. 'Plures,' "Fr. Gerard Hopkins: His Character," *Dublin Review* CLXVII (July), pp. 47–58.

1921

49. Kilmer, Joyce, "Manley Hopkins," *Circus and Other Essays* (N. Y.: Doran), pp. 180–85. [Reprinted from *Poetry,* Sept. 1914.]
50. Omond, T. S., *English Metrists* (Oxford: Clarendon Press), p. 263.
51. Sapir, Edward, "Gerard Manley Hopkins," *Poetry* XVIII (Sept.), pp. 330–336.

1922

52. Shuster, George N., *The Catholic Spirit in Modern Literature* (N. Y.: Macmillan), pp. 115–121.

1923

53. Porter, A. "Difficult Beauty," *Spectator* CXXX (Jan. 13), p. 66.
54. Maynard, Theodore, "Poems of Fr. Hopkins," *Freeman* VIII (Oct. 24), pp. 156–57.

1924

55. Putnam, Samuel, "Gerard Manley Hopkins," *Chicago Post,* (May 30).

1926

56. Leslie, Shane, *An Anthology of Catholic Poets,* 2nd ed., (N. Y.: Macmillan), Introd.
57. Lowe, E. A. and Frey, R., *Society of Pure English, Handwriting with Thirty-three Facsimile Plates and Artistic and Paleographical Criticisms* (London: Clarendon Press), Tract 23, pp. 97–98.
58. Maynard, Theodore, *The Book of Modern Catholic Verse* (N. Y.: Henry Holt), pp. 161–65.
59. Richards, I. A., "Gerard Hopkins," *Dial,* No. 131 (Sept.), pp. 195–203.

1927

60. Feeney, Leonard, S.J., "Father Hopkins' Mystic Songs," *In Towns and Little Towns* (N. Y.: America Press), p. 108.
61. Walsh, Thomas, *The Catholic Anthology* (N. Y.: Macmillan) pp. 292–96.
62. Richards, I. A., "Gerard Hopkins," *Cambridge Review* XLIX (Oct. 28), pp. 49–51.
63. Robinson, H. M., "Gerard Manley Hopkins: a Preface," *Commonweal* VII (Dec. 28), p. 869–71.

1928

64. Riding, Laura and Graves, Robert, *Survey of Modernist Poetry* (London: Wm. Heinemann), pp. 90–94.
65. Brown, Alec, "Gerard Hopkins and Associative Form," *Dublin Magazine* III (Apr.), pp. 6–20.

66. Lahey, G. F., S.J., "Gerard Manley Hopkins," *America* XXXIX (Oct. 6), pp. 619–20.

1929

67. Bridges, Robert, *Testament of Beauty* (Oxford: Clarendon Press).
68. Granger, Edith, ed., *An Index to Poetry and Recitations, a Practical Reference Manual,* Revised and enlarged (Chicago: A. C. McClurg), p. 221.
69. Richards, I. A., *Practical Criticism* (London: Kegan Paul, Trench, Trubner), pp. 80–89, 357.
70. North, Jessica Nelson, "Quality in Madness," *Poetry* XXXIV (Aug.), pp. 270–73.

1930

71. Carver, G., Eleanore, Sister, and Brégy, Katherine, editors, *The Stream of English Literature* (N. Y.: Heath) p. 351.
72. Empson, W., *Seven Types of Ambiguity* (London: Chatto & Windus), pp. 284–86.
73. Fathers of the Society of Jesus, University College, Dublin, *A Page of Irish History: Story of University College, Dublin* (1883–1909) (Dublin: Talbot Press).
74. Lahey, G. F., S.J., *Gerard Manley Hopkins: a Life* (London: Oxford U. Press).
75. Untermeyer, Louis, *A Critical Anthology* (N. Y.: Harcourt, Brace), pp. 159–167.
76. Woods, George B., *Poetry of the Victorian Period* (Chicago: Scott, Foresman), pp. 776–78; 1045.
77. Barrett, Alfred, S.J., "As the Air We Breathe," *Ave Maria* XXXI (Mar. 8), pp. 289–91.
78. Schneider, Isidor, "Gerard Manley Hopkins," *Nation* CXXX (April 16) pp. 456–58.
79. Lahey, G. F., S.J., "Hopkins and Newman," *Commonweal* XII (June 25), pp. 211–13.
80. Moore, T. S., "Style and Beauty in Literature," *Criterion* IX (July), pp. 591–603.
81. O'Brien, Justin, [review of *Life*], *Bookman* LXXI (July), p. 447.

82. Anon., "Gerard Manley Hopkins," *Times Literary Supplement* (July 17), p. 593.

83. Anon., "A Victorian Who Has Come into Fashion," *New York Times Book Review* (July 27), p. 12. [Review of *Life*.]

84. Binsse, H. L., "Gerard Manley Hopkins: Life and Work," *Saturday Review of Literature* VII (Aug. 9), pp. 33–34.

85. Sykes, Gerald, [review of *Life*], *New York Evening Post* (Aug. 9), pp. 5–6.

86. Dilly Tante [Stanley Kunitz], "Dilly Tante Observes," *Wilson Bulletin* V (Sept.), p. 61; (Dec.), p. 256–58.

87. Leahy, Maurice, "The Late Poet-Laureate and Father Gerard Hopkins," *Carmina*, No. 2 (Sept.), p. 22.

88. Underhill, Evelyn, "Gerard Manley Hopkins," *Spectator* CXLV (September 6), p. 318.

89. Burke, M. M., "Gerard Manley Hopkins," *Commonweal* XII (Sept. 10), pp. 459–60.

90. G. R., [review of *Life*], *America* XLIII (Sept. 10), p. 600.

91. Moran, E. A., "Hopkins: a Reply" [to M. M. Burke], *Commonweal* XII (Oct. 8), p. 582.

92. Pickman, Hester, "Gerard Manley Hopkins, S.J.," *Hound and Horn* IV (Oct.-Dec.), pp. 118–27.

93. Anon., "Preferences," *Canadian Forum* XI (Oct.), pp. 22–23.

94. Anon., "A Catholic Poet," *Commonweal* XIII (Nov. 12), pp. 32–33.

95. Zabel, M. D., "Gerard Manley Hopkins: Poetry as Experiment and Unity," *Poetry* (Dec.), pp. 152–161.

96. Anon., "Poems of Gerard Manley Hopkins," *Times Literary Supplement* (Dec. 26), p. 1099.

1931

97. Boner, Harold A., *Gerard Manley Hopkins* (M.A. Thesis, Columbia U., N. Y.).

98. Lahey, G. F., S.J., *The Prosody of Gerard Manley Hopkins and Robert Bridges* (M.A. Thesis, Fordham U., N. Y.).

99. Schappes, Morris U., "Gerard Manley Hopkins," *Symposium* II (Jan.), pp. 129–36.

100. Williams, Charles, "Gerard Manley Hopkins," *Times Literary Supplement* (Jan. 1), p. 12.

101. Anon., "Gerard Manley Hopkins' Poems," *Nation* CXXXII (Jan. 28), p. 105.

102. Turner, W. J., "Some Modern Poetry," *Nineteenth Century and After* CIX (Feb.), pp. 243–52.

103. Flanner, Hildegarde, "Gerard Manley Hopkins," *New Republic* LXV (Feb. 4), pp. 331–32.

104. Coblentz, S., "A Catholic Poet Comes into His Own," *Ave Maria* XXXIII (Feb. 7), pp. 161–63.

105. Grigson, Geoffrey, "A Poet of Surprise," *Saturday Review of Literature* CLI (Feb. 14), pp. 237–38.

106. Anon., [review of P], *Booklist* XXVII (Mar.), p. 322.

107. Little, Arthur, S.J., [review of P], *Studies* XXII (Mar.), p. 165–67.

108. Meagher, Margaret C., [review of P and *Life*], *Catholic World* CXXXII (Mar.), pp. 754–56.

109. Cowley, Malcolm, "The Resurrection of a Poet," *New York Herald Tribune Weekly Book Review* (Mar. 8), pp. 1, 6.

110. Deutsch, Babette, "Poems of Gerard Manley Hopkins," *New York Evening Post* (Mar. 14), p. 7.

111. O'Brien, Justin, "Gerard Manley Hopkins," *Bookman* LXXIII (Apr.), pp. 206–8.

112. Read, Herbert, "Gerard Manley Hopkins," *Criterion* X (Apr.), pp. 552–59.

113. Cock, A. A., "Gerard Manley Hopkins," *France-Grande Bretagne* (Apr. 19), pp. 92–6.

114. Pryce-Jones, Alan, "Gerard Manley Hopkins," *London Mercury* XXIV (May), pp. 45–52.

115. Hope, F., "Gerard Manley Hopkins," *Irish Ecclesiastical Record* XXXVII (June), pp. 561–70.

116. Grisewood, Harman, "Gerard Manley Hopkins," *Dublin Review* CLXXXIX (Oct.), pp. 213–26.

1932

117. Bridges, Robert, *Three Friends* (London: Humphrey Milford, Oxford U. Press), pp. 103–4; 120; 128; 239–41.

118. Leavis, F. R., *New Bearings in English Poetry* (London: Chatto & Windus), pp. 159–93.

118a. Olivero, F., *Correnti Mistiche della Letteratura Inglese Moderna* (Torino: Bocca).

119. Read, Herbert, *Form in Modern Poetry* (London: Sheed & Ward), pp. 44–55.

120. Kent, Muriel, "Gerard Manley Hopkins: Poet & Prosodist," *Bookman* LXXXI (Mar.), pp. 312–313.

121. Haugh, Irene, "Gerard Manley Hopkins," *Irish Monthly* LX (Apr.), pp. 220–27.

122. Roberts, Michael, "Notes on English Poets," *Poetry* XXXIX (May), pp. 271–79.

123. Stonier, G. W., "Gerard Manley Hopkins," *New Statesman* III (June 25), pp. 836–38.

124. James, Stanley B., "The Triumph of the Poet," *Irish Monthly* LX (Nov.), pp. 678–80.

1933

125. Drew, Elizabeth, *Discovering Poetry* (N. Y.: W. W. Norton), p. 82 ff., 110, 157.

126. Saintsbury, George, in Ward, A. W., and Waller, A. R., *Cambridge History of English Literature*, 2nd ed., (N. Y.: Macmillan) vol. 13, p. 234.

127. Evans, B. Ifor, *English Poetry in the Later Nineteenth Century* (London: Methuen), pp. 210–18.

128. Megroz, R. L., *Modern English Poetry* (London: Ivor Nicholson & Watson) pp. 18–19, 161 ff., 105–233.

129. Phare, E. E., *The Poetry of Gerard Manley Hopkins* (Cambridge U. Press). [N.B. This volume is referred to hereafter as "Phare."]

130. Read, Herbert, "The Poetry of Gerard Manley Hopkins," *English Critical Essays, Twentieth Century* (Oxford U. Press), pp. 351–74.

131. Stonier, G. W., *Gog and Magog and Other Critical Essays* (London: J. M. Dent & Sons), pp. 43–63.

132. Read, Herbert, "Poetry and Belief in Gerard Manley Hopkins," *New Verse* No. 1, (Jan.).

133. Anon., "Poetry in the Present," *Times Literary Supplement* (Feb. 9), p. 81–2.

134. Tierney, Michael, "Gerard Manley Hopkins' Meters," *Times Literary Supplement* (Feb. 16), p. 108.

135. Stanier, R. S., "Gerard Manley Hopkins' Meters," *Times Literary Supplement* (Feb. 23), p. 127.

136. House, Humphry, "Gerard Manley Hopkins' Meters," *Times Literary Supplement* (Mar. 2), p. 147.

137. Tierney, Michael, "Gerard Manley Hopkins' Meters," *Times Literary Supplement* (Mar. 9), p. 167.

138. Phillipson, Dom Wulstan, O.S.B., "Journals of Gerard Manley Hopkins," *Downside Review* LI (Apr.), pp. 326–48.

139. Kelly, Bernard, "The Joy of Chastity in the Poems of Gerard Manley Hopkins," *Blackfriars* XIV (Oct.), pp. 833–36.

140. Lahey, G. F., S.J., "Gerard Manley Hopkins," *Commonweal* XVIII (Oct. 20), pp. 581–84.

141. Scott, M. M., S.J., "Gerard Manley Hopkins," *Irish Monthly* LXI (Nov.-Dec.), pp. 715–20, 786–92.

142. Plomer, William, "Gerard Manley Hopkins," *Spectator* CLI (Nov. 17), p. 712.

143. Anon., [review of Phare], *Notes and Queries* CLXV (Nov. 25), p. 378.

144. Clarke, A., "The Poetry of Gerard Manley Hopkins," *Observer* (Nov. 26).

145. Browne, W., "Introduction to Hopkins," *Bookman* LXXXV (Dec.), pp. 228–29. [Review of Phare.]

1934

146. Bateson, F. W., *English Poetry and the English Language* (Oxford U. Press), pp. 117–18.

147. Bullough, Geoffrey, *The Trend of Modern Poetry* (London: Oliver & Boyd), pp. 23–25; 165–66.

148. Eliot, T. S., *After Strange Gods,* (N. Y.: Harcourt, Brace), p. 51.

149. Harvey, Sir Paul, ed., *Oxford Companion to English Literature* (Oxford: Clarendon Press), p. 381.

150. McGuire, D. P., *The Poetry of Gerard Manley Hopkins,* Pamphlet No. 2 (The English Association, Adelaide Branch).

150a. Selincourt, Basil de, *Oxford Lectures on Poetry* (Oxford: Clarendon Press).

151. Sitwell, Edith, *Aspects of Modern Poetry* (London: Duckworth), pp. 51–72.

152. Surtz, Edward, S.J., *Gerard Manley Hopkins' Poetry and the Spiritual Exercises of St. Ignatius* (M.A. Thesis, Xavier U., Cincinnati, Ohio).

153. Cock, A. A., "Gerard Manley Hopkins," *Wessex* III, pp. 95–7.

154. Wolff, L., "Gerard Manley Hopkins," *Revue Anglo-Americaine* XI, 546–47.

155. Anon., [review of Phare], *Month* CLXIII (Jan.), p. 93.

156. Anon., "The Poetry of Gerard Manley Hopkins," *Nation* CXXXVIII (Jan. 24), p. 109.

157. Anon., [review of Phare], *Times Literary Supplement* (Jan. 25), p. 57.

158. Deutsch, Babette, "Gerard Manley Hopkins," *New York Herald Tribune Weekly Book Section* (Jan. 28), p. 2.

159. Walton, E. L., "Gerard Manley Hopkins," *New York Times Book Review* (Jan. 28), p. 3. [Review of Phare].

160. Fairley, Barker, "A Survey and Commentary," *Canadian Forum* XIV (Feb.), pp. 186–87.

161. Benét, W. R., "The Phoenix Nest," *Saturday Review of Literature* X (Feb. 24), p. 508.

162. Tierney, Michael, "Studies in Literature: the Poetry of Gerard Manley Hopkins," *Studies* XXIII (Mar.), p. 180. [Review of Phare.]

163. Roberts, Michael, [review of Phare], *Adelphi* VIII (Apr.), p. 76.

164. Auden, W. H., [review of Phare], *Criterion* XIII (Apr.), pp. 497–500.

165. Downey, Harris, "Gerard Manley Hopkins, a Pioneer of Poetry," *Commonweal* XIX (Apr. 13), pp. 667–68.

166. [Casalandra], Sister Estelle, O.P., "The Tragedy of Gerard Manley Hopkins," *Rosary* XCV (May), pp. 21–24.

167. R., M. R., [review of Phare], *Oxford Magazine* (May 17), p. 714.

168. Meagher, Margaret C., [review of Phare], *Catholic World* CXXXIX (July), p. 499.

169. Brémond, André, S.J., "La Poésie Naïve et Savante de Gerard Hopkins," *Études* CCXXI (Oct.), pp. 23–49.

170. Slattery, J. J., "Some Bibliographical References to Gerard Manley Hopkins, S.J.," *Catholic Library World* V (Nov.), p. 36.

1935

171. Alexander, Calvert, S.J., *Catholic Literary Revival* (Milwaukee: Bruce), pp. 71–85.

172. Chambers, W. and R., *Biographical Dictionary of the Great of all Nations and All Times* (London: W. & R. Chambers).

173. Chew, Samuel C., [review of *Letters*], *Yale Review* XXV (Autumn), pp. 209–12.

174. Lewis, C. Day, *A Hope for Poetry* (Oxford: Blackwell), *passim*.

175. ———, "A Hope for Poetry," *Collected Poems* (N. Y.: Random House), pp. 167–76, [Reprint of above].

176. Hammerton, Sir J. A., ed., *The Concise Universal Biography* (London: Educational Book Co., Ltd.), p. 777.

177. Junkersfeld, Sister Mary Julienne, S.S.N.D., *History of the Critical Reception of the Poems of Gerard Manley Hopkins*, (M.A. Thesis, Loyola U., Chicago).

178. Kelly, Bernard, *The Mind and Poetry of Gerard Manley Hopkins* (London: Pepler & Sewell).

179. Roggen, F., "Gerard Manley Hopkins," *Studies in English Literature* (Imperial U. of Tokyo) XV, pp. 517–34.

180. Sargent, Daniel, "Gerard Manley Hopkins," *Four Independents* (N. Y.: Sheed & Ward), pp. 117–83.

181. Dobree, Bonamy, "Letters of Gerard Manley Hopkins," *Spectator* CLIV (Jan. 11), p. 53.

181a. Landier, Germain, "Lettres de G. M. Hopkins" [selections translated into French, with notes], *Mesures* [Paris] I (Jan.), pp. 100–109.

181b. Roditi, Edouard, "Poèmes de G. M. Hopkins" [English text of "Hurrahing in Harvest," "Duns Scotus's Oxford," "The Windhover," "Tom's Garland," with facing translations into French verse and general introductory critique], *Mesures* [Paris] I (Jan.), pp. 91–99.

182. Selincourt, Basil de, *Observer* (Jan. 20).

183. Stonier, G. W., "Current Literature Treats Hopkins," *New Statesman and Nation* IX (Jan. 26), p. 108.

184. Anon., [review of Letters], *Times Literary Supplement* (Jan. 31), p. 59.

185. Burdett, O., [review of Letters], *Nineteenth Century and After* CXVII (Feb.), pp. 234–41.

186. Keating, J., S.J., "Priest and Poet," *Month* CLXV (Feb.), pp. 125–36. [Review of Letters.]

187. Anon., [review of Letters], *Springfield* [Mass.] *Republican* (Feb. 24), p. 7.

188. Plowman, Max, "Gerard Manley Hopkins," *Times Literary Supplement* (Feb. 28), p. 124.

189. Turnell, G. M., "Homage to Gerard Manley Hopkins," *Colosseum* II (Mar.), p. 159.

190. Gallagher, Donald A., "The Originality of Gerard Manley Hopkins," *Fleur de Lis* (St. Louis U. Quarterly) (Mar.).

191. Plowman, Max, [Review of Letters], *Adelphi* IX (Mar.), pp. 356–61.

192. Roberts, Michael, "Reflections of Gerard Manley Hopkins," *London Mercury* XXXI (Mar.), pp. 480–81.

193. Vann, Gerald, O.P., "The Mind and Poetry of Gerard Manley Hopkins," *Colosseum* II (Mar.), pp. 156–8.

194. Walker, M. E. [review of Letters], *New York Times Book Review*, (Mar. 10), p. 2.

195. Hopkins, L. C., "Gerard Hopkins' Birthday," *Times Literary Supplement* (Mar. 14), p. 160.

196. Leslie, Shane, "Exquisite Doctor," *Saturday Review of Literature* XI (Mar. 16), pp. 549–50.

197. Deutsch, Babette, "Gerard Manley Hopkins, Poet and Pioneer," *New York Herald Tribune Weekly Book Section* (Mar. 17), pp. 1–2.

198. Abbott, C. C., "Gerard Manley Hopkins," *Times Literary Supplement* (Mar. 21), p. 176.

199. Lynam, Thomas J., S.J., "Self Portrait of a Poet," *America* LII (Mar. 23), p. 574. [Review of Letters.]

200. Brémond, André, S.J., "Art and Inspiration," *New Verse*, No. 14 (Apr.), pp. 5–12.

201. Devlin, Christopher, S.J., "Gerard Hopkins and Duns Scotus," *New Verse*, No. 14 (Apr.), pp. 12–17.

202. Griffith, Ll. Wyn, "Hopkins Influenced by Welsh Poetry," *New Verse*, No. 14 (Apr.), pp. 27–9.

203. Grigson, Geoffrey, "Blood or Bran: Hopkins and Hopkinsese," *New Verse*, No. 14 (Apr.), pp. 21–6.

204. House, Humphry, "More on Hopkins' Religious Life," *New Verse*, No. 14 (Apr.), pp. 3–5.

205. MacNeice, Louis, "A Comment," *New Verse*, No. 14 (Apr.), pp. 26–7.

206. Madge, Charles, "What is All This Juice? Hopkins and Victorian Conceptions of Nature," *New Verse*, No. 14, (Apr.), pp. 18–21.

207. Marsden, M., "The Letters of Gerard Manley Hopkins," *Music and Letters* XVI (Apr.), pp. 158–59.

207a. Phillipson, Dom Wulstan, O.S.B., "The Letters of Gerard Manley Hopkins," *Downside Review* LIII (Apr.), pp. 210–28.

208. Read, Herbert, [review of Letters], *Criterion* (Apr.), pp. 478–82.

209. Shewring, Walter J., "The Letters of Gerard Manley Hopkins" [review], *Blackfriars* XVI (Apr.), pp. 265–71.

210. Warren, C. Henry, "Gerard Manley Hopkins," *Fortnightly Review* CXLIII (Apr.), pp. 503–4.

211. Leslie, Shane, [review of Letters], *Ave Maria* XLI (Apr. 13), pp. 456–58.

212. Behn, I. E., "Gerard Manley Hopkins und seine Dichtung," *Hochland* [München] XXXII (May), pp. 148–69.

213. Kunitz, Stanley J., "Letters of Hopkins," *Wilson Bulletin* IX (May), pp. 491–92.

214. Lewis, C. Day, "Records of a Great Poet," *New Republic* LXXXIII (May 22), p. 52. [Review of Letters.]

215. Emerson, D., *Scholastic* XXVI (May 25), p. 10. [Note in Poetry Corner.]

216. Fairley, Barker, "Charles Doughty and Modern Poetry, A Comparison of Charles Doughty and Gerard Hopkins," *London Mercury* XXXII (June), pp. 128–33.

217. James, Stanley B., "Sacrifice of Song," *Catholic World* CXLI (June), pp. 290–95.

218. Turnell, G. M., "Gerard Manley Hopkins," *Colosseum* II (June), pp. 156–57. [Attack on *Spiritual Exercises*.]

219. Larsson, R., "Letters of Gerard Manley Hopkins," *Commonweal* XXII (June 21), pp. 219–21.

220. Downey, Harris, "The Letters of Gerard Manley Hopkins," *Virginia Quarterly Review* XI (July), pp. 458–61.

221. Zabel, M. D., "Hopkins in His Letters," *Poetry* XLVI (July), pp. 210–19.

222. Walker, M. E., "Four Independents," *New York Times Book Review* (July 7), p. 2.

223. Walton, E. L., "Portrait of a Poet," *Nation* CXLI (July 24), pp. 109–11.

224. Maynard, Theodore, "When the Pie was Opened," *Commonweal* XXII (Aug. 2), pp. 339–41.

225. Chew, Samuel C., [review of Letters], *Yale Review* XXV (Autumn), p. 209.

226. Keating, J., S.J., "Father Hopkins and the Spiritual Exercises," *Month* CLXVI (Sept.), pp. 268–70. [Reply to No. 218, Cf. No. 226.]

227. Leahy, Maurice, "Father Gerard Manley Hopkins, Jesuit and Poet," *Irish Monthly* LXIII (Sept.), pp. 567–76.

228. Leavis, F. R., [review] *Scrutiny* IV (Sept.), pp. 216–31.

229. Morrison, Theodore, "The Man of the Month," *Atlantic Monthly* CLVI (Sept.), pp. 6–8. [Review of Letters.]

230. Downey, Harris, "A Poem not Understood," *Virginia Quarterly Review* XI (Oct.), pp. 506–17.

230a. Gardner, W. H., "Early Poems and Extracts," *Criterion* XV (Oct.), pp. 1–17.

231. Meagher, Margaret C., "The Letters of Gerard Manley Hopkins," *Catholic World* CXLII (Oct.), pp. 119–20.

232. Anon., "Four Literary Converts," *Times Literary Supplement* (Nov. 30), p. 799.

233. Crehan, J. H., S.J., "Poetry and Religious Life; the Case of Gerard Manley Hopkins," *Month* CLXVI (Dec.), pp. 493–503.

234. Devlin, Christopher, S.J., "The Ignatian Spirit of Gerard Manley Hopkins," *Blackfriars* XVI (Dec.), p. 887–900.

1936

235. Atkins, Elizabeth, *Edna St. Vincent Millay and her Times* (Chicago: U. of Chicago Press), pp. 108–9; 205; 222–23.

236. Basil, Sister M., O.S.F., "Gerard Manley Hopkins," *Burnished Gold* I (Joliet, Ill: College of St. Francis), pp. 62–7.

237. Daiches, David, "Gerard Manley Hopkins and Modern Poets," *New Literary Values* (Edinburgh: Oliver & Boyd), pp. 23–51.

238. Deutsch, Babette, *This Modern Poetry* (N. Y.: W. W. Norton), pp. 10 ff., 31, 37, *passim*.

239. Dohmann, Sister Ottilia, S.C.C., *The Poetic Mind of Gerard Manley Hopkins* (Ph.D. Dissertation, Fordham U., N. Y.).

240. Pick, John, *The Religious Thought in the Poetry of Gerard Manley Hopkins* (Ph.D. Dissertation, U. of Wisconsin, Madison).

241. Gardner, W. H., "Wreck of the Deutschland," *Essays and Studies* of the English Association (Oxford: Clarendon Press) XXI, pp. 124–52.

242. Gilkes, Martin, *A Key to Modern English Poetry* (London: Blackie & Sons).

243. Grimsditch, Herbert S., "Gerard Manley Hopkins," *British Authors of the 19th Century,* ed. by Stanley Kunitz (N. Y.: H. W. Wilson), pp. 306–8.

244. Kelly, Blanche M., *The Well of English* (N. Y.: Harpers), pp. 278, 286–90, 366.

245. Mathew, David, *Catholicism in England from 1535–1935.* Portrait of Minority Group: Its Culture and Tradition (London: Longmans, Green), pp. 228–29.

246. Read, Herbert, "Gerard Manley Hopkins," *Defense of Shelley and other Essays* (London: Wm. Heinemann), pp. 111–44. [Reprint of Read's "The Poetry of Gerard Manley Hopkins," *English Critical Essays, Twentieth Century* (Oxford U. Press, 1933), pp. 351–74.]

247. Untermeyer, Louis, *Modern British Poetry* (N. Y.: Harcourt, Brace), pp. 96–104.

248. Yeats, W. B., "Gerard Manley Hopkins, S.J.," *Oxford Book of Modern Verse,* (N. Y.: Oxford U. Press), pp. XXXIX–XL, 17–24.

249. Wilson, Howard A., *Gerard Manley Hopkins' Prosody* (M.A. Thesis, State College of Washington).

250. Clarke, Egerton, S.J., "Gerard Hopkins, Jesuit," *Dublin Review* CXCVIII (Jan.), pp. 127–141.

251. Fletcher, John Gould, "Gerard Manley Hopkins: Poet or Priest?" *American Review* VI (Jan.), pp. 331–46.

252. Bliss, Geoffrey, S.J., "In a Poet's Workshop," *Month* CLXVII (Feb.), pp. 160–67. [On Hopkins' unfinished poem "On a Piece of Music."]

253. Downey, Harris, "Gerard Manley Hopkins," *Southern Review* I (Spring), pp. 837–45.

254. Leahy, Maurice, "A Priest-Poet: Father Gerard Manley Hopkins, S.J.," *Irish Ecclesiastical Record* XLVII (Apr.), pp. 355–68.

255. Anon., [review of P], *Boston Pilot* (May).

256. Kelly, Hugh, S.J., [review of Letters], *Studies* XXV (June), pp. 239–52.

257. Bliss, Geoffrey, S.J., "In a Poet's Workshop," *Month* CLXVII (June), pp. 528–35. [On Hopkins' unfinished poem, "The Woodlark."]

258. Gardner, W. H., "A Note on Hopkins and Duns Scotus," *Scrutiny* V (June), pp. 61–70.

258a. Ginneken, J. van, S.J., "Barbarous in Beauty," *Onze Taaltuin* V. (Juli), pp. 65–73.

259. Morley, C., "Wreck of the Deutschland," *Saturday Review of Literature* XIV (Aug. 15), p. 12.

260. Barrett, Alfred, S.J., "Critics, Communists, and Hopkins," *America* LVI (Oct. 31), pp. 90–91.

261. James, Stanley B., "Father Gerard Manley Hopkins, S.J.," *Sentinel of the Blessed Sacrament* (Sept.), p. 467.

262. Feeney, Leonard, S.J., "Father Hopkins and Professor Abbott," *America* LVI (Oct. 24), p. 68.

263. Millspaugh, C. A., "To Gerard Hopkins" [poem], *Commonweal* XXV (Nov. 13), p. 68.

264. Shaw, J. G., "Mr. Fletcher on Hopkins," *Commonweal* XXV (Nov. 13), pp. 69–71.

265. Young, G. M., "Forty Years of Verse," *London Mercury* XXXV (Dec.), pp. 112–22.

1937

266. Dicus, Sister Mary Vivian, *An Analysis of the Literary Importance of Gerard Manley Hopkins,"* (M.A. Thesis, U. of Wichita).

267. Durant, Rev. Albert, O.S.A., *The Concept of God in the Poetry of Gerard Manley Hopkins* (M.A. Thesis, Catholic U., Washington).

268. Groom, B., *The Formation and Use of Compound Epithets in English Poetry from 1579*, S.P.E. Tract XLIX, pp. 318–20.

269. Mansfield, Margery, "Gerard Manley Hopkins," *Workers in Fire* (New York: Longmans, Green), pp. 71, 130, 147–49, 161–65.

270. McCrossan, Sister Joseph Marie, *The Magic Baton of Gerard Manley Hopkins* (M.A. Thesis, Villanova College, Villanova, Pa.).

271. Muir, C., "The Notebooks of Gerard Manley Hopkins," *London Mercury* XXXV, pp. 511–12.

272. Noonan, James Joseph, *Evidences of the Supernatural in the Poetry of Gerard Manley Hopkins, S.J.*, (M.A. Thesis, Boston College).

273. Ogden, C. K., [editorial], *Psyche* XVI (London: The Orthological Institute), pp. 10–50.

274. Weygandt, C., "Latest Phases of English Poetry," *Time of Yeats* (N. Y.: Appleton-Century), pp. 386–428.

275. Kelly, Blanche M., "Immortal Diamond," *Catholic World* CXLIV (Jan.), pp. 481–82. [Excerpt from her book *The Well of English.*]

276. Anon., "Gerard Manley Hopkins' Papers—A Journal and Early Poems," *Times Literary Supplement* (Jan. 23), p. 56.

277. Feeney, Leonard, S.J., "A Further Comment," *America* LVI (Jan. 23), p. 380.

278. Stonier, G. W., "The Notebooks of Gerard Manley Hopkins," *New Statesman and Nation* XIII (Jan. 23), pp. 124–25.

279. Thornton, Francis B., "Gerard Manley Hopkins, Major Poet or Major Craftsman?" *America* LVI (Jan. 23), pp. 379–80.

280. Selincourt, Basil de, [review of N], *Observer* (Jan. 24).

281. Keating, J., S.J., "Disjecta Membra Poetae," *Month* CLXIX (Feb.), pp. 175–76.

282. Evans, B. Ifor, [review of N], *Manchester Guardian* (Feb. 5), p. 7.

283. Berchmans, Sister Louise, S.N.D., "Gerard Manley Hopkins," *America* LVI (Feb. 6), p. 425.

284. Gordon, David, "Superb? Absurd?" *America* LVI (Feb. 6), p. 425. [Reply to No. 279.]

285. Thornton, Francis B., "Hopkins Again," *America* LVI (Feb. 20), p. 475. [Reply to No. 284.]

286. Anon., [review of N], *Springfield* [Mass.] *Republican*, (Feb. 28), p. 7.

287. Cox, R. S., [review of N], *Scrutiny* (Mar.), pp. 455–56.

288. Croce, Benedetto, "Un Gesuita Inglese Poeta: Gerard Manley Hopkins," *Critica* [Napoli] XXXIII (Mar.), pp. 81–100.

289. Dobree, Bonamy, "The Hopkins Papers," *Spectator* CLVIII (Mar. 12), pp. 479–80.

290. Abbott, C. C., "Gerard Manley Hopkins," *Times Literary Supplement* (Mar. 13), p. 188.

291. ———, "Gerard Manley Hopkins: Letters," *Notes and Queries* CLXXII (Mar. 20), p. 210.

292. Cattani, Georges, "Notes sur Gerard Manley Hopkins," *Yggdrasill* (Mar. 25).

293. Flanner, Hildegarde, "Stations of the Cross," *New Republic* XC (Mar. 31), p. 243.

294. Lewis, C. Day., "Gerard Manley Hopkins, Poet and Jesuit," *Left Review* III (Apr.), pp. 172–75.

295. Maude, Mother Mary, [review of N], *Living Church* XCVI (Apr. 17), p. 495.

296. Feeney, Leonard, S.J., "Hopkins Without Comment," *America* LVII (Apr. 17), pp. 45–6.

297. MacManus, Francis, "Return of a Victorian," *Irish Monthly* LXV, pp. 327–35.

298. Pereira, I. J., Ineied, "The Notebooks and Papers of Gerard Manley Hopkins," *New Review* [Calcutta] (May).

298a. Pompen, A., O.F.M., "Gerard Manley Hopkins, S.J." *Onze Taaltuin* VI (Mei), pp. 95–102.

299. Troy, William, "Glorified from Within," *Nation* CXLIV (May 1), pp. 511–12. [Review of Letters.]

300. Holmes, John, "The Essential Soul of an English Poet," *Boston Evening Transcript* (May 15), p. 1. [Review of Letters.]

301. Deutsch, Babette, "Scholar, Priest, and Poet," *New York Herald Tribune Weekly Book Section* (May 16), p. 21. [Review of N.]

302. Gardner, W. H., "The Religious Problem in Gerard Manley Hopkins," *Scrutiny* (June), pp. 32–42.

302a. Kelly, Bernard, "Gerard Manley Tuncks," *Blackfriars* XVIII (June), pp. 424–9.

303. MacManus, Francis, "The Poet Who Knew Too Much," *Irish Monthly* LXV (June), pp. 389–99.

304. Shuster, George N., [review of N], *Commonweal* XXVI (June 4), p. 164.

305. Blackmur, R. P., "Text and Texture," *Virginia Quarterly Review* XIII, (Summer), pp. 449–53.

306. Walker, M. E., "In the World of Gerard Manley Hopkins," *New York Times Book Review,* (June 27), p. 6. [Review of N.]

307. MacNeice, Louis, "The Notebooks and Papers of Gerard Manley Hopkins," *Criterion* XVI (July), p. 698–700.

308. Moss, Ernest, "The Notebooks and Papers of Gerard Manley Hopkins," *Dublin Review* CCI (July), pp. 165–67.

309. Waterhouse, J. F., "Gerard Manley Hopkins and Music," *Music and Letters* XVIII (July), pp. 227–35.

310. Feeney, Thomas B., S.J., "Gerard Manley Hopkins, Priest and "Poet," *Boston Pilot* (July 3). [Reprint of radio address.]

311. Whitridge, Arnold, "Poet's Workshop," *Saturday Review of Literature* XVI (July 10), p. 20. [Review of N.]

312. Trueblood, C. K., "Esthetics of Gerard Manley Hopkins," *Poetry* L (Aug.), pp. 274–80.

313. Kelly, Blanche M., [review of N], *Catholic World* CXLV (Sept.), pp. 750–51.

314. Simons, John W., "Hopkins in his Sermons," *Commonweal* XXVI (Sept. 24), pp. 491–93.

315. Phillipson, Dom Wulstan, O.S.B., "Journals of Gerard Manley Hopkins," *Downside Review* LV (Oct.), pp. 526–38.

316. Forster, L., "Notebooks of Gerard Manley Hopkins," *English Studies* [Amsterdam] XIX (Oct.), pp. 236–39.

317. Gregory, Horace, [review of F], *Yale Review* XXVIII (Winter), p. 415.

1938

318. Botzum, W. A., "Hopkins," *Scrip* IX, pp. 23–25.

319. Louise, Sister, S.L., *Over the Bent World,* An Anthology of Verse (New York: Sheed & Ward), p. xv.

320. MacNeice, Louis, "Rhythm and Rhyme, a Personal Essay," *Modern Poetry* (London: Oxford U. Press), p. 115.

320a. Murphy, G., *The Modern Poet* (London: Sidgwick & Jackson).

321. Read, Herbert, "Gerard Manley Hopkins," *Collected Essays in Literary Criticism* (London: Faber & Faber), pp. 331–53. [Reprinted from *English Critical Essays, Twentieth Century* (Oxford U. Press), 1933, pp. 531–74.

322. Rodman, Selden, *A New Anthology of Modern Poetry* (N. Y.: Random House), pp. 120–24.

323. Slater, John, *Recent Literature and Religion* (N. Y.: Harper), pp. 185–86, 189–99.

324. Turnell, G. M., *Poetry and Crisis* (London: Sands, Paladin Press), p. 26 and *passim.*

325. Wild, Friedrich, "Letters of Gerard Manley Hopkins," *Anglia Beiblatt* XLIX, pp. 78–82.

326. Meyer, Gerard Previn, "For Gerard Manley Hopkins" [poem], *Commonweal* XXVII (Jan. 14), p. 318.

326a. Scrinivasa Iyengar, K. R., "Gerard Manley Hopkins," *New Review* (Calcutta) VII (Jan., Feb., Mar.), pp. 1–11; 115–25; 264–73.

327. Daly, James J., S.J., "Father Hopkins and the Society," *Thought* XIII (Mar.), pp. 9–13.

328. Harrold, Charles F., [review of F], *Modern Philology* XXXV (May), p. 440.

329. Anon., "Gerard Manley Hopkins—a Mind Entirely Religious," *Times Literary Supplement* (May 7), p. 312.

330. Dobree, Bonamy, "More Letters of Gerard Manley Hopkins," *Spectator* CLX (May 13), p. 880.

331. Stonier, G. W., "The Notebooks of Gerard Manley Hopkins," *New Statesman and Nation* XV (May 14), pp. 840–42.

332. Anon., "Gerard Manley Hopkins," *London Tablet* CLXXI (May 21), p. 666.

333. Heywood, Terence, "Hopkins and Bridges, on Trees," *Poetry Review* XXIX (May-June), pp. 213–18.

334. Anon., "Further Letters," *Blackfriars* XIX (June), pp. 465–67.

335. Coogan, Margery D., "Dare-Gale Skylark," *Fonthill Dial* (N. Y., College of Mount St. Vincent) (June).

336. Estrange, H. K., [review of F], *Month* CLXXI (June), pp. 569–70.

337. Evans, B. Ifor, [review of F], *Manchester Guardian* (June 24), p. 7.

338. Anon., [review of F], *New Yorker* XIV (June 25), p. 67.

339. James, Stanley B., "The Revolution in Literature," *Catholic Bookman* I (July-Aug.), pp. 386–88.

340. MacManus, Francis, "Further Letters of Gerard Manley Hopkins," *Irish Monthly* LXVI (July), pp. 508–10.

341. Phillipson, Dom Wulstan, O.S.B., "Journals of Gerard Manley Hopkins," *Downside Review* LVI (July), pp. 311–23.

342. Walker, R. S., "Introduction to the Poetry of Gerard Manley Hopkins," *Aberdeen University Review* XXV (July), pp. 232–43.

343. Pick, John, [review of F], *Commonweal* XXXVIII (July 8), pp. 302–3.

344. Fitts, Dudley, "A Poet's Letters," *Saturday Review of Literature* XVIII (July 9), p. 15.

345. Walker, M. E., "The Loneliness of the Priest," *New York Times Book Review* (July 10), p. 9. [Review of F.]

346. Gordon, David, "The Prose of Gerard Manley Hopkins," *America* LIX (July 16), pp. 335–56.

347. Hughes, Emily, "The Innovators," *Irish Monthly* LXVI (Dec.), pp. 820–24.

348. Bogan, Louise, "The Hidden Stream," *Nation* CXLVII (July 30), pp. 111–12. [Review of F.]

349. Williamson, Claude, "Gerard Manley Hopkins," *Pax* (July-Aug.).

350. Holmes, John, "The Unity of Hopkins as Letter-Writer and Poet," *Boston Evening Transcript* (Aug. 20), p. 1. [Review of F.]

351. MacColl, D. S., "Patmore and Hopkins: Sense and Nonsense in English Prosody," *London Mercury* XXXVIII (July-Aug.), pp. 217–24.

352. Deutsch, Babette, "Glimpses of a Rare Spirit," *New York Herald Tribune Weekly Book Section* (Aug. 21), p. 12.

353. Gordon, David, [review of F], *Catholic World* CXLVII (Sept.), p. 758.

354. Cox, R. S., [review of F], *Scrutiny* VII (Sept.), pp. 217–18.

355. Meagher, Margaret C., [review of F], *Catholic World* CXLVII (Sept.), pp. 758–59.

356. Maude, Mother Mary, [review of F], *Living Church* XCIX (Sept. 7), p. 214.

357. Gordon, David, "From Hopkins to Patmore, Poet," *America* LIX (Sept. 17), p. 573. [Review of F.]

357a. Panhuysen, J., "De Poesie van Gerard Manley Hopkins," *Boekenschouw* XXXII (Nov.), pp. 313–18.

358. Zabel, M. D., [review of F], *New Republic* XCVII (Nov. 30), p. 106.

359. Quinn, Kerker, "Portrait in Letters," *Poetry* LIII (Dec.), pp. 150–55. [Review of F.]

359a. Castelli, Alberto, *Scrittori Inglesi Contemporanei* (Messina).

1939

360. Coogan, Margery D., *The Nature Poetry of Gerard Manley Hopkins* (M.A. Thesis, Catholic U., Washington).

361. D'Arcy, Martin C., S.J., "Gerard Manley Hopkins," *Great Catholics,* ed. Williamson, (N. Y.: Macmillan), pp. 358–66.

362. Henderson, Philip, *The Poet and Society* (London: Secker & Warburg), pp. 103–31, and *passim.*

362a. Karp, Georg, *Germanische Formgefühl bei Gerard Manley Hopkins,* (Bottrop i.W.: Wilhelm Postberg).

362b. Kenmare, D., *The Face of Truth* (Oxford: Shakespeare Head Press), pp. 103–31.

363. Leishman, J. B., "Further Letters of Gerard Manley Hopkins," *Review of English Studies* XV, pp. 243–46.

364. Temple, William, *Genius in English Poetry* (London: Oxford U. Press).

365. Blackmur, R. P., "Mature Intelligence of an Artist," *Kenyon Review* I (Winter), pp. 96–99.

366. Williams, Charles, and Heywood, Terence, "Gerard Manley Hopkins and Milton," *Poetry Review* XXX pp. 307–8.

367. Hughes, Emily, "The Innovators," *Catholic Digest* III (Jan.), pp. 77–78. [Condensed reprint from *Irish Monthly* LXVI (Dec. 1938), pp. 820–24.]

368. Gordon, David, "Ex Voto Gerard Manley Hopkins" [poem], *Tablet* CLXXIII (Jan. 14), p. 54. [Reprinted in *America* LX (Mar. 18), p. 572.]

369. Brégy, Katherine, "Of Poets and Poetry," *Catholic World* CXLVIII (Feb., Mar.), pp. 522–30; 680–86; CXLIX (Apr.), pp. 73–80.

370. Binyon, Laurence, "Gerard Hopkins and His Influence," *University of Toronto Quarterly* VII (Apr.), pp. 264–70.

370a. Etman, A., "Haunting Rhythm," *Tijdschrift voor Taal en Letteren* XXVII (Apr.), pp. 30–7.

371. Robbins, R. H., "Choral Speaking at the Oxford Festivals," *Quarterly Journal of Speech* XXV (Apr.), pp. 227–35.

372. Caliri, Flavia, "Hopkins' Inspiration," *Ethos* (Emmanuel College, Boston), (Spring).

373. Caulfield, Jeanne, "Hopkins' Life," *Ethos* (Emmanuel College, Boston), (Spring).

374. Donovan, Mary, "Hopkins' Message," *Ethos* (Emmanuel College, Boston), (Spring).

375. Finlay, Ida, "Gerard Manley Hopkins, Poet and Priest," *Cornhill* CLIX (Apr.), pp. 467–78.

376. Murray, John, S.J., "Gerard Manley Hopkins," *Month*, CLXXII (Apr.), pp. 293–94.

377. Heywood, Terence, "On Approaching Hopkins," *Poetry Review*, (May), pp. 185–88.

378. Walsh, William T., "Sabotage on Parnassus," *America* LXI (May 6), p. 91.

379. Jones, Glyn, "Hopkins and Welsh Prosody," *Life and Letters Today* XXXIX (June), pp. 50–54.

380. Phillipson, Don Wulstan, O. S. B., "Journals of Gerard Manley Hopkins," *Downside Review* LVII (July), pp. 389–92.

381. Heywood, Terence, "Hopkins' Ancestry," *Poetry* LIV (July, Aug.), pp. 209–19; 271–79.

382. Gregory, Horace, [review of N and F], *Yale Review* XXVIII (Winter), pp. 415–18.

383. Anon., "The Pack of Autolycus," *Ethos* (Emmanuel College, Boston), (Nov).

383a. Peters, W., "Gerard Manley Hopkins," De Controverse rond zijn Persoon, *Studien* CXXXII (Nov.), pp. 448–59.

384. Daly, J. J., S.J., "One Way of Getting a Catholic Literature," *Thought* XIV (Dec.), pp. 537–38.

1940

385. Daiches, David, *Poetry and the Modern World* (Chicago: U. of Chicago Press), pp. 17–37 and *passim*.

386. Daly, James J., S.J., "Father Hopkins and the Society," *The Jesuit in Focus* (Milwaukee: Bruce), pp. 189–94. [Reprinted from *Thought*, Mar. 1938.]

387. Drew, Elizabeth, in collab. with John L. Sweeney, *Directions in Modern Poetry*, (N.Y.: W. W. Norton), *passim*.

388. Evans, B. Ifor, "Towards the Twentieth Century: Gerard Manley Hopkins and T. S. Eliot," *Tradition and Romanticism* (N.Y.: Longmans, Green), pp. 185–200.

389. Fraunces, John M., S.J., *The Meaning and Use of Inscape* (M.A. Thesis, Loyola U., Chicago).

390. Southworth, J. G., "Gerard Manley Hopkins," *Sowing the Spring: Studies in British Poets from Hopkins to MacNeice* (Oxford: Blackwell), pp. 15–32.

391. Wells, Henry, *New Poets from Old* (N. Y.: Columbia U. Press), pp. 35–43.

392. Pick, John, "The Growth of a Poet: Gerard Manley Hopkins," *Month* CLXXV (Jan., Feb.), pp. 39–46; 106–13.

393. Abbott, C. C., "Gerard Manley Hopkins: a Letter and Drafts of Early Poems," *Durham University Journal* XXXII (Jan.), pp. 65–73.

393a. Brémond, André, S.J., "Quelques Réflexions sur la Poésie et les Styles Poétiques. A Propos d'une Correspondance," *Études* CCXLII (Fév.), pp. 310–17.

394. Heywood, Terence, "Gerard Manley Hopkins: His Literary Ancestry," *English* III (Spring), pp. 16–24.

395. Applejoy, Petronius, "Hopkins Sets a Poetic Signpost," *Catholic World* CLI (May), pp. 184–90.

396. Feeney, Leonard, S.J., "By Way of Summary of Sorts," *America* LXIII (May 4), p. 104.

397. Chavez, Angelo, "To Gerard Manley Hopkins Accused of Exaggerated Marianism" [poem], *Spirit* VII (July), p. 74.

1941

398. Baldi, Sergio, *Gerard Manley Tuncks* (Brescia: Morcelliana).

399. Gardner, W. H., "Gerard Manley Hopkins as a Cywyddwr," *Transactions of the Honorable Society of Cymmrodorion,* Session of 1940 [London], pp. 184–88.

400. Dever, Joseph, "Gerard Manley Hopkins," *Stylus* (Boston College) LIV (Mar.), pp. 5–16.

401. Speaight, Robert, "Hopkins' Genius and Stature as a Major Poet," *Commonweal* XXXIII (Mar. 28), pp. 562–65.

401a. Matthai, A. P., "Hopkins the Jesuit," *New Review* [Calcutta] XIII (Apr.), pp. 306–317.

401b. Lind, L. Roberto, "Gerard Manley Hopkins: Poet Menor de la Edad Mediavictoriana," *Universidad de la Habana* XXXVI (Mayo), pp. 48–55.

402. Whitridge, Arnold, "Gerard Manley Hopkins," *University Review* (June), pp. 247–56.

403. Kite, E. S., "Conflict and Vision in Hopkins," *America* LXV (July 19), pp. 411–12.

404. Stanford, W. B., "Gerard Manley Hopkins and Aeschylus," *Studies* XXX (Sept.), pp. 359–68.

405. Daly, James J., S.J., "Conscience Among the Books," *America* LXVI (Oct. 25), pp. 73–4.

1942

406. Deferrari, Roy J., Brentano, Sister M. Theresa, Sheekey, Brother E. P., "Rosa Mystica and a Brief Biography of Gerard

Manley Hopkins," *Appreciation Through Reading*, II (Chicago: Wm. H. Sadlier), pp. 537–38.

407. Farrell, Sister Mary Pius, *Influence of the Liturgy on the Works of Gerard Manley Hopkins* (B.A. Thesis, Manhattan College, N. Y.).

408. Melchner, Sister M. Roberta, S.S.N.D., *Hopkins and the Common Man* (M.A. Thesis, Boston College).

409. O'Brien, Robert David, *The Critical Mind of Gerard Manley Hopkins* (M.A. Thesis, Boston College).

410. Pick, John, *Gerard Manley Hopkins, Priest and Poet* (London: Oxford U. Press).
[N.B. This volume is referred to hereafter as "Pick."]

411. Welch, Sister M. Charlotte, O.S.B., *The Unity of Gerard Manley Hopkins' Achievement* (M.A. Thesis, Loyola U., Chicago).

412. Anon., "Gerard Manley Hopkins, Priest and Poet," *Durham University Quarterly* XXXIV, pp. 34–5.

413. Sieveking, Lancelot, "Remarks about Hopkins," *Poetry Review* XXXIII, pp. 323–25.

414. Taylor, F., "Rebellious Will of Gerard Manley Hopkins," *Poetry* LIX (Feb.), pp. 270–78.

415. Pick, John, "Gerard Manley Hopkins: The Problem of Religious Poetry," *Stylus* (Boston College) LV (Feb.), pp. 14–21.

416. Bell, David, *Dafyd ap Gwilym*, Introductory Essay, "The Problem of Translation," *Y Cymmrodor* XLVIII (May), pp. 77–91.

417. Anon., "Prince of Celtic Bards, Singer of Love and Woodlands," *Times Literary Supplement* (May 30), p. 273.

418. Heywood, Robert, "A Sacramental View of the Universe," *Vineyard* (Libertyville, Ill.), (June).

418a. Tillemans, T., "Is Hopkins a Modern Poet?" *English Studies* XXIV (June), pp. 90–5.

419. Anon., "Gerard Manley Hopkins, a Poet's Conflict—the Divine and the Earthly," *Times Literary Supplement* (Sept. 26), p. 474.

420. Stonier, G. W., [review of Pick], *New Statesman and Nation* XXIV (Sept. 26), p. 207.

421. Turner, W. J., "Poet and Priest," *Spectator* CLXIX (Oct. 2), p. 318.

422. F.,H. L'A., [review of Pick], *Manchester Guardian* (Oct. 7), p. 3.

423. Turnell, G. M., "The Formation of Hopkins," *London Tablet* CLXXX (Oct. 17), p. 192.

424. Untermeyer, Louis, *Modern British Poetry,* 5th revised ed. (N.Y.: Harcourt, Brace), pp. 45–54.

425. K., D. L., "Poet Reinstated," *Month* CLXXVIII (Nov.), pp. 493–94.

426. Lamb, A. L. F., "Gerard Manley Hopkins: a Study," *Central Literary Magazine* (Nov.), pp. 50–55.

427. Anon., "Gerard Manley Hopkins, Priest and Poet," *Listener* XXVIII (Nov. 12), pp. 634–35.

428. Kelly, Hugh, S.J., [appreciation], *Studies* XXXI (Dec.), pp. 438–44.

1943

429. Casalandra, Sister Estelle, O.P., *Gerard Manley Hopkins—a Study in Spiritual Progress* (M.A. Thesis, Ohio State U., Columbus).

430. Noon, William T., S.J., *The Art Principles of Gerard Manley Hopkins, S.J.* (M.A. Thesis, Loyola U., Chicago).

431. Ashburner, P., [review of Pick], *Adelphi* XIX, pp. 127–28.

432. Lienhardt, R. G. [review of Pick], *Scrutiny* XI (Spring), pp. 220–24.

433. Little, Arthur, S.J., "Hopkins and Scotus," *Irish Monthly* LXXI (Feb.), pp. 47–59.

434. Rose, Leslie, "Plumage of Far Wonder," *Sentinel of the Blessed Sacrament* XLVI (Feb.), pp. 65–67.

435. Willy, M., [review of Pick], *English* IV, pp. 131–32.

436. Pick, John, "The Inspiration of Hopkins' Poetry," *America* LXVIII (Jan. 23), pp. 437–38.

437. Barry, John J., "Gerard Manley Hopkins," *Salesianum* XXXVIII (Apr.), pp. 55–66.

438. Darby, H. S., "Jesuit Poet—Gerard Manley Hopkins," *London Quarterly Review* CLXVIII (Apr.), pp. 110–22.

439. P., E. S., [review of Pick], *Springfield* [Mass.] *Republican* (Apr. 29), p. 8.

440. Stephenson, A. A., S.J., [review of Pick], *Dublin Review* CCXII (Apr.), pp. 170–174.

441. Hanlon, R. W., "Gerard Manley Hopkins: Priest & Poet," *Newsletter, Catholic Book Club* XXX (May), pp. 1–6.

442. Weyand, Norman, S.J., "Hopkins—Poet," *Books on Trial* II (May-June), p. 273. [Review of Pick.]

443. Pick, John [reply to R. W. Hanlon], *Newsletter, Catholic Book Club* XXX (June), pp. 1–2.

444. Greene, Marjorie, "Immortal Diamond," *Ethos* (Emmanuel College, Boston) XVI (June), pp. 127–32.

445. S. C., "Gerard Manley Hopkins, Priest and Poet," *Newsletter, Catholic Book Club* XXX (June), p. 1–2.

446. Shuster, George N., "The Varied Flavor of Hopkins," *Saturday Review of Literature* XXVI (June 13), p. 31.

447. Baker, Carlos, [review of Pick], *New York Times Book Review* (June 13), p. 10.

448. Abbott, C. C., [review of Pick], *Review of English Studies* XIX (July), pp. 311–13.

449. Hopkins, J. G. E., [review of Pick], *Columbia* XXII (July), p. 20.

450. Lilly, G., "Welsh Influence in the Poetry of Gerard Manley Hopkins," *Modern Language Review* XXXVIII (July), pp. 192–205.

451. Meagher, Margaret C., [review of Pick], *Catholic World* CLVII (July), pp. 439–41.

452. Weyand, Norman, S.J., [review of Pick], *New World* (July 9), p. 12.

453. Carey, Charles M., [review of Pick], *Ave Maria* LVIII (July 10), p. 58.

454. Westrup, J. A., "A Great English Song Writer," *Listener* XXX (July 22), p. 109.

455. Gardiner, Harold C., S.J., "Key to Genius," *America* LXIX (July 24), p. 439. [Review of Pick.]

456. Deutsch, Babette, "A Priest's View of a Poet," *New Statesman and Nation* CLVII (Aug. 28), p. 247.

457. Eberhart, Richard, "Heavenly-Mindedness," *Poetry* LXII (Sept.), pp. 347–53. [Review of Pick.]

458. Anon., "Gerard Manley Hopkins," *Notes and Queries* CLXXXV (Oct. 9), p. 240.

459. [Casalandra], Sister Estelle, O.P., "The Blessed Virgin Compared to the Air We Breathe," *Rosary* (Nov.).

460. Colligan, Geraldine, "The Mysticism of Hopkins," *Ave Maria* LVIII (Nov. 6), pp. 591–93.

461. [Casalandra], Sister Estelle, O.P., [review of Pick], *Torch*, (Dec.).

462. Lahey, G. F., S.J. [review of Pick], *Thought* XVIII (Dec.), pp. 721–2.

463. Parker, Mary, "Gerard Manley Hopkins: Poet of Design," *Mount Mary Quarterly* XIX (Winter), pp. 21–34.

1944

464. Gardner, W. H., *Gerard Manley Hopkins: A Study of Poetic Idiosyncrasy in Relation to Poetic Tradition*, vol. 1 (London: Secker & Warburg).

465. Grady, Thomas J., *The Poetic Principles of Gerard Manley Hopkins* (M.A. Thesis, Loyola U., Chicago).

466. Ruggles, Eleanor, *Gerard Manley Hopkins, a Life* (N. Y.: W. W. Norton).
[N.B. This volume is referred to hereafter as "Ruggles."]

467. Reid, J. C., *Gerard Manley Hopkins, Priest and Poet* (Wellington, New Zealand: Catholic Writers' Movement). [Pamphlet published as a centennial tribute.]

468. Hanson, W. J., "Gerard Manley Hopkins and R. W. Dixon," *London Quarterly and Holburn Review* CLXIX (Jan.), pp. 63–7.

469. Price, Fanny, "Gerard Manley Hopkins on Robert Bridges," *Notes and Queries* CLXXXVI (Jan. 15), p. 49.

470. Grady, Thomas J., "Windhover's Meaning," *America* LXX (Jan. 29), pp. 465–66.

471. Capellanus, "Windhover," *America* LXX (Feb. 12), p. 531.

472. Harding, H. N., "On First Looking into Gerard Manley Hopkins," *Poetry Review* (Mar.-Apr.), pp. 77–8.

473. Water, Charlotte Van de, "Poems to Remember: Windhover; with Biographical Note," *Scholastic* XLIV (Mar. 13), p. 20.

474. Jeremy, Sister Mary, "Gerard Manley Hopkins, 1844–1944" [poem], *Poetry* LXIV (Apr.), p. 11.

475. Anderson, Mary Ann, "Fruit of Silence," *Mundelein College Review* XIV (May), pp. 249–54.

476. [Casalandra], Sister Estelle, O.P., "Tragedy of Gerard Manley Hopkins," *Rosary* (May).

477. Anon., "Poet and Priest, Gerard Hopkins, 1844–1889, the Dare-Gale Skylark," *Times Literary Supplement* (June 10), pp. 282–84.

478. Churchill, R. C., "Gerard Manley Hopkins, Christian Socialist," *London Tribune* (June 10).

479. Leavis, F. R., "Gerard Manley Hopkins," *Scrutiny* XII (Spring), pp. 82–93.

480. House, Humphry, "Gerard Manley Hopkins: Poet-Priest," *Listener* (June 22), pp. 692–93.

481. D'Arcy, Martin C., S.J., "Gerard Manley Hopkins," *London Tablet* CLXXXIII (June 24), p. 308.

482. Kliger, S., "God's Plenitude in the Poetry of Gerard Manley Hopkins," *Modern Language Notes* LIX (June), pp. 408–10.

483. Brooks, Cleanth, "Gerard Manley Hopkins," *Kenyon Review* VI (Summer), p. 321.

484. McLuhan, Herbert Marshall, "The Analogical Mirrors," *Kenyon Review* VI (Summer), pp. 322–32.

485. Miles, Josephine, "The Sweet and Lovely Language," *Kenyon Review* VI (Summer), pp. 355–68.

486. Warren, Austin, "Instress of Inscape," *Kenyon Review* VI (Summer), pp. 369–82.

487. Whitehall, Harold, "Sprung Rhythm," *Kenyon Review* VI (Summer), pp. 333–54.
[N.B. The above listed titles from *Kenyon Review* are reprinted in No. 541.]

488. Bliss, Geoffrey, S.J., "Hopkins Centenary," *Month* CLXXX (July), pp. 233–40.

489. Hughes, Emily, "Ripples on a Pool: Influence of His Poetry," *Irish Monthly* LXXII (July), pp. 280–85.

490. Ridler, Anne, "Gerard Manley Hopkins," *Periodical* (Oxford) XXVI (July), pp. 109–13.

491. Turner, W. J., "Gerard Manley Hopkins (1844–1889)," *Spectator* CLXXIII (July 14), pp. 32–33.

492. Winstedt, Sir Richard, "Gerard Manley Hopkins," *Guardian* (July 21).
[Cf. No. 500 for controversy which followed.]

493. Hopkins, Gerard, "Gerard Manley Hopkins," *Times Literary Supplement* (June 24). [Letter establishing from family lists the date of Hopkins' birth as July 28, 1844.]

494. Anon., "Notre Dame Exhibit Honors Poet-Priest," *Catholic Review* (July 28).

495. Engle, Paul, [review of Ruggles], *Chicago Tribune Book Supplement* (July 30).

496. Currier, Isabel, [review of Ruggles], *Boston Traveller* (Aug. 2).

497. Anon., [review of Ruggles], *New Yorker* XX (Aug. 12), p. 56.

498. Kennedy, Leo, "Fine Life of the Jesuits' Poet," *Book Week* (Aug. 13), p. 9. [Review of Ruggles.]

499. Anon., "Poet's Poet," *Time* XLIV (Aug. 14), pp. 99–104. [Review of Ruggles.]

500. Davies, S. J., "Gerard Manley Hopkins: 'To What Serves Mortal Beauty?'," *Guardian* (Aug. 4). [Letter to Sir Richard Winstedt. Sir Richard's reply, Aug. 11. Further letter of Davies, Aug. 25.]

501. Gregory, Horace, "A Biography of Gerard Hopkins for the Centenary of a Poet who Died Unpublished and Unknown," *New York Herald Tribune Weekly Book Section* (Aug. 6), p. 5. [Review of Ruggles.]

502. Auden, W. H., "A Knight of the Infinite," *New Republic* CXI (Aug. 24), pp. 223–24.

503. Pick, John, "Gerard Manley Hopkins," *Commonweal* XL (Aug. 25), pp. 447–48. [Review of Ruggles.]

504. Leavis, F. R., "Revaluations (IV): Gerard Manley Hopkins," *Scrutiny* XII (Sept.), pp. 82–93.

505. Moore, Dom Sebastian, "Gerard Manley Hopkins and Duns Scotus," *Downside Review* (Sept.).

506. Spencer, Theodore, "Poet in Search of Inscape," *Saturday Review of Literature* XXVII (Sept. 2), p. 20.

507. Benét, W. R., "Gerard Manley Hopkins, Centenary Poem," *Saturday Review of Literature* (Sept. 2), p. 20.

508. Bischoff, A., S.J., "Tussaud Creation," *America* LXXI (Sept. 2), p. 539–40. [Review of Ruggles.]

509. McLuhan, Herbert Marshall, "Gerard Hopkins and His World," *New York Times Book Review* (Sept. 3), pp. 7, 14. [Review of Ruggles.]

510. Weyand, Norman, S.J., "Tributes to Famous Poet," *New World* (Sept. 15), p. 13.

511. Boyle, Robert, S.J., "Gerard Manley Hopkins," *America* LXXI (Sept. 30), p. 623.

512. Hughes, Riley, "Life of Hopkins, Sympathetic but Inadequate," *Books on Trial* III (Oct.-Nov.), p. 617. [Review of Ruggles.]

513. Abel, Darrel, "A Biography of Gerard Manley Hopkins," *South Atlantic Quarterly* XLII, pp. 415–17. [Review of Ruggles.]

514. Furness, Clifton J., "Gerard Manley Hopkins," *Atlantic Monthly* CLXXIV (Oct.), pp. 131–33.

515. Maritain, Jacques, "Poetic Experience," *Review of Politics* VI (Oct.), pp. 387–402. [Hopkins used as illustration.]

516. Thornton, Francis B., "The Wreck of the Deutschland," *Catholic World* CLX (Oct.), pp. 41–6.

517. Turner, Vincent, S.J., "Gerard Manley Hopkins: A Centenary Article," *Dublin Review* CCXV (Oct.), pp. 144–59.

518. Boyle, Robert R., S.J., "The Teaching of Hopkins," *Jesuit Educational Quarterly* VII (Oct.), pp. 91–5.

519. Bischoff, A., S.J., "Postscript on Hopkins," *America* LXXII (Oct. 14), p. 39.

520. Ehmann, Benedict, "The Poetry of Father Hopkins," *Catholic Courier* (Oct. 19), p. 15.

521. Shaw, J. G., "Oddities and Obscurities," *Canadian Register* (Oct. 28), p. 8.

522. Lienhardt, R. G., "Hopkins Commemorated," *Scrutiny* XII (Autumn), pp. 296–301. [Review of Gardner.]

523. Lowell, Robert, "A Note," *Kenyon Review VI* (Autumn), pp. 582–86.

524. MacGillivray, Arthur, S.J., "Gerard Manley Hopkins, Priest and Poet," *Poet Lore* L (Autumn), pp. 276–78.

525. Mizener, Arthur, "Victorian Hopkins," *Kenyon Review* VI (Autumn), pp. 590–606.

526. Warren, Austin, "Monument Not Quite Needed," *Kenyon Review* VI (Autumn), pp. 587–89. [Review of Ruggles.]

527. Stonier, G. W., "Hopkins," *New Statesman and Nation* XXVIII (Nov. 4), pp. 307–8.

528. ———, "Response to Gerard Manley Hopkins' Study in Variation," *Times Literary Supplement* (Nov. 11), p. 550.

529. Shewring, Walter J., "Gerard Manley Hopkins (1844–1944)," *Weekly Review* XL (Nov. 30), pp. 115–16.

530. Brown, Stephen, S.J., "A Catholic Approach to English Literature," *Irish Ecclesiastical Record* LXIV (Dec.), p. 373.

531. Hayes, John J., "Studies in Poetry," *Studies* XXXIII (Dec.), pp. 558–61.

532. Pick, John, "Centenary of Gerard Manley Hopkins," *Thought* XIX (Dec.), pp. 590–93.

533. Sale, W. M., "Gerard Manley Hopkins: Poet and Convert," *Poetry* LXV (Dec.), pp. 142–49.

534. Schoder, Raymond V., S.J., "Spelt from Sibyl's Leaves," *Thought* XIX (Dec.), pp. 633–48.

535. Quirk, Charles J., S.J., "Gerard Manley Hopkins (1844–1944)" [poem], *Catholic World* CLX (Dec.), p. 240.

536. H., R. B., [review of Ruggles], *Orate Fratres* XIX (Dec. 3), p. 47.

537. Anon., "Gerard Manley Hopkins (1844–1889)," *Listener* XXXII (Dec. 21), pp. 693–94.

1945

538. Brauns, M., S.J., "De dichter Gerard Manley Hopkins, S.J., by het eeuwfeest van zijn gerboorte (1844–1944)," *Streven* [Antwerpen], XII (Aug.), pp. 239–247.

539. Munoz Rojas, Jose A., "En el centenario de Gerard Manley Hopkins, S.J." (1844–1889), *Razón y Fe* CXXXII [Madrid], pp. 569–74.

540. Shapiro, Karl, *Essay on Rime* (N.Y.: Reynal), pp. 8, 15, 33, 34, 55.

541. Kenyon Critics, the, *Gerard Manley Hopkins* (N. Y.: New Directions Press). [Reprint of the articles on Hopkins in *Kenyon Review* for Summer and Autumn 1944, with additional biographical study by Austin Warren, and F. R. Leavis' "Metaphysical Isolation" reprinted from *Scrutiny* 1944.]

542. Wolfe, Ann F., "Impassioned Victorian Poet," *Saturday Review of Literature* XXVIII (Jan. 13), p. 26.

543. L., H. P. C., "To Gerard Manley Hopkins, S.J.," *Month* CLXXXI (Jan.), p. 65.

544. D'Arcy, Martin C., S.J., "Gerard Manley Hopkins," *Month* CLXXXI (Feb.), pp. 67–9.

545. Williams, Charles, "Gerard Manley Hopkins," *Time and Tide* (Feb 3).

546. Lowell, Robert [review of Ruggles], *Sewanee Review* LIII (Mar.), pp. 136–40.

547. Kirschbaum, Leo [review of Ruggles], *Modern Language Notes* LX (Mar.), pp. 199–200.

548. Gregory, Horace, "Living Poet, Deadly Critic," *Saturday Review of Literature* XXVIII (Mar. 24), pp. 38–9.

549. Meyer, Gerard Previn, "Poets and Dragonflies," *Saturday Review of Literature* XXVIII (Mar. 24), p. 10.

550. Howarth, R. G., "Yeats and Hopkins," *Notes and Queries* CLXXXVIII (May 15), pp. 202–4.

551. Pick, John, [review of Gardner], *Thought* XX (June), pp. 347–9.

552. Noon, William T., S.J., "Hopkins, Christian Humanist," *America* LXXIV (Oct. 20), pp. 73–75.

553. Harrold, Charles F., [review of Ruggles], *Journal of English and Germanic Philology* XLIV (Oct.), pp. 434–36.

554. Anon., "Pied Beauty," *Scholastic* XLVII (Nov. 19), p. 15.

555. Leahy, Maurice, "Laureate and Levite," *Epistle* (Winter), pp. 12–14.

555a. Fausset, H. I. A., "Gerard Manley Hopkins," *Poets and Pundits* (London: Jonathan Cape).

1946

556. Grierson, Herbert J. C., and Smith, J. C., "Twentieth Century Poetry Between the Wars, 1919–1939," *A Critical History of*

English Poetry (N. Y.: Oxford U. Press), pp. 553–54 and *passim*.

557. Carlson, Sister Marian Raphael, S.H.N., *Gerard Manley Hopkins and His Critics* (Ph.D. Dissertation, Loyola U., Chicago).

558. Cohen, Selma J., *The Poems of Gerard Manley Hopkins in Relation to His Religious Thought* (Ph.D. Dissertation, U. of Chicago).

559. Moira, Sister, S.C.N., *The Poetic Theory of Gerard Manley Hopkins, and its Relation to His Own Work* (M.A. Thesis, Notre Dame U., South Bend).

559a. O'Donnell, M. J., *Feet on the Ground*, being An Approach to Modern Verse (London: Blackie & Son).

560. Weiss, T., "Gerard Manley Hopkins . . . Realist on Parnassus," *Accent Anthology* (N. Y.: Harcourt, Brace), pp. 664–67.

561. Brauns, M., S.J., "Der Dichter Gerard Manley Hopkins," *Stimmen der Katholischen Welt* I (Bonn) pp. 204–211, 216. [Four of Hopkins' poems are translated into German, pp. 212–14 of same volume.]

562. K., L., [review of Kenyon Critics], *Bookweek* (Feb. 3), p. 2.

563. Pick, John, "Right Directions in Criticism," *America* LXXIV (Feb. 16), p. 539.

564. Anon., [review of Kenyon Critics], *New Yorker* XXII (Feb. 23), p. 90.

565. Pick, John, [review of Weiss, *Selections from Note-books of Gerard Manley Hopkins*], *Thought* XXI (Mar.), pp. 158–60.

566. Deutsch, Babette, "Studies of a Poet," *New York Herald Tribune Weekly Book Section* (Mar. 17), p. 12.

567. Mack, Maynard [review of Kenyon Critics], *Yale Review* XXXV (Spring), p. 539.

568. Schwartz, Delmore, "Poetry of Hopkins," *Nation* CLXII (Mar. 23), pp. 347–48.

569. Anon., "Habit of Perfection," *Catholic Worker* XIII (Apr.), p. 5.

570. Wyatt, E. V. R., [review of Kenyon Critics], *Commonweal* XLIV (Apr. 19), p. 20.

571. Connolly, Francis X., "Reaffirmation of Poetic Values," *Spirit* XIII (May), p. 57.

572. Meagher, Margaret C., [review of Kenyon Critics], *Catholic World* CLXIII (May), p. 163.

573. Anon., "God's Grandeur," *Land and Home* IX (June), p. 46.

574. Duffy, John, C.SS.R., "Gerard Manley Hopkins," *Spirit* XIII (July), pp. 88–91.

575. Grady, Thomas J., "A Great Poet," *Books on Trial* V (July-Aug.), p. 61.

576. Anon., [review of Kenyon Critics], *United States Quarterly* II (Sept.), p. 171.

577. Simons, John W., "The Credentials of the Catholic Poet," *Spirit* XIII (Nov.), p. 146.

578. Devlin, Christopher, S.J., "An Essay on Scotus," *Month* CLXXXII (Nov. 28), pp. 455–66. [Hopkins *passim*].

579. Silverstein, Henry, "Gerard Manley Hopkins," *Accent* VII (Winter 1946–7).

ALPHABETICAL INDEX TO A CHRONOLOGICAL HOPKINS BIBLIOGRAPHY

INDEX OF AUTHORS

Bonn, John Louis, S.J., U.S.N.R., A.B., M.A., D.O.A. (Boston College). Director of School of Expressional Arts and lecturer in the philosophy of literature, Boston College; author of *Canticle and Other Poems; So Falls the Elm Tree; And Down the Days; Jeremias; Life of Poetry; Joyful Mystery;* contributor to *Poetry, a Magazine of Verse, Reader's Digest, Tomorrow, America, Spirit, Thought.*

Boyle, Robert R., S.J., A.B. (University of Illinois). Engaged in theological studies at St. Mary's College (School of Divinity of St. Louis University); formerly instructor in English and Classics at Regis High School, Denver, Colorado; contributor to *Jesuit Educational Quarterly.*

Burns, C.A., S.J., A.B., M.A. (St. Louis University), M.A. (Western Reserve University). Professor of Religion, Loyola University (Chicago); formerly professor of Latin and Greek literature, Xavier University and John Carroll University; author of *The Glory of Sts. Peter and Paul's;* contributor to *Classical Bulletin.*

Carroll, Martin C., S.J., A.B. (Georgetown University), M.A. (Fordham University). Engaged in graduate work in English at the State University of Iowa; formerly instructor in literature, St. Joseph's College High School and Georgetown University; contributor to *America.*

MacGillivray, Arthur, S.J., A.B. (Boston College), M.A. (University of Minnesota). Head of English Department, Fairfield University; formerly instructor in English literature, Holy Cross College, Worcester, Massachusetts; author of *Sufficient Wisdom, A Book of Poems;* contributor to *Drink from the Rock, The Snob and the Saint,* and *I Sing of a Maiden* (anthologies), *America, Catholic World, Spirit.*

McNamee, Maurice B., S.J., M.A., Ph.D. (St. Louis University). Assistant professor in English, St. Louis University and Creighton University; graduate studies, Creighton University, Marquette University; contributor to *Thought, Modern Schoolman.*

Noon, William T., S.J., A.B. (Hamilton College), M.A. (Loyola

University, Chicago). Engaged in theological studies at Woodstock College; formerly instructor in English, Xavier High School, New York City; Stamford High School, Stamford-in-the-Catskills, New York; and Hudson High School, Hudson, New York; graduate studies, Columbia University; contributor to *America*.

Ong, Walter J., S.J., A.B. (Rockhurst College), M.A. (St. Louis University). Engaged in graduate work in English at Harvard University; formerly instructor in English at Regis College, Denver, Colorado; contributor to *Twentieth Century English* (book), *PMLA, Commonweal, Modern Schoolman, Modern Language Quarterly, America, Sewanee Review, Theological Studies, Speculum*.

Schoder, Raymond Victor, S.J., A.B., M.A. (Loyola University, Chicago), Ph.D. (St. Louis University). Final year of Jesuit ascetical studies ("Tertianship") at St. Beuno's, N. Wales; formerly instructor in literature, University of Detroit High School, Loyola Academy, Chicago; co-author of *A Reading Course in Homeric Greek*; contributor to *Studies* (Dublin), *Classical Journal, Theological Studies, Modern Schoolman, Classical Bulletin, America, Catholic World, Historical Bulletin, Jesuit Educational Quarterly, Classical Weekly, Thought, American Ecclesiastical Review*.

Watson, Youree, S.J., A.B. (Spring Hill College). Engaged in graduate work in philosophy at the Gregorian University (Rome); formerly instructor in literature, St. Charles College, Grand Coteau, Louisiana, and Jesuit High School, New Orleans; graduate studies, St. Louis University; contributor to *Thought, Magnificat, Jesuit Educational Quarterly, Review for Religious*.

Weyand, Norman, S.J., A.B., Ph.D. (St. Louis University). Assistant professor and chairman of Department of English, Loyola University, Chicago; formerly instructor in English, Xavier University and University of Detroit; graduate studies, Heythrop College, Chipping Norton, Oxon., Innsbruck University, Austria; contributor to *Month, Clare Market Review* (London University), *Historical Bulletin, Tablet* (London), *Modern Schoolman, Illinois Dental Journal, Jesuit Educational Quarterly*.

INDEX OF NAMES AND TITLES

Date Due

FEB 1 0 1959			
MAY 1 1959			
JUN 3 1959			
JAN 2 2 1960			
MAY 2 1 1962			
AUG 1 0 1962			
MAY 8 '64			
APR 2 7 '66			
DEC 0 8 1989			
⑬	PRINTED	IN U. S. A.	